AF823938

# Palgrave Studies in Maritime Economics

**Series Editors**
Hercules Haralambides, University of Paris 1 - Panthéon-Sorbonne, Paris, France; School of Maritime Economics and Management, Dalian Maritime University, Dalian, China
Elias Karakitsos, EN Aviation & Shipping Research Ltd, London, UK
Stig Tenold, Department of Economics, NHH – Norwegian School of Economics, Bergen, Norway

Palgrave Studies in Maritime Economics is a new, original and timely interdisciplinary series that seeks to be pivotal in nature and improve our understanding of the role of the maritime sector within port economics and global supply chain management, shipping finance, and maritime business and economic history. The maritime industry plays an increasingly important role in the changing world economy, and this new series offers an outlet for reviewing trends and developments over time as well as analysing how such changes are affecting trade, transport, the environment and financial markets. Each title in the series will communicate key research findings, shaping new approaches to maritime economics. The core audience will be academic, as well as policymakers, regulators and international maritime authorities and organisations. Individual titles will often be theoretically informed but will always be firmly evidence-based, seeking to link theory to policy outcomes and changing practices.

More information about this series at
https://link.springer.com/bookseries/15187

Claudio Ferrari · Hercules Haralambides ·
Sergio Prete · Alessio Tei
Editors

# Regulation and Finance in the Port Industry

## Lessons from Worldwide Experiences

palgrave
macmillan

*Editors*
Claudio Ferrari
Department of Economics
University of Genoa
Genoa, Italy

Sergio Prete
University of Bari Aldo Moro
Bari, Italy

Port Network Authority of the Ionian Sea
Taranto, Italy

Hercules Haralambides
University of Paris 1 - Panthéon-Sorbonne
Paris, France

School of Maritime Economics
and Management
Dalian Maritime University
Dalian, China

Alessio Tei
Department of Economics
University of Genoa
Genoa, Italy

School of Engineering
Newcastle University
Newcastle Upon Tyne, UK

ISSN 2662-6551 ISSN 2662-656X (electronic)
Palgrave Studies in Maritime Economics
ISBN 978-3-030-83984-0 ISBN 978-3-030-83985-7 (eBook)
https://doi.org/10.1007/978-3-030-83985-7

© The Editor(s) (if applicable) and The Author(s), under exclusive license to Springer Nature Switzerland AG 2022
This work is subject to copyright. All rights are solely and exclusively licensed by the Publisher, whether the whole or part of the material is concerned, specifically the rights of translation, reprinting, reuse of illustrations, recitation, broadcasting, reproduction on microfilms or in any other physical way, and transmission or information storage and retrieval, electronic adaptation, computer software, or by similar or dissimilar methodology now known or hereafter developed.
The use of general descriptive names, registered names, trademarks, service marks, etc. in this publication does not imply, even in the absence of a specific statement, that such names are exempt from the relevant protective laws and regulations and therefore free for general use.
The publisher, the authors and the editors are safe to assume that the advice and information in this book are believed to be true and accurate at the date of publication. Neither the publisher nor the authors or the editors give a warranty, expressed or implied, with respect to the material contained herein or for any errors or omissions that may have been made. The publisher remains neutral with regard to jurisdictional claims in published maps and institutional affiliations.

This Palgrave Macmillan imprint is published by the registered company Springer Nature Switzerland AG
The registered company address is: Gewerbestrasse 11, 6330 Cham, Switzerland

# Introduction: Book Rationale

*Essentially, all models are wrong, but some are useful.*

—Box G., Draper N. (1987). *Empirical Model-Building and Response Surfaces*, p. 424, Wiley.

The present volume has been developed starting from 2018 when we were involved in an assessment of different funding and planning schemes applied by EU ports. In gathering information on different practices, the editors recognised how different legislations and cultural elements did impact on planning practices and financial tools, giving port management bodies a quite diversified array of implementing strategies, independently from the governancemodel that most EU ports were actually subject to. As such, we thought that a volume collecting major case studies could increase current understanding on the link between planning tools, funding solutions, and regulatory practices, thus increasing current awareness beyond the traditional port governance literature. The rationale for the current volume is then linked to the necessity for a better understanding of the differences between general governance models and their local applications.

Another input we found out from the initial research which kicked off the current project was that the continuous modifications of port competitive arenas generated a series of rapid changes. These modifications were related to the merging of several port management organisations (one of the latest being the announced merge between Zeebrugge and Antwerp), the investments needed to cope with new technological standards (e.g. blockchain, ship and terminal automation, new energy sources), and the modifications of the competitive conditions of several interconnected markets (e.g. trade frictions among China, USA, and European Union; alliances; Belt and Road Initiative). All these elements pushed port regulators to either innovate governance models or promote stronger cooperations with main market players, as often done through the promotion of integrated solutions. In doing so, we spotted a clear critical issue: most of the traditional literature on port organisation and regulation is based on national case studies while most of the possible "lessons to be learnt" from these new applied solutions could be only based on comparisons among different experiences. The current book aims at filling this gap, providing the reader with the possibility to compare current regulatory and planning solutions in a vast set of port systems that cover all major world regions.

We are aware of the risks of promoting such comparisons, even when a vast sample of case studies—thanks to the contributions of many experts—is used: managing the development of such a project and assuring the consistency of the information provided have not been an easy task but we feel the final outcome is of incredible value.

One of the key findings of the current book is that several diverging trends can be observed in terms of port management tools even though general objectives (e.g. increase efficiency, attract investments) are often shared among different country regulators. Among the key trends, the most common ones are the different forms and levels of privatisation, the country openness to foreign investments and the links with macro-regional funding schemes.

Furthermore, the book—planned to include contributions from different scholars around the world—contains critical discussions of the elements that characterise port planning and management, as well as how those elements are driving investment decisions. The presence of a general (and more theoretical) part as well as specific country-based discussions improve the capability to compare theory with current practices, increasing the potential transferability of the outcomes as well as giving insights to both practitioners (e.g. regulators, potential investors) and policy makers.

The final aim of the book is to provide a guide for both scholars and practitioners on how different port organizational and regulatory contexts affect investment patterns and related financial tools. Academics can then use the book for better understanding and comparing different port regulatory frameworks, planning tools, and related financial solutions. Practitioners could be interested in the better understanding of different frameworks, as well, but their main interest will probably lie on the specification of relevant legislations and financial tools.

In our opinion, the present book also allows students to benefit from the insights of the book in order to allow them to find out how ports are managed and organised in different port regions and how these differences impact on the development strategies and related funding schemes.

The book organisation has been affected by both general book development issues (e.g. delays, merge of content among different chapters) and by the ongoing modifications of the port industry that were thought to be reflected in some of the book related parts.

Considering different audiences, the structure of the book is thought to provide value to students, mainly with a first part dedicated to general theory (Part 1) and policy comments and perspectives for the future of the industry (Part 3) and a second part that is dedicated to the application of general principles on specific port systems (Part 2). The Part 2 of the book is thought to generate most of the value for both practitioners and academics, given the relevant level of information included per port system, the wide range of represented countries, and the differences in industrial and trade structures.

While the book focuses on the link between planning, funding, and regulation of different port activities, a series of overarching issues have been indirectly mentioned in several chapters: the ongoing industry challenges in coping with the environmental issues has been highlighted by several authors either in the form of new investments for adapting port infrastructure to climate change or in mitigation strategies that might impact on funding schemes and regulatory tools. During the development phase of the book, for instance, several countries adopted the United Nations Sustainable Development Goals to be used in their port industry development strategies. Similarly, the International Association of Ports and Harbours (IAPH) reiterated many times how sustainability will represent a key issue for the future of port development and the related industry competitiveness.

As such, while the present book does not include a specific discussion on the environmental challenges, it provides an ample array of examples on how different national regulators are developing solutions to promote investments to boost port sustainability. Similarly, links with the new technologies currently under development and macro-regional investment issues—the most famous one being the Belt and Road Initiative—are all treated from a port system point of view in order to allow the readers to compare the local point of view, appreciating differences in both the perceived importance of the specific topic and the peculiarities of each national approach.

We are grateful for the many contributions included in the book: world experts gathered to contribute to the present volume with specific inputs and a unique understanding of local dynamics. While several colleagues directly contributed to the book, others indirectly participated towards a series of discussions, insights, and information sharing: we are thankful to all these silent contributors as well.

Last but not least: during the development of the present volume, Covid-19 pandemic kicked-off, impacting all our lives. This event did not just impact on different economic sectors but drastically change social and personal lives as well. A special (final) thought goes to all those friends and colleagues that have been impacted by the pandemic.

# Contents

# Notes on Contributors

**Michele Acciaro** is the Director of the Hapag-Lloyd Center for Shipping and Global Logistics (CSGL) and an Associate Professor for Maritime Logistics at the Department of Operations and Technology at Kühne Logistics University (KLU) in Hamburg. His recent research work focuses on container transport, port strategy, corporate sustainability in shipping and ports, and decarbonization.

**Jan Christoph Ahting** is an industrial engineer with a focus on the maritime sector. He holds a M.Sc. in Logistics (University of Applied Sciences Bremerhaven) and a diploma degree in Maritime Economics and Port Management (Jade University of Applied Sciences). Prior to entering academia, he worked for shipping companies and on port development. Being part of the research team "Maritime Logistics Workgroup" at Jacobs University, he was involved in EU projects.

**Giulia Arduino** She's a Port Economist with a Master's degree in Port Management and a Ph.D. in Logistics, Transport, and Territory. She's a professor at Tecnológico de Monterrey in Mexico and has published more than ten research papers and five chapters in transport-related books.

**Lauren Brand** is currently the President of the National Association of Waterfront Employers (NAWE), an industry association for marine terminal operator and stevedoring industries in the USA and prior to that led the Office of Ports and Waterways at the US Maritime Administration. As the President of NAWE, she strategically addresses operational safety, maritime policy, and regulatory issues.

**Pierre Cariou** is a Senior Professor in Maritime Shipping and Port Economics at Kedge Business School, France. His main research interests are shipping/port economics, liner shipping and port strategies, climate change policies, and maritime safety, topics on which he published more than 80 academic papers, and was involved in many public and private consultancy research projects.

**Chih-Ching Chang** is a professor and Executive Vice President at National Taiwan Ocean University and the former chairman of Taiwan International Ports Corporation (TIPC). His research field includes maritime law, shipping management, and port management.

**Shih-Liang Chao** is a professor in the Department of Shipping and Transportation Management at National Taiwan Ocean University. He had been working for Yang Ming Line and its dedicated terminal. His research focuses on the operation management of liner shipping and container terminals.

**Mihalis Chasomeris** is an Associate Professor at the Graduate School of Business and Leadership, University of KwaZulu-Natal. His fields of academic research and experience in international consultancy include the economic regulation of seaports, port governance and pricing, maritime transport economics, international trade, and transportation costs.

**Yang Chen** is a Professor of Strategy and Innovation and associate dean of College of Transport and Communications at Shanghai Maritime University, China. He obtained a Ph.D. degree from Fudan University and was once a visiting scholar at Harvard Business School. His research interest covers strategy, digitization, and innovation in shipping industry.

**Michaël Dooms** is an Associate Professor of Strategic Management at the Solvay Business School at the University of Brussels (VUB). He is a member of PortEconomics.eu and the Port Performance Research Network (PPRN). He has published in leading scientific journals such as the *International Journal of Project Management*, *Research in Transportation Business and Management*, *Maritime Policy and Management*, *Maritime Economics and Logistics*, *Journal of Transport Geography*, as well as leading practitioner-oriented magazines such as *Port Technology International*.

**Soner Esmer** is a Professor of Port and Maritime Logistics. He is specialized in the supply chain management, logistics, shipping, and port business. He has published widely in ports, shipping, and logistics and worked on many public and private projects and his research motivation comes from emerging debates in the supply chain.

**Laurent Fedi** is an Associate Professor in Maritime Law and Maritime Management at Kedge Business School, France. He currently leads different research projects notably on port governance, maritime safety, security, environmental protection, competition issues, and maritime digitalization. He already published more than 50 academic papers especially in maritime law.

**Claudio Ferrari** is Full Professor of Applied Economics at the University of Genoa, Italy, and member of the scientific board of the Italian Centre of Excellence for Integrated Logistics. He is the Director of the Ph.D. program in Marine Science and Technologies.

**Sanele Gumede** is a Senior Lecturer at the University of KwaZulu-Natal, where he teaches undergraduates economics and maritime economics to postgraduates. His research and supervision interests and consultancy experience include maritime transport economics, port governance and pricing regulation, and infrastructure pricing and valuation.

**Hercules Haralambides** is Distinguished Chair Professor of Maritime Economics and Logistics at Dalian Maritime University (China), and

Editor-in-Chief of the Maritime Economics and Logistics journal, published by Palgrave Macmillan (palgrave.com/41278). Other current affiliations include Texas A&M University (USA), Sorbonne University (France), and Erasmus University Rotterdam (The Netherlands).

**Hidekazu Itoh** is a Professor of Marketing with the School of Business Administration, and Adjunct Professor of Technology Management, Institute of Business and Accounting (IBA), Professional Graduate School, Kwansei Gakuin University, Japan. He obtained his Ph.D. from the Graduate School of Policy and Planning Sciences, University of Tsukuba, Japan, in 2003.

**Bart Kuipers** is a Senior Researcher in Port Economic at the Erasmus University (Rotterdam), being a seaport and logistics adviser of Erasmus UPT since 2008. Bart has worked at the Dutch Ministry of Transport, at TU Delft and TNO.

**Sashi N. Kumar** serves as the National Coordinator for Maritime Education and Training at the US Maritime Administration. Previously he served as the Academic Dean and Interim Superintendent at the US Merchant Marine Academy, Kings Point, NY. He holds a Master of Science in Maritime Management from Maine Maritime Academy and a Ph.D. in Maritime Economics from the University of Wales, Cardiff.

**Katie Lientz** is an economist who specializes in maritime transportation and the analysis of waterborne trade data at the US Maritime Administration. She holds a Master of Science in Natural Resource Economics from the Michigan Technological University and a Ph.D. in Policy Studies from Clemson University.

**Douglas McDonald** serves as the Director of the US Maritime Administration's Office of Policy and Plans. He leads a team of economists and analysts in support of the Federal agency's long-range plans, goals, and objectives.

**Axel Merkel** works as a researcher at the Swedish National Road and Transport Research Institute, department of transport economics. His research interests include maritime economics, port governance, and transport policy. He holds a Ph.D. in logistics from Molde University College, Norway.

**Jason Monios** is a Professor of Maritime Logistics at Kedge Business School, Marseille, France. His research areas include intermodal transport and logistics, port system evolution, port hinterlands, port and shipping governance and policy, institutional and regulatory settings, maritime sustainability, climate change adaptation, autonomous and electric vehicles, and urban freight transport and logistics.

**Denis Lewa Muganga** currently serves as the Director of Private Sector Investment Promotion at the Northern Corridor Transit and Transport Coordination Authority (NCTTCA) based in Mombasa, Kenya. Previously, he held the position of County Secretary and Head of Public Service at the County Government of Mombasa, as well as Principal Economist at the Kenya Ports Authority, and Senior expert roles at the IFC (World Bank Group) and the Government of Kenya (National Treasury).

**Ziaul Haque Munim** is an Associate Professor of Maritime Logistics at the University of South-Eastern Norway. His research interests include maritime economics and logistics, green shipping, supply chain management, and forecasting. Dr. Munim holds a Ph.D. degree from the University of Agder and a M.Sc. degree from the Vienna University of Economics and Business.

**David Guillermo Carrillo Murillo** He's a Civil Engineer with a "Master in Sciences" in Transport Economics and a Ph.D. in Business Economics and Engineering applied to transport and logistics. He has published 20 research articles and is an author of a book. He's a technical and financial consultant for port infrastructure and logistics internationally.

**Enrico Musso** is Full Professor of Applied Economics at the University of Genoa. Editor In Chief of the International Journal of Transport Economics, he has been appointed as Director of the Italian Centre of Excellence on Transport, Infrastructure, and Logistics.

**Athanasios A. Pallis** is a Professor in Management of Ports and Shipping, at the Department of Port Management and Shipping, National and Kapodistrian University of Athens, Greece. He is the President of the International Association of Maritime Economists (IAME), and the Vice-Chair of the Port Performance Research Network (PPRN). A founding member and co-director of *PortEconomics*, he co-authors the book *Port Economics, Management and Policy*.

**Sergio Prete** is Professor of Port Management at the University of Bari "Aldo Moro" (Italy) and President of the Port Network Authority of the Ionian Sea. Starting from 2011 he has carried out several managerial roles, among which the presidency of the Taranto Port Authority and the vice-presidency of the Italian Ports Association. In 2012, he was nominated Member of the "Expert Committee" of the Shanghai International Shipping Institute.

**Katharina Renken** works as Project Manager for the Terminal Partnering Program at Hapag-Lloyd. She provides global performance improvement support, employee trainings, and fosters the standardization process in container transport. Beforehand, Renken addressed sustainable ("green") maritime transport topics as a Senior Researcher while working and lecturing at Kühne Logistics University.

**Giovanni Satta** is an Associate Professor in Management and Finance at the University of Genoa, Italy. In the past, he has been a member of the IAME council and of the Port of Genoa management board.

**Seçil Sigali** is an Associate Professor Dr. of Accounting at Dokuz Eylul University, Maritime Faculty, Logistics Management Department, İzmir, Turkey. Seçil Sigalı's areas of expertise are Financial Reporting, Financial Analysis, Investments, Financial Management, Corporate Governance, Sustainability Reporting, Integrated Reporting, and Logistics Costs Analysis.

**Lars Stemmler** has been involved in port development as well as port finance and privatization as a consultant and project financier over the last 25 years. Lars is a visiting lecturer at various European universities in the field of maritime logistics. He holds a Ph.D. in European port policy and an M.Sc. in Logistics from Cranfield University.

**Alessio Tei** is an Associate Professor in Applied Economics at the Department of Economics of the University of Genoa. Previously, Alessio has worked at Newcastle University as Lecturer in Maritime Economics and he acted as visiting research at the University of Antwerp. During his career he has been invited as speaker and expert to several port and transport events.

**Beatriz Tovar** is a Full Professor at Las Palmas University. She is an expert in infrastructure and maritime economics and has been actively involved in contracts and research projects with the World Bank, CEPAL, etc. She has published in several international journals and is a member of the Editorial Boards of several journals.

**George K. Vaggelas** is an Associate Professor in Shipping and Transport Management, at the Department of Shipping, Trade and Transport, University of the Aegean, Greece. Author of several research studies dealing with port and shipping industry. George is also a member of the *PortEconomics* initiative.

**Thierry Vanelslander** (1975) is a professor at the Department of Transport and Regional Economics. His research is on economics in the port and maritime sector, land transport, and urban logistics. He is the chair of the WCTR SIGA2 (Ports and Maritime). Equally, he is the chair of the Freight and Logistics group within the ETC.

**Alan Wall** is an Associate Professor of Economics at the Department of Economics of the University of Oviedo and a member of the Oviedo Efficiency Group, a research team in the field of productivity and efficiency analysis. He has published in several international transport economics journals.

**Qiang Zhang** is an Associate Professor in the College of Transport and Communications at Shanghai Maritime University, China. He obtained his Ph.D. degree from SMU and was once a visiting scholar at Erasmus University Rotterdam and Transport and Environment. His research interests include port governance, port geography, and shipping decarbonization.

# List of Figures

# List of Tables

# Part I

## The Port Structure: Managerial and Operational Issues

# 1

# Port Governance Models and Their Historical Development

Claudio Ferrari, Hercules Haralambides, and Alessio Tei

## Introduction

Ports are key gates to coastal regions and their hinterlands. As such, they are infrastructure nodes representing strategic interchanges among different logistics chains, both at sea (i.e., commercial ships, cruise vessels, fishing boats, and yachts) and on land (e.g., road/rail transport,

C. Ferrari (✉) · A. Tei
Department of Economics, University of Genoa, Genoa, Italy
e-mail: ferrari@economia.unige.it

A. Tei
e-mail: alessio.tei@unige.it

H. Haralambides
University of Paris 1 - Pantheon-Sorbonne, Paris, France
e-mail: Iraklis.haralambides@univ-paris1.fr

School of Maritime Economics and Management, Dalian Maritime University, Dalian, China

© The Author(s), under exclusive license to Springer Nature Switzerland AG 2022
C. Ferrari et al. (eds.), *Regulation and Finance in the Port Industry*, Palgrave Studies in Maritime Economics,
https://doi.org/10.1007/978-3-030-83985-7_1

pipelines, industrial plants, leisure facilities, and touristic attractions) (Haralambides, 2021). Given their importance to a variety of different industries, the development of ports has often been influenced by several external factors (e.g., local and national politics and industry needs) as well as by the needs of port users (e.g., energy supply, vessel types and sizes, and cargo specialization). Thus, the complexity of port activities and the possibility of having ports that are either specialized (e.g., containers, cruise, fishing, and bulk cargo) or multipurpose ports have often shaped views on local port planning as well as its regulation.

At present, port systems handle the majority of world trade, both in terms of value and volume. UNCTAD, the Geneva-based United Nations Conference on Trade and Development, estimates that a consistent value of over 80% of total international trade is using seaports (UNCTAD, 2019). In the aftermath of the Covid-19 pandemic, seaborne trade had been regularly used as a proxy of the status of the world economy, by a number of international bodies (UNCTAD, 2020).

The economic role of ports makes them fundamental and strategic nodes in national and international logistics networks, being, as it may, essential elements for both industrial production chains and related consumption markets (Bottasso et al., 2014; Wilmsmeier et al., 2007). Together with this strategic role for the world economy, ports represent also key social and local assets for every hosting region, in terms of generating local value-added (e.g., increasing local accessibility and connectivity to remote areas), employment, and incomes. Moreover, ports have recently assumed a new role in important policy measures, aiming to mitigate the environmental impact of transport operations (e.g., through the development of the so-called *Motorways of the Sea*) (Casaca & Marlow, 2007).

From a historical viewpoint, the strategic significance of the port industry both for foreign trade and national industrial development has led many national governments to seek an active involvement in the development and control of port infrastructure. In more recent times,

A. Tei
School of Engineering, Newcastle University, Newcastle Upon Tyne, UK

however, the scarcity of public financial resources; the unwillingness of the public sector to assume the market risk of specialization; the limited ability of the public administration to run complex, risky, and increasingly commercialized activities, such as those of container terminals; the interest of carriers in having their own *dedicated terminals*; and the increasing appetite of the private sector (Global Terminal Operators—GTO) in the often very lucrative port terminal investments have given ways to the devolution of decision-making authority from the 'centre' to the 'periphery'.[1] A period of national port reforms has thus started, which is still underway in most countries.

Port reforms range from the simple commercialization of port operations to corporatization, and all the way to full port privatization (Baird, 1995, 2002; Everett & Robinson, 2006; Haralambides, 2017). A part of the extant literature (e.g., Baird, 2004, 2013; Everett & Pettitt, 2006) has indeed claimed that port reforms kicked-off when the financial needs of the port business exceeded either the capability or the willingness of the public sector to accommodate them. Finally, it should also be said that the private sector's involvement in port business has often given rise to conflict between port and city administrations, particularly municipalities, many of which still believe that it ought to be themselves the lawful managers of 'their' ports.[2]

Thus, in spite of the increasing incursion of the private sector in port business, the importance of ports for the local economy still represents a political and regulatory factor, resisting the more pervasive forms of reform (full privatization). This has created a heterogeneity of, one could say, *customized* regulatory solutions, in an effort to reconcile the new needs of trade and industry with local context and in this way allow public bodies to still be involved in port planning and control, either directly or indirectly, depending on the specific local circumstances

[1] A reversal of this trend can however be observed at the time of writing, i.e., a *recentralization* of decision-making powers, through the integration of regional ports under a single authority. The trend is championed by China, followed by Italy and other European countries.

[2] During his years as the manager of the Italian port of Brindisi, Professor Haralambides vividly remembers the then-mayor of the city, and member of the port's supervisory committee, never missing an opportunity to declare that he did not participate in committee meetings just in order to raise his hand and vote, but he was coming there to actually manage the port!

(World Bank, 2001). In the European Union, in particular, such a kaleidoscope of port laws and regulations has not allowed the bloc to devise comprehensive policies on such important matters as port competition; pricing; accounting; financing; state-aids; reporting; and transparency (Haralambides & Acciaro, 2015). Each and every time such an attempt was made by the European Commission, it was invariably met with the by now infamous assertion of ports in unison: 'each port is different, and one size fits all solutions is not possible'.

Given the complexity of the topic, the present book aims at discussing local port regulations and governance in the light of both industrial development and port planning. We try to understand if there might be common solutions to differing local problems. In doing so, the main industrial trends and challenges are discussed in the first part of the book, comprising topics such as regulatory frameworks, governance models, and industry integration. The second part of the book focusses on describing the main port models worldwide, highlighting major trends in port regulation, as applied by major ports. The third and last part of the book summarizes our main findings and addresses the main challenges of the port sector going forward.

The intrinsic relationship of ports with their hinterland, and the need to serve efficiently their client firms there, have necessitated the development of innovative port designs; the specialization of port infra- and superstructure; the internal reorganization of ports; new governance models; and modern management methods. Whereas ports in past centuries were acting as 'emporiums' of break-bulk goods, developing multipurpose facilities capable of handling the majority of ships at their berths, today ports comprise a number of specialized terminals that handle different types of ships, in specialized facilities, and by dedicated equipment (Baird, 2004). The most notable example of this is offered by container terminals and the containerization of cargo. But of course, specialized terminals do abound for the handling of cars; fruit; chemicals; and a miscellany of bulk cargoes.

The automation of operations at 'standardized', specialized terminals has had another important effect on ports and their surrounding communities. Whereas the former general cargo ports were a beehive of economic activity and creators of substantial value-added, specialized terminals, most notably container terminals, are becoming simple *thoroughfares*: gateways, whose induced impacts do not remain locally but are dissipated throughout the global supply chain, from the mainland China exporter to the European importer (Benacchio et al., 2001). The limited local impacts (including employment) of automated terminals have often been the cause of the reluctance of governments to finance port investments, thus making way to the private sector. On the more positive side of the picture, however, the facilitating role of ports—mostly in terms of reducing transport costs to and from their hinterlands and forelands—has attracted industrial activity and international distribution centres in and around the port domain, thus creating important port clusters of commerce, manufacturing, research, and education (for a discussion of this and similar aspects, interested readers are directed to Haralambides, 2017). Moreover, one could also argue that the limited economic impacts of automated ports are compensated by their impact on the seamless cargo flows of global supply chains traversing the port and connecting its hinterland to important foreign forelands.

Specialization, in essence containerization, has also had a most noticeable effect on terminal layout and, consequently, on new organizational paradigms and management styles (Goss, 1990a, 1990b). Such changes have aimed to optimize terminal characteristics to the new realities, including berths and quays built to handle specialized vessels; storage yard layouts, to provide specific cargo services; road and rail connections; sea accessibility; and approach channels and turning basins. Furthermore, the usually limited terminal space—obliging terminals to stack containers x-high—and the unswerving demand of shippers and carriers to move containers through the port as quickly as possible, has given impetus to advanced IT systems and operations research algorithms, aiming to minimize time; motion, rehandling; and environmental impacts of port activity.

We might be amiss at this juncture not to mention that port land is a scarce commodity with alternative uses and, often, high opportunity cost. To conform with trade growth projections, and the spectacular sizes of modern ships (see below) and cargohandling equipment, ports require either the conversion of old facilities into new ones (e.g., from warehouses traditionally used for general cargo to stacking yards, currently needed in the container business) or the creation of 'new port land', wherever this is possible, usually through its reclamation from the sea, or through the establishment of 'dry-ports' in the seaport's hinterland. In both cases, cargohandling equipment and internal terminal vehicles need to be upgraded too, among others, these days, through electrification.

Figure 1.1 compares the traditional multipurpose terminal (indented) layout with the new 'containerized' one.

Figure 1.2 presents the increase in ship sizes (measured in average Gross Tonnage—GT) of new buildings, entering the shipping market. As can be seen, starting from the 1980s, all major shipping sectors (i.e., container, tanker, dry bulk, and passenger ships) have experienced an exponential growth in ship sizes. The impact of this trend on port planning is significant, as is those ships' needs for efficient cargohandling operations, as well as for safe and quick port turnaround. Figure 1.3 shows an example of different terminal layout designs, of ports that have attempted to adjust their infrastructure to different market needs (i.e., land reclamation at the bottom right and top left of the figure).

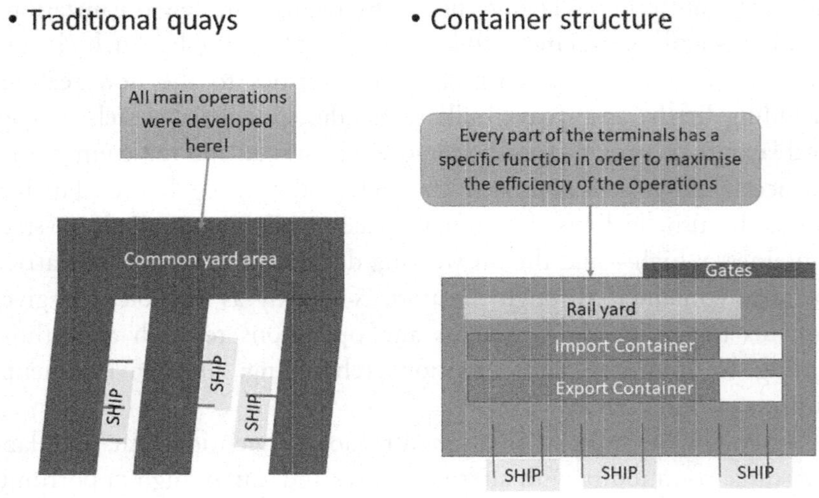


**Fig. 1.1** Different terminal layouts

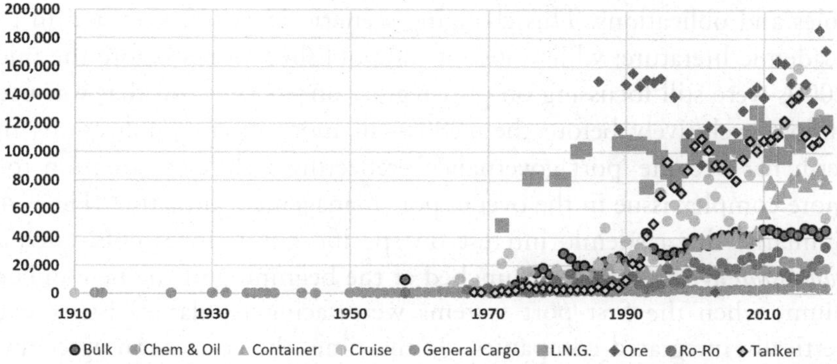


**Fig. 1.2** Average newbuilding gross tonnage per year for major ship types (1910–2019) (*Source* Own elaboration from Clarkson-Sin data, 2019)

**Fig. 1.3** Example of land reclamation undertaken to adapt old terminals to new uses (*Source* Google Maps, 2020)

## Switching from Port Reform to Port Governance

Until the 1980s, most ports were operated and managed by public bodies known as Port Authorities (PA). The privatization wave that started in late 1970s (Baird, 1995; Everett & Robinson, 2006) created the need for elaborate regulations and regulatory models capable of taking into account the complex interactions between a number of (international) companies which were required to meet public tender rules and obligations. This changing scenario is well represented in the academic literature: while most of the published works before the mid-2000s were still focussing on port regulation—a keyword that was used almost exclusively before the 1980s—in more recent publications the term has become 'port governance', reflecting a shift of attention to a more complex issue in the overall port management literature (Fig. 1.4). Similarly, the academic interest on specific governance tools, such as *concession agreements*, was launched at the beginning of the new millennium, when the first port systems were facing regulatory issues with vertically integrated companies. At the time, the concession agreement was the only administrative tool to regulate and monitor long-term management practices at the 'privatized' port areas.

Together with the establishment of novel managerial solutions, both academic (Goss, 1990a, 1990b) and international organizations (e.g., World Bank, 2001) have repeatedly tried to schematize the characteristics of different governance models. Table 1.1, versions of which, admittedly, have been going around a lot in the literature, shows a summary of key port governance characteristics, categorized as in World Bank (2001).

Among the governance models of Table 1.1, the landlord model is prevalent in most countries around the world, representing a middle road

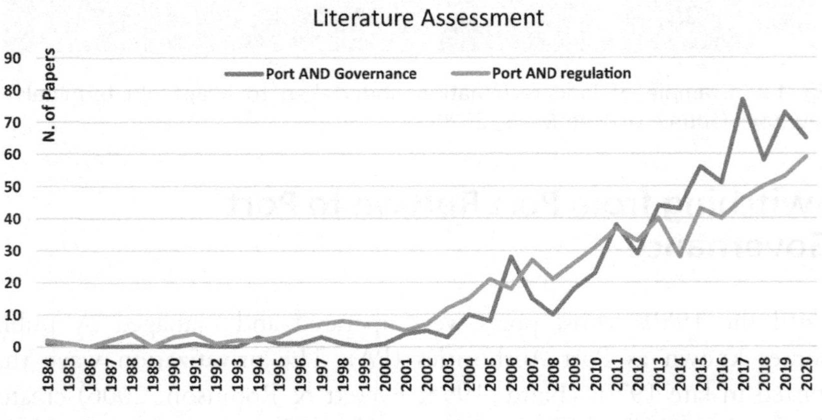


**Fig. 1.4** Summary of the main elements affecting port regulation (*Source* Own elaboration from Scopus, 2020)

**Table 1.1** Summary of main governance responsibility

| Port / Activity | Public port | Tool port | Landlord port | Private port |
|---|---|---|---|---|
| Port Administration | | | | |
| Nautical Management | | | | |
| Nautical Infrastructure | | | | |
| Port infrastructure | | | | |
| Superstructures | | | | |
| Cargo handling activities | | | | |
| Pilotage | | | | |
| Towage | | | | |
| Mooring | | | | |
| Dredging | | | | |
| Other functions | | | | |

| Private responsability | Either public or private | Public responsability |
|---|---|---|

(or an intermediate step) between public and private port administration and control. Here, the Port Authority, i.e., the manifestation of the public sector, retains only regulatory and planning authorities, including the leasing of port areas (landlord) to private port operators. The latter engage mostly in cargohandling operations through concessions awarded by the PA.

Given the impossibility to immediately achieve solutions satisfying all involved stakeholders, conflicts usually occur in the aftermath of national port reforms, and a series of further waves of reforms have as a matter of fact taken place in many countries (e.g., Spain, France, Italy, Brazil, and China). Moreover, notwithstanding the above classic categorization of port models (i.e., public, tool, landlord, and private), a scattered landscape still seems to exist, in which, more than one governance model can be found even within the same national port system (Debrie et al., 2013; van der Lugt et al., 2017). This situation can be explained either by the introduction of subsequent cyclical phases of reforms, that generated asymmetric applications of the rules, or by the related complexity of port management, that allowed different authorities to customize their port ecosystems in alignment with local needs. This aspect has also been discussed in the context of the ongoing structural issues, such as *climate crisis* and the Covid-19 pandemic, by different authors (e.g., Notteboom & Haralambides, 2020) highlighting the need of strengthening local aspects within port governance and business models.

Because of the possibility of tailoring governance models to local needs, as also mentioned in Brooks and Pallis (2012), theoretical approaches to port governance are often too far away from reality, and only through specific case studies and factual comparisons can the differences between port systems be effectively shown. As already mentioned above, *complexity* has often been listed as one of the reasons for the ineffective harmonization policies, as happened in the EU. In the second part of the book, we show examples of such misalignment: although most governance systems are inspired by the above four key governance models, they often diverge quite substantially, depending on local characteristics and cultural needs.

## Port Governance Critical Issues

Often, revisions of governance models have been introduced to facilitate port development, seizing the opportunities that a rapidly changing market is offering. Notwithstanding such intentions, some authors have questioned the capability of certain port reforms to have effectively achieved the stated goals (e.g., Baird, 2013; Parola et al., 2017). As mentioned above, waves of port governance reforms have taken place in recent decades, triggered by concerns that existing governance structures were unsuitable to fully exploit the potential of seaport systems.

This implies that, even if not explicitly detailed in policy documents, the objectives of seaports have been subsequently identified and implicitly included in specific port reform goals. Naturally, of course, such goals are not totally independent from the underlying governance model.

A tentative list of goals is presented in Table 1.2. Next to each goal there is a list of possible key performance indicators (KPI) that allow one to assess if the described action is actually able to pursue the goal it was intended to achieve.

The pride of a port manager, each time traffic in their port grows, seldom goes unnoticed, nor does their effort to make this appears like their own doing, i.e., the result of their own good management. But *generic* KPIs, such as those listed in Table 1.2, are influenced by a host of other factors, and as such they risk being only weakly dependent on port governance and performance. In the case of our proud manager and the related throughput statistics—as an indicator of a governance model that performs well in terms of fostering economic growth and the development of the maritime regions around the seaport—the mere fact that throughput increases do not necessarily imply the success of policies (or managers), for such increases could be attributable to several other factors, like an economic growth in the hinterland which has led to a greater demand for imports and export flows; congestion in neighbouring ports; or even an improvement in the accessibility of the seaport, due to an increased capacity of road and rail infrastructure. As such, any statement about the adequacy or inadequacy of the governance model loses its meaning and, in this context, it is also often pointless to try and compare such KPIs among seaports, national or international, for the simple reason that it is difficult to 'define the market' (i.e., hinterland and foreland) to which the KPI should apply.

**Table 1.2** Goals and KPIs of port policies

| Goals of port policy | KPIs |
|---|---|
| Reduction of public involvement in seaports | • Number of privatized ports<br>• Number of terminal concessions awarded<br>• Number of port authorities corporatized |
| Increase port efficiency | • Rate of containers moved per crane/hour<br>• Number of containers moved per day by rail or truck |
| Maximize the value added of seaports | • Increase in the value added for port operators or for port supply chains |
| Fostering the economic growth of the port region | • Impact on GDP<br>• Number of jobs created |
| Favouring private participation in port investments | • Percentage of private capital in port investment<br>• Number of PPPs |

*Source* Authors' elaboration based on the literature review

In fact, without an adequate set of planned outcomes and related benchmarking indicators, it is impossible to ascertain the extent to which the objectives of a certain policy have been achieved or not. Notwithstanding this, the design of a set of indicators, aiming at recording the impacts—both intended and unintended—of port policies, is not without merit. To put it differently, it is important to have a set of KPIs, as well as statistics (in real-time or up to date), consistent with the objectives to be monitored, so as to be able to put in place an effective control system of goals, and the actions taken to achieve them.

In practice, opinions on the adequacy of a port's performance, or governance model, are often based on fuzzy and unquantifiable sentiments of port actors and the overall port community. And although no such opinion is sufficient by itself to assess the actual performance of the port system, together they are sufficient to describe the appeal of the port towards its clients, namely the shipping companies and the cargo owners.

The problem of quantifying KPIs of different port systems, and the extent to which these are unequivocally accepted by all port stakeholders, has often been linked to another key element of most port reforms.

In the past—and to an extent today—, ports, their development, and operations were in the hands of the public sector. Ports were offering public services, with some of those (e.g., towage, pilotage, and mooring) considered to be *public service obligations* (PSO). In such environments, the concept of *efficiency* assumes a different meaning and the concept of *profitability* or *cost-recovery* may not enter the picture at all (Haralambides, 2017). Today, however, modern port systems consist of a difficult balance between public and private interests (for instance, environmental, safety and security concerns, vis à vis cargohandling operations, profitability, and risk-taking of private stevedores). Reconciling public and private interests, and agreeing on performance indicators accepted by both, has often been a riddle permeating every economic reform, far beyond the port sector. Interestingly, even after reforms, friction continues, for instance, between shipowners and port labour, or between shipowners and nautical-technical service providers (towage, pilotage, and mooring). Many may still remember the European dockers' strikes in the 1990s against port privatization (Baird, 2004), as well as the disputes that sometimes occur on the terms of a concession, or the assignment of port terminal areas (Goss, 1990a). Finally, the need for a balance between public port ownership and control on the one hand, and different stakeholders' interests on the other, has often been linked to the discussion on the growing market power of certain port actors, such as Global Terminal Operators (Musso et al., 2000), or to the tendency towards vertical or horizontal integration (Notteboom et al., 2017). The public–private 'balancing act', and the sometimes hopeless job of the port manager, is also exemplified by the way their decisions are restricted due to the popular classification of ports into hubs of national interest, regional ports, and specialized ports of local interest (Wang et al., 2021).

The tools for regulating port activity, especially whenever specific goals need to be achieved, or conflicts to be managed, are therefore a key element of both port regulation and planning. As said above, the identification of the appropriate KPIs and of the ways to promote them among port stakeholders represent today some of the major challenges of most port authorities (Ferrari et al., 2019). In this sense, concession agreements have often been interpreted (Saeed & Larsen, 2010; Theys et al., 2010) as a way of aligning planning and regulation, at the same time making the port attractive to new investment.

Given the challenge of reconciling planning and regulation (and apparently port financing too), the current book looks inquisitively to different national experiences, paving the way, hopefully, to novel approaches and insights for policy-makers.

## Need for Insights

At the danger of becoming repetitive, we again stress that the different national approaches to the practical implementation of port governance models (the landlord model most notably) have prevented regulators from designing and promulgating common port policies in the areas that *do* matter, like competition, pricing, and the treatment of state-aids and public investment. This failure is particularly visible in the European Union whereas, around the world, perhaps the World Trade Organisation (WTO) should have something to say in cases where public money is spent to develop private facilities (e.g., container terminals), thus distorting competition with ports in neighbouring countries (Haralambides, 2002). This is particularly so when, as said above, the economic impacts of automated port investments may be fairly limited.

As regards the financing itself of port investments, while most port reforms do not take explicitly into consideration relevant funding schemes and financial issues, governance models impact directly on the capability and interest of private and public operators to invest in the port business, and they thus indirectly impact on the attractiveness that such port businesses are capable of guaranteeing.

This aspect has been particularly highlighted by several authors (Parola et al., 2012; Theys et al., 2010), whenever port concessions have been examined. Concessions represent a key element of most landlord models, but their application has been heterogeneous in terms of legal characteristics, constraints, and related operational aspects and contract terms (for instance, business exclusivity; long-term benefits; concession fee; contract duration; renewal; awarding process; and the future relationship of the investor with the port authority). Thus while, formally, regulatory tools appear the same, their application is not. This scattered scenario, and the uncertainty it produces, may be the source of asymmetric information (ITMMA, 2008) that impedes appetites for port investment. This element is critical for all port systems under transition, in which specific rules need to be set, defining national capabilities for attracting funding in a strategic industry, such as that of ports.

Thus, while it might be easy to observe the functioning and effects of different port governance models (World Bank, 2001), understanding regulatory limitations and different applications of 'common' solutions is a much wider challenge that can be approached only through an effective description of the impact of currently applying solutions. Given the issues discussed above, Fig. 1.5 summarizes the main elements that have affected—and are still influencing—the different solutions to port regulation as well as to port planning.

The present book aims at providing such insights, hopefully helping policy-makers and port operators to understand how to better use different regulatory tools, as a way to boost port planning and the efficiency of port operations, among others by using the most effective financing solutions in relation to the desired goals. The book provides

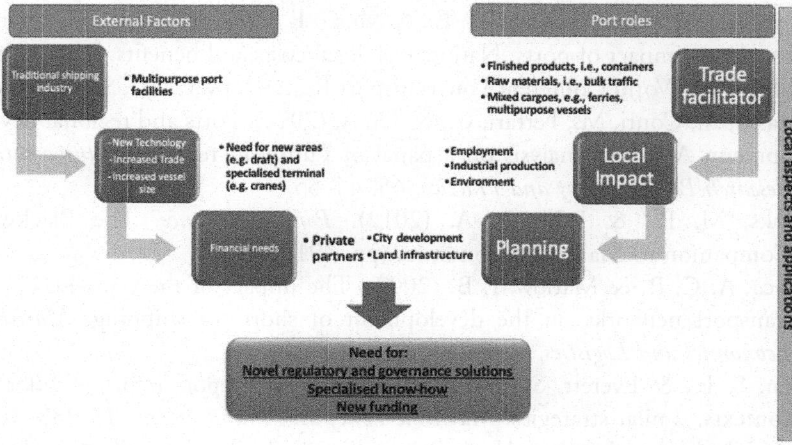


**Fig. 1.5** Summary of the main elements influencing the regulation of ports (*Source* Authors' elaboration)

valuable input for extant policy challenges, merging theoretical discussions with lessons learnt from applied regulatory systems. The aim here is to transfer knowledge and insights both from the academic state-of-the-art and from past experiences on the capability of relevant national champions to sustain port competitiveness and value for their local communities.

## References

Baird, A. J. (1995). Privatisation of trust ports in the United Kingdom: Review and analysis of the first sales. *Transport Policy, 2*, 135–143.

Baird, A. J. (2002). Privatization trends at the world's top-100 container ports. *Maritime Policy and Management, 29*, 271–284.

Baird, A. J. (2004). Public goods and the public financing of major European seaports. *Maritime Policy and Management, 31*, 375–391.

Baird, A. J. (2013). Acquisition of UK ports by private equity funds. *Research in Transportation Business and Management, 8*, 158–165.

Benacchio, M., Haralambides, H. E., & Musso E. (2001, July 22–27). On the economic impact of ports: National vs. local costs and benefits. Proceedings of the 9th World Conference on Transport Research (WCTR), Seoul, Korea.

Bottasso, A., Conti, M., Ferrari, C., & Tei, A. (2014). Ports and regional development: A spatial analysis on a panel of European regions. *Transportation Research Part a: Policy and Practice, 65*, 44–55.

Brooks, M. R., & Pallis A. A. (2012). *Port governance*. The Blackwell Companion to Maritime Economics (pp. 491–516).

Casaca, A. C. P., & Marlow, P. B. (2007). The impact of the trans-European transport networks on the development of short sea shipping. *Maritime Economics and Logistics, 9*, 302–323.

Chen, S. L., & Everett, S. (2014). The dynamics of port reform: Different contexts, similar strategies. *Maritime Policy and Management, 41*, 288–301.

Debrie, J., Lavaud-Letilleul, V., & Parola, F. (2013). Shaping port governance: The territorial trajectories of reform. *Journal of Transport Geography, 27*, 56–65.

Everett, S., & Pettitt, T. (2006). Effective corporatization of ports is a function of effective legislation: Legal issues in the existing paradigm. *Maritime Policy and Management, 33*, 219–232.

Everett, S., & Robinson, R. (2006). Chapter 12 Port reform: The Australian experience. *Research in Transportation Economics, 17*, 259–284.

Ferrari, C., Puliafito, P. P., & Tei, A. (2019). Dynamics in terminal concessions: The role of performances. *Maritime Economics and Logistics, 21*, 99–110.

Goss, R. O. (1990a). Economic policies and seaports: 3. Are port authorities necessary? *Maritime Policy and Management, 17*(4), 257–271.

Goss, R. O. (1990b). Economic policies and seaports: 4. Strategies for port authorities. *Maritime Policy and Management, 17*, 273–287.

Haralambides, H. E. (2002). Competition, excess capacity and the pricing of port infrastructure. *International Journal of Maritime Economics, 4*, 323–347.

Haralambides, H. (2017). Globalization, public sector reform, and the role of ports in international supply chains. *Maritime Economics and Logistics, 19*, 1–51.

Haralambides. (2021). *Containerization and the port industry*. The Elsevier Transport Encyclopedia.

Haralambides, H., & Acciaro, M. (2015). The new European port policy proposals: Too much ado about nothing? *Maritime Economics and Logistics, 17*, 127–141.

ITTMA—Institute of Transport and Maritime Management Antwerp. (2008) The Awarding of seaport. Terminals in Europe: Results from ITMMA Survey Commissioned by ESPO, Antwerp.

Mangan, J., Lalwani, C., & Fynes, B. (2008). Port-centric logistics. *The International Journal of Logistics Management, 19*, 29–41.

Musso, E., Ferrari, C., & Benacchio, M. (2000). Cooperation in maritime and port industry and its effects on markets structure. In C. Brebbia & J. Olivella (Eds.), *Maritime engineering and ports II* (pp. 91–100). WIT Press.

Notteboom, T. E., & Haralambides, H. (2020). Port management and governance in a post-COVID-19 era: Quo vadis? *Maritime Economics & Logistics, 22*, 329–352.

Notteboom, T. E., Parola, F., Satta, G., & Pallis, A. (2017). The relationship between port choice and terminal involvement of alliance members in container shipping. *Journal of Transport Geography, 64*, 158–173.

Parola, F., Ferrari, F., & Tei, A. (2012). Managing port concessions: Evidence from Italy. *Maritime Policy & Management, 39*, 45–61.

Parola, F., Ferrari, F., Tei, A., Satta, G., & Musso, E. (2017). Dealing with multi-scalar embeddedness and institutional divergence: Evidence from the renovation of Italian port governance. *Research in Transportation Business and Management, 22*, 89–99.

Saeed, N., & Larsen, O. I. (2010). Container terminal concessions: A game theory application to the case of the ports of Pakistan. *Maritime Economics and Logistics, 12*, 237–262.

Theys, C., Notteboom, T. E., Pallis, A. A., & de Langen, P. W. (2010). The economics behind the awarding of terminals in seaports: Towards a research agenda. *Research in Transportation Economics, 27*, 37–50.

UNCTAD. (2019). *Review of maritime transport 2019*. UNCTAD.

UNCTAD. (2020). *Review of maritime transport 2020*. UNCTAD.

Van der Lugt, L., Dooms, M., & Parola, F. (2013). Strategy making by hybrid organizations: The case of the port authority. *Research in Transportation Business and Management, 8*, 103–113.

van der Lugt, L. M., de Langen, P. W., & Hagdorn, L. (2017). Strategic beliefs of port authorities. *Transport Reviews, 37*, 412–441.

Wang, C., Haralambides, H., & Zhang, L. (2021). Sustainable port development: the role of Chinese seaports in the 21st century Maritime Silk Road. *International Journal of Shipping and Transport Logistics, 13*(1/2), 2021.

Wilmsmeier, G., Hoffmann, J., & Sanchez, R. J. (2007). The impact of port characteristics on international maritime transport costs. *Research in Transportation Economics, 16*, 117–140.
World Bank. (2001). *Port reform toolKit*. World Bank.

# 2

# Institutions, Port Planning and Finance

**Enrico Musso and Alessio Tei**

## Introduction

Ports have traditionally dragged the attention of national policymakers, mainly because of their need for special regulation and funding as well as for their role in regional economies. Moreover, the connection between port activities and different local and national economic aspects often generates the interest of both public and private actors, either towards different cooperative solutions (e.g. Public–Private Partnerships)

E. Musso · A. Tei (✉)
Department of Economics, University of Genoa, Genoa, Italy
e-mail: alessio.tei@unige.it

E. Musso
e-mail: enrico.musso@unige.it

A. Tei
School of Engineering, Newcastle University, Newcastle Upon Tyne, UK

© The Author(s), under exclusive license to Springer Nature Switzerland AG 2022

C. Ferrari et al. (eds.), *Regulation and Finance in the Port Industry*, Palgrave Studies in Maritime Economics,
https://doi.org/10.1007/978-3-030-83985-7_2

or impacting on possible conflicts and trade-offs. Although those connections are often perceived as statistics, the balance among different market players—and the related interests—varies considerably over time, often in accordance with the industry modifications (e.g. containerisation and trade patterns). The importance of such infrastructure has often been translated in several dedicated national laws—in most countries defined as "Port Law"—that impact on regulation, funding schemes and on different organisations of national and local port systems. These legal levels often generate a multi-layered regulation in which national and local rules co-exist, all shaping the particular port environment in terms of capability for performing certain activities and in allowing stakeholders to efficiently operate within the port premises.

Such elements are often discussed in academic literature by referring to the generics of the port governance models. Often such discussions are treated at macro-level (i.e. national port organisation), neglecting local elements that heavily impact on the actual implementation of different models, potentially forming a wide array of solutions in terms of internal organisation and capability to attract investments. Within this general framework, Baltazar and Brooks (2006) showed how the principles of the port devolution that characterised most countries starting from the 1980s were justified by similar needs but outcomes were very heterogeneous, depending on local elements.

Port investments are considered a key competitive factor in modern port economics, affecting the port development, the planning of alternative activities and the capability to finance alternative solutions either directly or indirectly affecting the array of potential development projects that a port management body can deploy. Despite the relative importance and general agreement on these factors, Musso et al. (2006) highlighted how the actual deployment of different investments—and their capability to achieve the foreseen results—is strictly dependent on the relations, synergies and conflicts among the numerous stakeholders involved in the investment process, stressing the role of institutions for correctly balancing different interests. As such, understanding how institutions could impact on the actual implementation of port governance models and how the planning of activities can be aligned with its actual deployment is both paramount and tricky. This latter issue is linked to the potential trade-offs that have been highlighted by literature, often in relation with the assessment of the rationale for different port reforms (e.g. Estache et al., 2002; Everett, 2003; Tongzon et al., 2015) and their actual impact on port performance. Even if there is a consensus in the primary reason pursued by most port governance modifications (i.e. increased port efficiency), the capability of actually achieving such goal is often disputable and strongly dependent on the smooth implementation of such reforms and their acceptance within the port community. Levelling the playing field is often more complicated than originally planned by policymakers.

For instance, several scholars argue that the commonalities and differences in European port performance can be linked to the differentiated governance applications even though most countries adopt the same governance model, i.e. the landlord model. This issue being often considered more relevant than the geographical location of different ports. Several modifications introduced by different EU national legislators had the adaptation and modernisation of port systems as primary goal, often in connection with the changes occurred in competing port ranges (e.g. Ferrari et al., 2015). Because of this issue, many policy papers (e.g. Haralambides et al., 2001) argue that the European Commission primary goal should be the introduction of common rules within the European Union, reviewing the reasons for the past failing attempts and proposing a regulatory approach consistent with the different national port experiences: the historical development of different port institutions along with national culture do play a role in the different implementation of governance models, forming hidden barriers to potential innovative solutions. This latter element is of particular importance, and it is often observed in many port-related aspects: Ferrari et al. (2015) compared similar regulatory tools applied in EU ports, highlighting how similar labels (e.g. concession agreement) are often linked to different legal and operational characteristics, generating asymmetric rights and duties for port stakeholders in different ports and justifying differentiated capabilities for ports of better adapting to the market development. Despite this, cultural barriers and local interests have opposed to a wide reform of the EU port sector, often in connection with differentiated trade-offs in accepting common rules: any port reform needs to be developed together with the port community that is going to be regulated with such rules and lobbying activities are often fundamental for the success of such reform processes, as demonstrated by the several experiences described in this book and by the several attempts for an EU common port policy.

Thus, the conservatism that is often linked to the port and shipping industry (Arduino et al., 2013) when it comes to innovating the business, could be translated—whenever the focus of the discussion comes to governance models—into the impact of local traditions (and commercial interests) on the application of governance models.

As such, before detailing the different solutions adopted by different countries, the current chapter discusses the role of institutions in the implementation of different governance models and the impact that such differences have on port planning and finance.

## Institutions Towards Path Dependence

Starting from the 1980s, most countries have experienced a series of port reforms: the majority has experienced a tendency in promoting private participation in port operations, often in the hope of achieving higher efficiency levels and a reduced public debt due to the needed port investments (e.g. Everett, 2002). As pointed out by Dooms et al. (2013), policymakers engaged on a path of continuous assessment of the applied regulatory frameworks, including who and what mattered in decision-making when implementing transport infrastructure projects. This issue is particularly visible whenever public–private partnerships are promoted. Within this reviewing continuous activity, port models in recent decades have been associated with the weakening of the public control and an increased role of corporatised port actors. This evolution of the port environment incentivised researchers to undertake studies on whether institutions mattered in port reforms, governance and planning (e.g. Debrie et al., 2013; Dooms et al., 2013). Similarly, several scholars have tried to better assess the reasons for a dichotomy that can be observed looking at different experiences. On the one hand, a general convergence in more privatised systems and on the other hand a simultaneous tendency in customised solutions that generated a variety of applications of governance models often labelled using the same name: "landlord model".

Due to the tendency of labelling differentiated approaches under a relatively small group of governance model categories, Suykens (1985) investigated the link between different regulatory choices and achieved advantages, underlining how ports reaching similar efficiency gains had found to respond to dissimilar systems for governance: thus, no unique optimal recipe can be actually identified.

Bergantino et al. (2013) highlighted how the contextualisation of port operations can help in better understanding the performance of different activities since many general—context related—factors heavily impact on the capability of port stakeholders to efficiently use the traditional port production inputs (e.g. quay, yard and labour). The abovementioned study highlights how, once contextual elements (e.g. operational environment and regulatory issues) have been taken into account, pure managerial efficiency can be understood more clearly while often efficiency studies are often biased by context-related elements. Managers' performance, ceteris paribus, is more evenly distributed than it seemed from the analysis of the raw efficiency levels often performed by generalised assessments. Thus, in accordance with Bergantino et al. (2013), ignoring the role of general economic conditions and political regimes of ports' functioning (together with the local infrastructural endowment) does lead to misleading results. As such, the evaluation of different governance models as well as their capability of achieving the promised results is often connected to the possibility of being adapted to the local context and being internalised by relevant stakeholders.

The presence of a general "port governance convergence", with a relatively low number of solutions, has generated a plethora of studies that were focused in understanding the process of actual implementation of port reforms as well as on evaluating factors that impact on the actual achievement of the regulatory goals.

A study promoted by Tongzon et al. (2015), for instance, highlighted that port governance is normally associated with the implementation process dependent on the paths that were established by the broader institutional framework in which the ports are located. This latter aspect ensures differentiated solutions aiming at maximising the collaboration with local stakeholders. On the one hand, port reforms are often driven by external benchmarks (e.g. World Bank Port Reform Tool Kit) but they often have to deal with local cultural heritage and institutional dependence. Within this framework, Ng and Pallis (2010) proposed a port reform scheme (Fig. 2.1) in which the original structure of the port organisation initially planned by the regulator is actually modified and "mitigated" by the local institutional background and—as such—by all relevant stakeholders that impact on the actual implementation of the foreseen governance model.

Such "mitigation" factor is often implicitly recognised in most of the papers describing reform processes or differentiated local applications of national rules (e.g. Debrie et al., 2013; Parola et al., 2017). Within the field of the Economic Geography (e.g. Hall, 2003; Mackinnon et al., 2009), the impact of such institutional dependence is often linked to a convergence path in which all stakeholders affect the final outcome of an organisational change generating a result that can also be quite different from the optimal outcome originally planned. For instance, Reveley and Tull (2012), assessing New Zealand and Australia port reform processes, highlight how "*economic and political actors' purposive decisions pushed the development of port institutions down a pathway which became hard to step off: institutional lock-ins impeded strategic flexibility and the growth of port productivity; inefficient macro- and micro-level institutional arrangements reduced*" regional port efficiency. On the one hand, the "institutionalisation" of port reforms mitigates conflicts that otherwise could generate economic losses, strikes and other issues; on the other hand, it generates unexpected outcomes, risking to slow down the achievement of the foreseen reform targets.

Thus, Notteboom et al. (2013) investigated the impact of path dependence in seaport governance, mainly focusing on the notion of "lock-in" effect. Institutional lock-ins are normally defined as hidden barriers to innovation generated by the presence of specific steps to be followed within the organisation in order to smoothly implement any form of reform and the possibility to have unexpected outcomes due to the internal interactions of differentiated actors within the related institution. Applied to the port context, institutional lock-ins often impact on the capability of regulators to implement modifications in the port

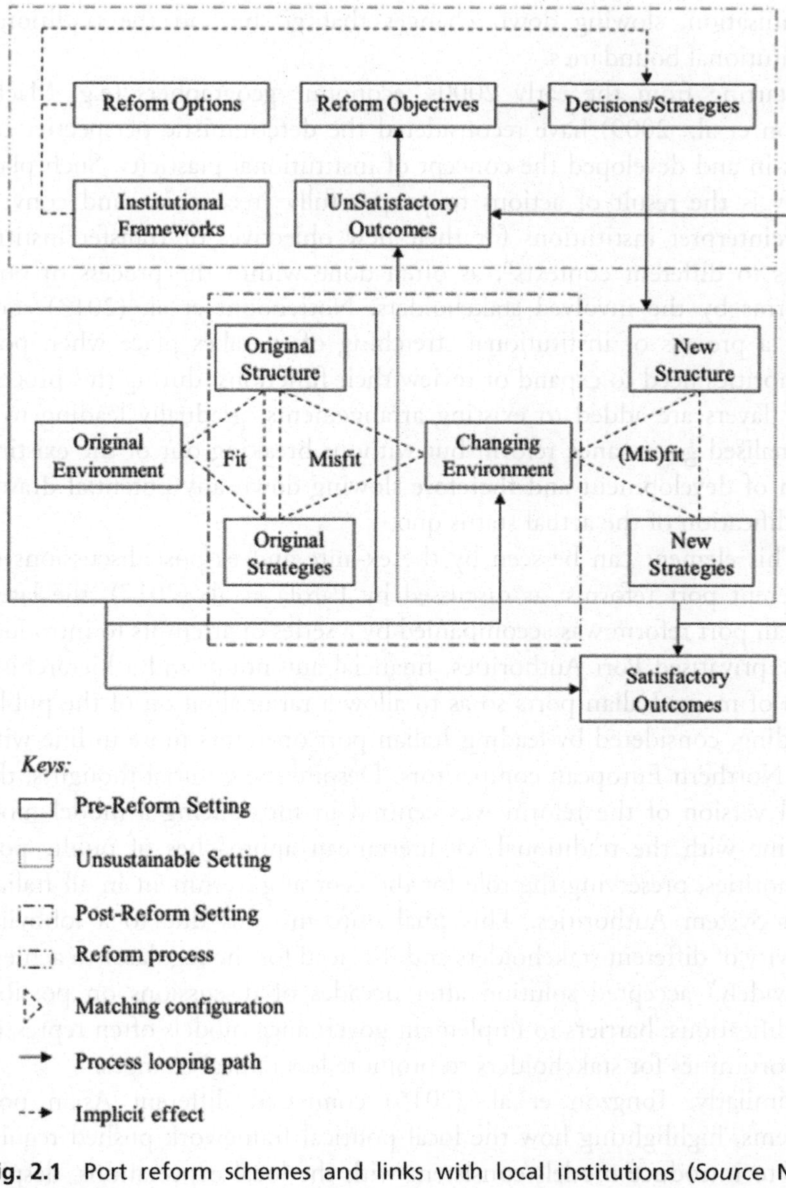


**Fig. 2.1** Port reform schemes and links with local institutions (*Source* Ng & Pallis, 2010)

organisation, slowing down changes that go beyond the traditional institutional boundaries.

Starting from the early 2000s, economic geographers (e.g. Mackinnon et al., 2009) have reconsidered the deterministic perspective on lock-in and developed the concept of institutional plasticity. Such plasticity is the result of actions to purposefully "recombine and convert or reinterpret institutions for their new objectives or transfer institutions to different contexts", as often done within the process of port reforms by the involved stakeholders. Notteboom et al. (2013) state that a process of institutional stretching often takes place when port authorities need to expand or review their functions: during this process new layers are added to existing arrangements, gradually leading to a formalised governance reform but without breaking out of the existing path of development and therefore slowing down any potential drastic modification of the actual status quo.

This element can be seen by the ex-ante and ex-post discussions of different port reforms: as discussed by Parola et al. (2017), the latest Italian port reform was accompanied by a series of attempts to introduce fully privatised Port Authorities, financial autonomy and a hierarchisation of major Italian ports so as to allow a rationalisation of the public funding, considered by leading Italian port operators more in line with the Northern European competitors. Despite these initial thoughts, the final version of the reform was centred in introducing a model more in line with the traditional Mediterranean approaches of public port authorities, preserving the role for the central government in all Italian Port System Authorities. This final outcome was due to a lobbying activity of different stakeholders and the need for the regulator to achieve a "widely" accepted solution after decades of discussions on possible modifications: barriers to implement governance models often represent opportunities for stakeholders to promote less radical changes.

Similarly, Tongzon et al. (2015) compared different Asian port systems, highlighting how the local political framework pushed regulators to introduce models consistent with the local expectations, despite an initial array of alternative solutions.

Thus, port reforms are often the outcome of explicit and implicit negotiations between the regulator and the different stakeholders, with the aim of achieving a solution both accepted by the different port communities and in line with the cultural and organisational characteristic of the port region.

The abovementioned discussion underlines how stakeholders play an important role in defining the actual setting of the port and its capability of fulfilling long-term goals. While general port reforms have been impacted by the role of institutions, it is important to highlight how these attitudes often impact on the daily port business in the aftermath of different reforms: the mitigating effect of institutions on port governance modifications often generate smooth implementation strategies as well, assuring minor impacts on the operability of different ports and then assuring the sustainability for the changed regulatory framework.

## Finance, Planning and National Interests

The path dependency related to the formulation and implementation of port governance models, often impact on the capability of different port systems to innovate and to achieve long-term goals.

These critical issues occur whenever governance models are linked to the planning capabilities of different port management bodies and in their possibility of achieving their intended goals. González-Laxe et al. (2015) investigate the different perspectives that public institutions might have in improving port performance when compared to other port stakeholders. In assessing differentiating factors, the cited authors highlight how public and private stakeholders often have conflicting objective functions often determining misaligned behaviours, especially when it comes to achieving long-term objectives. Among the long-term goals, environmental related issues have recently used as one of the main examples of this misaligned behaviours. For instance, Becker et al. (2012) link the role of port institutional challenges to the capability of different ports to introduce effective solutions not only for mitigating environmental impacts of maritime activities but also for adapting port infrastructure to climate change and therefore to implement long-term investment programmes. In fact, while mitigation strategies are often welcome by all relevant port stakeholders—given their role for marketing purposes as well—adaptation investments are often seen as unproductive intervention with long-run benefits but short-term costs in relation to infrastructure operability. Conflicts among stakeholders that do not necessarily share the same values (e.g. public vs private actors) or business horizon (e.g. concession agreement duration) often generate hidden barriers to such investments, if such expenditures do not directly benefit a clear set of the stakeholders involved.

Similarly, Raimbault (2019) highlights the role of regional institutions in promoting hinterland connections: this seems particularly important if linked with the concept of port regionalisation: strong connections with inland regions become more and more strategic for ports and the role those external institutions play in the implementation of such connections is strategically important for the long-term prosperity of the port. Because of this, whenever the governance model allows port management bodies to promote cooperation agreements, port management bodies try to pursue collaborations with other infrastructure managers in order to strengthen hinterland connections, often providing these connections as distinctive competitive advantages of such ports. Whenever this latter solution is not allowed, port management bodies try to strengthen links with the different regional institutions in order to implicitly promote coordinated efforts in the provision of effective links to/from the port. Within the recent industry development, the role of external stakeholders, often operating in the hinterland, is becoming more and more fundamental for the port industry and the differentiated limits of the alternative governance models generated an array of collaborative behaviours with the different stakeholders involved, often impacting the role of institutions within the port and posing a push for further evolution in the deployment of novel governance solutions. This element has been also highlighted by the recent wave of new investments in technologies—such as block chain, the automation of terminal operations and the Internet of Things—where the capability of effectively deploying such technologies is either promoted or limited by the local stakeholders that represent a key factor in the delays of the industry in promoting such solutions (e.g. Bavassano et al., 2020).

## Conclusions

Institutions play an important role in defining the implementation of the chosen port governance model. While most of the papers assessing port reforms in different national contexts refer to institutions only as the regulators promoting the new port law, all port stakeholders actually play a role on the final port organisation, impacting the planning of port layout as well as the balance among different market players. Such element has been fundamental in justifying the differences in terms of local rules and regulations, particularly among different port communities ideally applying the same model. On the one hand, we observe a convergence to a more privatised port system, on the other local institutions assure a "customisation" of the chosen governance solution. Because of this, the comparison of different experiences represents a key element for understanding the root cause of current situations as well as for better identifying limits and opportunities that port systems might have in implementing further round of reforms.

The correct understanding of the role played by path dependence, linked to institutional lock-in, may shed lights on the role of such phenomenon in shaping the organisation of ports and on the possibility for actually implementing either drastic modifications in respect to the status quo or achieving specific goals. Within this issue, the balance of conflicting interests within the stakeholders' community might impact the achievement of the port's long-term goals as well as the capability for the port management bodies to correctly implement the internal strategies. Understanding the role of institutions is then fundamental for correctly comparing different local and national experiences as well as for using such experiences for planning future port reforms.

## References

Arduino, G., Aronietis, R., Crozet, Y., Frouws, K., Ferrari, C., Guihery, L., Kapros, S., Kourounioti, I., Laroche, F., Lambrou, M., Lloyd, M., Polydoropoulou, A., Roumboutsos, A., Van de Voorde, E., & Vanelslander, T. (2013). How to turn an innovative concept into a success? An application to seaport-related innovation. *Research in Transportation Economics, 42*(1), 97–107.

Baltazar, R., & Brooks, M. (2006). Port governance, devolution and the matching framework: A configuration theory approach. *Research in Transportation Economics, 17*, 379–403.

Bavassano, G., Ferrari, C., & Tei, A. (2020). Blockchain: How shipping industry is dealing with the ultimate technological leap. *Research in Transportation Business & Management, 34*, 100428.

Becker, A., Inoue, S., Fischer, M., & Schwegler, B. (2012). Climate change impacts on international seaports: Knowledge, perceptions, and planning efforts among port administrators. *Climatic Change, 110*(1), 5–29.

Bergantino, A., Musso, E., & Porcelli, F. (2013). Port management performance and contextual variables: Which relationship? Methodological and empirical issues. *Research in Transportation Business & Management, 8*, 39–49.

Debrie, J., Lavaud-Letilleul, V., & Parola, F. (2013). Shaping port governance: the territorial trajectories of reform. *Journal of Transport Geography, 27*, 56–65.

Dooms, M., Verbeke, A., & Haezendonck, E. (2013). Stakeholder management and path dependence in large-scale transport infrastructure development: The port of Antwerp case (1960–2010). *Journal of Transport Geography, 27*, 14–25.

Estache, A., Gonzalez, M., & Trujillo, L. (2002). Efficiency gains from port reform and the potential for yardstick competition: Lessons from Mexico. *World Development, 30*, 545–560.

Everett, S. (2003). Corporatization: A legislative framework for port inefficiencies. *Maritime Policy and Management, 30*, 211–219.

Ferrari, C., Parola, F., & Tei, A. (2015). Governance models and port concessions in Europe: Commonalities, critical issues and policy perspectives. *Transport Policy, 41*, 60–67.

González-Laxe, F., Freire-Seoane, M., & Montes, C. (2015). Port policy and port choice: The Spanish case. *International Journal of Transport Economics, 44*, 529–553.
Hall, P. V. (2003). Regional institutional convergence? Reflections from the Baltimore waterfront. *Economic Geography, 79*, 347–363.
Haralambides, H., Verbeke, A., Musso, E., & Benacchio, M. (2001). Port financing and pricing in the European Union: Theory, politics and reality. *International Journal of Maritime Economics, 3*, 368–386.
Mackinnon, D., Cumbers, A., Pike, A., Birch, K., & Mcmaster, R. (2009). Evolution in economic geography: institutions, political economy and adaptation. *Economic Geography, 85*, 129–150.
Musso, E., Ferrari, C., & Benacchio, M. (2006). Port investment: Profitability, economic impact and financing. *Research in Transportation Economics, 16*, 171–218.
Ng, A. K., & Pallis, A. (2010). Port governance reforms in diversified institutional frameworks; generic solutions, implementation asymmetries. *Environment and Planning A, 42*, 2147–2167.
Notteboom, T., De Langen, P., & Jacobs, W. (2013). Institutional plasticity and path dependence in seaports: Interactions between institutions, port governance reforms and port authority routines. *Journal of Transport Geography, 27*, 26–35.
Parola, F., Ferrari, C., Tei, A., Satta, G., & Musso, E. (2017). Dealing with multi-scalar embeddedness and institutional divergence: Evidence from the renovation of Italian port governance. *Research in Transportation Business & Management, 22*, 89–99.
Raimbault, N. (2019). From regional planning to port regionalization and urban logistics. The inland port and the governance of logistics development in the Paris region. *Journal of Transport Geography, 78*, 205–213.
Reveley, J., & Tull, M. (2012). Institutional path dependence in port regulation: A comparison of New Zealand and Australia. In G. Harlaftis, S. Tenold, & J. M. Valdaliso (Eds), *The world's key industry* (pp. 158–179). https://link.springer.com/book/10.1057%2F9781137003751.
Suykens, F. (1985). Administration and management at the Port of Antwerp. *Maritime Policy and Management, 12*, 181–194.
Tongzon, J., Ng, A. K., & Shou, E. (2015). Institutions, transport infrastructure governance, and planning: Lessons from the corporatization of port authorities in East Asia. *Environment and Planning C: Government and Policy, 33*, 1467–1483.

# Part II

## National Port Systems vis à vis Global Shipping

# 3

# Port Finance and Regulation in Kenya

Michaël Dooms and Denis Lewa Muganga

## Introduction

In this chapter, we discuss the case of the Kenyan port system from the angle of Port Finance and Regulation. In East Africa, Kenya and its Port of Mombasa at the Indian Ocean are not only crucial for the economic development of the country itself but historically also as a key gateway for landlocked countries such as Uganda, Rwanda and Burundi. For these hinterland destinations, the region is characterized by an increasing

M. Dooms (✉)
Department of Business, Vrije Universiteit Brussel, Brussels, Belgium
e-mail: michael.dooms@vub.be

D. L. Muganga
Northern Corridor Transit and Transport Coordination Authority (NCTTCA), Mombasa, Kenya

© The Author(s), under exclusive license to Springer Nature Switzerland AG 2022

C. Ferrari et al. (eds.), *Regulation and Finance in the Port Industry*, Palgrave Studies in Maritime Economics,
https://doi.org/10.1007/978-3-030-83985-7_3

degree of port competition with, e.g. the presence of the ports of Dar-Es-Salaam (Tanzania) and the port of Djibouti (Djibouti). In what follows, we discuss Kenya's port system and performance, after which we describe the main port regulation and finance instruments. We also offer some forward-looking elements. When it comes to research on African countries, the usual challenges in terms of quality and availability of data apply. For this chapter, we were able to use internal documents of the Kenya Ports Authority such as financial, business and master plans. We largely focus on the period since 2000 and on the Port of Mombasa, the main operational commercial port at present.

## Description of Kenya's Port System

### Brief History of Port Governance in Kenya

Kenya Ports Authority (KPA) is a state-owned body under the Ministry of Transport established by an Act of Parliament of 20 January 1978 with the mandate to maintain, operate, improve and regulate all scheduled seaports situated along Kenya's coastline and lake ports (Government of Kenya, 2014a). It is one of the institutional successors of the former East African Railways and Harbours Corporation which entailed rail and harbour interests both on the infrastructure and operations level in Kenya, Tanzania and Uganda. Following the break-up of the East African Community, the corporation was broken up into three parts. In Kenya, it was chosen to create three companies: the Kenya Ports Authority (KPA), Kenya Cargo Handling Services (KCHS) and Kenya Railways. Following reforms in the next decades, KPA and KCHS were merged (1986) and a separate maritime authority, Kenya Maritime Authority (KMA), was created (2004).

In the Kenyan context, only one national port (the Port of Mombasa) is currently fully operational and runs commercial operations under a service port regime. All other ports are small in size and their operations are not yet fully functional. These include Shimoni, Kisumu, Lamu and the Old Mombasa Port. However, there are plans to revitalize Shimoni and Kisumu, alongside a large greenfield development in

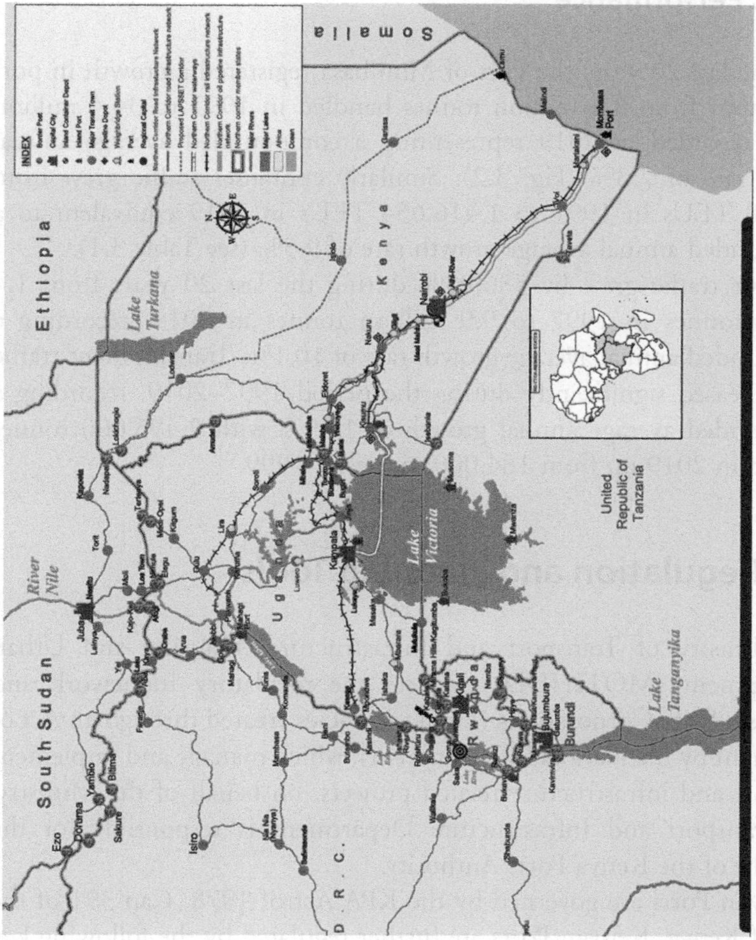


**Fig. 3.1** Kenyan ports and their hinterland connections (*Source* Map provided by NCTTCA)

Lamu (for a full discussion on Kenya's port governance system, we refer to Dooms & Farrell, 2017). Figure 3.1 shows the transport infrastructure system originating from the port of Mombasa.

### Traffic Performance

Over the last 20 years the Port of Mombasa registered a growth in port throughput from 8.4 million tonnes handled in 1997 to 34.4 million tonnes recorded in 2019 representing a compounded average annual growth rate of 7.3% (Fig. 3.2). Similarly container traffic grew from 230.698 TEUs in 1997 to 1.416.654 TEUs in 2019 equivalent to a compounded annual average growth rate of 9.5% (see Table 3.1).

Transit traffic grew by 586.95% during the last 20 years from 1.4 million tonnes in 1997 to 9.9 million tonnes in 2019, recording a compounded annual average growth rate of 10.1%. Transhipment traffic also increased significantly during the period 1997–2019, recording a compounded average annual growth of 13.9% with 2.495.000 tonnes handled in 2019 up from 184.000 tonnes in 1999.

## Port Regulation and Planning Tools

The Ministry of Transport and Infrastructure, Housing and Urban Development (MOTIHUD) oversees the regulatory framework and supervises State Corporations (Public Agencies created through an Act of Parliament by the National Government), which manage and implement transport and infrastructure-related projects, on behalf of the Ministry. The Transport and Infrastructure Department is responsible for the oversight of the Kenya Ports Authority.

Kenyan Ports are governed by the KPA Act of 1978, Cap 391 of the Laws of Kenya. Kenyan Ports are further regulated by the following key laws and regulations:

1. East African Harbours Regulations
2. Customs Management Act

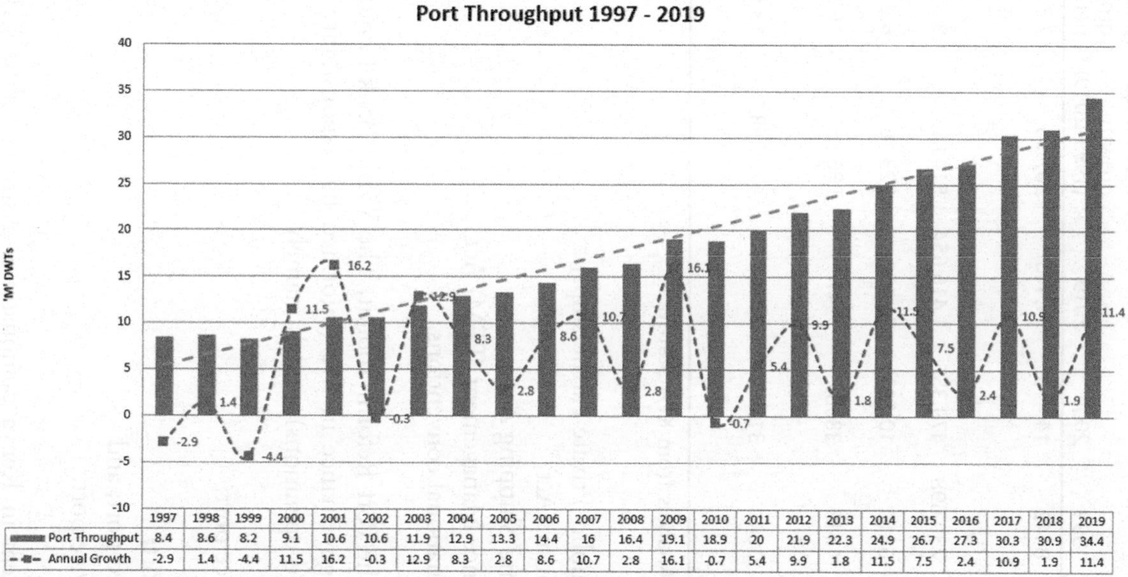


**Fig. 3.2** Port throughput 1997–2019 (*Source* Authors Analysis from KPA Statistics)

**Table 3.1** Mombasa Port performance overview

| | 1999 | 2009 | 2019 | Percentage growth (1999–2019) | Average annual growth percentage |
|---|---|---|---|---|---|
| Port throughput ('000' tonnes) | 8442 | 14,419 | 34,440 | 307.96 | 7.3 |
| Container traffic (TEUs) | 230,698 | 479,355 | 1,416,654 | 514.07 | 9.5 |
| Local ('000' DWT) | 6810 | 10,293 | 21,998 | 223.16 | 6.0 |
| Transit traffic ('000' tonnes) | 1448 | 3808 | 9947 | 586.95 | 10.1 |
| Transshipment traffic ('000' tonnes) | 184 | 318 | 2495 | 1225.98 | 13.9 |

*Source* Authors Analysis from KPA Statistics

3. PPP Act (Public–Private Partnerships)
4. Kenya Maritime Act
5. Merchant and Shipping Act
6. Public Finance Management (PFM) Act
7. Other international conventions.

According to the Port Reform Toolkit, The World Bank Group (2003) classifies port governance in five (informed by responsibility for port investments and operations) models, namely

1. Public service port;
2. Tool port;
3. Landlord port;
4. Corporatized port; and
5. Private Service port.

The ports system in Kenya demonstrates a strong public service port model, where all port facilities and infrastructure are publicly funded (i.e. by the Kenya Ports Authority), except for a few private investments under long-term lease arrangements. However, over time, there has been an intended strategic shift towards the landlord port model, where specific port facilities have been offered in concession through public–private partnerships (PPPs). The 1978 KPA Act, Part V Section 18 and 19, confirms the financial management principles applying to both port operations (operating expenses) and borrowing for infrastructure development (capital expenses), while Part VI Section 20 and 21 defines the framework for accounts and reports, specifying guidelines for annual accounts and annual reports and financial years.

As provided in the Act, the KPA has a duty to ensure that its businesses are conducted according to commercial principles. The KPA may also, subject to the direction given to the Board by the Minister responsible for finance, invest any surplus funds in such securities as the Board may deem fit.

The KPA raises revenues through specific charges stipulated in the KPA tariff book, which is revised and approved every five years. The tariff contains fees and charges to be paid by port users for cargo handling and storage services, marine services and ship dues and general services. In terms of revenue split, stevedoring (33%) and wharfage (33%) are the main revenue categories. Container handling (8%), shore handling (12%) and other revenue (14%) complete the revenue split, according to the 2016/2017 annual report (KPA, 2017).

As per law, the KPA is forbidden to assign its property by way of security for borrowed money. It is also mandatory in the KPA Act that any loan will have to be authorized/guaranteed by the Government of Kenya (GOK). The debt is however not consolidated in the National Debt, instead it will be shown in the KPA Books as a direct loan to the port authority.

Section 31(1) of the Public Financial Management (PFM) Act, which is the law guiding management of resources held by all public institutions in Kenya, provides that 'The Cabinet Secretary shall submit to Parliament, every four months, a report of all loans made to the national government, national government entities and county governments, in accordance with Article 211(2) of the Constitution'.

The PFM Regulations also provide for the administration, control and management of grants extended to public entities.

Other governance tools outside KPA include:

- The Mombasa Port Charter which outlines key performance targets and is agreed upon by different stakeholders (Port Authority, Maritime Authority, Shipping Agents, etc.), with weekly follow-up meetings to discuss operational issues.
- The activities within the Northern Corridor Transit and Transport Agreement (NCTTA), a regional cooperation treaty which is enforced by a proper authority. The NCTTA covers 6 countries (Burundi, Rwanda, DR Congo, South-Sudan, Uganda and Kenya) and needs to guarantee and improve landlocked country access to the port of Mombasa, by improving both infrastructural and operational aspects of various transport supply chains. It has a proper authority overseeing the implementation of the Agreement.

With regard to port planning, the port has issued master plans for the port of Mombasa since 2004, with updates in 2009, 2015 and 2019, supported by external consultants. These are translated by KPA corporate staff into five-year strategic and business plans, which include capital investment budgets, as well as measures undertaken to ensure organizational improvements such as ICT and HR related, aimed at transforming the organization. For smaller ports such as Kisumu and Shimoni, separate master plans and feasibility studies were recently commissioned as part of the overall Kenya Ports masterplan.

The Lamu Port development, on the other hand, is managed by a separate authority (LAPPSET corridor authority), with a separate board of directors. However, it is expected that KPA will manage the new port once it is completed, although other parties (both private as well as port authorities from other countries) have expressed their interest.

# Financial Tools

## General Discussion

All ports in Kenya are regulated by national law: the KPA Act, Cap 391, of the Laws of Kenya. As indicated above, Mombasa Port is currently the only commercial Port in Kenya, while all other ports are small in nature and only undertake small-scale trade, with minimal revenues generated per annum. In 2014, however, the County Government of Mombasa (CGM) initiated a legislative process of reviewing the management and regulation of the Port of Mombasa, as well as revenue sharing between the KPA and the CGM, proposing to charge two dollars per tonne of cargo that passes through the Port of Mombasa. This proposal follows a longer term latent tension between the national government and local stakeholders on the alleged costs and benefits from the presence of the port, where a large flow of tax and dividends is generated towards the national government and redistributed accordingly, with CGM in recent times more explicitly claiming that it does not get its fair share of the net benefits, and questioning their social support for port activities (see Dooms & Farrell, 2017; Hoyle, 1997). This tension has been escalated by the recent move by CFSs (Container Freight Stations) to relocate economic activity to Nairobi, due to the shift of cargo to the Inland Container Depot (ICD) in Nairobi through the SGR (Standard Gauge Railway) project.

## Emerging Local Policies

The CGM developed two legislations, the Mombasa County Port Authority Bill 2014, and the Ferries and Harbors Bill 2014 (Government of Kenya, 2014b, 2014c). The Memorandum on the Mombasa County Port Authority Bill stated that the bill was necessitated by the need to have a body which would oversee collection of revenue in matters related to transport and shipping, which would in turn improve the county government's revenue. The latter bill sought to allow the CGM to identify vessels in the harbor and allow for revenue collection from vessels landing cargo.

Revenue collection was therefore the main focus of the introduction of this law and the establishment of the KPA. However, Regulatory Impact Assessment (RIA) in Kenya requires that laws and regulations should only be reviewed to enhance health, safety, security and environmental protection, and not be driven by a revenue motive. Despite the draft laws getting approval at the local county level, they were rejected by the Attorney General at the national level.

## Limited Success of Port PPPs Despite the Elaborated Framework

Regarding opportunities for PPPs and funding mechanisms through private sector partnerships, the Government, through the Vision 2030, Kenya's national long-term development strategy covering the period 2008 to 2030, places great emphasis on creating a productive infrastructure in the country's journey towards poverty reduction as well as social, political and economic transformation. Kenya faces a significant infrastructure-financing deficit estimated at $2.1 billion annually, which constrains growth and development. Sustained expenditures of almost four billion dollars per year will be required to meet the country's infrastructure needs. The World Bank Group estimates that increasing infrastructure financing could improve Kenya's per capita growth rate by three percentage points (World Bank, 2019).

Responding to this challenge, the Government of Kenya, through the National Treasury, made infrastructure development and public service provision through Public–Private Partnerships (PPP) a priority mechanism that can help it address this major infrastructure funding gap and achieve the benefits of successful PPP investments. Major successes of PPPs include substantial private investment; transfer of significant risk to the private sector; improving access to infrastructure; creating higher quality assets with better operation and maintenance and helping achieve better value for money.

Established initially under the Public Procurement and Disposal (Public–Private Partnership) Regulations in 2009, the Kenyan government has in the recent past been committed to improving and strengthening the PPP framework for private sector participation in the country. Several accomplishments are notable:

a. The adoption of a PPP Policy in 2011 to articulate the government's commitment to PPPs and to provide a basis for the enactment of a PPP Law;
b. The enactment of the PPP Act on 8 February 2013;
c. The gazettement of the National PPP Regulations on 19 December 2014;
d. The development of PPP Regulations for the County Governments; and
e. The development of a PPP Manual.

To support the delivery of the country's PPP agenda, a number of institutions have been created under the PPP Act of 2013 (Government of Kenya, 2014d). They include:

a. PPP Committee;
b. PPP Petition Committee;
c. PPP Unit; and
d. PPP Nodes within the Ministries, Government Agencies and County Governments.

The KPA has made a commitment to expand its infrastructure through PPP funding options, including the appointment of a senior management team to form a PPP Node (as defined in the PPP Act 2013), which is a special task force within the organization concerned with the management of PPP projects.

However, players in the ports sector have largely been local, due to the lack of success in establishing PPP projects. The initial attempt was on Concessioning of the second Container Terminal at the Port of Mombasa. This was however not successful. A study was then conducted on the possibility of developing and operating Kisumu Port through

PPP. The findings of the study however indicated that it was not viable as a PPP project as it would require substantial public investments to increase private sector interest. Also the main international lenders and investors in the country (Japan and China) have not shown interest for those reasons.

Negotiations are now ongoing to engage a private party to operate Lamu Port, whose first three (3) berths are currently under development. A feasibility study has also been completed for Shimoni Port to confirm viability for PPP investment. The report has been submitted to the PPP Unit for approval before progressing. A fishing port and multipurpose facility have been proposed for Shimoni. More recently, the county government of Kwale, the county immediately to the south of Mombasa, has confirmed its interest to operate Shimoni port, with assistance from KPA under the form of provision of capacity building (training and education). Overall, it seems that PPPs as an instrument to further port development in Kenya have been difficult to implement. Recent research by Humphreys et al. (2019), under the auspices of the World Bank, confirms the continued drive towards vertical integration driven by the public sector in East African ports. For Kenya, in particular, the research explicitly points to contradictions between policy objectives on increased private sector participation and the actual policy implementation, with KPA pursuing further interests and capability development in cargo handling operations.

FDIs in the ports sector have been minimal, except for loans advanced to KPA for the development of various port facilities such as berths, access roads, among others. The main player in these loans has been JICA (Japan International Cooperation Agency).

Other actors providing investment aid are TMEA (Trade Mark East Africa), a multi-country funded development aid agency which provides technical assistance as well as partial investment aid for, e.g. new equipment purchases as well as rehabilitation of existing, older berths or environmental-related projects.

On the hinterland side, the most prolific foreign intervention was the construction of a new railway line (Standard Gauge Railway or SGR), financed through a state-to-state loan of the Chinese government, including investment in a new marshalling yard at the port of Mombasa.

The SGR was a game changer that totally transformed cargo handling at the port of Mombasa. It plans to evacuate up to 40% of all import cargo from the port, up from the 2% previously evacuated by the old railway line.

Overall, KPA's self-financing capacity stays relatively high due to its monopolistic position in the provision of port infrastructure and cargo handling services, making an after-tax profit between 25 and 70 million USD annually (KPA, 2017).

## Critical Discussion and Conclusion

The elements presented in the previous section suggest that despite the presence of frameworks to allow foreign investment in port development (such as the PPP Act and its implementation), the level of private investment in the port area in a strict sense has remained very limited to non-existent. On the other hand, there are clear signs that inward investment related to port development will increase in the future.

First, at the level of hinterland connections, the investment and operation of the Standard Gauge Railway (SGR) between Nairobi and Mombasa (opened in 2018) has been financed by an approximately 3.2 billion USD loan (about 50% commercial and 50% concessional) from China's Exim Bank. Given Kenya's status as a lower middle-income economy, conditions for favourable funding by other institutions have become more stringent, with the country turning to Asian countries for financing (in particular China and Japan). Likewise, stretch targets for the use of the SGR make part of the contract between both governments and have led to legislative initiatives by the GOK with (1) outright obligations for cargo owners to use the railway (2) preferential, subsidized tariffs for rail use. It remains to be seen whether this situation is sustainable in the longer term.

Second, the impact of the SGR on the local economic development of the city of Mombasa has been largely considered to have a strong short-term negative economic impact on the region as road trucking, clearing and forwarding and other port-related business have either completely disappeared (e.g. employment at Container Freight Stations outside the port area) or re-located to Nairobi (given the presence of the Inland Container Depot that acts as an extended gate dry port) (County Government of Mombasa, 2019). This evolution has contributed to a further loss of legitimacy of port activities in the local community and with the local government, which is seeking its own ways to get financial benefits from the port's presence. On the other hand, new opportunities have been identified locally, with the development of Special Economic Zones (SEZs), in particular, the Dongo Kundu area of more than 1.300 hectares (a development suggested by the 2015 KPA masterplan authored by JICA). Here, financing and investment by the Japanese International Cooperation Agency (JICA) for an amount of approximately 400 million USD has been secured, of which about 15% as a grant and the remaining part as a soft loan.

As a result, inward foreign investments or financing flows are mainly linked to projects outside the port area itself, but with a clear and direct impact on the port's performance, as the SGR is considered as efficiency enhancing, as well as improving the environmental profile of the port through a modal shift; the Dongo Kundu SEZ development will most likely contribute to the development of cargo volumes, as inward foreign investments in manufacturing activities, one of the GOK main objectives, are expected.

Finally, critical reflections are needed on the future business and revenue model of the KPA, if the governance model is tending increasingly to a landlord model. Even in the current situation of a public service port acting as a monopoly, financial stress and lack of self-financing capacity might be expected as, due to the efficiency enhancement through SGRs, and the development of ICDs, substantial revenue flows relating to demurrage of cargo at either port or ICD locations are decreasing. With regard to the Dongo Kundu SEZ development, it is unclear whether the KPA will also collect revenues under the form of leases or concessions (or the outright sale of land). Likewise, as for the Dongo Kundu and for Lamu Port development, it appears that robust business cases allowing sufficient short-term revenue to cover the loans are lacking, given the 'on-and-off' interest of foreign investors (e.g. for Lamu there have been several proposals submitted to GOK for the operation of the infrastructure, but never materialized). In sum, a shift towards the landlord model, coupled to delayed implementation of large-scale development projects, might substantially change the financial relations within the Kenyan port industry, and if ill-implemented lead to the financial instability of the local actors involved. However, at present, there is little evidence that GOK is heading towards structural reform and/or disinvestment in port operations.

## References

County Government of Mombasa. (2019). *Assessment report on the socio-economic impact of the operationalization of the standard gauge railway on the Port City of Mombasa.* Study executed by MBEC Consultants in collaboration with the University of Nairobi.

Dooms, M., & Farrell, S. (2017). Lions or gazelles? The past, present and future of African port authorities: The case of East Africa. *Research in Transportation Business & Management, 100*(22), 135–152.

Government of Kenya. (2014a). KPA Act 1978.

Government of Kenya. (2014b). Mombasa County Government—Mombasa Port Authority Bill.

Government of Kenya. (2014c). Mombasa County Government—Mombasa Ferries and Harbors Bill.

Government of Kenya. (2014d). Public Private Partnership (PPP) Act 2013.

Hoyle, B. (1997). *Ports, port cities and coastal zones: Development, interdependence and competition in East Africa.* Koninklijke Academie voor Overzeese Wetenschappen (67p.).

Humphreys, M., Stokenberga, A., Herrera Dappe, M., Iimi, A, & Hartmann, O. (2019). *Port development and competition in East and Southern Africa: Prospects and challenges.* The World Bank Group. (185 p.).

Kenya Ports Authority. (KPA). Annual Bulletin of Statistics (2003–2019).

Kenya Ports Authority (KPA). (2017). Annual report 2016–2017.

The World Bank Group. (2003). *Port reform toolkit* (English). World Bank. Accessed at http://documents.worldbank.org/curated/en/120991468762301637/Port-reform-toolkit

The World Bank Group. (2019). *Kenya: Enabling private-sector participation in infrastructure and social services.* April 2018. Accessed at https://www.worldbank.org/en/about/partners/brief/kenya-enabling-private-sector-participation-in-infrastructure-and-social-services

# 4

# Regulation, Governance and Infrastructure Pricing in South Africa's Ports Sector

Mihalis Chasomeris and Sanele Gumede

## South Africa's Ports System

South Africa is geographically located on strategic maritime trade routes. It is at the centre of major east–west and north–south routes and has the potential to expand its role in global seaborne commerce. South Africa's ports also serve as a vital trade gateway to neighbouring countries. It is the second-largest economy in Africa with a Gross Domestic Product of about US$350 billion in 2017. The province of Gauteng contributes approximately 35% to South Africa's Gross Domestic Product. In 2017,

M. Chasomeris (✉)
Graduate School of Business and Leadership, University of KwaZulu-Natal, Durban, South Africa
e-mail: chasomerism1@ukzn.ac.za

S. Gumede
School of Accounting, Economics and Finance, University of KwaZulu-Natal, Durban, South Africa

© The Author(s), under exclusive license to Springer Nature Switzerland AG 2022

C. Ferrari et al. (eds.), *Regulation and Finance in the Port Industry*, Palgrave Studies in Maritime Economics,
https://doi.org/10.1007/978-3-030-83985-7_4

if the Gauteng's provincial economy were to be ranked as a country, it would be the sixth largest in Africa (Statistics South Africa, 2018). Hence, a large percentage of cargo volumes are generated by Gauteng. The county's aggregated ranking on the Logistics Performance Index (Arvis et al., 2018), for the period 2012–2018, was 29 out of 167 countries. The UNCTAD (2018) Liner Shipping Connectivity Index shows that South Africa has improved from 23.13, in 2004, to 40.11, in 2018. Despite this improvement, its overall country ranking of 32, in 2004, declined to 44th place, out of 178 countries, in 2018. The capacity of container vessels has been increasing, therefore requiring fewer vessels to carry more TEUs. As a result, vessel arrivals to South Africa's ports have been declining.

Figure 4.1 presents the approximate location of South Africa's eight commercial ports. South Africa's port cargo volumes doubled from 40 million metric tonnes, in 1969–1970, to 80 million tonnes, in 1977–1978, and doubled again to reach 160 million tonnes by the mid-1990s

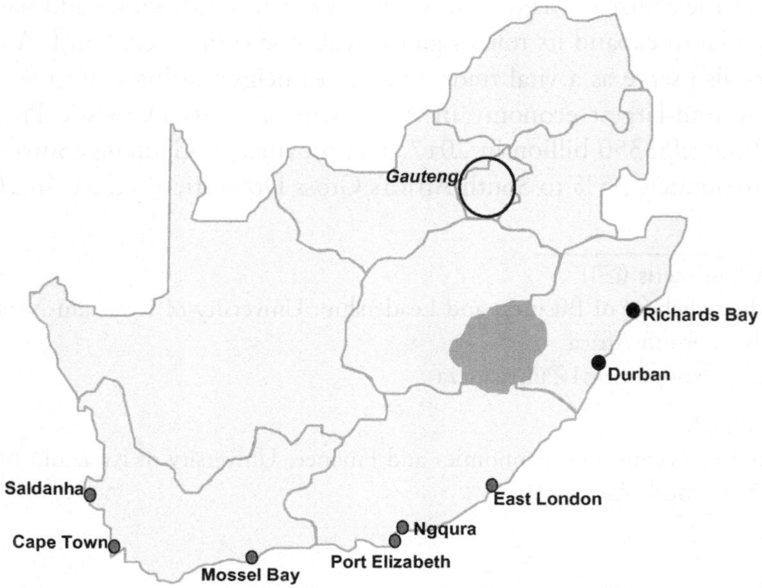


**Fig. 4.1** National ports statistics 2017 (*Source* Authors adjusted using the map from the National Department of Transport, 1998)

(Jones, 2002). In 2017, the country's eight commercial ports handled over 227 million metric tonnes, 4.63 million TEUs and had 9821 vessel arrivals (see Table 4.1). The Port of Richards Bay handles the highest volumes of cargo of about 100 million tonnes. It features a multipurpose terminal and is renowned for its multi-product dry bulk handling facilities, and its privately operated bulk coal terminal was the largest in the world for about three decades. However, the Port of Durban is the busiest multipurpose port in Africa and handled total cargoes of about 42 million tonnes, more than 455,000 vehicles and about 2.7 million TEUs in 2017. Therefore, Durban handles much higher valued cargo than Richards Bay. Cargo values flowing through the Port of Durban are estimated to be about two-thirds of the total value of cargo through the country's ports. The Port of Saldanha handles about 70 million tonnes of mainly bulk cargo, the majority of which is iron ore.

In 2015, South Africa imported 19.7 million tonnes of crude oil, that is, about 83% of its crude oil requirements with the remainder produced locally (South African Energy Sector Report, 2018). Crude Oil imports enter through Durban (76.5%), Cape Town (22%) and Mossel Bay (1.5%) (South African Market Insights, 2017).

TNPA provides services to customers in five market segments as shown in Table 4.2. Over the four fiscal years, Table 4.2 shows port volume trends and that the containers market segment contributed the highest annual revenues to TNPA, followed by dry bulk, liquid bulk, automotive (vehicles) and break-bulk. The trends in profits and investments are discussed below under the heading of Revenue Required Pricing Methodology and Tariff Structure.

## Port Governance and Regulation

South Africa has a distinct, and controversial, system of port governance and regulated port authority pricing. All eight commercial ports in the country are owned by a single landlord, Transnet's National Ports Authority (TNPA) that provides infrastructure and marine services. TNPA (2012, 56) summarises its overall objectives as "ensuring the competitiveness of the South African ports system and support economic

**Table 4.1** South African port statistics, 2017

| | Richards Bay | Durban | East London | Ngqura | Port Elizabeth | Mossel Bay | Cape Town | Saldanha | Total |
|---|---|---|---|---|---|---|---|---|---|
| Cargo landed | 5,865,440 | 31,474,614 | 1,094,452 | 19,309 | 133,0965 | 993,393 | 246,2623 | 4,974,436 | 48,215,232 |
| Cargo shipped | 93,832,438 | 10,095,505 | 98,114 | – | 807,2654 | 751,022 | 945,637 | 64,970,407 | 178,765,778 |
| Transhipment cargo | 80,075 | 85,964 | 2871 | 120,388 | 132 | – | 586,170 | 1010 | 876,609 |
| Total cargo handled | 99,777,953 | 41,656,082 | 1,195,437 | 139,696 | 9,403,752 | 1,744,415 | 3,994,430 | 69,945,853 | 227,857,619 |
| TEUs landed | 5370 | 1,164,172 | 30,334 | 172,616 | 42,705 | – | 139,724 | – | 1,790,256 |
| TEUs shipped | 9777 | 1,127,022 | 32,924 | 176,441 | 39,917 | – | 375,059 | – | 1,753,211 |
| TEUs transhipped | 94 | 408,784 | 66 | 457,033 | 85,661 | – | 139,724 | – | 1,091,362 |
| Total TEUs handled | 15,241 | 2,699,978 | 63,324 | 806,090 | 168,283 | – | 881,913 | – | 4,634,829 |

| | Richards Bay | Durban | East London | Ngqura | Port Elizabeth | Mossel Bay | Cape Town | Saldanha | Total |
|---|---|---|---|---|---|---|---|---|---|
| Vehicles landed | 52 | 260,084 | 17,878 | – | 58,074 | – | 11 | – | 336,099 |
| Vehicles shipped | 49 | 144,085 | 92,942 | – | 66,911 | – | 26 | – | 304,013 |
| Vehicles tran-shipped | – | 51,205 | – | – | 132 | – | 41 | – | 51,378 |
| Total vehicles handled | 101 | 455,374 | 110,820 | – | 125,117 | – | 78 | – | 691,490 |
| Vessel arrivals | 1850 | 3323 | 312 | 485 | 937 | 350 | 2031 | 533 | 9821 |
| Vessel gross tonnage | 72,207,967 | 121,429,871 | 10,303,627 | 31,032,920 | 29,453,538 | 2,600,807 | 49,866,339 | 35,818,157 | 352,713,226 |

*Notes* 1. Cargo is measured in metric tonnes, 2. Vehicles are measured in units
*Source* Authors compiled using data from Transnet National Port Authority (2018)

**Table 4.2** Port volumes and TNPA revenues and profit before taxtrends

| Segments | Measures | 2016 | 2017 | 2018 | 2018/19 | 2020 Target |
|---|---|---|---|---|---|---|
| Containers | 000 TEUs | 4439 | 4466 | 4778 | 4682 | 4902 |
| | R million | 3778 | 3690 | 4186 | 4239 | |
| Break-bulk | million tonnes | 7.57 | 6.6 | 7.1 | 6.2 | 7.6 |
| | R million | 250 | 220 | 253 | 208 | |
| Liquid bulk | million tonnes | 41.7 | 41 | 44.5 | 41.1 | 40.4 |
| | R million | 698 | 679 | 768 | 700 | |
| Dry bulk | million tonnes | 170,79 | 179 | 180.6 | 179,0.4 | 190.9 |
| | R million | 1070 | 1130 | 1283 | 1298 | |
| Vehicles | units | 697,048 | 666,810 | 676,508 | 722,791 | 724,141 |
| | R million | 534 | 359 | 370 | 403 | |
| Average tariff increase | % | 4.8 | 0 | 6 | −6.27 | 4.8 |
| Profit before tax | R million | 4089 | 2934 | 3815 | 7481 | |

*Source* Transnet (2017, 2018, 2019)

growth as mandated by its role as a state-owned company". TNPA dictates port investments and the types of cargo that can be handled in each port, therefore suppressing competition between ports. TNPA is one of the five divisions within Transnet SOC Ltd., a state-owned logistics company. Transnet Port Terminals (TPT) is the public port operator that holds 21 terminal operator licenses. Transnet Freight Rail (TFR) essentially owns and operates the country's freight rail business and Transnet Engineering (TE) is the backbone of the country's railway industry and is focussed on manufacturing, repair and maintenance of railway rolling stock, spares and associated transport equipment. Transnet Pipelines (TPL) is a regulated monopoly that transports petroleum and gas products (Transnet, 2017). The Department of Public Enterprises (DPE) is the sole shareholder of all South Africa's state-owned companies (SOCs), including Transnet SOC Ltd. DPE's objectives are to ensure that all SOCs are sustainable and profitable within the legislative framework and contribute to the country's economic growth.

TNPA, as a monopoly, is subject to price regulation by the Ports Regulator of South Africa. The National Ports Act 12 of 2005 provided for the establishment of the Ports Regulator to regulate TNPA. The Ports Regulator does not regulate other divisions in the Transnet group, including TPT. Hence the regulation of TNPA is frustrated and undermined. An Economic Regulation of Transport bill that will establish a single Transport Economic Regulator has been published for comments. It envisions that the Ports Regulator will be dissolved and its resources transferred to the single Transport Economic Regulator. The Ports Regulator presently reports to the National Department of Transport (NDoT). The NDoT is responsible for all transport and logistics policy formulation and implementation in accordance with the country's socio-economic and political objectives. The current uncoordinated government port objectives of the NDoT and DPE create governance confusion and have the potential to weaken policy implementation and the country's ports system (Gumede & Chasomeris, 2017a; Havenga et al., 2017).

## Public and Private Sector Participation in Ports

TNPA issues port permits and port terminal operating licenses as well as monitors the productivity and performance of terminal operators. The Port Reform Toolkit (World Bank, 2007) recommends that port authorities should be independent and not have shares (ownership) in terminal operations. Likewise, the National Ports Act (2005) recommended that TNPA must be incorporated as a subsidiary of the Transnet group. More than a decade later, TNPA remains, controversially, a division within the Transnet group. Port stakeholders have governance concerns that TNPA is responsible for issuing license to both TPT, their sister division within Transnet, as well as to competing private terminal operators. TNPA is responsible for approximately 750 property leases. There is a total of 91 terminal licenses, 21 of these are owned by TPT.

Table 4.3 compares public–private sector market share of cargo handling operations. TPT remains the single operator of car (on wheels) terminals, and from 2010 to 2016 it increased its market share of container handling from about 97 to 98% and bulk cargo handling from

**Table 4.3** Public and private sector market share, a comparison of 2010 and 2016

| Service | TNPA | | Port operations | | | |
|---|---|---|---|---|---|---|
| | | | TPT | | Private sector | |
| Year | 2010 (%) | 2016 (%) | 2010 (%) | 2016 (%) | 2010 (%) | 2016 (%) |
| Marine services | 100 | 100 | | | | |
| Bulk cargo handling | | | 37 | 52 | 63 | 48 |
| Break-bulk cargo handling | | | 78 | 69 | 22 | 31 |
| Container handling | | | 97 | 98 | 3 | 2 |
| Car (on wheel) handling | | | 100 | 100 | 0 | 0 |

*Source* Compiled by Gumede and Chasomeris (2017a) using data from URBAN-ECON (2010), Gumede and Chasomeris (2015), and Havenga et al. (2017)

37 to 52%, while break-bulk handling market share has decreased from 78 to 69%. TNPA is the sole provider of marine services.

## Revenue Required Pricing Methodology and Tariff Structure

South Africa's system-wide, largely uniform, port authority pricing methodology means that there is one TNPA tariff book with a set of prices that applies to all eight commercial ports, regardless of the diverse circumstances at each port. The uniform cargo dues tariff structure does not allow port managers to offer lower prices in underutilised ports in order to attract traffic, and no ability to adjust prices to deal appropriately with traffic in congested ports, in the case where identical activities are offered. Furthermore, the system-wide uniform port authority pricing means that port users pay for infrastructure that they may not directly benefit from. For example, port users in Durban may be subsidising infrastructure investment at the Port of Ngqura. Such cross-subsidisation is permitted by the Ports Regulator, provided that it is considered in the best interests of the country's economic and developmental objectives. TNPA has a Market Demand Strategy with a purpose to create infrastructure ahead of demand. Port infrastructure investment plans are proposed by TNPA to the Local Port Consultative Committees (PCC) for approval by the local and national PCC.

The Ports Regulator was established in 2007. Since 2009/2010, TNPA has submitted a tariff application to the Ports Regulator annually. The Ports Regulator invites port users and other stakeholders to comment on the application. The Ports Regulator then assesses the application and the stakeholders' comments and makes a decision in accordance with the regulatory framework. TNPA and the Ports Regulator have presently agreed to use a Required Revenue (RR) method to determine the annual total revenue that TNPA may raise through annual adjustments to the port tariffs. The method ensures that port users pay for all infrastructure investments, as well as operating costs, and allows TNPA to make a risk-adjusted rate of return on port assets (as calculated by a weighted average cost of capital formulae that uses a capital asset pricing model) (Gumede & Chasomeris, 2018). Concerns have been raised that the RR model may incentivise port capital expenditure (investments), bloat operating expenditure and set port prices at levels that are not in the best interests of the country's economic development objectives (Chasomeris, 2015; Gumede & Chasomeris, 2017b). The RR method continues to allow TNPA to make an annual profit in excess of ZAR two billion. Both TNPA and the Ports Regulator confirm that the RR model is not designed for ports; however, since the National Ports Act (2005) is silent on the pricing methodology to be used, neither exclude any particular method and in the absence of a better method, the RR model is used (Ports Regulator, 2011).

Table 4.2 shows the average TNPA tariff increase allowed by the Ports Regulator for 2015/2016–2018/2019. In 2018/19, TNPA applied for a tariff increase of 4.21%. However, the Ports Regulator determined that there should be an overall average tariff decrease of 6.27%. The main reasons for this significant difference are as follows. Firstly, a change in the valuation of assets methodology that resulted in the R15.8 billion reduction in the RAB. Secondly, an R721 million reduction in the return on equity that caused the WACC to decrease from 6.8 to 6.55%. Finally, an R205 million reduction in depreciation due to the implementation of the Financial Capital Maintenance method of asset valuation that uses the actual remaining useful life of the asset (Ports Regulator, 2018). TNPA (2018) raised concerns that a significant reduction in the RAB and annual revenues may affect their financial sustainability. However, the Ports Regulator (2018) argued that the reduced tariff still allowed for 92% of the applied for revenue that includes the large infrastructure expenditure required for the acceleration of economic growth.

The tariff structure determines the distribution of costs and revenues over the different port user groups. Historically, ad valorem wharfage was 1.78% on imports and 0.89% on exports. It was abolished in 2002 and replaced with per-unit pricing. However, largely due to the legacy of ad valorem pricing, TNPA prices are still below the benchmarked mean for low-value bulk commodities like coal and iron ore, and above the mean for high-value containerised commodities and automotive vehicles. Vessel charges are also below the benchmarked mean and the required tariff revenues are raised from the tariffs charged to port tenants and cargo owners (Gumede & Chasomeris, 2018; Ports Regulator, 2017).

The Ports Regulator (2015) estimates that cargo owners contribute approximately 60% of the current total revenue of TNPA, while tenants and shipping lines contribute 22% and 18%, respectively. The Ports Regulator (2015) proposes that the long-term end state of distribution of port costs should be that cargo owners contribute 35%, tenants 29% and shipping lines 36%. The long-term distribution is a proposed ten-year implementation plan, starting in the 2017/2018 tariff year. Therefore, to move gradually over the ten years (or more), towards the long-term distribution, the Ports Regulator (2015) estimates an annual real price decrease for cargo owners of about 5.2%, while prices for shipping lines and tenants are estimated to increase by about 7.2% and 2.8%, respectively.

Indeed, for 2019/2020, although the Ports Regulator (2018) decided on an overall average tariff decrease of 6.27%, specific changes to the tariffs included: no change to the 2018/19 marine services and related tariffs; a 10% decrease to all container dues and RoRo cargo dues; a 10% increase to coal export cargo dues; and stipulated upper limit price caps for all break-bulk, dry bulk and liquid bulk cargo dues.

## Discussion and Conclusion

Several competition concerns and conflicts of interest are evident within Transnet and the ports sector. These are perpetuated and exacerbated by the failure to implement Section 3(2) of the National Ports Act (2005). In essence, TNPA should be incorporated under the name "National Ports Authority (Pty) Ltd" with Transnet as the sole shareholder. More than 14 years since the passing of the Act, TNPA remains, controversially, a division rather than a subsidiary of Transnet SOC Ltd. This has hindered sound governance, pricing and regulation of South Africa's ports (Gumede, 2018). A further perceived conflict of interest is that currently the members of the TNPA Deemed Board are the same as the members of the Transnet Board (Transnet, 2019). Therefore, there may be instances where board decisions of the Transnet group supersede the best interests of the TNPA division and port stakeholders. Indeed, from 2010 to 2014, about R16.7 billion was transferred from the TNPA division to the Transnet group. Hence, port users argue that they are cross-subsidising less profitable divisions of Transnet.

There is underinvestment in South Africa's ports. It appears that TNPA revenues and profits are not being sufficiently re-invested into the ports system. For example, the Ports Regulator (2016) showed over the six-year period from 2010 to 2015 that TNPA had a cumulative underspend on their Capital expenditure programme of more than R8.6 billion.

TNPA makes significant profit margins, the highest within the Transnet group. Table 4.2 shows that from 2016/17 to 2018/19 annual profit before tax increased 155% from just over R2.9 billion in 2017 to more than R7.4 billion in 2019. Over the same period, TNPA was granted an increase in CAPEX from R4.1 billion to R5.4 billion. Actual capital expenditure, however, declined 55% from just over R2 billion to R905 million (see Fig. 4.2). The decline in investment into the ports system is not consistent with TNPA's planned increases in capital expenditure and is a major concern to port users, the Ports Regulator and TNPA. Nevertheless, there is renewed hope as TNPA has a six-year (2019/20–2024/25) capital investment plan with a total value of R35.6 billion. The investment plan allocates more than R7.2 billion to the

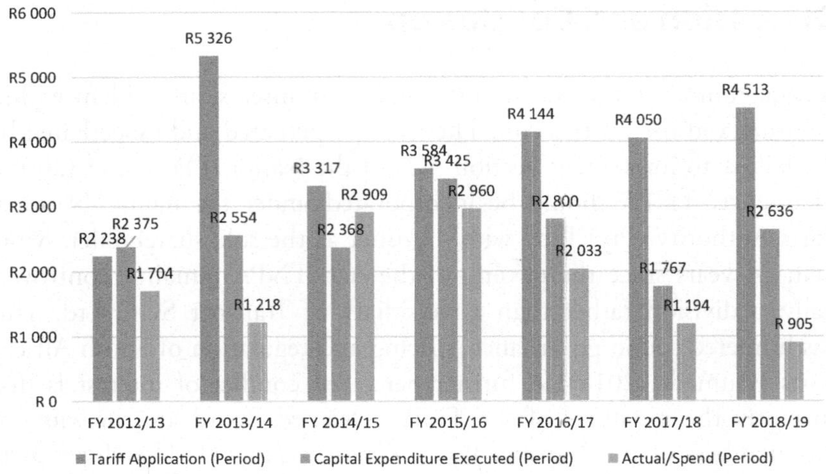


**Fig. 4.2** Capital expenditure in South Africa's ports, 2012/13–2018/19 (*Source* Authors generated using data from TNPA [2019])

containers market segment, R4.4 billion to liquid bulk, R2.4 billion to dry bulk and R1.9 billion to break-bulk (Transnet, 2019). Examples of major projects over the next three years include: Berth deepening at the Durban Container Terminal, expansion of the Cape Town Container Terminal, a manganese export terminal project as well as an automated mooring system at the Port of Ngqura, replacement of six tugs, acquisition of replacement and new helicopters and investment into ship repair initiatives at six ports (TNPA, 2019).

There has been slow progress in port governance and regulation, hindered by fears that incorporating TNPA would mean a significant reduction in Transnet assets and profits and "could constitute an event of default under some of Transnet's funding agreements" (Transnet, 2016: 19). Nevertheless, such incorporation should improve port governance, regulation and pricing as well as the level of investment, productivity and competitiveness of South Africa's ports.

**Acknowledgements** We thank Debbie Chasomeris for formatting and editorial assistance in writing this article.

## References


Arvis, J., Ojala, L., Wiederer, C., Shepherd, B., Raj, A., Dairabayeva, K., & Kiiski, T. (2018). *Connecting to compete 2018: Trade logistics in the global economy, the logistics performance index and its indicators* (6th ed.). The World Bank [Online]. Available at https://openknowledge.worldbank.org/bitstream/handle/10986/29971/LPI2018.pdf. Accessed 30 Nov 2018.

Chasomeris, M. G. (2015, June). Port infrastructure pricing: A critique of the revenue required methodology. *International Journal of Transport Economics, XLII*(2), 153–170.

Department of Energy. (2018). South African Energy Sector Report (2018). Available at http://www.energy.gov.za/files/media/explained/2018-South-African-Energy-Sector-Report.pdf. Accessed 10 Oct 2019.

Gumede, S. (2012). *Assessing stakeholders' perspectives of maritime ports pricing in South Africa*. Master of Commerce Full Masters Dissertation, University of KwaZulu-Natal.

Gumede, S. (2018). *South Africa's seaport governance and pricing: Dilemmas and reforms*. Unpublished PhD Thesis, University of KwaZulu-Natal.

Gumede, S., & Chasomeris, M. (2015). Maritime port pricing and governance: Trends and stakeholder comments. *Journal of Economic and Financial Sciences, 8*(1), 47–62.

Gumede, S., & Chasomeris, M. (2017a, June 27–30). *Regulation of South Africa's ports: Dilemmas and reforms*. International Association of Maritime Economists Conference, Kyoto.

Gumede, S., & Chasomeris, M. G. (2017b). A critique of South Africa's National Ports Authority's revenue required pricing methodology. *International Journal of Transport Economics, 44*(4).

Gumede, S., & Chasomeris, M. (2018). Pricing strategy and tariff structure for a port authority: A case study of South Africa. *Maritime Policy & Management, 45*(6), 756–769.

Havenga, J., Simpson, Z., & Goedhals-Gerber, L. (2017). International trade logistics costs in South Africa: Informing the port reform agenda. *Research in Transportation Business and Management, 22*, 263–275.

Jones, T. (2002, June 5). *Invisible hand effective when Prices in line with true costs*. The Mercury, Highroad for KZN.

*National Ports Act. (2005). National Ports Act No. 12 of 2005.* https://www.portsregulator.org/images/documents/national_ports_act.pdf. Accessed 12 Dec 2018.

Ports Regulator. (2011). *Record of decision: Tariff application by the national ports authority for the tariff year 2011/2012* [Online]. Available at http://www.portsregulator.org/ports_reg_011.htm. Accessed 23 May 2012.

Ports Regulator. (2015). *Tariff strategy for the South African ports system 2015/16* [Online]. Available at http://www.portsregulator.org/images/documents/PRSA-Tariff-Strategy-2015-2016.pdf. Accessed 26 Aug 2015.

Ports Regulator. (2016). *Five year public regulatory review* (2015/16). Ports Regulator of South Africa.

Ports Regulator. (2017). *Global Pricing Comparator Study (GPCS).* [Online]. Available at https://www.portsregulator.org/images/documents/Global-Pricing-Comparator-Study-2017-18.pdf. Accessed 12 Aug 2018.

Ports Regulator. (2018). *Record of decision: Tariff application by the National Ports Authority for the Tariff Years 2019/20–2011/22* [Online]. Available at https://www.portsregulator.org/doc/record-of-decision-npa-tariff-application-2019_20.pdf. Accessed 28 Nov 2018.

South African Market Insights. (2017). *South Africa's crude oil imports. Where is it coming from*? [Online]. Available at https://www.southafricanmi.com/blog-23oct2017.html. Accessed 26 Nov 2018.

Statistics South Africa. (2018). *If South Africa's provinces were independent states* [Online]. Available at http://www.statssa.gov.za/?p=11092. Accessed 7 Nov 2018.

TNPA. (2012). *Tariff Application Financial Year 13/14: Tariff application to the Ports Regulator in terms of the National Ports Act* (Act No. 12 of 2005), September [Online]. Available at http://www.portsregulator.org. Accessed 19 Oct 2013.

TNPA. (2015). *Tariff Application Financial Year 15/16: Tariff application to the Ports Regulator in terms of the National Ports Act* (Act No. 12 of 2005), August [Online]. Available at http://www.portsregulator.org. Accessed 10 Oct 2015.

TNPA. (2018). Transnet National Ports Authority tariff application for financial year 2019/20 [Online]. Available at https://www.portsregulator.org/economic/tariffs/2019-20-tnpa-tariff-application. Accessed 5 Nov 2018.

TNPA. (2019). *NPA tariff application roadshow presentation.* Available at https://www.portsregulator.org/doc/NPA-Tariff-Application-Roadshow-Presentation-2019.pdf Accessed 11 Oct 2019.

Transnet National Port Authority. (2018). *Port statistics* [Online]. Available at https://www.transnetnationalportsauthority.net/Commercial%20and%20Marketing/Pages/Port-Statistics.aspx. Accessed 14 Mar 2018.

Transnet. (2016). *Annual financial statements 2016* [Online]. Available at https://www.transnet.net/InvestorRelations/AR2016/2016/downloads/TRANSNET-AFS-2016.pdf. Accessed 4 Nov 2017.

Transnet. (2017). *Transnet national ports authority investor relations 2018*. Available at https://www.transnet.net/InvestorRelations/AR2017/OD%20Reports/8335_Transnet%202017_NPA%20HR.pdf. Accessed 11 Oct 2019.

Transnet. (2018). *Transnet national ports authority investor relations 2018*. Available at https://www.transnet.net/InvestorRelations/AR2018/TNPA.pdf. Accessed 11 Oct 2019.

Transnet. (2019). *Transnet national ports authority investor relations 2019*. Available at https://www.transnet.net/InvestorRelations/AR2019/Transnet%20National%20Ports%20Authority.pdf. Accessed 11 Oct 2019.

UNCTAD. (2018, October 3). *Liner shipping connectivity index (2004–2018)*, United Nations Conference on Trade and Development, Geneva [Online]. Available at https://unctad.org/en/PublicationsLibrary/UNCTAD_Liner_Shipping_Connectivity_Index_2004-2018.xlsx. Accessed 25 Nov 2018.

URBAN-ECON. (2010). *Economic review of participation in ports operation and services in South Africa: Economic review document*. Ports Regulator of South Africa.

World Bank. (2007). *Port reform toolkit* (2nd ed.). The International Bank for Reconstruction and Development.

# 5

# Regulation and Finance in the Port Sector: Current Practices and the Future of Port Development in Mexico

Giulia Arduino and David Guillermo Carrillo Murillo

## National Port System Description

The history of Mexican Ports has started since 1519 when Spanish conquers founded the first port in Continental America: Veracruz. The development of the history of Mexican Ports was followed by the establishment of 102 ports and 15 independent terminals (out of a port) (Fig. 5.1).

The reason for this development is due to the strategic location of the country, near the biggest economy in the world, and with access to two oceans. Therefore, the potential port growth and its relation to

G. Arduino
Tecnológico de Monterrey, Mexico City, Mexico

D. G. Carrillo Murillo (✉)
DTP Consultores, Mexico City, Mexico

© The Author(s), under exclusive license to Springer Nature Switzerland AG 2022

C. Ferrari et al. (eds.), *Regulation and Finance in the Port Industry*, Palgrave Studies in Maritime Economics,
https://doi.org/10.1007/978-3-030-83985-7_5

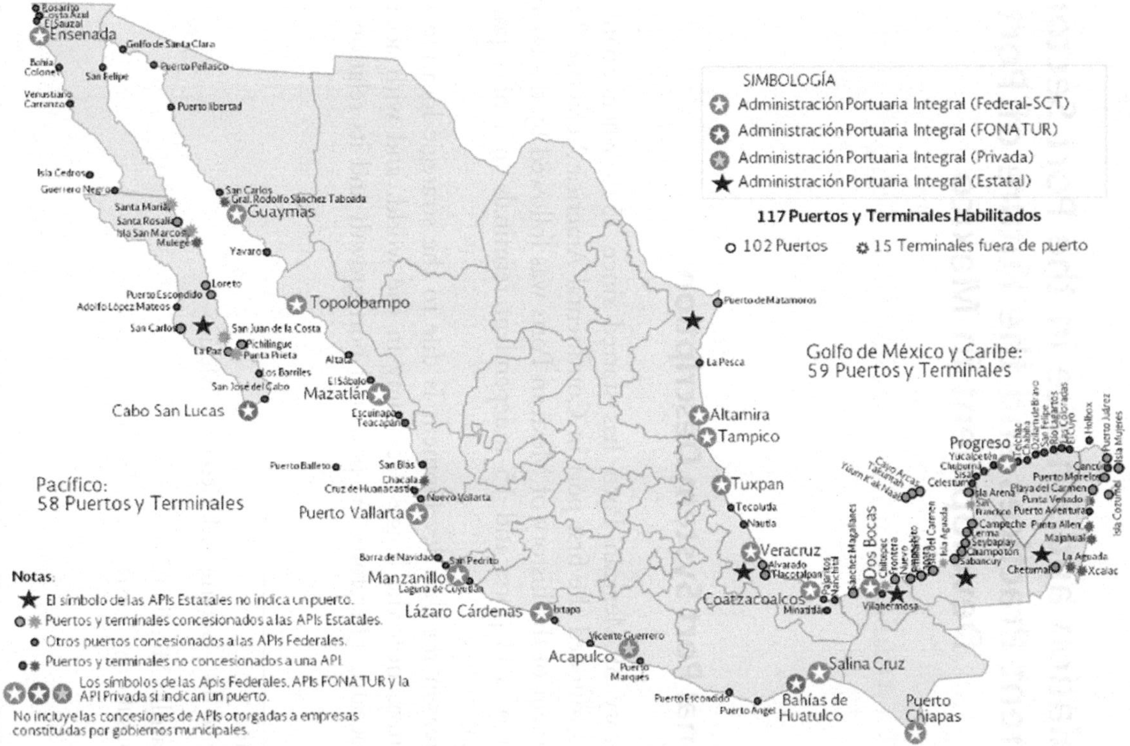


Fig. 5.1 Mexican port system (*Source* Mexican Ministry of Communications and Transportation, 2018)

the dynamics of the economy have been always the core of the development for the country (Mexican Ministry of Communications and Transportation, 2018).

From the creation of the port of Veracruz until 1991, the ports were publicly managed and developed (Estache, 2004).

With the development of the seaborne trade, Mexico followed a growing trend in order to adapt to the foreign trade. The current seaport throughput of the main ports in Mexico is shown in Tables 5.1 and 5.2.

As one may observe in the previous tables, only two ports on the Pacific coast and six ports on the Gulf and Caribbean coasts perform all the port activities. This is due to the historical oil monopoly owned by the government that decides which ports handle oil derivatives.

In total, the ports of the Pacific coast loaded and unloaded 128 mio tonnes while the ports of the Gulf and Caribbean coast handled almost 180 mio tonnes, for a total of almost 308 mio tonnes in 2017 (Tables 5.3 and 5.4).

There are two ports on the pacific coast and five ports on the Gulf and Caribbean coasts considered as the busiest ports handling more than 20 mio tonnes in 2017. In total, they represent almost 60% of the total tonnage loaded and unloaded in ports for the whole country (Mexican Ministry of Communications and Transportation, 2018).

For total container throughput, three busiest Mexican ports handled more than one mio TEUs in 2017: Manzanillo, Lázaro Cárdenas and Veracruz.

The reason behind the barely inexistence of cabotage activities is due to historical restrictions for this activity in the country. Cabotage for ports has been forbidden for international reciprocity purposes. While in other countries cabotage is only allowed for ships built and/or registered in the country, Mexico has been trying to release this activity for containers—empty and full. Thus, only two Mexican Ports received national cargo—Mazatlán and Salina Cruz.

**Table 5.1** Total tonnage per port and activity on the Pacific Coast

| Port | General cargo | | Dry bulk | | Liquid bulk | |
|---|---|---|---|---|---|---|
| | Bulk | Containers | Agricultural | Mineral | Oil/Derivates | Other fluids |
| Rosarito | | | | | 2,734,541 | |
| El Sauzal | 99,521 | 1,427,646 | | | | |
| Ensenada | 255,282 | | | 702,408 | | 185,354 |
| Isla de Cedros | 422 | | | 13,817,341 | | |
| Guerrero Negro | | | | 6,967,175 | | |
| San Carlos | 41,073 | | | | 121,941 | |
| La Paz | 1,258,519 | | | | 1,115,731 | |
| Pichilingue | 1,994,648 | | | 291,966 | 41,615 | |
| San Juan de la Costa | | | | 1,123,629 | | |
| Isla San Marcos | 17,014 | | | 2,142,521 | | |
| Punta Santa María | | | | 964,708 | | |
| Santa Rosalía | 25,103 | | | | | |
| Puerto Libertad | | | | | | |
| Guaymas | 144,578 | 187,636 | 550,952 | 4,193,613 | 2,453,841 | 331,043 |
| Topolobampo | 1,969,479 | | 1,887,444 | 985,528 | 2,208,254 | |
| Mazatlán | 1,955,730 | 467,391 | | | 2,308,212 | |
| Manzanillo | 1,680,280 | 20,538,195 | 1,563,009 | 4,190,808 | 3,321,307 | |
| Cuyutlán | | | | | | 2,965,043 |
| Lazaro Cárdenas | 2,190,787 | 7,783,598 | 280,613 | 16,137,791 | 2,677,333 | 720,215 |
| Acapulco | 66,553 | | | | 628,939 | |
| Salina Cruz | 5557 | 22,978 | 9500 | | 7,818,273 | |
| Puerto Chiapas | 44,136 | 258,487 | 132,347 | 3750 | | |
| | 11,748,682 | 30,685,931 | 4,423,865 | 51,521,238 | 25,429,987 | 4,201,655 |

*Source* Mexican Ministry of Communications and Transportation (2018)

## Port Regulation and Planning Tools

In 1989, the Mexican government created an entity that grouped all commercial port services to be performed in Mexican ports and separated it from the regulation and management of the ports (Alarco, 1996).

**Table 5.2** Total tonnage per port and activity on the Gulf and Caribbean Coast

| Port | General cargo | | Dry bulk | | Liquid bulk | |
|---|---|---|---|---|---|---|
| | Raw | Containers | Agricultural | Mineral | Oil/ Derivates | Other fluids |
| Altamira | 3,900,835 | 7,078,973 | 644,425 | 5,295,881 | | 4,923,072 |
| Tampico | 1,407,632 | 11,537 | 52,200 | 1,246,089 | 5,070,423 | 10,000 |
| Tuxpan | 103,302 | 94,944 | 1,347,511 | 407,956 | 11,228,261 | 1,531,012 |
| Veracruz | 3,483,027 | 11,074,046 | 7,494,542 | 2,999,488 | 1,755,207 | 996,351 |
| Coatzacoalcos | 677,636 | 149,417 | 1,385,699 | 1,465,059 | 23,469,274 | 1,752,458 |
| Frontera | | | | | | |
| Dos Bocas | 2,163,072 | | 23,000 | 5629 | 31,122,320 | 23,860 |
| Isla del Carmen | 133,602 | | | | | |
| Seybaplaya | 12,229 | | | | | |
| Lerma | 510 | | | | 614,257 | |
| Cayo Arcas | | | | | 27,759,162 | |
| Progreso | 112,062 | 522,203 | 2,002,719 | 80,033 | 2,938,320 | 20,750 |
| Las Coloradas | | | | | | |
| Punta Sam | 428,655 | | | | | |
| Isla Mujeres | 428,655 | | | | | |
| Puerto Morelos | 4336 | 36,602 | | | | |
| Cozumel | 835,934 | | | | | |
| Punta Venado | 835,934 | | | 8,470,239 | | |
| | 14,527,421 | 18,967,722 | 12,950,096 | 19,970,374 | 103,957,224 | 9,257,503 |

*Source* Mexican Ministry of Communications and Transportation (2018)

**Table 5.3** Busiest Mexican ports in total tonnage

| Port | 2017 | Share (%) |
|---|---|---|
| Manzanillo | 31,293,599 | 10.17 |
| Lázaro Cárdenas | 29,790,337 | 9.68 |
| Altamira | 21,843,186 | 7.10 |
| Veracruz | 27,802,661 | 9.04 |
| Coatzacoalcos | 28,899,543 | 9.39 |
| Dos Bocas | 33,337,881 | 10.84 |
| Cayo Arcas | 27,759,162 | 9.02 |
| Busiest ports | 179,630,340 | 58.39 |
| Mexico's total | 307,641,698 | 100.00 |

*Source* Mexican Ministry of Communications and Transportation (2018)

**Table 5.4** Principal Mexican ports in TEUs throughput

| Port | Containerised cargo | | |
|---|---|---|---|
| | International | Cabotage | Total |
| Ensenada | 230,185 | | 230,185 |
| Guaymas | 16,031 | | 16,031 |
| Mazatlán | 46,334 | 2046 | 48,380 |
| Manzanillo | 2,830,370 | | 2,830,370 |
| Lazaro Cárdenas | 1,149,079 | | 1,149,079 |
| Salina Cruz | 708 | 1596 | 2304 |
| Puerto Chiapas | 47,702 | | 47,702 |
| Altamira | 803,222 | | 803,222 |
| Tampico | 926 | | 926 |
| Tuxpan | 9180 | | 9180 |
| Veracruz | 1,117,304 | | 1,117,304 |
| Coatzacoalcos | 19,992 | | 19,992 |
| Progreso | 91,318 | | 91,318 |
| Puerto Morelos | 9345 | | 9345 |
| Total TEU | 6,371,696 | 3642 | 6,375,338 |

*Source* Mexican Ministry of Communications and Transportation (2018)

Even though private participation was possible according to the law, almost every port service was performed by public firms, turning the former port model into the service port (Rodríguez, 1999).

The reason behind this phenomenon was the power of Unions in ports, a situation that conditioned the growth of port throughput (Martínez, 1994).

In 1993, Port Administrators were established under the name of "Autoridad Portuaria Integral" or "API". Since then, they perform as concession holders for the port precinct and the port activities as Parastatal Firms (DOF, 2016).

At the beginning, the APIs continued to perform port activities but gradually, through the "cession of rights for operational activities", they assigned the port activities to private firms. Nowadays, none of the operational services is provided by any API in Mexico.

In terms of Port Governance, several bodies perform different port activities. Table 5.5 indicates the main governance bodies for Mexican Ports.

As shown in the Table 5.5, each API responsible for the port concession has the responsibility to veil for the future development of the port. Therefore, planning is crucial for APIs and they are obliged to present the Port's Master Development Program every 10 years with a revision every five years by the Ministry of Communications and Transportation.

Once each API prepares the Port's Master Development Program, it should be authorised or modified by the Ministry of Communications and Transportation (SCT), based on the policies and programs for the development of the national port system.

In case such modifications cause any damage to the concessionaire or group of terminals, the government through the Ministry of Communications and Transportation will duly compensate for those damages (Mexican Ministry of Communications and Transportation, 2018).

**Table 5.5** Governing bodies for Mexican ports

| Seaport activity | Governance body |
|---|---|
| Navigation Authority | Harbour captaincy |
| Entrances and exits regulation | Customs |
| Police of the port—land and sea | Secretary of marine |
| Concession owner | Port administration |
| Monitoring of environmental issues | Federal Attorney for Environmental Protection |
| Port regulation | Ministry of Communications and Transportation |

*Source* Authors' own elaboration

## Financial Tools

Mexican financial laws for port infrastructure allow several ways to finance projects. The traditional way to finance port infrastructure is through the cession of rights scheme. A fundamental condition for granting the cession of rights is to create a private firm with the sole purpose of providing port services. In this way, the financing of the port infrastructure is opened to private capitals through these private firms (DOF, 2016).

Furthermore, the recent Public–Private Partnership (PPP) Mexico's Act opens the door for different types of port infrastructure financing. The Act is formulated as an umbrella of options that enables different types of PPPs including the concession and Projects for the provision of services (PPS). PPSs are implemented whenever a project with social profitability needs subventions to achieve financial profitability (DOF, 2018a).

The Act is the government's first effort to open traditional financial schemes not only through the cession of rights but also to increase the umbrella of options to finance port infrastructure. By the way, all the resources necessary for the development of the port infrastructure are secured through trusts. Even the collection of grants and donations from local governments as land or financial resources must be deposited in the trusts.

Another way to finance the port infrastructure is through the Development Bank in Mexico called Banobras, which can act as the entity that provides the subsidies in accordance with the Bank's development programs. But Banobras can also act as a fiduciary for the development of port projects. As an example, we can mention that the Mexican Bank for the Development of Foreign Trade (Bancomext) has collaborated with Banobras in the financing for the development of the Port Terminal of Tuxpan with SSA Mexico placing 340 million USD (BANCOMEXT, 2018).

Other ways for acquiring subventions may be the national budget that is voted and modified by the Mexican deputies and senators every year. However, this strategy involves several political decisions and usually takes more time to get subventions.

Examples of funding options are present in all terminals and ports operating in Mexico.

First, there are purely private terminals outside ports that are operating for the sole purpose of a firm, usually in the mining sector to export minerals.

Second, APIs tender available port areas whenever a particular firm is interested in providing a port service, once the cession of rights is given, the designated firm is responsible for finding the financing for the project. In that case, there is only one restriction imposed by the government, the firm should be registered and established in Mexico. Once this status changes, the cession of rights will be cancelled and this risk will be assigned directly to the owner of the cession of rights. This clause includes the issuance of bonds and the restriction is limited to 49% of bonds owned by foreigners. The issuance of bonds requires a permit from the Ministry of Economy with respect to:

- Specific sectors; and
- Foreign capital limit to provide public services.

Third, there is a private concessionaire from a federal port: the Acapulco API.

As we can see, the financing for port infrastructure projects is open to the private sector and it can be combined with subventions from the Mexican Development Bank and State contributions.

Furthermore, the most recent extension of the Port of Veracruz had an 80% of private financing and 20% of the national budget for a total of 31 billion pesos. The first phase of this project allows to increase the port operations on fluids, general cargo, containerised cargo, agricultural bulk and mineral bulk with more than 120 ha for all terminals and 2.5 km of berths with a depth from 15.5 to 20 m, and a breakwater to protect the terminals of 4.3 km long (SEMARNAT, 2018).

By the way, only one terminal is still in the bidding process and five terminals own the cession of rights that allowed private participation in the financing of this extension of the Port of Veracruz.

To conclude, the link between funding and the development of port projects is due to the cession of rights model implemented by the APIs as they own the concession of port services in Mexico (DOF, 2016).

## Links Between Local and National Port Regulation and the International Framework of Ports

Aside from Federal APIs, concessions were given for Local APIs (owned by States) that follow the steps of Federal APIs through the cession of rights.

This framework positions APIs as purely managers for the development of Mexican ports, and State or Local Port Authorities as managers, and in some cases operators of Mexican Ports (Tables 5.6 and 5.7).

Therefore, it is possible to affirm that the Mexican law allows different Public–Private Partnerships for ports with the limits imposed by the Foreign Investment Law, which determines a 49% participation for an API, port services such as ship piloting, shipping firms involved in the commercial exploitation of vessels for inland navigation and cabotage, with the exception of tourist cruises and exploitation of dredges and naval artefacts for the construction, conservation and port operation (DOF, 2018).

However, the Law allows for a participation of more than 49% with the authorisation of the Mexican Commission of Foreign Investments in port services for vessels to carry out their inland navigation operations, such as towing and mooring (DOF, 2018).

By the way, the API Acapulco is operated by a joint venture in which two firms operate all port services, mainly service to cruises. The joint venture is formed by TMM (Mexican Firm) and SSA (American Firm), both firms are registered in Mexico and so, there is no limit for the direct investment source (API Acapulco, 2018).

Concerning liners and trump vessels, they are all equally served and there are no specific requirements to entry to Mexican ports, the usual requirements for every port are controlled by Federal Attorney

**Table 5.6** Mexican ports of the Pacific Coast

| Mexican port | State | Concession type | Port authority |
|---|---|---|---|
| Rosarito | Baja California | Federal | Not assigned |
| El Sauzal | Baja California | Federal | API Ensenada |
| Ensenada | Federal | Federal | |
| Isla de Cedros | Baja California | Federal | Not assigned |
| Guerrero Negro | Baja California Sur | State | API Baja California Sur |
| San Carlos | Baja California Sur | State | |
| La Paz | Baja California Sur | State | |
| Pichilingue | Baja California Sur | State | |
| San Juan de la Costa | Baja California Sur | State | |
| Isla San Marcos | Baja California Sur | State | |
| Punta Santa María | Baja California Sur | State | |
| Santa Rosalía | Baja California Sur | State | |
| Puerto Libertad | Sonora | Federal | Not assigned |
| Guaymas | Sonora | Federal | API Guaymas |
| Topolobampo | Sinaloa | Federal | API Topolobampo |
| Mazatlán | Sinaloa | Federal | API Mazatlán |
| Manzanillo | Colima | Federal | API Manzanillo |
| Cuyutlán | Colima | Federal | |
| Lazaro Cárdenas | Michoacán | Federal | API Lazaro Cárdenas |
| Acapulco | Guerrero | Private | API Acapulco |
| Salina Cruz | Oaxaca | Federal | API Salina Cruz |
| Puerto Chiapas | Chiapas | Federal | API Puerto Chiapas |

*Source* Mexican Ministry of Communications and Transportation (2018)

for Environmental Protection and Immigration, the API itself and the Customs.

The relationship between the development of ports and cities in Mexico is different from this relationship in other regions of the world. Since the ports are mainly federal, the development of cities is not related to the growth of the port. Although some APIs or Port Authorities contribute with some social investments, these are limited to the API's ability to finance waterfront pedestrian infrastructure that is mainly touristic. Mexican ports used to distribute the value of the port in cities in the past. Today, they are merely nodes as a result of competitiveness in the hinterlands (Zepeda Ortega et al., 2017). The Mexican ports

**Table 5.7** Mexican ports of the Gulf and Caribbean coasts

| Mexican port | State | Concession | Port authority |
|---|---|---|---|
| Matamoros | Tamaulipas | State | API Tamaulipas |
| Altamira | Tamaulipas | Federal | API Altamira |
| Tampico | Tamaulipas | Federal | API Tampico |
| Tuxpan | Veracruz | Federal | API Tuxpan |
| Veracruz | Veracruz | Federal | API Veracruz |
| Coatzacoalcos | Veracruz | Federal | API Coatzacoalcos |
| Frontera | Tabasco | State | API Tabasco |
| Dos Bocas | Tabasco | Federal | API Dos Bocas |
| Isla del Carmen | Campeche | State | API Campeche |
| Seybaplaya | Campeche | State | |
| Lerma | Campeche | State | |
| Cayo Arcas | Campeche | State | |
| Progreso | Yucatán | Federal | API Progreso |
| Las Coloradas | Yucatán | Federal | |
| Punta Sam | Quintana Roo | Federal | API Quintana Roo |
| Isla Mujeres | Quintana Roo | Federal | |
| Puerto Morelos | Quintana Roo | Federal | |
| Cozumel | Quintana Roo | Federal | |
| Punta Venado | Quintana Roo | Federal | |

*Source* Mexican Ministry of Communications and Transportation (2018)

compete to serve the main central cities of the country and the development of the cities around the ports is behind the development of the same ports. In some port cases, the surrounding cities limit their expansion in spatial terms. As such, the expansion of the ports has developed outside those cities, but it has been integrated into the enclosure of the ports under API administrations. This is the case of the ports of Coatzacoalcos, Ensenada, Lázaro Cárdenas, Manzanillo, Mazatlán and Veracruz.

## Critical Discussion: How Can Port Regulation and Financial Practices Affect Local Port Development?

Port regulation in Mexico is aligned to reduce barriers to international trade in the country and to strengthen the national economy. Therefore, the deregulation process for the port sector in the early 1990s is a milestone for the development of the local port, opening the window to promote international collaboration at the organisational and financial level. In fact, the improvement of port services is a success factor that allowed the attraction of foreign investments for logistics and commerce.

Concerning the development of local ports, the APIs are completely free to plan and develop port services, but they need the approval of the General Coordination of Ports and Merchant Marine of the Ministry of Communications and Transportation. The importance of this approval is to align the planning of the ports' development with the Federal Policy related to the maritime and port sectors.

Port cooperation, port agreements and MOUs are generally established for the case of commercial activities that require the cooperation of two ports. Take the case of liners that need to load and unload containers in several ports, or the case of cruise ships that must navigate on international waters to offer casino services, both cases need an agreement between the ports to implement those services.

Another case of port cooperation is limited to knowledge sharing and in this case several ports have cooperated through national agreements, e.g. the list of MOUs signed at the Interamerican Commission of Ports (ICP, 2018).

## Conclusions

Mexican ports allow for several schemes of port financing. Port Administrators or APIs own the concessions of ports services and port infrastructure development. The port services are offered by private firms through the APIs' cession of rights. Nevertheless, port infrastructure development still needs the approval of the centralised government and this issue limits the financing capacity of APIs to spread their growth to the cities around them.

## References


Alarco, G. y. (1996). Límites económicos a la privatización portuaria: el caso mexicano 1992–1995. *Gestión y Política Pública*, 66.

API Acapulco. (14 de 10 de 2018). *Administración Portuaria Integral Acapulco.* Obtenido de. www.apiacapulcoport.com

BANCOMEXT. (12 de 10 de 2018). *Banco Mexicano de Comercio Exterior.* Obtenido de El desarrollo de puertos mexicanos recibe financiamiento de IFC. https://www.bancomext.com/notas-de-interes/10228

DOF. (19 de 12 de 2016). *Diario Oficial de la Federación.* Obtenido de Ley de Puertos. http://www.diputados.gob.mx/LeyesBiblio/pdf/65_191216.pdf

DOF. (15 de 06 de 2018a). *Diario Oficial de la Federación.* Obtenido de Ley de Asociaciones Público Privadas. http://www.diputados.gob.mx/LeyesBiblio/pdf/LAPP_150618.pdf

DOF. (15 de 06 de 2018b). *LEY de Inversión Extranjera.*. Obtenido de http://www.diputados.gob.mx/LeyesBiblio/pdf/44_150618.pdf

Estache, A. e. (2004). Sources of efficiency gains in port reform: A DEA decomposition of a Malmquist TFP index for Mexico. *Utilities Policy*, 10.

ICP. (26 de 10 de 2018). *Comisión Interamericana de Puertos.* Obtenido de. https://www.google.com/url?sa=t&rct=j&q=&esrc=s&source=web&cd=4&ved=2ahUKEwjAjqqzgqjfAhXRna0KHZOvB-QQFjADegQIBxAC&url=http%3A%2F%2Fscm.oas.org%2Fdoc_public%2FSPANISH%2FHIST_17%2FCIP01045S02.doc&usg=AOvVaw3VeOwiwksgyjfNLe_JrnrK

Martínez, G. e. (1994). *Desregulación económica (1989–1993).* Fondo de Cultura Económica.

Mexican Ministry of Communications and Transportation. (22 de 09 de 2018). *Administración Portuaria Integral* . Obtenido de https://www.gob.mx/fop/acciones-y-programas/administracion-portuaria-integral-api

Rodríguez, E. (1999). Regulación de los sectores de infraestructura y energéticos en México. En P. e. Spiller, *La regulación del Sistema Portuario Mexicano* (pp. 229–262). Editorial Porrúa.

SEMARNAT. (14 de 05 de 2018). *Secretaría de Medio Ambiente y Recursos Naturales.* Obtenido de Nuevo Puerto de Veracruz, ejemplo de sustentabilidad. https://www.gob.mx/semarnat/articulos/nuevo-puerto-de-veracruz-ejemplo-de-sustentabilidad

Zepeda-Ortega, I. E., Angeles-Castro, G., & Carrillo-Murillo, D. G. (2017). Infraestructura portuaria y crecimiento económico regional en México. *Economic Social Territory, 17*(54), 337–366. ISSN 2448-6183. https://doi.org/10.22136/est002017806.

# 6

# U.S. Port Governance and Investment

Sashi N. Kumar, Lauren Brand, Katie Lientz, and Douglas McDonald

## Introduction

U.S. ports serve as vital hubs that link domestic and international waterborne freight to a multimodal transportation network of roads, rail lines, and pipelines. Annually, these ports handle nearly 2.4 billion short tons of domestic and international cargo and receive 82,000 calls from commercial vessels.[1] As the amount of freight handled by U.S. ports

[1] Based on 2016 waterborne commerce data obtained from the U.S. Army Corps of Engineers (see USACE, 2017) and 2015 vessel call data for U.S. ports obtained from the U.S. Maritime Administration (see MARAD, 2015). Only self-propelled, cargo-carrying vessels are included in MARAD's vessel call statistics.

S. N. Kumar (✉) · L. Brand · K. Lientz · D. McDonald
Maritime Administration, Washington, DC, US
e-mail: shashi.kumar@dot.gov

© The Author(s), under exclusive license to Springer Nature Switzerland AG 2022

C. Ferrari et al. (eds.), *Regulation and Finance in the Port Industry*, Palgrave Studies in Maritime Economics,
https://doi.org/10.1007/978-3-030-83985-7_6

is expected to rise,[2] ensuring that the nation's surface transportation system is equipped to handle future trade volumes is of paramount importance. Although many U.S. ports are already working to accommodate larger vessels, there are other critical investments ports must make in order to efficiently move anticipated future freight volumes. These include enhanced connectivity with other surface transportation modes, improved first and last-mile connections, and the incorporation of automated technologies into port operations.

Among policymakers, there is a growing awareness that freight fluidity is critical to the nation's economic sucess and that ports, both large and small, are vital for that. However, the process of enhancing connectivity between ports and the broader freight transportation network is inherently challenging. U.S. ports are not only geographically diverse but vary broadly in the amount of cargo they handle, the industries they serve, and the types of intermodal connections they require.[3] In 2016 alone, there were 8200 individual docks in the U.S. handling international or domestic trade, and approximately 86-percent of the cargo volume moving through these docks was non-containerized (USACE, 2017). The process of integrating this diverse group of ports into an intermodal surface transportation system will require extensive planning to address a range of unique infrastructure needs. Accordingly, this chapter will examine two interrelated issues: (1) the governance structures that currently influence U.S. port operations, and (2) how port governance in the U.S. is influencing investment in infrastructure projects. The chapter concludes with a summary outlook on facilitating future infrastructure investments in U.S. ports.

---

[2] According to the U.S. Bureau of Transportation Statistics, the weight of waterborne freight handled by the U.S. transportation system is expected to increase by 38 percent between 2015 and 2045 (U.S. BTS, 2016).

[3] Port terminals in the U.S. can generally be placed into eight different categories based on their cargo handling needs or the industries that they support: containerized, break bulk, bulk, or roll-on/roll-off (Ro-Ro) cargos; commercial fishing; cruise ships; and the space launch industry.

**Table 6.1** Top 10 U.S. Ports by Tonnage Handled

| Port | Average Annual Short Tons (2013–2017) |
|---|---|
| 1.Port of South Louisiana, LA | 260,408,433 |
| 2.Houston, TX | 242,507,427 |
| 3.New York, NY and NJ | 129,088,628 |
| 4.Beaumont, TX | 88,564,522 |
| 5.New Orleans, LA | 87,209,677 |
| 6.Corpus Christi, TX | 83,212,957 |
| 7.Long Beach, CA | 82,298,745 |
| 8.Baton Rouge, LA | 70,370,979 |
| 9.Port of Virginia, VA | 66,285,406 |
| 10.Los Angeles, CA | 61,515,112 |

*Source* U.S. Army Corps of Engineers

## Port Governance Structures

The U.S. port sector consists of both public and privately owned ports that vary broadly in the management of their day-to-day operations. Most major ports in the U.S. are owned by public port authorities, and their operational structure usually takes on one of three forms; that of an operating port, a landlord port, or a hybrid of both the landlord and operating port models (see Table 6.1).[4] Public ports are usually owned by a state, county, or city. In some special cases, a port may be owned by a bi-state entity (*e.g.*, the Port of New York and New Jersey) or by a special taxing district (*e.g.*, Port Canaveral in Florida). In general, port authorities, regardless of the level of government in which they are affiliated, are governed by a board. The board may be comprised of elected officials, individuals appointed by a senior elected official (*e.g.*, individuals appointed by a state Governor, or the Mayor of a city), or a combination of both elected officials and other appointed board members. Port authorities play an integral role in the planning, financing, and revenue-generating activities of the ports they oversee. In addition, port authorities engage in a range of business-related activities, including applying for grants, issuing bonds, and autonomously levying

[4] Unlike many other countries, port lands in the United States may be owned by a City, a County, a Special Taxing District, a bi-State public authority or a State-owned entity, each with its own charter that specifies rules and regulations governing land use.

**Table 6.2** Common Operational Structures of U.S. Public Ports

| Operational Structure | Characteristics | Example(s) |
|---|---|---|
| Operating Port | Owned and operated by a public entity that is responsible for both the operation of port terminals and providing virtually all port services | Port of Charleston<br>Port of Savannah<br>Port of Boston<br>Port of Houston |
| Landlord Port | A port authority will maintain ownership of the basic port infrastructure, while a privately owned lessee is responsible for executing the day-to-day operations of the facility | Port of Los Angeles<br>Port of Long Beach<br>Port of New York: New Jersey<br>Port of Baltimore<br>Port of New Orleans |
| Hybrid (Operating and Landlord) Port | Some port facilities are operated through lease agreements and others are operated by the port authority | Alabama State Port Authority (Port of Mobile) |

facility charges approved by their Board of Commissioners. On the other hand, privately owned ports usually fall into one of two categories; those operated solely for the use of their owner and those that are operated for public use. The Port of Fernandina, in the state of Florida, is one example of a port that is both privately owned and operated but provides terminal service to a range of customers. Although private ports are usually owned by corporate entities, they are still subject to Federal laws and regulations that may impact their operations (Table 6.2).

The U.S. is somewhat unique in that there is no Federal ports system or national ports policy that guides or manages the port planning activities or day-to-day operations.[5] Instead, port authority boards generally determine the policies and overall vision that will guide a port's planning and operations. The U.S. federal government does, however, retain exclusive jurisdiction over the navigable waterways of the U.S., including

[5] The only exception to this is the Federal coordination of a National Port Readiness Network (NPRN) that consists of select, strategically chosen commercial ports that support military force deployment during national emergencies including humanitarian aid and disaster relief activities.

harbors, and maintains regulatory authority over a range of port-related matters, including the safety of port and vessel operations, environmental and security matters, and matters related to fair competition among shippers and marine terminals. Perhaps most notably, Federal involvement in U.S. ports includes collecting the Harbor Maintenance Tax (HMT); a fee that is assessed on all imports, domestic shipments, and passengers.[6] After these fees are collected by U.S. Customs and Border Protection (U.S. CBP), they are deposited into the Harbor Maintenance Trust fund, which is then used to pay for congressionally authorized harbor maintenance projects.[7] Accordingly, port authorities rely heavily on the Federal government to both fund and conduct maintenance activities, including dredging, on the harbors and channels that provide direct access to their terminals.[8]

## Infrastructure Needs

Recent developments both internal and external to the U.S. have influenced the need for port infrastructure investments. Over the past decade, the nation has had a sustained period of economic growth that has been accompanied by consistent population growth (U.S. Census Bureau, 2017).[9] Not only is the population growth expected to continue, but freight traveling on all modes of the U.S. transportation network is also expected to rise (U.S. BTS, 2017; Vespa et al., 2018). These factors have

[6] The Harbor Maintenance Tax (HMT) is assessed based on the value of each shipment. Shippers must pay 0.125% of the value of all commercial cargo that is shipped through maritime ports (U.S. CBP, 2017). The list of ports and areas where cargo is subject to the HMT can be found in U.S. Code of Federal Regulations, 19 CFR 24.24. This list consists almost exclusively of coastal and Great Lakes ports. An excise tax, known as the Inland Waterways Fuel Tax (IWFT), is passed against self-propelled vessels operating at harbors and ports on the inland waterways. Receipts from the IWFT are deposited into the Inland Waterways Trust Fund to fund (up to 50% in most cases of) the construction of inland waterways infrastructure such as locks and dams.

[7] For a discussion of the controversies related to the use of HMT funds, see Kumar (2002).

[8] Although the U.S. Army Corps of Engineers (USACE) is responsible for the maintenance of navigable waterways, ports are generally responsible for any dredging or other maintenance activities that take place at (or near) berths.

[9] According to the U.S. Bureau of Economic Analysis (BEA), U.S. gross domestic product (GDP) has increased steadily since 2009 (U.S. BEA, 2018).

tested and will continue to test, the limits of U.S. ports. In addition, the widened Panama Canal (completed in July 2016) has fueled efforts among U.S. East and Gulf Coast ports to accommodate *neopanamax* vessels that are now routinely transiting the canal. U.S. ports have largely been proactive in addressing infrastructure needs related to the handling of larger vessels. For example, prior to the opening of the expanded locks, no ports along the Gulf of Mexico were capable of accommodating containerships of 6000-TEU or greater in size. Today, the ports of Houston, Mobile, and New Orleans regularly service vessels with capacities greater than 6000-TEU. Many ports on the U.S. East Coast have also responded similarly by investing in additional berth space, larger cranes, and initiating plans for the construction of new terminals (see Wang & Pagano, 2015). In addition, several dredging projects are expected to take place at East Coast ports in the near future, including at the Ports of Savannah and Charleston, where the inner harbors of these ports will be deepened to 47 and 52-feet, respectively (see Fig. 6.1 for current maximum channel depths at U.S. ports). Dredging projects such as these will help to ensure that U.S. ports are equipped to handle both increasing cargo volumes and larger vessels.

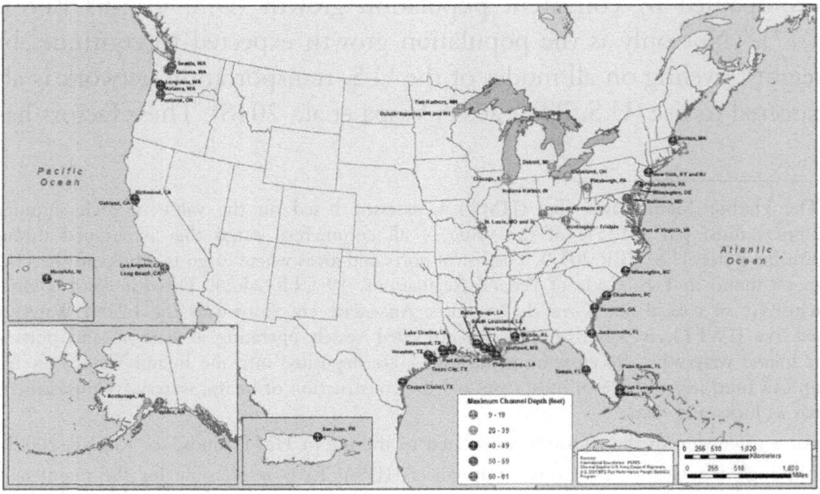


**Fig. 6.1** Maximum channel depths at selected U.S. ports

Events taking place in U.S. energy markets have also influenced port infrastructure needs. In December of 2015, Congress lifted a decades-old ban on U.S. exports of crude oil. Since then, exports of U.S.-produced crude oil have increased substantially; from less than a half-million barrels per day in January of 2016 to an average of 2 million barrels per day during the third quarter of 2018 (U.S. EIA, 2018a). Similarly, U.S. ex,ports of liquefied natural gas (LNG) quadrupled during 2017 and are likely to continue this trajectory as four additional export terminals become operational by 2021 (U.S. EIA, 2018b, 2018c). For U.S. ports, handling this growing volume of energy exports is likely to require a variety of infrastructure investments. This is particularly true on the Gulf Coast, where channel depths for accommodating fully laden very large crude carriers (VLCC) are highly desirable. The Port of Corpus Christi is working to address this limitation and has entered into a P3 agreement to fund over $1 billion in improvements, including dredging, that would allow them to service fully laden VLCCs (Druzin, 2018).[10] Privately owned offshore oil terminals provide another option for transferring crude oil to and from VLCCs. The Louisiana Offshore Oil Port (LOOP) has been loading VLCCs with U.S. produced oil since early 2018 (Moore, 2018) and a deep-water crude oil export facility off Corpus Christi is already in the licensing and planning stages. Private investments in these offshore facilities could become more common as exports of crude oil continue to rise.

U.S. ports are also looking at ways to minimize the impacts of LNG vessel traffic on their harbors and channels. In Corpus Christi, port officials are working with the U.S. Army Corps of Engineers (USACE) to secure funds to widen the ship channel which would allow two-way traffic and improve traffic flow as LNG carriers transit the channel (Musser, 2017). As additional LNG export terminals become operational, other Gulf Coast ports may need to take similar steps to reduce potential bottlenecks.

Although the infrastructure challenges created by larger vessels have been well-documented, there are other important infrastructure needs

---

[10] Proposed dredging at the Port of Corpus Christi will still require the approval of the U.S. Army Corps of Engineers.

at U.S. ports that must also be addressed. This includes the need for improved intermodal connectivity which is an issue critical to ensuring that ports can efficiently handle their inbound and outbound cargo movements. According to a recent survey, eighty percent of ports anticipate investing at least $10 million in their port's intermodal connectors before the year 2025 (AAPA, 2015). U.S. ports are particularly in need of adequate on-dock or near-dock rail access and other intermodal projects that will enhance "first and last mile" connectivity (AAPA, 2018). In addition, operational technologies are playing an increasingly important role in many U.S. ports, as automated cargo-handling equipment and gate appointment systems have allowed ports to more efficiently utilize their existing storage space and reduce drayage as well as truck turnaround times. Ports are increasingly turning to technology to reduce the environmental footprint of their landside activities. Several U.S. ports are actively testing the use of electric trucks and cargo-handling equipment, while two battery-powered trucks are already conducting yard operations at the Port of Oakland (Link-Wills, 2018). These are just some of the improvements that ports will be looking to fund in the coming years. Other recent innovations in freight transportation, including autonomous trucks, the digitalization of port operations, and the use of blockchain technology are also expected as these technologies become more developed.[11]

## Planning and Funding Tools

Recognizing a need for improved freight system planning, U.S. Congress recently passed legislation requiring states to formulate comprehensive freight plans that will identify significant freight system goals and priority projects. They should provide critical guidance as to how state agencies expect to develop and maintain their freight transportation infrastructure, including ports and their intermodal connectors. Congress has

---

[11] In the context of ports, "digitalization" refers to the process of using information technology to electronically collect, store, and analyze data related to all aspects of a port's performance, including the cargo booking process, vessel calls, cargo handling, truck arrivals and turn times (Port of Rotterdam, n.d.).

also established two federal transportation discretionary grant programs, including one program that is specifically oriented toward freight-related projects.[12] Although neither of these programs is port-specific, port authorities are eligible to apply for federal transportation grants to help fund a range of infrastructure projects. In recent years, the Federal government has funded a variety of such port projects, including many projects that will enhance intermodal connectivity at port facilities. Notably, transportation grant programs administered by the Federal government often require, or strongly encourage, applicants, to share in the cost of the project by requiring non-Federal matching funds.

Although the U.S. federal government does not offer a credit assistance program tailored specifically to ports, they are eligible to participate in existing transportation infrastructure finance programs that are administered by the U.S. Department of Transportation. Both the Transportation Infrastructure Finance and Innovation Act (TIFIA) and the Railroad Rehabilitation and Improvement Financing (RRIF) programs can be used by ports to finance intermodal transfer facilities, on-dock rail, and other projects that will improve access into and out of ports. Programs such as these can provide ports with access to direct loans, loan guarantees, and standby lines of credit, and often favor projects that are likely to attract private investment through P3 agreements. However, port-participation in TIFIA and RRIF has been low, which is partially attributable to the complex nature of applying to these credit assistance programs (AAPA, 2015). Even without federal assistance, port authorities are increasingly turning to P3s to finance infrastructure improvements. These P3 arrangements usually involve concessions that are awarded to private entities who will then construct and operate new port facil,ities, usually under a long-term lease agreement. Efforts by U.S. ports to seek out private partners for infrastructure projects have resulted in an influx of foreign investment into U.S. ports. Estimates suggest that most port terminals in the U.S. are now operated by foreign entities

[12] The BUILD and INFRA grant programs both provide dedicated, discretionary grant funding for transportation projects.

(Kaplan, 2006); this is a trend that is likely to continue as many ports prepare themselves to accommodate increasing cargo volumes.[13]

Other public financing mechanisms available to port authorities include municipal bonds that are secured by port operating revenues, income from a tenant lease or concessionaire agreement, or local tax revenues. In addition, port authorities or other government agencies may issue private activity bonds, which allow public entities to finance privately owned port projects being developed for public use (AAPA & MARAD, 2017). Commercial lending markets are also evolving to meet the needs of port owners, as it is now possible to obtain bank loan financing for port infrastructure projects (AAPA and MARAD). Whether these loans are more cost beneficial than municipal financing options depends on a variety of factors including market conditions, as well as the term and size of the loan (AAPA and MARAD).

## Summary Outlook

Many U.S. ports are already planning for improvements that will allow them to accommodate future increases in waterborne trade. These projects are often intermodal in nature and are designed to increase throughput, improve first and last-mile connections, and relieve road congestion. In fact, 77 percent of U.S. ports are already planning for on-dock, near-dock, or rail access improvements that will need to take place within the next decade (AAPA, 2018). This suggests that there is still significant work to be done before U.S. ports are fully integrated into our surface transportation system. Although there are a variety of mechanisms in place to finance these necessary improvements, the process of planning for infrastructure projects and securing public and private investment is inherently challenging. Given the disparate nature of U.S. ports, each port project is likely to be different and encounter its own set of unique challenges. As a result, it is important that all port owners have access to the necessary tools and expertise to secure financing for their

[13] As an example, twelve out of thirteen container terminals in the ports of Los Angeles and Long Beach in Southern California have some level of foreign ownership.

projects. The Federal government is beginning to recognize this need and has responded by establishing a resource center, the Build America Bureau, which provides technical expertise to public entities looking to utilize credit assistance programs or P3 agreements to finance their transportation infrastructure projects.

From a planning perspective, there are several steps that can be taken by policymakers and port owners, and operators to ensure that the ports are ready to accommodate future economic growth. Throughout the government, it is imperative that ports are thoroughly incorporated into all planning efforts related to surface freight transportation. For States, this means that ports and their intermodal connectors should be included in State Freight Plans. Preparers of State Freight Plans should identify ports and related intermodal facilities that are experiencing mobility issues and thoroughly document these bottlenecks. In addition, States should ensure that ports are included in all efforts to conduct outreach or collect feedback related to their freight plans. Likewise, ports of all sizes should engage in their own planning efforts, which should include the formulation of asset management plans and the use of "firewalled" savings accounts for future infrastructure investments.

## References

American Association of Port Authorities. (2015). *Post Surface Transportation Infrastructure Survey: The State of Freight*. Retrieved from http://aapa.files.cmsplus.com/StateofFreight_Report_final.pdf

American Association of Port Authorities. (2018). *The State of Freight III*. Retrieved from http://aapa.files.cms-plus.com/PDFs/State%20of%20Freight%20III.pdf

American Association of Port Authorities and the U.S. Maritime Administration (MARAD). (2017). *Port Planning and Investment Toolkit*. Retrieved from http://aapa.files.cms-plus.com/PDFs/Toolkit/Introduction%20and%20Users%20Guide.pdf

Brooks, M. R., & Pallis, A. A. (2012). Port governance. In W. K. Talley (Ed.), *The Blackwell companion to maritime economics*. Blackwell Publishing Ltd.

Committee on the Marine Transportation System (CMTS). (2017). *Federal Funding Handbook for Marine Transportation System Infrastructure*. Retrieved from https://www.cmts.gov/downloads/2017_CMTS_Federal_Funding_Handbook_for_MTS_Infrastructure.pdf

Druzin, R. (2018). Port of Corpus Christi, Carlyle to team up for Texas VLCC terminal. *San Antonio Express-News*. Retrieved from https://www.expressnews.com/business/eagle-ford-energy/article/Port-of-Corpus-Christi-Carlyle-to-team-up-for-13346547.php

Kaplan, E. (2006). The UAE purchase of American port facilities. Retrieved from https://www.cfr.org/backgrounder/uae-purchase-american-port-facilities#chapter-title-0-9

Kumar, S. (2002). The U.S. Harbor Maintenance Tax Controversy: Is there a solution? *International Journal of Maritime Economics, 4*(2), 149–163.

Link-Wills, K. (2018). Oakland sees second trucker turn to all-electric rig. *American Shipper*. Retrieved from https://www.americanshipper.com/news/oakland-sees-second-trucker-turn-to-allelectric-rig?autonumber=72915&via=news-page-top-news

Moore, K. (2018). Louisiana Offshore Oil Port loads first oil for export. *WorkBoat*. Retrieved from https://www.workboat.com/news/offshore/louisiana-offshore-oil-port-loads-first-oil-export/

Musser, L. (2017). Seizing LNG supply chain opportunities. *Seaports Magazine, 46,* 10–16.

Port of Rotterdam. (n.d.). Step by step towards a digital port. Retrieved from https://www.portofrotterdam.com/en/port-forward/step-by-step-towards-a-digital-port

U.S. Army Corps of Engineers. (2017). The U.S. Waterway System: 2017 Transportation Facts and Information. Retrieved from https://publibrary.planusace.us/#/series/Fact%20Cards

U.S. Bureau of Transportation Statistics. (2016). DOT Releases 30-Year Freight Projections. Retrieved from https://www.bts.dot.gov/sites/bts.dot.gov/files/legacy/bts13_16.pdf

U.S. Bureau of Transportation Statistics. (2017). DOT Releases 30-Year Freight Projections. Retrieved from https://www.bts.gov/newsroom/dot-releases-30-year-freight-projections

U.S. Bureau of Economic Analysis. (2018). National Income and Product Accounts: Table 1.1.5 Gross Domestic Product. Retrieved from https://apps.bea.gov/iTable/iTable.cfm?reqid=19&step=2#reqid=19&step=2&isuri=1&1921=survey

U.S. Census Bureau. (2017). Annual Estimates of the Resident Population: April 1, 2010 to July 1, 2017. Retrieved from https://factfinder.census.gov/faces/tableservices/jsf/pages/productview.xhtml?pid=PEP_2017_PEPANNRES&prodType=table

U.S. Customs and Border Protection. (2017). What is the Harbor Maintenance Fee (HMF)? Retrieved from https://help.cbp.gov/app/answers/detail/a_id/283/~/what-is-the-harbor-maintenance-fee-%28hmf%29%3F

U.S. Energy Information Administration. (2018a). U.S. Exports of Crude Oil. Retrieved from https://www.eia.gov/dnav/pet/hist/LeafHandler.ashx?n=PET&s=MCREXUS1&f=M

U.S. Energy Information Administration. (2018b). U.S. liquefied natural gas exports quadrupled in 2017. Retrieved from https://www.eia.gov/todayinenergy/detail.php?id=35512

U.S. Energy Inforamtion Administration. (2018c). U.S. liquefied natural gas export capacity to more than double by the end of 2019. Retrieved from https://www.eia.gov/todayinenergy/detail.php?id=37732

U.S. Maritime Administration (MARAD). (2015). Vessel Calls in U.S. Ports, Selected Terminals and Lightering Areas. Retrieved from https://www.maritime.dot.gov/data-reports/data-statistics/data-statistics

Vespa, J., Armstrong, D. M., & Medina, L. (2018). Demographic Turning Points for the United States: Population Projections for 2020 to 2060. Retrieved from https://www.census.gov/content/dam/Census/library/publications/2018/demo/P25_1144.pdf

Wang, G., & Pagano, A. M. (2015). Select U.S. Ports Prepare for Panama Canal Expansion. Report prepared for the Commercial Real Estate Development Association. Retrieved from https://www.naiop.org/-/media/Research/Research/Research-Reports/Select-US-Ports-Prepare-For-Panama-Canal-Expansion/PortsReport_FINAL_010915_rvsd.ashx

# 7

# Regulation and Finance in the Bangladesh Port Industry

Ziaul Haque Munim

## Bangladesh Port System

"Two thousand years ago, the Indian subcontinent was a point of departure and destination for merchants and mendicants from across the Arabian Sea and the Bay of Bengal" (Paine, 2014, p. 1). The Bay of Bengal accommodates several important world ports, e.g. Chittagong, Colombo, Kolkata-Haldia, Chennai etc. The existence of Chittagong Port of Bangladesh can be traced back to the fourth century B.C (CPA, 2010). Later, the port appeared on Ptolemy's map in the second century A.D. The Arab traders travelled to Chittagong frequently during the ninth century. During those days, the Yemeni and Arab traders used Chittagong Port to trade with India, Sumatra-Java (Indonesia) and China in the East, and Greece in the West. During the sixteenth and

Z. H. Munim (✉)
Faculty of Technology, Natural and Maritime Sciences, University of South-Eastern Norway, Horten, Norway
e-mail: ziaul.h.munim@usn.no

© The Author(s), under exclusive license to Springer Nature Switzerland AG 2022

C. Ferrari et al. (eds.), *Regulation and Finance in the Port Industry*,
Palgrave Studies in Maritime Economics,
https://doi.org/10.1007/978-3-030-83985-7_7

seventeenth centuries, the Portuguese settled in Chittagong surrounding the port. In 1552, De Barros, one of the first Portuguese chroniclers of Asia, described Chittagong as "the most famous and wealthy city of the kingdom of Bengal" because the port attracted traffic from all of the eastern region (Banglapedia, n.d.). Later in 1760, during the British period, the port became part of the British East India Company. The present location of the port was established in 1887, and four terminals were built by 1910. After the British left the region in 1947, Chittagong Port became part of East Pakistan, and the Chittagong Port Trust was formed in 1960. The current governing body, Chittagong Port Authority (CPA), was established in 1976 after Bangladesh became an independent country in 1971.

Today Bangladesh has three seaports (hereafter, ports): Chittagong, Mongla and Payra. The government has also been planning to develop a deep-sea port since the last decade, but only recently has confirmed to develop the port in Matarbari in collaboration with the Japan International Cooperation Agency (JICA) (Hamid, 2018). Figure 7.1 depicts the location of the existing three ports along with the proposed deep-sea port and the major river and inland ports. Among the existing ports, Chittagong Port is the largest one and handles over 90% of the country's international seaborne trade (CPA, 2017). Currently, Chittagong ranks 64th in the world's top 100 ports list.[1] The Mongla Port is the second largest port of the country, located about 90 km from the western part of the Bay of Bengal. Although Mongla started operation in 1950 as Chalna Port, the current governing body, Mongla Port Authority (MPA), was established in 1987. The third port of the country, Payra Port was initiated in 2013 by the Government of Bangladesh to boost economic activities in the South-West region of the country. The distance between Mongla and Payra is about 120 km. The fourth port, Matarbari, the first deep-sea port of the country is under construction approximately 100 km south of Chittagong Port. As the port operation in Payra is still in the early stage, and Matarbari is only under construction, Fig. 7.2 presents container and cargo handling statistics of Chittagong and Mongla Port.

[1] https://lloydslist.maritimeintelligence.informa.com/one-hundred-container-ports-2019.

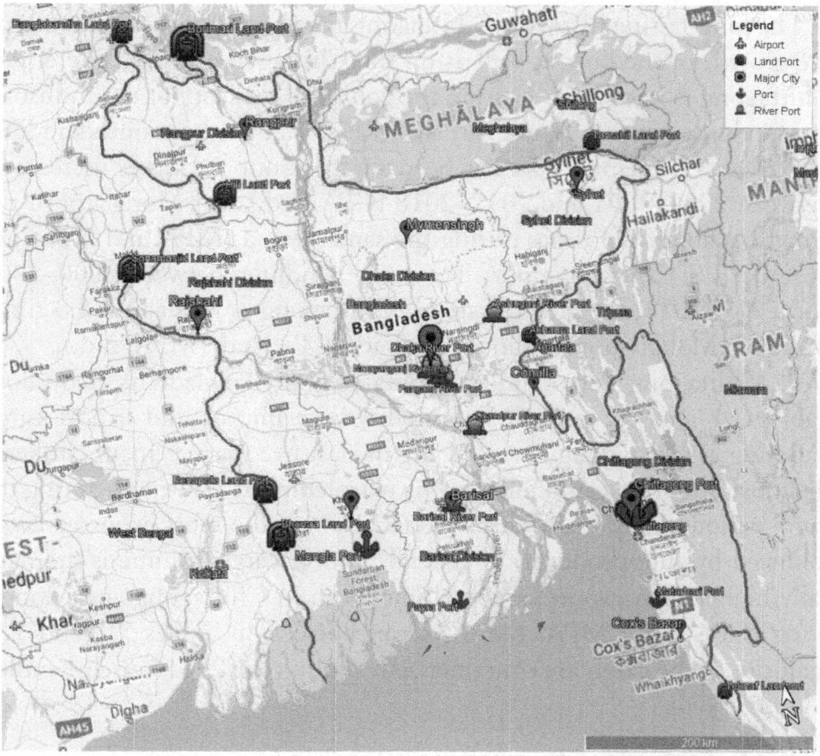


Fig. 7.1 Major sea, river and inland ports (icon size is scaled based on throughput) (*Source* Author's own elaboration using Google Earth Pro)

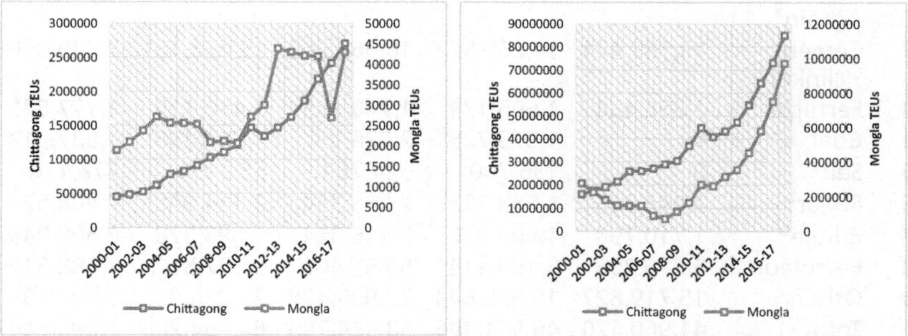


*(a) Container handling*

*(b) Cargo handling*

**Fig. 7.2** Container and cargo handling statistics (*Source* CPA [n.d.] and MPA [n.d.])

The long-lasting history of Chittagong Port has a positive influence on the growth of the port as well as on the Chittagong region. The city of Chittagong is known for hosting the country's majority of the industrial production activities. As we can see in Fig. 7.2, the container handling growth in Chittagong port has been sharp, about 5.9 times increase in between 2000–2001 and 2017–2018 (CPA, n.d.). For Mongla port, the growth is about 2.3 times during the same period (MPA, n.d.), but not as smooth as Chittagong port. For cargo handling, between 2000–2001 and 2017–2018, the growth rate for Chittagong port is about 5.3 times while for Mongla port is about 3.5 times (CPA, n.d.; MPA, n.d.).

As Chittagong Port handles the majority of Bangladesh's trade flow, Tables 7.1 and 7.2 present commodity-wise import and export cargo handling at Chittagong Port. During the last five years, cement clinker is the most imported cargo followed by petroleum. As for export during the same period, ready-made garments (RMG) are the most exported cargo followed by Jute products. In general, import cargo volume is dramatically higher than export cargo volume, both in Chittagong and Mongla ports (CPA, n.d.; MPA, n.d.). As can be seen in Tables 7.1 and 7.2, majority of the cargo are containerized. Among the 2611 vessels handled

**Table 7.1** Commodity-wise import cargo handling (metric tons)

| Sl no | Commodity | 2013–2014 | 2014–2015 | 2015–2016 | 2016–2017 | 2017–2018 |
|---|---|---|---|---|---|---|
| 1 | Food grain[a] | 2,072,156 | 2,955,454 | 3,963,718 | 5,047,751 | 6,783,355 |
| 2 | Cement clinker | 13,580,424 | 14,209,572 | 16,962,003 | 19,628,181 | 21,492,163 |
| 3 | Fertilizer | 1,256,454 | 1,605,124 | 1,740,385 | 1,416,115 | 1,777,825 |
| 4 | Coal | 0 | 1,375,725 | 2,226,397 | 1,364,436 | 1,527,312 |
| 5 | Salt | 0 | 136,700 | 324,760 | 551,956 | 778,178 |
| 6 | Sugar[b] | 2,044,215 | 1,989,353 | 2,095,344 | 2,134,908 | 2,468,556 |
| 7 | Edible[b] | 1,710,798 | 1,904,320 | 2,456,364 | 1,996,578 | 2,508,948 |
| 8 | Petroleum | 5,576,296 | 6,169,314 | 5,655,407 | 7,027,510 | 7,788,517 |
| 9 | Others[c] | 15,719,827 | 18,595,844 | 22,900,408 | 27,296,850 | 32,925,593 |
| | **Total** | **41,960,170** | **48,941,406** | **58,324,786** | **66,464,285** | **78,050,447** |

[a]Approximately 20–30% containerized [b]Approximately 3–5% containerized [c]Approximately 70–80% containerized
*Source* CPA (2018)

**Table 7.2** Commodity-wise export cargo handling (metric tons)

| Sl no | Commodity | 2013–2014 | 2014–2015 | 2015–2016 | 2016–2017 | 2017–2018 |
|---|---|---|---|---|---|---|
| 1 | Jute[a] | 190,071 | 165,287 | 157,635 | 212,353 | 20,480 |
| 2 | Jute products[a] | 808,741 | 813,599 | 706,938 | 821,677 | 722,800 |
| 3 | Leather goods[a] | 31,477 | 35,787 | 30,211 | 30,644 | 35,912 |
| 4 | Tea[a] | 495 | 490 | 48 | 0 | 0 |
| 5 | Garments[a] | 2,653,198 | 2,760,449 | 2,788,000 | 2,973,724 | 3,422,571 |
| 6 | Frozen goods[a] | 173,429 | 123,846 | 94,299 | 121,893 | 110,555 |
| 7 | NAPTHA | 79,618 | 76,952 | 68,256 | 104,954 | 18,500 |
| 8 | AMMONIA | 14,000 | 40,004 | 40,800 | 15,000 | 19,083 |
| 9 | Others[b] | 1,387,348 | 1,823,572 | 2,085,447 | 2,429,514 | 2,441,564 |
| | **Total** | **5,338,377** | **5,839,986** | **5,971,634** | **6,709,759** | **6,791,465** |

[a]100% containerized [b]Approximately 80–95% containerized
*Source* CPA (2018)

by Bangladeshi ports in 2018, 51% are container, 29% dry bulk, 18% liquid bulk and 2% Ro-Ro (UNCTAD, n.d.a).

While the majority of the country's trade happens through Chittagong and Mongla port, there are also 23 inland ports and 22 river ports in Bangladesh (Ministry of Shipping, 2018). Figure 7.3 presents the share of cargo handled by Chittagong, Mongla, inland and river ports for the fiscal year 2017–2018. A negligible share of trade, 0.37 million tons, is carried out by the airports of the country (Ministry of Shipping, 2018). All Bangladesh ports can be categorized as gateway ports since transhipment volumes to India and Nepal are negligible.

Mongla Port's rather slow growth in comparison to Chittagong is most likely due to its poor transport connection with major cities, particularly with Dhaka (see Fig. 7.1). In contrast, Chittagong Port is well connected to most major cities of the country via road, rail and inland water transport (IWT). Figure 7.4 shows Chittagong's cargo clearance share via different transport modes. Despite being less environmentally friendly, road transport has the highest share. Noteworthy, before the 1965 Indo-Pak war, the share of IWT was much higher as most of Chittagong port's cargo was transported to other parts of Bangladesh as well as to the North Western region of India using IWT.

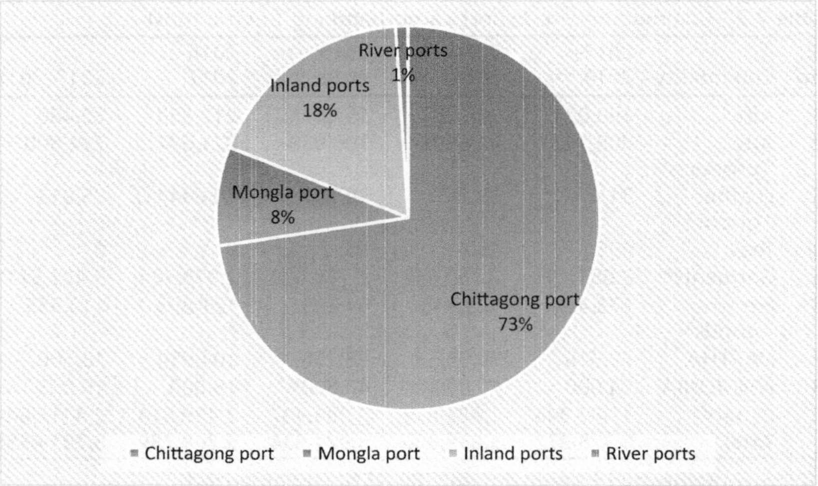


**Fig. 7.3** Port category-wise cargo handling share 2017–2018 (*Source* CPA [n.d.]; MPA [n.d.]; Ministry of Shipping [2018])

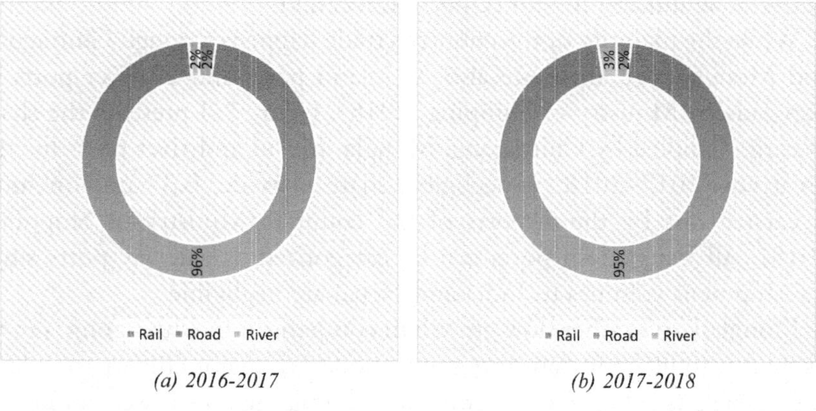


**Fig. 7.4** Cargo clearance from Chittagong Port by transport mode (TONs) (*Source* CPA [2018])

Meanwhile, Bangladesh is performing well in terms of overall port sector development in comparison to ports of similar scale in neighbouring countries. In terms of container throughput, Chittagong (64) ranks better than Karachi (83), Kolkata and the ports of Myanmar.[2] In the same vein, based on port liner shipping connectivity index (PLSCI) value in 2018, Chittagong (13.31) is better than Kolkata (8.62), Mumbai (6.91) and Rangoon ports (10.19), although larger regional ports such as Nhava Sheva (44.24), Mundra (46.05), Karachi (31.10), Colombo (63.52) performs better (UNCTAD, n.d.b). With a PLSCI value of 4.35 in 2018, Mongla is lagging behind. Moreover, in 2018, Bangladesh ranks 107th in the logistics performance index (LPI), better than most of the regional countries such as Myanmar (108), Sri Lanka (122) and Pakistan (136).[3]

## Port Regulation and Planning

All ports of Bangladesh, including inland and river ports, are under the administrative control of the Ministry of Shipping of the Government of the People's Republic of Bangladesh (Ministry of Shipping, 2018). Despite this, different port governance models are evident. One of the reasons is that ports function as autonomous entities under the oversight of the Ministry of Shipping. Host municipalities of the ports cannot exercise any control, financially or non-financially, over the ports. However, ports usually deliver some form of service to their respective municipalities which they consider as corporate social responsibility (CSR), e.g. CPA maintains several roads in the Chittagong city.

As much of the port regulation and planning depend on governance, the port governance models of Bangladeshi seaports are summarized in Table 7.1 based on the governance model categorization of the *World Bank Port Reform Toolkit* (World Bank, 2007). Depending on the degree of public–private participation in four port functions, which are, infrastructure, superstructure, port labour and other port operations, there are four-port governance models: service, tool, landlord and private (ibid.). Until now, service and tool port model are dominant in Bangladesh (i.e.

[2] Kolkata and ports of Myanmar not in the list of top 100 ports. See https://lloydslist.maritimeintelligence.informa.com/one-hundred-container-ports-2019.

[3] https://lpi.worldbank.org/international/aggregated-ranking.

Table 7.3 Port governance model in Bangladesh

| Function[a] | Chittagong | Mongla | Payra | Matarbari |
|---|---|---|---|---|
| Infrastructure | Public | Public | Public | Public |
| Superstructure | Public | Public | Private | Public |
| Port labour | Private | Public | Private | Private |
| Other operations | Mostly Private | Mostly Public | Mostly Private | Mostly Private |
| *Dominant governance model* | *Tool port* | *Service port* | *Landlord port* | *Tool port* |

[a]All functions adapted from World Bank Port Reform Toolkit 2007, Module 3, p. 21

in Mongla and Chittagong). However, with the recently signed Public–Private Partnerships (PPPs) projects for Mongla and Payra ports, landlord port model will soon be evident in the Bangladesh port industry. Meanwhile, the landlord model has already been existent among the inland (dry) ports of the country, for example, in Teknaf and Sonamosjid. Local private company, United Group, operates and manages the Teknaf Landport under concession agreement with the Bangladesh Land Port Authority (BLPA). Under similar terms, the Panama Sonamasjid Port Link Ltd. operates and manages the Sonamosjid Landport. The under-construction deep-sea port, Matarbari, is expected to be governed under the tool port model (Table 7.3).

From the port planning perspective, all ports have their own planning department and can undertake port planning activities themselves. However, plans exceeding BDT 10 Crore[4] need to be approved by the Ministry of Shipping. The government usually undertakes short, mid and long-term plans for all ports. Currently, the government has put the development of Payra Port in one of its "10 Fast Track" projects. For the master plan preparation of the port, the government has already commissioned approximately Euro 134.52 million to a Dutch company named the Royal Haskoning DHV and Bangladesh University of Engineering and Technology (Dhaka Tribune, 2019). For Payra Port, the short-term plan is to initiate small-scale port operations and undertake all necessary

[4] *Roughly Euro 1 million.*

preparations such as customs clearance facilities, banking, implementation of ISPS code, VHF communications etc. (PPA, n.d.). The mid-term plan is to operate at least one multipurpose and one bulk terminal (ibid.). Finally, the long-term plan is to make the port fully operational by 2023 and develop a port city by establishing an exclusive economic zone (EEZ), shipyard, local airport and eco-tourism (ibid.). According to the Public—Private Partnership Authority (PPPA) of Bangladesh, at least three projects of Payra Port—Payra Port dredging, coal terminal and container terminal development, are being considered for PPP (PPPA, n.d.).

For Chittagong Port, under the supervision of CPA and Ministry of Shipping, a detailed strategic master plan has been developed recently by HPC Hamburg Port Consulting (Germany), KS Consultants Limited (Bangladesh) and Sellhorn Ingenieurgesellschaft (Germany) (Asian Development Bank, 2015). The proposed master plan covers port development scenarios until 2043 (HPC, 2015). The estimated handling volume at Chittagong Port in 2043 is expected to be 124 million tonnes, which is an increase of 82 million tonnes relative to 2012 (ibid.). However, the port is currently experiencing capacity issues (Munim, 2020; 2019; Munim et al., 2019). To further meet estimated demand, HPC (2015) recommended upgrading two of Chittagong's container terminals (i.e. NCT and CCT) while transferring the operations of GCB terminal to modern container and multipurpose terminals. As such, HPC (2015) suggested the development of three new container terminals (i.e. KCT1, MPT and BCT) which are financially sound from a port asset management perspective and profitable. The port authority has already taken initiatives, and several new container and multipurpose terminal constructions are ongoing (CPA, 2018).

As handling throughput in Mongla Port has grown steadily in recent years (see Fig. 7.2), the government has initiated several capacity expansion projects. Mongla Port currently has two new container terminals under development. An agreement has been signed between MPA and Powerpack Ports Limited (The Independent, 2016). This is a PPP project, and Powerpack Ports Limited will maintain and operate the terminals for 30 years following a concession agreement under landlord governance model.

Furthermore, to keep pace with the projected port throughput growth of Bangladesh (HPC, 2015), the Matarbari port is under development following a PPP project between CPA and JICA. JICA will hand over the port to CPA after completion. CPA sources confirm that Matarbari will be governed according to the same model as Chittagong, that is, the tool port governance model.

## Financial Tools

Generally, the Ministry of Shipping of Bangladesh has been the main source of funding for new port developments in Bangladesh. Yearly budgets for port development are approved in the national budget for the upcoming fiscal year in the parliament. Once operational, ports usually finance their own development and expansion projects from their revenue but need approval from the Ministry of Shipping for larger projects. This holds for the tool and service ports of the country, Chittagong and Mongla (as depicted in Table 7.1). Over the years, CPA saved a fund of approximately Euro 1.04 billion (as of 2017) from their profits (CPA, 2017). Additional to current port revenues, CPA also earns substantial interest from banks on the saved fund (ibid.). Thus, CPA can finance their future projects smoothly using their own fund. Although the same behaviour is expected from Mongla Port, however, due to lack of funds, their current and upcoming projects cannot be financed by their own fund. Currently, the government has financed seven projects in Mongla Port worth Euro 31 million, which are in the development stage, three projects worth Euro 66.6 million are under implementation stage, and few projects are under approval process worth Euro 292.5 million[5] (The Independent, 2016).

Financial tools for the two to be built container terminals at the Mongla Port and one at the Payra Port are different than the ones discussed already. As these terminals are being developed under PPP projects, private firms are financing these projects. Not much detail is

---

[5] *BDT 310 Crore ≈ Euro 31 million, BDT 666 crore ≈ Euro 66.6 million, BDT 2925 Crore ≈ Euro 292.5 million.*

publicly available on the future governance model of Payra Port, but port officials confirm that it is going to be governed under the landlord model. Meanwhile, Powerac Ports Limited, a local private firm, will be developing two container terminals at Mongla Port as well as operate those terminals under a 30 years concession contract (The Independent, 2016). The estimated cost of the project is USD 52.74 million (ibid.). Powerac will share profits with MPA as per agreement. Finally, for the first stage development of the Matarbari Port, the full cost will be covered by JICA without any repayment terms (JOC, 2018). The same was confirmed by a CPA official.

## Links Between Local and National Port Regulation and the International Framework of Ports

International organizations have been involved in the Bangladesh port industry since the 1980s. Organizations like the World Bank, Asian Development Bank and JICA play a key role in providing funds for port development projects in Bangladesh. In 1982, the World Bank sanctioned USD 60 million to Chittagong Port for the construction of two multipurpose terminals to cope up with the rising container throughput in the early 1990s (World Bank, n.d.). Recently, the World Bank has provided USD 507 million for private companies to improve infrastructure quality in Bangladesh that includes container terminal and land port development projects (World Bank, 2017a). The Asian Development Bank financed the strategic master plan project for Chittagong Port, which outlined the overall framework for future port development (Asian Development Bank, 2015). When it comes to financing from the World Bank or Asian Development Bank, port authorities, particularly the CPA is reluctant to avail those funds. One reason is that CPA has their own funds to finance future projects. Another reason, rather interesting, is that funds from those organizations are first availed by the government at a lower interest rate, then later given as a loan to the ports with a higher interest rate.

Only recently the Bangladesh government started to embrace private participation in seaport development projects, the first project being the development of two terminals at Mongla Port (PPPA, n.d.). Moreover, PPPs have been considered for Payra Port dredging, coal terminal and container terminal development (PPPA, n.d.). The dredging deal has been granted to the Belgian company Jan De Nul (JDN) for Euro 550 million (World Maritime News, 2017). Further detail of the coal and container terminal development projects is not yet available. Meanwhile, JICA is financing the deep-sea port project in Matarbari, which is currently under the design stage; the estimated cost is not yet publicly available. The initial establishment at Matarbari Port will have only one container terminal and one multipurpose terminal, but there will be enough room for further expansion. Furthermore, it is allegedly heard that PSA Singapore will be developing a new container terminal under the umbrella of Chittagong Port, the Bay Container Terminal. According to UNCTAD (2017), more than 80% of the world's container terminals are operated by private organizations nowadays. Although Bangladesh lags behind neighbouring countries with respect to privatization (World Bank, 2017b; Munim et al., 2019), multiple PPP projects for port development undertaken recently is paving the way ahead.

## Critical Discussion

As discussed in the previous section, the Bangladesh port industry has been embracing private involvement recently. However, the majority of the private organizations involved in port development projects in Bangladesh are local firms. The neighbouring countries of Bangladesh, such as Pakistan, India and Sri Lanka, have involved some of the world's largest global terminal operators (GTOs), such as DP World, Hutchison Ports and PSA Singapore, in their port development and operation (Munim et al., 2019). According to the World Bank (2017b), Asian Development Bank (2015) and Munim et al. (2019), Bangladesh can win from meaningful private investment into the port sector. Many GTOs have already expressed their interests in future port development projects. However, due to national protectionism, ports authorities and governments are reluctant to acquire support from foreign entities. A long history of foreign control (i.e. Portuguese, British, Pakistani) of the country's largest port may have contributed to the development of such a mindset. However, it seems this scenario might change in the near future.

The major port of the country, Chittagong Port, is one of the highest technically efficient ports in the world but suffers greatly in terms of service quality (Munim, 2020; 2019; Wu & Goh, 2010). In a port competitiveness survey from the users' perspective, Munim and Schramm (2018) found that port facilities and efficiency, service quality and green port management of Chittagong Port are the three factors with the lowest scores. Improvement in these factors can be achieved from meaningful private involvement in port development and operation. Private intervention in port operation increases efficiency of port operation, reduces pressure on public sector budget, reduces labour costs, introduces cutting-edge technology and know-how, increase land-utilization and can introduce competition among ports or terminal (Bagchi & Paik, 2001; Baird, 2000; UNCTAD, 2017), which can contribute significantly to the competitiveness of a port.

Access to private funding frees up government funds that can be used for other purposes. Still, the Bangladesh government has been continuously investing in port, land port and river port development parallel to private firms. This ensures faster transport network development. As such, the Shipping Minister praised the government's support to develop the country's port infrastructure (The Independent, 2016). Despite increasing participation from local private firms, port development plans need to be approved by the Ministry of Shipping before implementation, particularly large projects. The government authority scrutinizes and monitors development plans as private firms will transfer back the developed port to the government at the end of their concession agreement.

Both Chittagong and Mongla are currently serving as a gateway port but entails unexplored potential to become a regional intermodal transhipment hub. Munim and Haralambides (2018) explored the potentials of the Bangladesh port to serve the pseudo-landlocked regions of North-east India and neighbouring landlocked countries Nepal and Bhutan. While there exists a great economic potential, the service quality of

Chittagong and Mongla through capacity expansion is obvious. In this circumstance, GTOs can play an important role by employing the latest technologies, knowledge and experience from large-scale port operation worldwide. In addition, Munim et al. (2019) found that landlord port yields maximum surplus compared to tool or service port model in the context of Bangladesh. As mentioned earlier, CPA and the government of Bangladesh are sceptical towards GTOs' interventions in the port industry. Such a defensive attitude is not new for small ports (Haralambides, 2002). However, ports like Busan, ranked 6th in the world in 2017,[6] also faced a similar situation to Chittagong Port in the early 1990s and overcame through PPP projects (Bagchi & Paik, 2001). Thus, there lies enormous potential for Bangladesh ports to gain from PPPs involving GTOs.

## References


Asian Development Bank. (2015). Bangladesh: Strategic master plan for Chittagong Port. Last accessed on December 25, 2018, from https://www.adb.org/projects/45078-001/main#project-pds

Bagchi, P. K., & Paik, S. K. (2001). The role of public-private partnership in port information systems development. *International Journal of Public Sector Management, 14*(6), 482–499.

Baird, A. J. (2000). Port privatisation: objectives, extent, process, and the UK experience. *International Journal of Maritime Economics, 2*(3), 177–194.

Banglapedia. (n.d). Chittagong city. Retrieved on December 20, 2018, from http://en.banglapedia.org/index.php?title=Chittagong_City

CPA. (2010). Chittagong Port Authority Yearbook 2010. Chittagong.

CPA. (2017). Chittagong Port Authority Annual Report 2016–2017. Chittagong.

CPA. (2018). Chittagong Port Authority Annual Report 2017–2018. Chittagong.

CPA. (n.d). Container and cargo handling statistics. Chittagong Port Authority, Chittagong.


---

6 https://lloydslist.maritimeintelligence.informa.com/one-hundred-container-ports-2017.

Dhaka Tribune. (2019). Deal inked to prepare Payra Port master plan. Last accessed on October 3, 2019, from https://www.dhakatribune.com/bangladesh/development/2019/02/14/deal-inked-to-prepare-payra-port-master-plan

Hamid, N. (2018). Matarbari port to be turned into a deep-sea port. Retrieved on December 20, 2018, from https://www.thedailystar.net/frontpage/matarbari-port-be-turned-deep-sea-port-1515973

Haralambides, H. E. (2002). Competition, excess capacity, and the pricing of port infrastructure. *International Journal of Maritime Economics, 4*(4), 323–347.

HPC. (2015). Strategic master plan for Chittagong Port. Chittagong, Bangladesh: Hamburg Port Consulting GmbH.

JOC. (2018). Matarbari port's expansion goal is 8,000 TEU ships by July 2023. Last accessed on December 24, 2018, from https://www.joc.com/port-news/asian-ports/port-chittagong/matarbari-port%E2%80%99s-expansion-goal-8000-teu-ships-july-2023_20180123.html

Ministry of Shipping. (2018). Annual report of Ministry of Shipping 2017–2018. Retrieved on December 20, 2018, from https://mos.portal.gov.bd/sites/default/files/files/mos.portal.gov.bd/annual_reports/8f422406_aaeb_428d_8676_afb3914fc5d4/Anual%20Report%20of%20MoS%202017-2018.pdf

MPA. (n.d.). Container and cargo handling statistics. Mongla Port Authority, Mongla.

Munim, Z. H. (2020). Does higher technical efficiency induce a higher service level? A paradox association in the context of port operations. *The Asian Journal of Shipping and Logistics, 36*(4), 157–168.

Munim, Z. H., & Haralambides, H. (2018). Competition and cooperation for intermodal container transhipment: A network optimization approach. *Research in Transportation Business & Management, 26*, 87–99.

Munim, Z. H., & Schramm, H.-J. (2018). Does port competitiveness effect users' competitiveness? Evidence from a major gateway port. *The Annual conference of the International Association of Maritime Economists (IAME) 2018*. September 11–14, 2018. Mombasa, Kenya.

Munim, Z. H., Saeed, N., & Larsen, O. I. (2019). 'Tool port' to 'landlord port': A game theory approach to analyse gains from governance model transformation. *Maritime Policy & Management, 46*(1), 43–60.

Paine, L. (2014). *The sea and civilization: A maritime history of the world*. Atlantic Books Ltd.
PPA. (n.d.). Welcome to Payra Port Authority. Last accessed on December 24, 2018, from http://ppa.gov.bd/site/page/baa1e3c7-9aaa-41ce-92be-b8fa8eb38582/Welcome-to--Payra-Port
PPPA. (n.d). Public Private Partnership Authority. Last accessed on December 24, 2018, from http://www.pppo.gov.bd/projects.php
The Independent. (2016). Two jetties of Mongla Port to be developed worth $52.74m. Last accessed on December 24, 2018, from http://www.theindependentbd.com/arcprint/details/56915/2016-08-22
UNCTAD. (2017). Review of maritime transport. United Nations Conference on Trade and Development. Geneva, Switzerland.
UNCTAD. (n.d.a). Port call and performance statistics: Number of arrivals, time spent in ports, vessel age and size, annual. Last accessed on October 3, 2019, from https://unctadstat.unctad.org/wds/TableViewer/tableView.aspx?ReportId=170027
UNCTAD. (n.d.b). Port liner shipping connectivity index, annual. Last accessed on October 3, 2019, from https://unctadstat.unctad.org/wds/TableViewer/tableView.aspx?ReportId=170026
World Bank. (2007). Port Reform Toolkit. 2nd Ed. The International Bank for Reconstruction and Development/The World Bank, Washington, DC, USA.
World Bank. (2017a). World Bank Provides $507 Million Financing to Improve Infrastructure in Bangladesh. Last accessed on December 25, 2018, from http://www.worldbank.org/en/news/press-release/2017/04/05/world-bank-provides-507-million-financing-to-improve-infrastructures-in-bangladesh
World Bank. (2017b). Bangladesh Can Win from Reforms, Private Investment in Ports. Last accessed on December 25, 2018, from http://www.worldbank.org/en/news/press-release/2017/04/27/bangladesh-can-win-from-reforms-private-investment-in-ports
World Bank. (n.d.). Chittagong Port Project. Last accessed on December 25, 2018, from http://projects.worldbank.org/P009426/chittagong-port-project?lang=en&tab=overview

World Maritime News. (2017). Payra Port Signs USD 647 Mn Dredging Deal. Last accessed on December 24, 2018, from https://worldmaritimenews.com/archives/237802/payra-port-signs-usd-647-mn-dredging-deal/

Wu, Y.-C. J., & Goh, M. (2010). Container port efficiency in emerging and more advanced markets. *Transportation Research Part E: Logistics and Transportation Review, 46*(6), 1030–1042.

# 8

# The Chinese Port System: Current Organization and Investment Solutions

Qiang Zhang and Yang Chen

## Introduction

Since undergoing "Reform and Opening-up Policy" in 1978, China's economy has experienced rapid and stable growth. International trade between China and the rest of the world has also increased fast. China's foreign trade volume has grown from 35.5 billion yuan in 1978 to 30.51 trillion yuan in 2018 (China Daily, 2019). Due to the large scale of foreign trade, Chinese ports, which are key nodes in the global supply chain and connect China with the international transport network, have attracted considerable investment and become national "growth poles"

Q. Zhang (✉) · Y. Chen
Shanghai Maritime University, Shanghai, China
e-mail: qiangzhang@shmtu.edu.cn

Y. Chen
e-mail: chenyang@shmtu.edu.cn

© The Author(s), under exclusive license to Springer Nature Switzerland AG 2022

C. Ferrari et al. (eds.), *Regulation and Finance in the Port Industry*, Palgrave Studies in Maritime Economics,
https://doi.org/10.1007/978-3-030-83985-7_8

that serve as economic catalysts. Currently, China is home to 7 of the 10 largest ports in the world (United Nations Conference on Trade and Development, 2018). In 2017, the total container throughput of national ports reached 238 million TEUs (Ministry of Transport, 2018).

Improvements in port regulation, finance, planning are the critical reasons for the success of the Chinese port industry. To achieve a complete understanding of the Chinese port industry, the current organization and investment solutions in the Chinese port industry must be reviewed.

The structure of the remainder of this chapter is as follows: Sect. "Chinese Port System and Its Basic Governance Structure" provides a general description of China's national port system and basic port governance structure. In Sect. "Local Port Development: Planning and Financial Tools", financial and planning tools are discussed from a local port development perspective alongside the effects of regional port integration reform. In Sect. "International Collaborations: The "Bring in" and "Going Global" Strategies", international collaborations in the Chinese port domain are presented. Section "Conclusions" provides the conclusions.

## Chinese Port System and Its Basic Governance Structure

China's ports form the world's largest cargo handling system, with the annual cargo throughput exceeding 10 billion tons. According to the Ministry of Transport (MOT) of the People's Republic of China, there are 25 seaports and 28 inland waterway ports listed as national main ports in China (MOT, 2004). Compared with inland waterway ports, seaports play a more crucial role in Chinese foreign trade. In 2017, the total throughput of foreign trade goods reached nearly 4.1 billion tons, of which approximately 3.7 billion tons was handled in seaports (MOT, 2018). In terms of the geographical locations of Chinese seaports, there exist five seaport clusters from the north to the south, namely the Bohai Rim, Yangtze River Delta, Southeast Coast, Pearl River Delta, and Southwest Coast seaport clusters. These clusters jointly constitute eight transportation systems (i.e., coal, crude oil, iron ore, containerized cargo, grain, commercial vehicle, land-island roll-on/roll-off [RORO], and passenger transportation), which are classified according to the specific cargo category split (MOT, 2006). Table 8.1 lists the main cargo categories of the traffic handled in Chinese ports. Over the past two decades, Chinese ports have maintained a relatively stable pattern of cargo category split that is dominated by bulk cargo. Notably, containerized cargo has grown fast to become the second-largest category exceeding liquid and general cargo.

Continual heavy investment (Fig. 8.1) has been a crucial driving force behind the development of China's ports. Due to this investment, new terminals have been built and old ones have been upgraded. In 2000, there existed 784 berths at the level of 10,000 tons and above (MOT, 2001). Comparatively, in 2017, there existed 2366 berths at the same level, among which 1948 berths were located along the coastline (MOT, 2018). Regarding the main bodies of port investment, the biggest investor has changed from the central government to local port enterprises. In the 1980s, the central government dominated port investment. Today, the financial input of the central government accounts for less than 1% of the total port investment, whereas investment from local port enterprises accounts for more than 50% (Wang, 2011). Other important sources of funding for port construction include the special fund for ports from the MOT, loans from domestic banks, foreign investment from overseas companies, and funds from local governments.

Shaped by national port reforms at the end of the 1980s and early 2000s, the current port governance structure is mainly characterized by decentralization from the central government and the separation of governmental functions from port enterprise management. More specifically, all ports directly controlled by the MOT and jointly managed by the MOT and local governments are devolved to the local governments where the ports are located. The local port authority, which begins to act as a pure port regulator, is responsible for port administrative management, whereas the local port corporation is responsible for the commercial functions and is a pure business entity operating the port. Furthermore, this basic port governance structure was reinforced by the *Port Law of 2004*. In recent years, under the umbrella of port integration

**Table 8.1** Cargo category split of the traffic handled in Chinese ports

| Cargo category | 2000 | | 2005 | | 2010 | | 2015 | |
|---|---|---|---|---|---|---|---|---|
| | Througput (Million tons) | Proportion (%) | Througput (Million tons) | Proportion (%) | Througput (Million tons) | Proportion (%) | Througput (Million tons) | Proportion (%) |
| Bulk cargo | 1163 | 52.7 | 2756 | 56.8 | 5153 | 57.7 | 7361 | 57.7 |
| Liquid cargo | 347 | 15.7 | 584 | 12.0 | 854 | 9.6 | 1081 | 8.5 |
| General cargo | 417 | 18.9 | 614 | 12.7 | 954 | 10.7 | 1242 | 9.7 |
| Containerized cargo | 211 | 9.6 | 694 | 14.3 | 1532 | 17.2 | 2455 | 19.3 |
| RORO cargo | 67 | 3.0 | 205 | 4.2 | 439 | 4.9 | 611 | 4.8 |
| Total | 2205 | 100 | 4853 | 100 | 8932 | 100 | 12,750 | 100 |

*Source* Compiled by authors based on Statistical Bulletins of Chinese Transport Industry Development

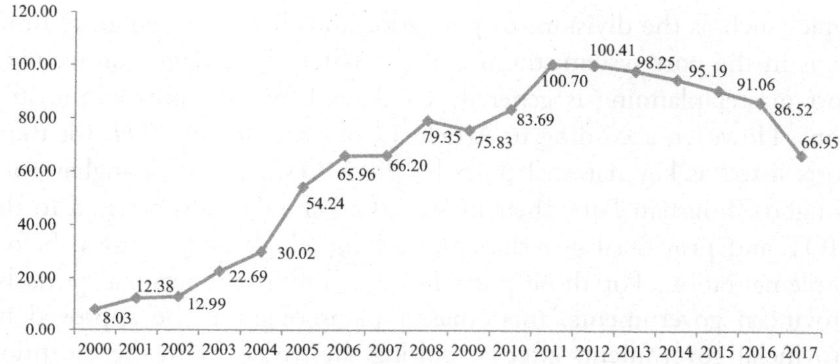


**Fig. 8.1** Annual investment in China's seaport construction (billions of RMB) (*Source* Created by authors based on Statistical Bulletins of Chinese Transport Industry Development)

(Wang et al., 2015), this port governance structure has followed a more incremental evolution path, in which new rules, procedures or functions are gradually added to existing institutions (Notteboom & Yang, 2017). For example, provincial port groups and port administrations are newly established in some provinces (Huo et al., 2018).

## Local Port Development: Planning and Financial Tools

### Planning Tools Used by Local Ports

According to the *Port Law of 2004* and *Port Planning Regulation of 2008*, port planning consists of two basic sub-types, namely port layout planning and port master planning. Port layout planning generally adopts a holistic review and allocates the roles and main functions of several ports in a certain geographical scope. The MOT plays a dual role on account of being responsible for national port layout planning and providing suggestions for regional port layout plans submitted by port administrations at the provincial level. Compared with port layout planning, port master planning is considerably more specific and covering topics such as the divisions of port areas and their corresponding functions in the port system, the use of shorelines, hinterland connectivity. Port master planning is generally conducted by local port administrations. However, according to Article 11 of *Port Law of 2004*, for those ports listed as key national ports by the MOT, such as Shanghai port, Ningbo-Zhoushan Port, their master plans should be submitted to the MOT and provincial governments seeking advice and approval before implementation. For those ports listed as important regional ports by provincial governments, their master plans ought to be approved by provincial governments after consulting the MOT. With the exception of key national ports and important regional ports, master plans of ports of less importance only need to be approved by local governments and put on record by provincial governments. Therefore, it is fair to claim that the involvement of the MOT and upper governments in the master planning of different ports vary according to their different degree of importance.

In summary, port planning in China is characterized by layering and decentralization. The MOT, local governments, and local port administrations play different roles in the planning of different ports at different scales. Decentralization is closely related to the center-stage positions enjoyed by local governments and local port administrations in terms of port governance. With the exception of national port layout planning, local port administrations generally have a substantial role in all other port planning, especially port master planning for individual ports.

In China, planned port construction projects, particularly projects with specialized berths for coal, ore, oil, and gas, and specialized container terminals, require approval from Development and Reform Commission (DRC) before implementation. Due to the reforms aimed at administrative decentralization, in December 2016, the right of approval for port projects was devolved from the national DRC to provincial level DRCs, which enhanced local autonomy in port planning.

Legislatively, local port enterprises are not involved in port planning. However, they still can affect port planning processes to a certain extent by lobbying local port administrations, which is especially true for large operators.

## Financial Tools Used by Local Ports

Today, there exist six main investment bodies in the Chinese port domain, among which internal funds from local port enterprises, loans from domestic banks and funds from local governments are in predominant positions (Wang, 2011). In recent years, the financial tools used by local ports have become increasingly diversified. An increased number of financial tools are discussed and applied, such as public–private partnership (PPP) models, issuance of stocks, and asset-backed security models. Among them, PPP models are the most advocated. According to *Opinions on Deepening the Reform of the Transportation Infrastructure Sector's Investment and Financing System* promulgated by the MOT in 2015, private enterprises are encouraged to invest in transportation infrastructure through PPP models. Specifically, built-operate-transfer (BOT), built-transfer, and transfer-operate-transfer models are encouraged under different circumstances. For example, construction of the No. 9 and No. 10 berths in the comprehensive port zone of the Port of Huanghua was conducted using BOT model. In this case, a special purpose vehicle (SPV) was jointly established by the state-owned Cangzhou Port Corporation and private investors, and 72% of the SPV's registered capital is owned by private parties.[1]

With the increasing number of local port enterprises being listed on the market, stock issuance has become a potential option for local ports to raise capital for promoting port construction projects. For example, in June 2015, Beibu Gulf Port Co., Ltd. issued 120 million shares to certain investors, through which it raised 2.7 billion RMB. These funds were mainly used to acquire berth assets and undertake further construction.[2]

In general, the development of the Chinese capital market and enhancement of the financial capacity of China's local port enterprises have made local ports more accessible for financing and also have made it easier to raise money for port upgrades and expansions.

---

[1] *Note*: Detailed information about this case can be retrieved at http://www.hebcz.gov.cn/ppp/pppxmk/2016rzlt/2016sh_jtys/201609/t20160921_262287.html (In Chinese).

[2] *Note*: Detailed information about this case can be retrieved at http://m.sohu.com/a/74651164_233920 (In Chinese).

## Impact of Recent Regional Port Integration Reforms

The global and domestic economic slowdown and industrial structural changes significantly influenced the demand for transportation over Chinese waterways. Consequently, the problem faced by China has switched from port capacity shortage to over-capacity (Notteboom & Yang, 2017). To mitigate the fierce inter-port competition caused by over-capacity and to efficiently utilize regional port resources, in 2015, the MOT initiated a pilot reform in the Guangxi Beibu Gulf, which aimed at substantially improving regional cross-city port integration through the establishment of a provincial port administration. Inspired by this pilot reform, other provinces began to explore the possibility of synergizing local port enterprises within their jurisdictions. Zhejiang Province is a representative example, with its regional port integration reform acknowledged and selected as a national demonstration case by the MOT. The uniqueness of the Zhejiang case is this is the first in China to have concurrently established a Provincial Port Corporation as the unified port operator and a special provincial port administrative agency as the unified port regulator. Consequently, the provincial level has begun to have increased power in regional port development. The system in Zhejiang has been studied and repeated by many other coastal provinces, such as Hainan, Jiangsu, and Liaoning. Outside of China, increasing involvement by upper levels of government in port governance matters has also been observed in countries such as the United States, Italy, and Brazil (Zhang et al., 2018).

The following three aspects regarding the effects of Chinese regional port integration reform are noteworthy. First, port planning, particularly port master planning, is no longer solely focused on individual ports. Provincial port administrations provide complete consideration to all ports in their jurisdictions and conduct overall planning to ensure rational functional division and reasonable port resource allocation among ports. Second, the newly established Provincial Port Corporation has merged port enterprises at the municipal level through equity transfer agreements, which indicates that this new entity has a sizeable asset scale and strong financial capacity. Thus, the Provincial Port Corporation likely has a large number of financial tools available. Third, the best practices in port operations can be easily shared by different port enterprises in the region because of the information sharing brought by integration. Port efficiency can probably be further improved by following such practices.

## International Collaborations: The "Bring in" and "Going Global" Strategies

The "bring in" and "going global" strategies have been effective approaches for enhancing international collaborations in China since the 1980s. A review of international collaborations in the Chinese port domain in the past 40 years indicates that "bring in" strategy predominated in the early 30 years, whereas the past 10 years have seen the prevalence of the "going global" strategy.

More specifically, in the 1980s–2000s, the public sector lacked sufficient funds to finance capital-intensive port projects at a pace that could meet the requirements of Chinese manufacturing output (Wang et al., 2004). Furthermore, Chinese ports were eager to introduce the best practices from foreign port enterprises to improve domestic port efficiency. These facts meant that attracting foreign investment in Chinese ports was considerably encouraged. In 1985, the State Council officially promulgated the *Interim Regulation on Preferential Treatment to Sino-Foreign Joint Ventures on Harbour and Wharf Construction* to grant tax incentives to Sino foreign port joint ventures. The first foreign participation occurred in 1987 when a container terminal joint venture was established by the US-funded Encinal Terminals Company and the Nanjing Port Authority (MOT, 2009). By 2001, 25 container terminals were jointly owned, managed, or operated by foreign companies (Wang et al., 2004). Among the foreign port enterprises entering the Chinese market, Hutchison Port Holdings and the Port of Singapore Authority outperformed their rivals and became the main sources of foreign investment (MOT, 2009). Their success can be partially attributed to their ethnic Chinese backgrounds (Wang et al., 2004). In 2002, the year after China's accession into the

World Trade Organization, China repealed the regulation on the proportion limits of foreign investment in port joint ventures, which allowed the establishment of exclusively foreign-owned port enterprises.

With the significant development of China's port enterprises, some have gradually realized the importance of "going global" strategy and have begun to ambitiously expand their global business networks to further enhance their competitive advantages. COSCO SHIPPING Ports Limited (CSP) and China Merchants Port Holdings (CMPort) are two pioneers in overseas port investment among Chinese port enterprises. By the end of 2017, CSP had invested in 12 foreign terminal companies,[3] such as Piraeus Container Terminal S.A. in Greece, and Euromax Terminal Rotterdam B.V. in the Netherlands. Comparatively, CMPort has created a port network portfolio spanning 36 ports in 18 countries and regions, including Colombo International Container Terminal Limited in Sri Lanka, and Lomé Container Terminal S.A. in Togo.[4] In addition to these global port operators, large local port enterprises, such as Shanghai International Port Group (SIPG), have actively explored the overseas port market. For instance, SIPG acquired a 25% stake in Belgium's multi-user Zeebrugge Container Terminal from APM Terminals (APMT) in 2010.[5] Moreover, in May 2015, SIPG obtained the right to run the new Port of Haifa in northern Israel for 25 years beginning in 2021. From the perspective of geographical scope, ports that have received investment from China are mainly located in Asia, Africa, and Europe. China's current Belt and Road Initiative (BRI), as a geo-economic policy, has driven Chinese port enterprises in "going global."

The switch from "bring in" to "going global" reflects the evolution in the role of Chinese port enterprises within the global maritime transportation network. Under-invested foreign ports have benefited from the sufficient funds and advanced port management practices of the

---

[3] *Source*: CSP's official website https://ports.coscoshipping.com/en/Businesses/Portfolio/#OverseasTerminals (accessed 20.12.2018).

[4] *Source*: CMPort's official website http://www.cmport.com.hk/EN/about/Profile.aspx?from=2 (accessed 20.12.2018).

[5] *Note*: CSP acquired SIPG's 25% stake in 2017 via a deal with APMT and finally took over APMT Zeebrugge.

Chinese port industry. For example, since the operations commenced at the Piraeus Container Terminal (PCT) which is a CSP subsidiary, the Piraeus port has experienced a major increase in throughput and become one of the largest container ports in Europe. The influence of CSP's involvements has been catalytic (Pallisand & Vaggelas, 2017). In the future, on one side, many provincial port enterprises established under the regional port integration reforms are expected to participate in international collaborations with foreign ports as they seek to improve their global port service network and increase their financial capacities. On the other side, China's port market is becoming increasingly open, and an increased number of foreign port enterprises and shipping companies are projected to become involved in port projects in China to secure their market shares. For example, APMT made a deal with Ningbo-Zhoushan Port Corporation in 2015 to jointly invest and operate the No. 3 to No. 5 berths of the Meishan Phase I Container Terminal Project for establishing a transfer and distribution center for the Maersk Line in northeast Asia.

## Conclusions

Chinese ports have attained notable achievements over the past 40 years. The four decades have also witnessed the evolution of the Chinese port governance structure and investment solutions. China's *Port Law of 2004* established a fundamentally institutional framework that set basic principles such as decentralization and the separation of governmental functions from port enterprise management. Port planning in China is characterized by layering and localization. Local port enterprises can partly affect port planning by lobbying local port administrations. The financial tools used by local ports have become increasingly diversified. The central government no longer dominates port investment, whereas investment from local port enterprises accounts for more than 50% of the total port investment. With the development of China's capital market and the enhancement of the financial capacity of China's local port enterprises, local ports have become more accessible to the capital market, which has made it easier to raise money for port construction.

Regional port integration reforms have been carried out by a number of provinces aiming at mitigating the fierce inter-port competition caused by over-capacity and improving the utilization efficiency of regional port resources. International collaborations promoted by the "bring in" and "going global" strategies have constantly facilitated the development of Chinese ports. In the early stages, foreign participation provided funds and advanced management knowledge to Chinese ports. Subsequently, Chinese port enterprises have invested in overseas ports and shared best practices in port operations. International collaborations in the port domain are expected to continue under the umbrella of China's BRI.

## References

China Daily. (2019). China's foreign trade up 9.7% in 2018. https://www.chinadaily.com.cn/a/201901/14/WS5c3bee95a3106c65c34e43a1_1.html. Accessed 15 January 2019.

Huo, W., Zhang, W., & Chen, S. L. (2018). Recent development of Chinese port cooperation strategies. *Research in Transportation Business & Management, 26*, 67–75.

Ministry of Transport. (2001). Bulletins of statistics on the development of Chinese transportation industry in 2000 (Its Chinese edition can be retrieved at: http://www.docin.com/p-28291588.html). Accessed 16 December 2018.

Ministry of Transport. (2004). The public announcement of the list of Chinese main ports (Its Chinese edition can be retrieved at: http://www.110.com/fagui/law_115044.html). Accessed 16 December 2018.

Ministry of Transport. (2006). National layout plan of seaports (Its Chinese edition can be retrieved at: http://www.gov.cn/gzdt/2007-07/20/content_691642.htm). Accessed 16 December 2018.

Ministry of Transport. (2009). 30 years of reform and opening in Chinese transportation industry: The volume of waterway transportation. China Communications Press (In Chinese).

Ministry of Transport. (2018). Bulletins of statistics on the development of Chinese transportation industry in 2017 (Its Chinese edition can be retrieved at: http://zizhan.mot.gov.cn/zfxxgk/bnssj/zhghs/201803/t20180329_3005087.html). Accessed 16 December 2018.

Notteboom, T. E., & Yang, Z. (2017). Port governance in China since 2004: Institutional layering and the growing impact of broader policies. *Research in Transportation Business & Management, 22,* 184–200.

Pallis, A. A., & Vaggelas, G. K. (2017). A Greek prototype of port governance. *Research in Transportation Business & Management, 22,* 49–57.

United Nations Conference on Trade and Development. (2018). Review of Maritime Transport. https://unctad.org/en/pages/PublicationWebflyer.aspx?publicationid=2245. Accessed 15 January 2019.

Wang, C., Ducruet, C., & Wang, W. (2015). Port integration in China: Temporal pathways, spatial patterns and dynamics. *Chinese Geographical Science, 25*(5), 612.

Wang, J. J., Ng, K. Y., & Olivier, D. (2004). Port governance in china: A review of policies in an era of internationalizing port management practices. *Transport Policy, 11*(3), 237–250.

Wang, W. (2011). The analysis of the investment and financial models of port constructions. *Chinese Waterway Transportation, 2,* 40–41 (In Chinese).

Zhang, Q., Geerlings, H., Makhloufi, A. E., & Chen, S. (2018). Who governs and what is governed in port governance: A review study. *Transport Policy, 64,* 51–60.

# 9

# Development of Japan's Port System

Hidekazu Itoh

## Introduction to Japan's Port System

### The Maritime Transport Market

Japan is an island country with a long coastline (35,275 km). Urban areas such as Tokyo and Yokohama on the Tokyo Bay, Nagoya on the Ise Bay, and Osaka and Kobe on the Osaka Bay, are located on the Pacific coast (Fig. 9.1). Most port activities are also concentrated on the Pacific coast side (Table 9.1). Japan's international trade depends on maritime transportation. Over 99% (99.1% in exports and 99.8% in imports) of cargo was freighted by maritime transport (ton base) in 2014 (Policy Bureau, MLIT). In value base, about 24% (26.6% in exports and 22.4% in imports) of high-value goods such as semiconductors and electronic

H. Itoh (✉)
Kwansei Gakuin University, Nishinomiya, Japan
e-mail: hito@kwansei.ac.jp



© The Author(s), under exclusive license to Springer Nature Switzerland AG 2022
C. Ferrari et al. (eds.), *Regulation and Finance in the Port Industry*, Palgrave Studies in Maritime Economics,
https://doi.org/10.1007/978-3-030-83985-7_9

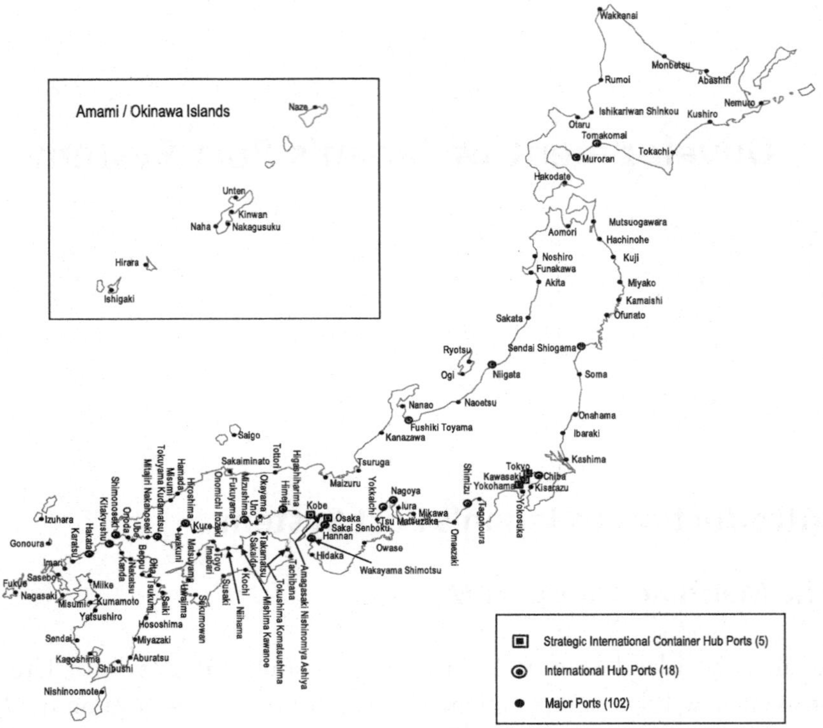


**Fig. 9.1** The location of Japanese ports (*Source* Ports and Harbours Bureau, MLIT [2018])

products were freighted by air transport in 2014. With the overseas transfer of manufacturing capabilities and globalization of supply chains, the relative volume (ton base) of imports has been declining (Fig. 9.2).

However, Japan's domestic freight traffic is different from international freight traffic. The amount of domestic cargo (ton base) freighted by truck in 2014 was 91.3% (59.2% in 1950). The related share of maritime transport was 7.8% in 2014 (9.4% in 1950). Domestic freight traffic (ton base) is dominated by road transportation; however, the related share of maritime transport is significant in freight turnover (i.e., ton-kilometer). Maritime transport accounted for 44.1% of domestic freight turnover in 2014, which implies that the average transportation

**Table 9.1** Cargo handling ranking at Japanese ports (in 2016)

(a) Total cargo volume (unit: 10 thousand tons)

| Ranking | Name of Port | Total | Export | Import | Domestic | Ferry |
|---|---|---|---|---|---|---|
| 1 | Nagoya | 19,326 | 5271 | 7576 | 6066 | 412 |
| 2 | Chiba | 15,433 | 953 | 8281 | 6200 | |
| 3 | Yokohama | 10,912 | 3062 | 3831 | 4019 | |
| 4 | Tomakomai | 10,560 | 107 | 1597 | 3170 | 5687 |
| 5 | Kitakyushu | 9853 | 722 | 2514 | 2321 | 4297 |
| 6 | Kobe | 9831 | 2331 | 2842 | 1881 | 2778 |
| 7 | Mizushima | 8675 | 949 | 4563 | 3163 | |
| 8 | Tokyo | 8595 | 1337 | 3473 | 2873 | 913 |
| 9 | Osaka | 8203 | 936 | 2475 | 1663 | 3129 |
| 10 | Kawasaki | 8197 | 901 | 4404 | 2892 | |

(b1) International container volume

| Ranking | Name of Port | Thousand TEUs |
|---|---|---|
| 1 | Tokyo | 4251 |
| 2 | Yokohama | 2521 |
| 3 | Nagoya | 2491 |
| 4 | Kobe | 2141 |
| 5 | Osaka | 1952 |
| 6 | Hakata | 844 |
| 7 | Kitakyushu | 449 |
| 8 | Shimizu | 445 |
| 9 | Tomakomai | 201 |
| 10 | Yokkaichi | 179 |

(b2) Domestic container volume

| Ranking | Name of Port | Thousand TEUs |
|---|---|---|
| 1 | Kobe | 661 |
| 2 | Tokyo | 484 |
| 3 | Naha | 464 |
| 4 | Osaka | 264 |
| 5 | Yokohama | 260 |
| 6 | Nagoya | 167 |
| 7 | Kagoshima | 125 |
| 8 | Hakata | 122 |
| 9 | Tomakomai | 116 |
| 10 | Hiroshima | 104 |

*Note* Domestic container handling does include the feeder handlings inside Japan
*Source* Japanese Ports Statistics

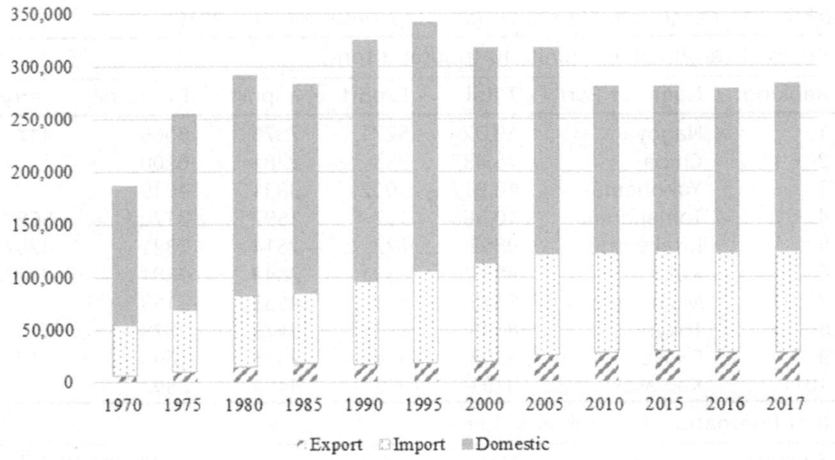


**Fig. 9.2** The changes of port handling volume at Japanese ports (*Source* Japanese Ports Statistics) (unit: 10 thousand tons)

distance of maritime transport is much longer (496 km) than road transport. In addition, the share of maritime transport has not changed in the last 70 years after World War 2 (WW2) (41.0% in 1950). On the other hand, the share of railway transport has been decreasing drastically (ton-kilometer 50.3% in 1950 and only 5.0% in 2014) following changes (heavy industry to light industry) in Japan's industrial structure and shifting of location from the mountainside to the Pacific coast side.

Maritime transport remains the dominant mode for handling international cargo as a quarter of export goods are carried by liner service (mostly containerized, others are tramper services). However, for imports, transporting cargo by liner service is less than 5% because imported goods are mostly oil and coal. Most cargo handled by domestic maritime transport is for industrial use (Table 9.2).

**Table 9.2** The share of goods at Japanese ports (in 2016)

| Category of products (unit: 10 thousand tons) | Export | | Import | | Domestic | |
|---|---|---|---|---|---|---|
| | Volume | % | Volume | % | Volume | % |
| **Total** | **28,645** | **100.00** | **95,133** | **100.00** | **98,557** | **100.00** |
| Agriculture, Fishery | 139 | 0.49 | 4485 | 4.71 | 1495 | 1.52 |
| Forestry | 73 | 0.25 | 3324 | 3.49 | 650 | 0.66 |
| Mining | 1564 | 5.46 | 51,228 | 53.85 | 28,356 | 28.77 |
| Metal and Machinery | 16,156 | 56.40 | 5142 | 5.41 | 24,319 | 24.68 |
| Chemical industry | 6707 | 23.42 | 22,931 | 24.10 | 34,224 | 34.72 |
| Light industry | 667 | 2.33 | 2023 | 2.13 | 2568 | 2.61 |
| Miscellaneous manufactures | 1054 | 3.68 | 4230 | 4.45 | 559 | 0.57 |
| Special goods | 2274 | 7.94 | 1707 | 1.79 | 6317 | 6.41 |
| Unclassified | 11 | 0.04 | 62 | 0.06 | 69 | 0.07 |

*Note* The cargo carried by railway and car ferries is not included
*Source* Japanese Port Statistics

## Classification of Japanese Ports

After the "Port and Harbor Act (PHA)" was amended in 2011 (see next section for details), Japan's ports were classified as follows (Table 9.3) based on the role and position (see below) in the PHA and the form on management and construction. (1) Strategic international ports include the ports of Tokyo, Yokohama, Kawasaki, Osaka, and Kobe, which serve as hubs for long-distance international container transport in international maritime transport networks. They often link the international maritime cargo transport networks directly with the domestic maritime cargo transport networks and require high-priority actions for boosting their international competitiveness. (2) Central international ports include the ports of Chiba, Nagoya, Kitakyushu, and Hakata that serve as hubs for international maritime cargo transport or ocean freight transportation networks. The main difference between strategic international ports and central international ports is the ability to handle/collect cargo, and transship container cargo to/from the other domestic ports acting as hubs for domestic feeder networks. (3) Major ports are significant as they are associated with the interests of the nation excluding (1) and (2). (4) Regional ports are ports other than (1), (2), and (3). Until

**Table 9.3** The classification at Japanese ports (in 2018)

| Category | Total Number | Port Management Body (PMB) | | | |
|---|---|---|---|---|---|
| | | Prefectures | Municipalities | Port Authority | Others [a] |
| (1) Strategic International port | 5 | 1 | 4 | 0 | 0 |
| (2) Central International port | 18 | 11 | 4 | 0 | 3 |
| (3) Major port | 102 | 82 | 16 | 1 | 3 |
| (4) Regional port | 808 | 504 | 304 | 0 | 0 |

*Note1* [a]Smaller internal organization
*Note2* The table does not include 61 ports by a prefectural governor on the basis of PHA Article 56
*Source* Second clause of Article 2, Port and Harbor Act, as of April 1, 2018

2011, strategic international ports (five ports) and central international ports (18 ports) were categorized as "specific major ports" with "major ports" in the PHA. The historical change in the classification is discussed in the next section.

## The Japanese System of Port Management

### Port and Harbor Act (PHA)

Until WW2 and after the Meiji period (1868), Japan's national government was responsible for developing and operating ports. Although major transport acts (railways, roads, and aviation) were enacted before WW2, Japan's laws for ports were enacted only in 1950 (after WW2) following strong negotiations between bodies concerned (Kawasaki et al., 2015). Japan's PHA was first enacted in 1950 to transfer the responsibility of port administration from the national government to a port management body (PMB) established by a local government. In the act, PMB means a port authority or local public entity. After WW2, major Japanese ports such as Yokohama and Kobe were taken over by the General Headquarters (GHQ) of the allied forces.

The purpose of the PHA was to manage and operate ports for developing transport infrastructure and contribute to the growth of both national and local economies. In addition, the PHA supported strong export-oriented economic growth after WW2 (Doi, 2003). In the Act, the "Port Authority" established by the local government(s) or local public bodies is defined as the port administrator, requested by the GHQ to prevent transferring ports for military purpose (Kuroda, 2014), and is similar to the port authority system in the United States (US). However, after WW2, due to financial constraints, the local governments and prefectures managed most of the ports. Moreover, except the port of Niihama in Ehime Prefecture, which has a historical background and is managed by a port authority organized by the city of Niihama and Sumitomo group, all other ports are managed by the local governments because of Japan's unique style of infrastructure management (Kawasaki et al., 2015; see next section also).

## Port Management and Classification of Operations

The management and operation of ports are classified into four types based on construction, ownership, and operation of infra-and-superstructure between the PMB and port (terminal) operator (Table 9.4). In leased home (tool port), PMB constructs and owns the infrastructure (berthing facilities). In addition, a leased home is divided into two categories for the superstructure (gantry and yard cranes, container yard, sheds, and warehouses). In term-leased land (landlord port), the port operator constructs the superstructure and the infrastructure. For a detailed discussion, see Ducruet and Itoh (2020), which discusses the classification and characteristics of major ports in the world. Most Japanese ports are classified as "leased home with equipment" in terms of publicness as social capital. In general, *public money* is used for developing ports as public projects for infra-and-super-structures. Therefore, since the use of public berth was on the "first come, first served" basis,

**Table 9.4** The classification of port management organization and operational form

| | | | 1. Government | 2. Leased home | | 3. Term-leased land | | 4. Ownership |
|---|---|---|---|---|---|---|---|---|
| | | | | With equipment | Without equipment | | | |
| Development plan and permission | | | PMB | PMB | PMB | PMB | PMB | Operator |
| Construction | Infra- | Non-profit | PMB | PMB | PMB | PMB | PMB | Operator |
| | | Profit | | | | Operator | Operator | |
| | Super- | | | | Operator | | | |
| Ownership | Infra-non-profit | | PMB | PMB | PMB | PMB | PMB | Operator |
| | Infra-profit | | | | | | Operator | |
| | Super- | | | | Operator | Operator | Operator | |
| Operating | | | PMB | Operator | Operator | Operator | Operator | Operator |
| Example | | | Tanjung Priok (Indonesia), Laem Chabang (Thailand), Durban (South Africa), Haifa (Israel) | Kaohsiung, (Taiwan) Busan (Korea), ***Japanese ports***, Seattle (USA), Chinese ports, Dubai (UAE) | European major ports (Rotterdam, Humbug), Los Angeles, Long Beach, NY/NJ (USA), ***Japanese international ports*** * | Hong Kong | Kaohsiung (Taiwan), Busan (Korea), Leam Chabang (Thailand), Jawaharlal Nehru Port (India) | Singapore (after privatization), UK, New Zealand |

*Note* [a]Japanese international ports (Hanshin, Yokohama and Kawasaki) by (specified) Port Operating Companies
*Source* Kurihara (2014)

Table 9.5 The reform of Japan's port system

| Year | Key word | Purpose |
|---|---|---|
| 1950 | Port and Harbor Act | Transfer of port management from national government to port management body (port authority or local public entity) |
| 1967 | Port Terminal Corporation (*Kohdan*) | Investing "private money" for container terminal development due to international trade promotion, and exclusive terminal use |
| 1982 | Port Terminal Corporation (*Kohsha*) | Increasing the share of "public money" for container terminal developments, and applying "public privatization" |
| 1995 | Central and Core ports | Constructing the Japan's port network by 10 central ports at 4 bay areas and 8 core ports |
| 2005 | Super Central ports | Enhancing international competitiveness with Asian ports by high standard terminals' developments and integrated terminal operations |

the system was far from user needs in terms of efficiency. Under the situation, specifically, systems such as dedicated berths for specific goods (after 1959) and prioritized usage on the main routes (after 1963) were applied to port users until the development of containerization because of the huge expansion in port handling generated by economic growth. Some reforms on the PHA, and the related laws and regulations were carried out after containerization (Table 9.5). The following sub-sections discuss the evolution of Japan's port management system and port policy.

## The Evolution of Port Management System by Containerization

However, the progress made by ports in handling volumes by *containerization* needs specific container berths for major shippers and more efficient handling and development of bigger berths and terminals. As the PMB (i.e., the local government) could not develop container terminals with only *public money*, the national government established the system of public corporation (*Kohdan* in Japanese) or Port Terminal Corporation (PTC) (Table 9.6) for developing container terminals using *private money*, which is from fiscal investment and loan program by the national government, and private placement bond. Moreover, the public corporation leases terminals to operators, that is, the related departments of shipping lines, for their exclusive use. The Keihin International Trade Public Corporation at Tokyo Bay and Hanshin International Trade Public Corporation at Osaka Bay were established in 1967, and these two port corporations constructed 33 container berths by 1982. Investment in the terminals was as follows: 10% from the national government, 10%

**Table 9.6** The port development system

| | | National Government | Port Management Body (PMB) | Port Terminal Corporations (PTC) etc. | Shipping Lines or Terminal Operators |
|---|---|---|---|---|---|
| Long-term National Port and Harbour policy | | ● | | | |
| Basic Policies on Port and Harbour Development and Use | | ● | | | |
| Port Planning | | Screening | ● | | |
| Construction of Port facilities | Public | ● | ● | | |
| | PTC | Interest-free loans | Interest-free loans | ● | Lease charges |
| | Private | | | | ● |
| Management | | | ● | ● | ● |
| Operations | | | | | ● |

*Note* PTCs were established to develop and manage container terminals. The term "Port Terminal Corporations etc." includes private container terminal companies
*Source* International Policy Planning Office, Ports and Harbours Bureau, MLIT (2013)

from PMB (the local government), 40% from subletting loans, and 40% was raised through borrowings.

In 1982, the public corporation was repealed following reforms in the Japan's administrative system. The two corporations were taken over by four new public corporations (*Kohsha* in Japanese; the ports of Tokyo, Yokohama, Osaka, and Kobe). The new public corporations implemented similar funding scheme for developing container berths at 12 m water depth. However, the funding scheme for developing them at 13–14 m water depth included 20% from the national government, 20% from PMB, 30% from subletting loans, and 30% raised from borrowings. Funding for developing berths over 15 m water depth was as follows: 30% from the national government, 30% from PMB, 20% through subletting loans, and 20% from borrowings. However, to meet the increasing costs for developing deeper water depths and higher berth standards, the share of *public money* increased.

## Framework for International Strategic Ports

Given the situation, container handling volumes at Japanese ports were under pressure as compared with leading Asian ports. Therefore, in 1995, Japan's Ministry of Land, Infrastructure, Transportation and Tourism (MLIT), Ministry of Transport until 2001, opened a new framework and enacted "Ports in the Age of Global Exchange," focusing on constructing a network of central ports and core ports for strengthening regional production and consumption activities associated with the neighboring Asian countries after globalization. The outline of the framework is as follows: (1) developing four bays or "central" port areas, (2) eight "core" ports, (3) designing nearly 20 regions as international distribution ports in remote areas, and (4) developing port services and information technologies (Table 9.7). However, in the 1990s, transshipment of cargo at the port of Busan in S. Korea to/from Japan's eastern and western regional ports, especially the Sea of Japan, was expanding with the development of container terminals and feeder services connecting Busan (Xu & Itoh, 2018).

**Table 9.7** Selection and concentration at Japanese ports

| Before 2005 (since 1995) | | After 2005 |
|---|---|---|
| Central port areas (4 bays) | Core 8 ports | Super Central ports |
| **Tokyo Bay** (Tokyo, Yokohama, Kawasaki) | Tomakomai<br>Niigata | **Keihin port** (Tokyo Bay) |
| **Ise Bay** (Nagoya, Yokkaichi) | Sendai-Shiogama<br>Hitachinaka | |
| **Osaka Bay** (Osaka, Kobe) | Shimizu<br>Hiroshima | **Hanshin port** (Osaka Bay) |
| **North Kyushu** (Shimonoseki, Kitakyushu, Hakata) | Shibushi<br>Naha | |

As discussed above, public corporations (*Kohdan* and *Kohsha* in Japanese) used borrowing to develop container terminals. However, the lease charge for terminal operators kept increasing with the rising costs of construction, and higher lease charge affected overall competitiveness between Asian ports. Therefore, following the reconstruction plan for rehabilitation and recovery after the Great Hanshin earthquake in 1995, container berths were developed as public projects (i.e., *public money*) from 1998 onward. However, terminal operators always used exclusively the berths developed by the PMB. The *new* system changed the concept of pubic nature and started steering toward "public privatization."

Moreover, the MLIT designated five major ports as "super central ports" for enhancing international competitiveness with Asian ports and revised the PHA in 2005 (Table 9.7). The framework is as follows: (1) developing next-generation high standard container terminals, (2) integrated operations by large-scale terminal operators, and (3) national government supports for targeting 30% reduction in port handling costs, and one-day lead-time reduction for global competition. As dedicated operators manage container terminal(s) for shipping lines, or "cost centers" in Japan, the MLIT enacted the port policy for fostering terminal operators who run integrated terminals (berths more than 1000 m long in total) as "profit sectors" for competing with Asian ports. The national government provided financial support for a lending system for container berths, handling machinery, and a fixed assets tax. As a result, by 2005, large-scale container terminal operators (i.e., mega terminal operators) were established at four major ports, except Tokyo port. In addition to container ports, the MLIT also designated international bulk ports for commodities (cereals, ironstone, and coal) mainly at regional ports as import ports for supporting economic activities and livelihoods since 2009.

## Japanese Port Development and Operations

### Port Planning and Development

The port administrator (i.e., the local government) has to prepare "port plans" for handling port development, usage, maintenance at ports and neighboring areas, and consider the views of key people relevant to the plan at the local port council as it is a public service. Moreover, the port administrator must submit the plan to the MLIT. The national council of transport policy and the sub-groups for ports and harbors, established under the MLIT, assesses and deliberates the plans submitted by local governments based on the national port policies. The MLIT can request revisions in the plan based on the national port policy and ministerial ordinances.

Local public bodies manage and operate ports, but the plans need MLIT approval because port development requires advanced technologies and large budgets for constructing various port facilities including berths connecting to the land and sea systems. The national government is involved in planning and developing ports, as described in the national laws. In fact, based on the regulations, the national and local governments divide the construction costs for planning ports (Table 9.8).

### Port Operating Company System Since 2011

After Japan enacted the PHA in 1950, except dedicated container terminals, the local governments manage and operate public ports. However, a part of the PHA was amended to separate management and operations

**Table 9.8** Portion of port development costs borne by the central government (CG) and port management body (PMB)

| | Water area and outlying facilities | Berthing facilities | Port traffic facilities |
|---|---|---|---|
| **International Strategic ports and Major International ports** | | | |
| CG works project | CG 5.5/10; PMB 4.5/10<br>The CG, however, bears 2/3 for breakwaters and shipping channels | CG 5.5/10; PMB 4.5/10<br>The CG, however, bears 2/3 for retrofitting of gateway ports (resistant earthquake) | CG 2/3; PMB 1/3 |
| Subsidized projects | CG 5/10; PMB 5/10<br>The CG, however, bears 4/10 or less of the cost of the basin for small craft and other small facilities | | CG 5/10 |
| **Major ports** | | | |
| CG works project | CG 5.5/10; PMB 4.5/10 | | CG 5.5/10; PMB 4.5/10 |
| Subsidized projects | CG 5/10; PMB 5/10<br>The CG, however, bears 4/10 or less of the cost of the basin for small craft and other small facilities | | CG 5/10 or less |
| **Local ports** | | | |
| Subsidized projects | CG 4/10; PMB 6/10 | | |

*Note* CG: Central Government, PMB: Port Management Body
*Source* International Policy Planning Office, Ports and Harbours Bureau, MLIT (2013)

and to improve port management efficiency by incorporating the "private" sector's expertise or the Port Operating Company System in 2011 (Table 9.9). Based on the system, "strategic international ports" (five ports, or "super central ports" in 2005, Table 9.7) and "central international ports" (18 ports) can select a specifically designated port operating company per port. Until the amendment in 2011, strategic international ports and central international ports were classified into "specific major ports" in the PHA. However, in 2011, these 23 ports were promoted from specific major ports to "international ports" in the PHA (Table 9.3).

All the strategic international ports designated (especially) port operating companies until January 2014. In addition, in October 2014, the

Table 9.9 New port operational system (container terminal)

| | Public system | Terminal corporation system | New system (since 2011) |
|---|---|---|---|
| Type of use | Public use | Exclusive use | Common use, preferential use |
| User fees | Relatively inexpensive | Relatively expensive | Relatively inexpensive |
| Efficiency of use | Low | High | High |
| Improvement of quay walls | Public (national government, PMB) | Terminal corporation (leases by ship owners) | Public (national government, PMB) |
| Improvement of inland sites | PMB | Terminal corporation (leases by ship owners) | PMB |
| Onshore structure and facility development | PMB | Terminal corporation (leases by ship owners) | Terminal corporation (the national government and the PMB supply partial support through interests-free loans) |

(continued)

**Table 9.9** (continued)

| | Public system | Terminal corporation system | New system (since 2011) |
|---|---|---|---|
| Operation | Port operators (unspecified) | Port operators (connected with the ship owners) | Flexible, unified management by a terminal corporation, including the quay walls (Allows comprehensive use of the quay walls and other facilities.)<br>Unified management of common terminal operations, employing a high-intensity system and coordinated operation with the onshore yards; common use and high-intensity use by multiple maritime and harbor transport companies |

*Source* International Policy Planning Office, Ports and Harbours Bureau, MLIT (2013) two companies operating the ports of Kobe and Osaka (Hanshin port) established the Kobe-Osaka International Port Corporation, which was designated by the MLIT. The corporation operates container terminals at the Hanshin port in an integrated manner. In January 2016, the two companies operating the ports of Yokohama and Kawasaki also established the Yokohama-Kawasaki International Port Corporation, which was designated by the MLIT as (only) a port operating company for the Keihin port. However, the port of Tokyo, which is the largest port in Japan for imports, did not join the company because it wanted to work intensively on investments in port facilities and functional enhancement for the massive demand generated at the Tokyo metropolitan area, and the Tokyo Port Terminal Corporation (*Kohsha*) had already been privatized in 2009.

In addition, for corresponding national challenges with broad-based cargo handling by constructing the "privatization" system for operating ports by the national government, the PMB (local government), and a private company, the Japanese government proposed amendments for making it possible for the national government to invest directly in Port Operating Companies at (only) strategic international ports. In December 2014, the Japanese government invested in a (specified) port operating company at Hanshin port. After WW2, initially, Japan's national government was directly involved in operating ports.

## Public–Private Partnerships in Japan's Port Management

Since 1950, most PMBs in Japan are local governments (Table 9.3). In addition, the form of the organization and operations are basically the "leased home with equipment" type (Table 9.4). Alternatively, the operation of a port (container) terminal is handled by private companies (i.e., terminal operators of shipping lines) paying the lease charges to the PTC at major ports (Table 9.6). Private companies were not allowed to invest in any port infrastructure.

In 1999, after the Act on Promotion of Private Finance Initiative (PFI) was established, a private company could lease a berth at a port from the

PMB on a long-term basis, develop, and operate a superstructure (i.e., a gantry crane) at the terminal. In addition, the right to operate public facilities or the system of concession was established after the PFI Act was revised in 2011. Broadly, most of the services created by PFI operations are covered by public money (tax) and most of the operations are build-transfer-operate (BTO) type of agreements as they involve buildings and housing for the public sector (Kawasaki et al., 2015).

As of January 2018, 194 PFI operations were listed on the MLIT. Most of the operations are government buildings and public housing (BTO). Only three operations involved the development and operation of container terminals (Hitachinaka and Hibiki container ports) and the development of berthing facilities for pleasure boats at Hiroshima. The first two cases of container ports are build-operate-transfer (BOT) type. The contract terms are 20 years for Hitachinaka and 25 years for Hibiki, and their operation is based on a two-tier system with the pier land developed by public operations and others developed by a PFI operator, and self-support accounting. However, the case of Hitachinaka in Ibaraki Prefecture is still working. The private company (currently, Ibaraki Port Authority Corporation) was established in September 1997 based on the PFI Act at the international container terminal of Hitachinaka District (formerly, the port of Hitachinaka) of the port of Ibaraki in Ibaraki Prefecture, which is a major international port, and the company started operating and managing them in April 2000.

The case of Hibiki is the project at Hibiki District of the port of Kitakyushu in Fukuoka Prefecture (Kyushu Island). In 2000, the city of Kitakyushu decided to adopt PFI for the development of a container yard and gantry cranes at the Hibiki container terminal. A mega-operator, the PSA (Port of Singapore Authority) first held a stake in the project, and the Hibiki Container Terminal (HCT) Co. Ltd., a joint venture, was established as a PFI operator in April 2004, and the company started operating and managing them in April 2005. The handling volumes were targeted at 1.125 million TEUs (twenty-foot equivalent units) a year based on the advantage of establishing shipping networks with China and South Korea.

However, just two years later, HCT reported bankruptcy in 2007 due to less handling volumes expected before the operations started.

Watanabe (2015), a chapter in Kawasaki et al. (2015), noted the serious contractual problem associated with the project. Overall, although HCT had to take the downward risk of handling demand, the city of Kitakyushu showed interest in covering the risk before the agreement with HCT. As a result, the city of Kitakyushu entered into a contractual agreement with HCT for purchasing the company's assets in September 2007 due to insufficient estimation for handling demand.

In addition to the case of PSA at HCT, the ICTSI (International Container Terminal Services), which is a Manila-based global port management company, established Naha International Container Terminal, Inc., which had a 10 year-contract of terminal operation with Naha PTC at the port of Naha in Okinawa prefecture, with local port transport agents in 2005, and entered the operation at the container terminal. This was the second case on terminal operation by foreign capitalization. However, ICTSI withdrew from the operation completely in 2015 due to less handling volumes too.

As discussed above, including the port operating companies at Hanshin port and the ports of Yokohama and Kawasaki, the (container) ports by PFI are positioned as "leased home without equipment" (Table 9.4). However, the Japanese ports differ from European ports in that the Japanese national and regional governments share the ownership and responsibility of land and infrastructure.

Finally, although concession is one form of public–private partnership, it is not present in Japan's port sector. However, the Kansai Airport Group started operating the Kansai International Airport (KIX) and the Osaka International Airport (ITM) in April 2016, and affiliated the Kobe Airport (UKB) into the group in April 2018 using concession. In addition, private companies operate the airports of Sendai and Takamatsu through a concession contract. The framework of a concession is a common tool used for operating airports, and the Japanese government has started to invest directly (partially) in private companies handling seaport operations.

## Discussion

Since Japan's port development has a public service aspect, and most ports are managed by local governments, it is quite difficult to differentiate between them (or balancing the development of Japanese ports) for competing with Asian ports. For example, as a national policy, the Korean government has been investing in the port of Busan for collecting transshipped containers at the port and emerging as a "hub port" in Northeast Asia. Busan handled about 75% of Korean container throughputs in 2017. Japan's national government has been approving unbiased "port plans" proposed by the PMB (mainly, the local governments) and is extending financial support for their development. However, with the progress in global economic growth, containerization, and stagnation in Japan's maritime networks, the government is engaging in the management of ports. It is investing directly in privately operated companies at major ports, that is, at Hanshin port and the ports of Yokohama and Kawasaki (Keihin port, excluding the port of Tokyo) for securing trunk lines to North America and Europe versus major Asian ports, especially the port of Busan.

**Acknowledgements** This research has received financial support from Kwansei Gakuin University Special Research Fund in 2019.

## References

Doi, M. (ed.). (2003). *Economics of ports and regions*. Taga-Shuppan (in Japanese).

Ducruet, C., & Itoh, H. (2020). Introduction to global container shipping market. In R. Shibasaki, H. Kato & C. Ducruet (Eds.), *Global logistics network modelling and policy: Quantification and analysis for international freight* (pp. 3–30).

International Policy Planning Office, Ports and Harbours Bureau, Ministry of Land, Infrastructure, Transport and Tourism. (2013). *Ports and Harbours in Japan 2013*.

Kawasaki, Y., Terada, K., & Tezuka, K. (eds.). (2015). *Operation and competition of container ports*. Seizando-Shoten Publishing (in Japanese).
Kurihara, Y. (2014). *The global trend of port service industry*. Mitsui & Co. Global Strategic Studies Institute (in Japanese).
Kuroda, K. (ed.). (2014). *Port policy in Japan*. Seizando-Shoten Publishing (in Japanese).
Xu, H., & Itoh, H. (2018). Density economies and transport geography: Evidence from the container shipping industry. *Journal of Urban Economies, 105,* 121–132.

# 10

# The Taiwanese Port System: Current Organization and Investment Solutions

Shih-Liang Chao and Chih-Ching Chang

## Taiwan's Port Systems: An Overview

An island state at the west edge of the Pacific Ocean, Taiwan has seen its shipping industry play a pivotal role in its economic development. To facilitate transporting passengers and cargoes, Taiwan built several ports with different purposes, i.e., international commercial ports, domestic commercial ports, industrial ports, yacht ports, and other special facilities (Shyu et al., 2017). International commercial ports are critical interfaces linking Taiwan to other ports worldwide. According to the Ministry of Transportation and Communications (MOTC), Taiwan has seven international commercial ports (MOTC, 2018) (see Fig. 10.1), of which Kaohsiung Port was positioned as a hub port that services

S.-L. Chao (✉) · C.-C. Chang
Department of Shipping and Transportation Management, National Taiwan Ocean University, Keelung, Taiwan
e-mail: alexchao@email.ntou.edu.tw

© The Author(s), under exclusive license to Springer Nature Switzerland AG 2022
C. Ferrari et al. (eds.), *Regulation and Finance in the Port Industry*, Palgrave Studies in Maritime Economics,
https://doi.org/10.1007/978-3-030-83985-7_10

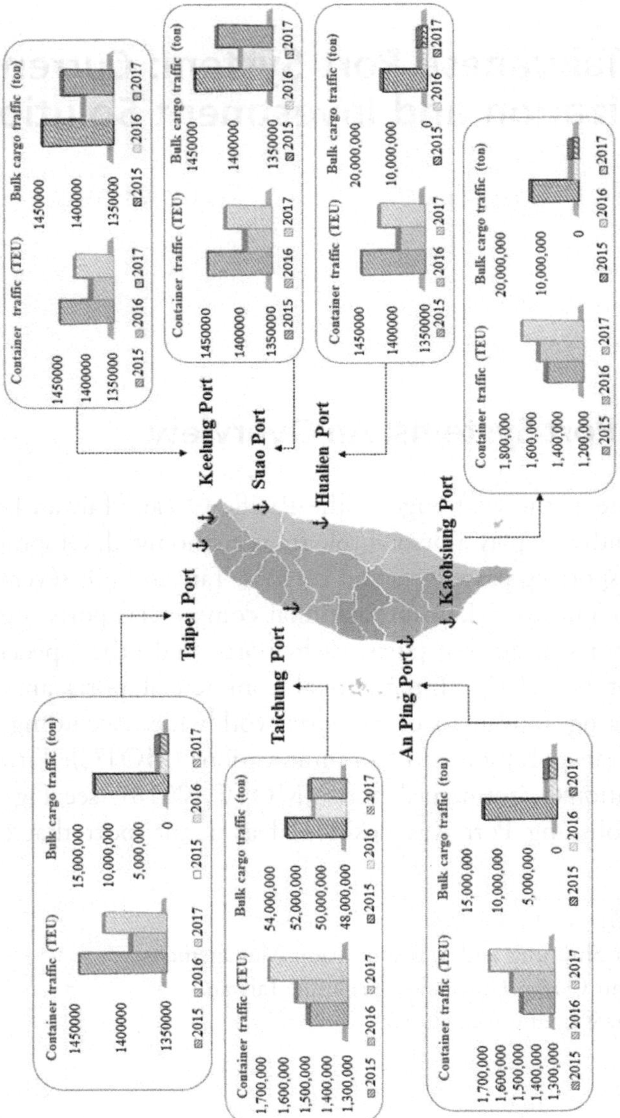


Fig. 10.1 Taiwan's international commercial ports (*Source* TIPC [2018])

large vessels sailing between continents. In addition, Kaohsiung Port also planned to conduct intelligent global logistics and accommodate cruise ship tours. Meanwhile, Keelung Port was set to cater to container vessels and luxury cruise ships sailing through Asian ports. Taipei Port, which was built to relieve the bulk cargo traffic at Keelung Port, aimed to cater to container vessels in the Asian regional market. As part of its future core business plans, Taipei Port also seeks to develop a diversified logistics operations business such as express delivery by sea, sea/air intermodal transport, and car logistics. Located in the middle of Taiwan's west coastline, Taichung Port focuses on facilitating the transport of passengers between Taiwan and China. It also aims to take advantage of the large hinterland to strengthen its ability to service dry bulk cargoes and energy-related transport as part of its main business. The other three international commercial ports are positioned to accommodate vessels carrying goods relating to the regional market and ferry passengers. Besides the aforementioned international commercial ports owned and operated by governmental port authorities, Taiwan has two privately owned industrial ports: Mai-Liao Port and Ho-Ping Port. These two ports were established for handling import and export cargoes of Mai-Liao and Ho-Ping industrials zones, respectively. The following are further details about Taiwan's international commercial ports:

(1) Keelung Port: Keelung was developed as a port in the seventeenth century when it was occupied by the Dutch. Since then, the port has seen a gradual increase in cargoes. Because of its wider role in servicing a large portion of northern Taiwan, it was built as a commercial port in 1886. While its advantageous geographical location improved its business in the nineteenth century, the insufficient draft and the lack of foreland for port operations have limited the port's ability to serve large cargo ships. As a result, in 1999, an auxiliary port—Taipei Port—was built to accommodate large container ships in the north Taiwan area. Currently, Keelung Port has 57 wharves that service cargo ships and large cruise ships. In 2017, the port's throughput was 17,464,002 tons. In terms of containers, 1,418,327.75 twenty-foot equivalent units (TEUs) were processed

in 2017, of which 753,072.75 TEUs were imported, and 640,551 TEUs were exported, showing a balanced trade situation.

(2) Taichung Port: Located in the middle of Taiwan's west coast, Taichung Port is a typical artificial port that was planned during the Japanese occupation. However, this project was not carried out until the 1970s because of World War II. As Taiwan's second-largest port with 50 wharves, Taichung Port currently caters to bulk cargoes including grain, coal, LNG, petroleum, and chemical goods, as its large port area can accommodate a large number of silos and warehouses. In terms of containers, it processed a total of 1,660,663 TEUs of containers in 2017, 806,158 TEUs of which were imported, and 854,505 TEUs were exported.

(3) Kaohsiung Port: The largest port in Taiwan, Kaohsiung Port was originally a small fishing village from 1522 to 1566. It was first developed in 1624 by the Dutch when they occupied Taiwan. In 1895, the Chinese government ceded Taiwan to Japan by signing the Treaty of Shimonoseki. The Japanese further enhanced the port's infrastructure to facilitate the transportation of bulk goods. Based on its excellent geographical characteristics and location, Kaohsiung Port played an important role in East Asia during the 1990s. In 1999, it was ranked as the world's third-largest container port, outranked only by Hong Kong and Singapore. Although Taiwan still had economic growth after 2000, its throughput grew slowly when Taiwan's labor-intensive industries started to migrate abroad. In 2017, Kaohsiung Port was ranked as the 15th-largest port in terms of container traffic. Its focal feature is its business model; it leases most of its terminals to major world liner carriers (see Table 10.1). This strategy enabled carriers and their members to set up a transshipment hub at the port. To service large container ships, the Kaohsiung port area has expanded with new terminals in recent years; in 2011, Terminal 6 went fully operational. With four deep-water wharves with a 16.5-m draft, Terminal 6, which is now operated by the Yang Ming Group, can handle modern large containers with a carrying capacity of approximately 13,000 TEU. Furthermore, Terminal 7, which is expected to simultaneously accommodate five large ships carrying 22,000 TEUs of containers with five berths, is now under

**Table 10.1** Container terminals leased to liner carriers in Kaohsiung Port

| Berth No | Length (meter) | Number of gantry cranes | Depth | Lessee |
|---|---|---|---|---|
| 63 | 275 | 2 | 14.5 | Wan Hai Line |
| 64 | 245.46 | 2 | 14.5 | Wan Hai Line |
| 65 | 351.5 | 2 | 14.5 | OOCL |
| 66 | 408.5 | 3 | 14.5 | OOCL |
| 68 | 320.16 | 3 | 15.5 | APL |
| 69 | 320 | 4 | 15.5 | APL |
| 70 | 320.6 | 4 | 14 | Yang Ming Group |
| 76 | 320 | 2 | 14 | Hanjing |
| 77 | 355 | 4 | 15 | Hanjing |
| 78 | 320 | 3 | 15 | Hanjing |
| 79 | 355 | 4 | 15 | Evergreen |
| 80 | 340 | 2 | 14 | Evergreen |
| 81 | 120 | 2 | 14 | Evergreen |
| 108 | 375 | 3 | 17.6 | Yang Ming Group |
| 109 | 375 | 3 | 17.6 | Yang Ming Group |
| 110 | 375 | 3 | 17.6 | Yang Ming Group |
| 111 | 375 | 3 | 17.6 | Yang Ming Group |
| 115 | 276.86 | 3 | 17.6 | Evergreen |
| 116 | 320.02 | 3 | 17.6 | Evergreen |
| 117 | 320 | 2 | 17.6 | Evergreen |
| 118 | 320 | 2 | 14 | Hyundai |
| 119 | 320 | 3 | 14 | Hyundai |
| 120 | 320 | 3 | 14 | TIPC[a] |
| 121 | 320 | 3 | 14 | TIPC[a] |

[a]Taiwan International Ports Corporation

construction. The first phase of Terminal 7 is scheduled to be fully operational by 2023. Taking advantage of state-of-the-art technology and facilities, Terminal 7, which was leased to the Evergreen Group for 50 years, is set to enhance Kaohsiung Port's throughput.

(4) Taipei Port and Suao Port: These two auxiliary ports of Keelung Port play different roles in supporting its business. Taipei Port, which had been called Tamsui Port until 1999, was built mainly to relieve the pressure on Keelung Port while servicing large container ships because of insufficient draft and yard capacity. With four deep-water wharves with a draft of 16 meters and a large yard area equipped with 40 automatic rail-mounted gantry cranes, Taipei Port can efficiently accommodate large modern container ships. In 2017, the container

traffic handled at the port reached 1,561,743 TEUs, of which 758,566 TEUs were imported, and 803,177 TEUs were exported. In addition to one large container terminal, Taipei Port has 16 other wharves to service dry bulk ships, general cargo ships, and chemical ships. Suao Port, meanwhile, was built in 1965 as a small commercial port. It was upgraded to an international commercial port in 1983 through a land reclamation project that increased the land area by 80 hectares. Without dedicated wharves and gantry cranes to exclusively handle container ships, Suao Port's role is to mitigate the crowded vessel traffic in Keelung Port by offering additional wharves to handle dry bulk and chemical ships.

(5) Hualien Port: Hualien Port was built in 1939 to serve the eastern part of Taiwan, but it was out of commission until 1956 because its main facilities were destroyed during World War II. In 1963, after the completion of an expansion project, it was upgraded to an international commercial port. Because there are very few manufacturing firms in eastern Taiwan, Hualien Port aims to provide wharves and storage facilities to ships carrying chemicals, cement, and bulk and general cargoes. This port does not have wharves and gantry cranes dedicated to container ships.

(6) Anping Port: A historic port built in the 1800s, Anping Port was positioned as an auxiliary port of Kaohsiung Port to accommodate ships and cargo traffic. Because of draft constraints, only ships with less than 12-meter drafts can be handled in this port. It mainly accommodates medium and small ships sailing throughout the intra-Asia region. It currently has 17 wharves, of which 15 are for public use, servicing passenger ships, bulk ships, general cargo ships, and chemical ships. The other two wharves are leased to a private firm to accommodate its chemical ship fleets.

## The Commercial Port Law and Relevant Regulations

The Commercial Port Law (CPL) is the primary regulation governing the private and public sectors in Taiwan's port industry, including shipping companies, stevedoring companies, customs brokers, port companies, terminal operators, Taiwan International Ports Corporation (TIPC), the Maritime and Port Bureau (MPB) and the MOTC. The CPL covers issues such as port governance, planning, construction, management and operations, safety, pollution prevention, stevedore and tally clerk administration, salvage and wreck removal, and port state control in Taiwan ports. The main contents of the CPL are shown in Table 10.2.

Article 75 of the CPL stipulates that "for those commercial port safety and management matters which involve international affairs, the competent authorities (i.e., MOTC) may refer to international conventions, agreements, as well the rules, methods, standards, suggestions of the annex of those conventions, and promulgate domestic regulations or rules." This provision enables Taiwan's government to adopt appropriate rules to cope with changes in international conventions and comply with mandatory rules as provided by such conventions. For example, Taiwan's government announced that starting January 1, 2019 (one year earlier than that provided by the International Maritime Organization [IMO]), all ships and vessels operating in Taiwan's seven international commercial ports are required to use fuel with a maximum of 0.5 percent m/m sulfur or install marine scrubbers as agreed by the IMO. As of 2018, the CPL has been amended nine times since it was enacted. Meanwhile, the CPL also authorized the public sector, such as the MPB, to formulate enforcement rules to address practical issues. This mechanism enables Taiwan to act in line with the global maritime industry by rapidly integrating the latest international regulations into national rules.

**Table 10.2** The main contents of Taiwan's CPL

| |
|---|
| 1. Port governance |
| (1) Competent authorities: Ministry of Transportation and Communications (MOTC) |
| (2) A state-owned enterprise operating and managing Taiwan's international ports: Taiwan International Ports Corporation Ltd (TIPC) |
| (3) Matters involving public power: governed by the Maritime and Port Bureau (MPB) under the MOTC |
| (4) Domestic commercial ports: operated and managed by the MPB or designated authorities |
| (5) Matters concerning public order and fire services within port areas: the port police and harbor fire brigade of each port |
| 2. Planning and construction |
| (1) Overall planning and development plan: initiated by the TIPC, the MPB, and the designated authorities, after consulting city governments where the ports are located to be submitted to the Executive Yuen for approval |
| (2) Land needed for a commercial port: requisitioned according to relevant laws |
| (3) Construction, restoration, or destruction of building and facilities within the commercial port areas: administrated by port authorities such as the TIPC and the MPB |
| 3. Operation and management |
| (1) Public infrastructures, such as breakwater and navigational channels: entrusted to commercial port authorities to construct and maintain |
| (2) Other facilities within the port areas: could be constructed and operated by the TIPC or operated by government- or private-owned enterprises through investment or rental agreements with the TIPC |
| (3) The construction and maintenance of commercial port public infrastructures: paid by the Port Construction Fund |
| (4) Commercial port authorities should levy commercial port service fees to be submitted to the Port Construction Fund |
| 4. Safety and pollution prevention |
| (1) Prior declaration of ship entrance or departure |
| (2) Right to reject a ship's application for entrance into the port |
| (3) Adoption of emergency measures to prevent danger or avoid disaster |
| (4) Berth or anchorage arrangement for ships staying in port areas and emergency measures to be taken |
| (5) Measures for ships carrying dangerous goods |
| (6) Rules for navigation, operation, or berthing within port areas |
| (7) Activities that are prohibited or need prior consent |
| (8) Duties and measures concerning pollution prevention |
| (9) Disaster prevention plans and their implementation |
| (10) Port facility security plan, its assessment, and deficiency corrections |
| 5. Stevedore and tally clerk administration |
| Rules for the licensing and administration of stevedores and tally clerks |

(continued)

**Table 10.2** (continued)

| |
|---|
| 6. Salvage, wreck removal, and port state control |
| (1) Shipowners' duties for their ship salvage operations and the MPB's right to adopt contingency or response measures |
| (2) Reporting and approval of salvage plan before salvage operation |
| (3) Establishment of coastal radio service and Task Control Center |
| (4) Implementation of port state control |

## Port Planning Tools

In Taiwan, the overall planning of commercial ports takes place every five years and consists of three phases. First, the external and internal economics and maritime environments are reviewed. For the external environment, the development of world trade, ship tonnage, and ship types is studied carefully. Meanwhile, the current situation and future plans focusing on equipment, facilities, and the throughput of ports in the West Pacific and China are also investigated. Afterward, the situation of Taiwanese ports included in the services of major liner carriers and alliances is surveyed. Next, the internal environment is analyzed by reviewing the social-economic indexes and current traffic status of cargoes and passengers in the last decade. In terms of cargoes, the annual throughputs of containers and general and bulk cargoes handled by each port in Taiwan in the last decade are also collected and analyzed. Meanwhile, passenger traffic in each port is also surveyed in terms of international trips, domestic trips, and trips between Taiwan and China. The second phase, which is the essence of the entire planning procedure, establishes a regression model to forecast cargo volume growth in terms of bulk cargo, general cargo, and containerized cargo. The estimated growth in cargo volume is then allocated to each port as the future demand. The third phase involves checking the equilibrium between future supply and demand for each port and suggesting plans for adjusting each port's area and facilities based on these observations. For example, the TIPC and the MOTC may adjust investment plans and budget allocations based on port policy prioritization and a particular port's business demands.

## Financial Tools Used by Taiwan's Ports

Taiwan's port authorities have been corporatized since March 2012, integrating four harbor bureaus (Keelung, Taichung, Kaohsiung, and Hualien) into the state-owned TIPC, which operates and manages the country's seven international commercial ports. Matters concerning public power (such as retaining a foreign ship for serious violations of navigation regulations or threats to the marine environment) and security are governed by the MPB under the MOTC. Taiwan amended its CPL to implement this policy.

The financial resources for Taiwan's port construction and administration mainly come from (1) the TIPC's budget; (2) the Port Construction Fund; (3) investments from other public entities or private sectors based on models provided by CPL (e.g., private sectors investing in and running terminals in port areas), as well as projects based on the Promotion of Private Sector Participation in Public Construction Law (e.g., the build-operate-transfer [BOT] model); and (4) privately owned industrial ports (e.g., Mia Liao Port and Hoping Port).

In January 2012, Taiwan's government combined the former "Taiwan Province Government-owned Traffic Construction Fund" and the "Wharf Workers Retirement Fund" to create the Port Construction Fund. It is administrated by the MPB and aims to promote port service quality, improve port facilities, enhance port competitiveness, support environmental sustainability, and create income to replenish the fund itself. To ensure that the Port Construction Fund is sound and continuously promotes the development of Taiwan's commercial ports, Taiwan's port authorities, including the TIPC and the MPB, are mandated to carefully assess port construction in terms of priority in accordance with the necessity and urgency of the development plan when allocating fund's annual budget.

According to the CPL and its bylaws, the Port Construction Fund is derived from government subsidies through a budget process, commercial port service fees, income from the lease of property, or the creation of land superficies by the TIPC or other entities, contributions from the TIPC's annual surplus, income from domestic commercial port operations, former commercial port construction fees, fructus of the fund, and other relevant resources. Among these, commercial port service fees must be used solely for the construction and maintenance of international commercial ports. The MPB is required to collect the commercial port service fees based on the gross tonnage of ships calling at a Taiwan port, the number of passengers departing from it, and the tonnage of goods to be loaded and unloaded.

The major expenditures of the Port Construction Fund include (1) the provision of breakwaters, navigational channels, turning basins, navigation aids, public roads, information platforms, gate control systems, and other commercial port infrastructures; (2) expenditures related to port planning, research projects, port security, administration, participation in international organizations, and investments in port facilities as required by port development policies or international conventions; (3) necessary expenditures to meet port development needs, such as port connection roads, energy-saving and pollution prevention facilities, port traffic control facilities, and port land acquisition; (4) expenses regarding the operation of domestic commercial ports run and administrated by the MPB; and (5) expenditures related to administration and general affairs.

According to the Taiwan International Ports Corporation Establishment Law, the TIPC is required to assign 10% of its net profits (after taxes) to a mandatory surplus reserve fund. At the TIPC's discretion, additional percentages of the net profits may be assigned to a separate special surplus reserve fund and the Port Construction Fund. These accumulated profits can be used for further investments in Taiwan ports. Furthermore, the TIPC is required to allocate 18% of its net profits to the municipal or county governments of its seven international commercial ports. This money can be regarded as a subsidy to local governments for improving or maintaining the relevant infrastructure outside the port areas.

## Link Between Local and International Frameworks

Although Taiwan is not currently a member of the IMO, it has been monitoring the development of international maritime regulations and operating in line with the latest standards. Taiwan constantly integrates all newly revised or announced international regulations into local regulations and implements them effectively. For example, to maintain species diversification and prevent water pollution, the IMO passed the International Convention for the Control and Management of Ships' Ballast Water and Sediments (BWM) in 2004. After the threshold was determined through an agreement among 30 countries in 2016, the total ship fleets accounting for more than 30% of the world's total gross tonnage, the BWM was officially enacted in 2017. To gear Taiwan toward compliance with international conventions, the MPB has been studying the implementation process and the content of the BWM since 2013. In addition, the Regulations on Ship Equipment and Rules Governing Port Services at International Commercial Ports were amended in accordance with the BWM in 2015 to provide the source of law for implementation in Taiwan.

As a member of the world marine society, Taiwan has been maintaining a proactive attitude toward the development of shipping-related international regulations. All regulations that are relevant to the organization have branched out into local acts or rules for implementation in line with those of other countries. Besides the BWM, in 2017, the MPB announced it would begin to follow the latest resolution of the Maritime Safety Committee (MSC) and the Marine Environment Protection Committee (MEPC) by issuing or revising the Polar Ship Certificate, the Cargo Ship Safety Construction Certificate, the Cargo Ship Safety Certificate, the International Route Passenger Ship Safety Certificate, the International Water Pollution Prevention Certificate, and the National Water Pollution Prevention Certificate. Meanwhile, the Regulations Seafarers' Training, Examination and Application for Certification and the Vessel Fire Safety Regulations were also amended in accordance with the International Convention on Standards of Training,

Certification and Watchkeeping for Seafarers (STCW) and the International Convention for the Safety of Life at Sea (SOLAS) to comply with the latest standards set by the IMO.

As for international investment in the port industry, no incentive program exists to encourage foreign direct investment in Taiwan ports. Foreign companies stand in the same position as any Taiwanese operator in publicly bidding for declared port operation or investment projects.

## Current Regulatory and Financial Structure Affecting Port Development

To facilitate port development and operations and enhance ports' social and economic functions, Taiwan's government established the Port Construction Fund to finance the construction and maintenance of the public infrastructure of Taiwan ports based on the CPL. Taiwan's CPL provides the following rules for the financial structure, investments, and operation of port facilities:

(1) Land acquisition: This is the key element of port development and operations. The land areas in Taiwan's ports, including newly reclaimed ones, are owned by the central government, which allows the TIPC to establish superficies on lands (Article 7). The TIPC pays an annual rent of around NT$1.3 billion (US$0.43 billion) to the Port Construction Fund to use specific land areas. It is also required to pay land value taxes to the government. The tax rate is 1% of the government-announced land value.

(2) Port infrastructure and superstructure investment and operations: According to Articles 10 and 11 of the CPL, the infrastructure in Taiwan's international commercial port areas, such as breakwaters, waterways, information platforms, and gate control of free-trade port zones, are entrusted to the TIPC for their construction and maintenance. The TIPC is allowed to solely operate the ports' infrastructure and superstructure, such as terminal facilities, and can also act as a landlord enabling other public entities or private sectors to

lease, invest in, and/or operate these port land areas and/or superstructure facilities. These operators pay rent and other port charges to the TIPC, and the TIPC then pays superficies rent to the Port Construction Fund. The selection procedures for these operators, rent benchmark, performance management, and dispute settlement methods are promulgated by the MOTC.

(3) Port tariff and pricing policy: The maximum amount and collectible items related to port charges, which are levied by the TIPC, the MPB, and other port operators running Taiwan's port facilities, can be fixed and altered by the TIPC, the MPB, and other government authorities, subject to MOTC approval.

With regard to BOT projects for Taiwan's ports, the Promotion of Private Sector Participation in Public Construction Law provides certain incentives for encouraging private investments in major public-use facilities, including investments in port infrastructure and superstructure, as long as the investment amount is not less than NTD$2 billion (about US$67 million). The available incentive measures include government assistance in acquiring privately owned land (only applicable to projects initiated and planned by government agencies), the relaxation of financing restrictions on major construction loans, profit tax relief on investment expenditures, a five-year exemption from profit income taxes and land value taxes, and preferential tariff concessions for imported machinery and equipment, among others.

Article 8 of the abovementioned law provides the following models for private sector participation:

(1) BOT, wherein a private institution invests in the construction and operation of new facilities and, upon expiration of the concession period, transfers the ownership of such facilities to the government.
(2) Build-transfer-operate 1 (BTO1), in which a private institution invests in the construction of facilities and, upon completion, surrenders ownership to the government without compensation. The government lets the private institution operate such facilities, and after the concession period expires, the right to operate reverts back to the government.

(3) BTO2, wherein a private institution invests in the construction of facilities. Upon completion of the construction, the government acquires ownership by paying the construction expenses in a lump sum or in installments. The government then allows the private institution to operate the infrastructure. When the concession period expires, the right to operate reverts back to the government.
(4) Rehabilitate-operate-transfer (ROT), in which a private institution invests in the extension, reconstruction, and/or repair of existing facilities and operates them. Upon expiration of the concession period, the right to operate reverts back to the government.
(5) Operate-transfer (OT), wherein a private institution operates facilities built and invested in by the government. After the expiry of the concession period, the right to operate reverts back to the government.
(6) Build-operate-own (BOO), in which a private institution invests in the construction of facilities on private land provided by the private institution itself. It has ownership of such facilities after construction and then operates the infrastructure itself or permits a third party to do so.
(7) Any other model approved by the appropriate authorities.

So far, there are two major BOT projects in Taiwan's ports. One is the Taipei Port Container Terminal (TPCT), which was established on July 25, 2003, for the construction and operation of seven container terminals in Taipei Port, four of which have been put into use. Its concession period is 50 years, with an initial investment of around NT$20 billion. The other project is the Kao Ming Container Terminal (KMCT) (i.e., the sixth container terminal of Kaohsiung Port), which was established on September 20, 2007, based on an investment project called "Phase I of the Kaohsiung Port Intercontinental Container Terminal." The concession period is also 50 years. The KMCT has four berths, with a total length of 1500 meters and a land depth of 475 meters, and the designed draft is 16.5 meters. Its initial investment amount was NT$39.7 billion.

In addition, Taiwan has two privately owned industrial ports, the Mai-Liao Industrial Port and the Ho-Ping Industrial Port, which were invested in, constructed, and fully operated by private sectors. They are based on Article 30 of the Statute for Upgrading Industries, which allows industrial zone investors to construct industrial ports, subject to governmental approval. These industrial ports can only provide services for importing and exporting various materials in the industrial zone to be used by manufacturers in that zone. This statute was repealed on May 12, 2010, so no other industrial ports will be constructed in the future.

## Business Models of Taiwan's Ports and Promoting International Collaboration

The TIPC is authorized by law to run the following businesses or operations: (1) all planning, development, and management activities conducted within commercial port areas; (2) the management and provision of services related to ocean shipping within commercial port areas; (3) the development and management of port free-trade zones; (4) the development and management of tourism and recreation businesses; (5) the investment, reinvestment, and management of relevant domestic and overseas businesses; and (6) other relevant transportation, construction, and tasks designated and approved by the appropriate authorities.

Under such circumstances, the TIPC's business scope mainly focuses on developing and running local ports as a state-owned company. Nevertheless, it is still capable of facilitating international collaboration or investments in Taiwan's port areas, such as the investment made in the Mitsui Outlet Park in Taichung Port and a joint venture with the Taiwan International Windpower Training Corp. Ltd. The TIPC may also be involved in overseas investment projects and participates in some international joint venture projects, such as Pt Formosa Sejati Logistics, which runs an inland terminal in Indonesia, and Taiwan Foundation International Pte. Ltd., which acts as a holding company for overseas investments.

## References

Ministry of Transportation and Communications. (2018). Taiwan, R.O.C., "Ports and Harbors: Facilitating Trade and Shipping". https://www.motc.gov.tw/ch/home.jsp?id=727&parentpath=0,1,717

Shyu, S.-S., Cheng, L.-Y., Shiau, C.-M., Wu, K.-L., Liu, Y.-C., Thum, B.-H., Chang, S.-M., & Tsai, R.-H. (2017). The Integrated Overall Development Plan of Taiwan's Ports (2017~2021), Institute of Transportation, Ministry of Transportation and Communications, Taiwan, R.O.C.

Taiwan International Ports Corporation. (2018). *Business statistics*. https://kl.twport.com.tw/chinese/Form.aspx?n=182F1F096AD23D0C

# 11

# Regulation and Finance in the Port Sector: Current Practices and Future Port Development: The Belgian Case

Thierry Vanelslander

## National Belgian Port System Description

Belgium has historically always been located at the crossroads of important international trading routes. Also today, the country keeps that role, functioning as a transshipment hub for a large amount of traffic entering and leaving Europe. As the majority of international trade travels by sea, it is evident that Belgium must possess a substantial number of large seaports to be able to play its international trading role.

Depending on the definition used from Vanelslander (2005), Belgium features between two and six seaports (Fig. 11.1). First, if the criterion of the location is used (at sea versus inland), Belgium has two real seaports: Zeebrugge and Ostend, as those are the two located directly at

T. Vanelslander (✉)
Department of Transport and Regional Economics,
University of Antwerp, Antwerp, Belgium
e-mail: thierry.vanelslander@uantwerpen.be

© The Author(s), under exclusive license to Springer Nature Switzerland AG 2022
C. Ferrari et al. (eds.), *Regulation and Finance in the Port Industry*, Palgrave Studies in Maritime Economics,
https://doi.org/10.1007/978-3-030-83985-7_11

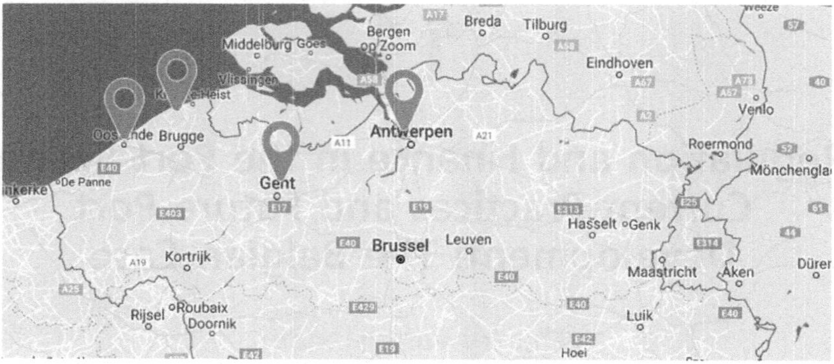


**Fig. 11.1** Belgian seaports (*Source* GeoBasis-DE/BKG [2018])

sea (Fig. 11.1). Second, if the criterion of hinterland size is used, there are three seaports that qualify, as their hinterland exceeds the borders of the small country which Belgium is: Antwerp, North Sea Port Flanders (Ghent) and Zeebruges. North Sea Port is an interesting and relatively unique case at global scale, as it is the result of a recent cross-border merger between the seaports of Ghent and Zeeland Seaports. The latter in turn was the product of the merger between the two Dutch ports of Flushing and Terneuzen. Third and finally, if the ship type is used as a distinguishing criterion, with the requirement that seagoing ships should be able to access, Belgium counts six seaports: Ostend, Zeebruges, North Sea Port, Antwerp, Genk, Liège and Brussels. The latter three indeed can host seagoing ships, but with strong draught and size limitations. For Genk and Liège, access goes via the Albert Canal, connecting the port of Antwerp directly to Liège. The Albert Canal is a Class VIb waterway, allowing for ships up to 6000 tonnes cargo capacity. It was built during the 1930s. For Brussels, access goes via the Sea Canal. The latter has a similar size as the Albert Canal.

Given the nature of the book, only seaports will be considered according to the hinterland criterion, which implies that this chapter limits itself to Antwerp, Ghent and Zeebruges.

Antwerp is connected to the North Sea through the river Scheldt, which takes about 100 km of sailing distance. The first traces of Antwerp as an international port date back to the twelfth century. Antwerp benefits from cross-border international imports and exports. In 1585, under the Spanish reign, the port was turned into an inland port, with the closure of the river Scheldt. As of the 1800s, the port industrializes, which gives it its immediate source of cargo. In 1930, the expansion of the port starts in the northern direction, up until the Dutch border. In 1970, works start on the Antwerp Left Bank, the newest expansion area for the port. In 2005, the large new dock on Antwerp's Left Bank, the Deurganckdock, was ready for service. In 2016, the Kieldrecht Lock comes into operation: the biggest lock in the world, which gives a better access to Antwerp's Left Bank, which till then was accessible only through one smaller lock (Port of Antwerp, 2018).

Antwerp is a tidal port due to the river Scheldt: ships with a draught up to 13.10 m can reach the port irrespective of the tide. At high tide, ships with a draught up to 15.50 m can access. Moreover, the older docks in the port are all behind locks, as a protection against the tide. Only the right-bank Europe and North Sea Terminal as well as the newly built Deurganckdock terminals are in front of the locks (Vlaamse Havencommissie, 2018a).

The port of Ghent also has its access to the sea via the river Scheldt, be it that this port is located closer to the sea. However, given that a long sailing stretch through the Canal Ghent-Terneuzen is required before reaching the river Scheldt, the total approach time to Ghent is about the same as to the port of Antwerp. Ghent has during the ages sought various access ways to the sea, either through existing rivers or through manmade canals. The shift in access ways was needed due to sanding of existing rivers, and political troubles with neighbouring country The Netherlands. Ghent is a tide-independent port, even though part of its access way runs through the river Scheldt: its major limitation is the Canal Ghent-Terneuzen, which only allows ships with a draught up to 12.50 m. In 2022, the port is due to get a new lock, which will alleviate the strong draught limitation (Vlaamse Havencommissie, 2018b).

The port of Zeebruges finally is located at sea. This port too has a long history. For thousands of years, the city of Bruges was directly located at and later on connected with the sea via a natural access. Sanding and political troubles here too create the need to build canal connections, after which Belgian King Leopold II in 1895 decides to build a new port, Zeebruges, at the sea. The port suffers heavily under the two world wars but got rebuilt each time. Also, its missing hinterland connections via rail and inland waterway were gradually introduced. Zeebruges has a lock, which does not at all limit its coastal potential of receiving the biggest ships in the world (Port of Zeebruges, 2018; Vlaamse Havencommissie, 2018c).

Of the three considered Belgian seaports, Antwerp is by far the biggest one, with about 74% of the Belgian maritime traffic in tonnage in 2017 (Table 11.1, including Port of Ostend). The port plays an important role also in the Hamburg—Le Havre range in nearly all major traffic flows (containers, ro/ro, coal, iron ore, agribulk, fertilizer, energy gases, steel and forest products). The port is a market leader in conventional cargo and has an important position in container handling. About 38% of the port's throughput is dry and liquid bulk (Vlaamse Havencommissie, 2018a).

Ghent disposes of specialized terminals for warehousing and distribution of grain, coal, ore, petroleum products, fertilizers, juices, cars, forest

**Table 11.1** Throughput (1000 tonnes) of Belgian seaports

| Antwerp | | North Sea Port Flanders | Zeebruges | Ostend | Total |
|---|---|---|---|---|---|
| 1980 | 81,935 | 18,424 | 14,189 | 3760 | 118,308 |
| 1990 | 10,201 | 24,439 | 30,349 | 4552 | 161,349 |
| 2000 | 13,099 | 24,039 | 35,475 | 4307 | 194,815 |
| 2005 | 16,006 | 22,222 | 34,591 | 7669 | 224,541 |
| 2006 | 16,739 | 24,144 | 39,474 | 7812 | 238,818 |
| 2007 | 18,295 | 25,102 | 42,077 | 7984 | 258,112 |
| 2008 | 18,942 | 27,028 | 42,024 | 8478 | 266,953 |
| 2009 | 15,781 | 20,787 | 44,866 | 5370 | 228,833 |
| 2010 | 17,816 | 27,257 | 49,601 | 4935 | 259,952 |
| 2011 | 18,719 | 27,192 | 46,958 | 3844 | 265,186 |
| 2012 | 18,413 | 26,302 | 43,544 | 3197 | 257,172 |
| 2013 | 19,097 | 25,955 | 42,832 | 1819 | 261,579 |
| 2014 | 19,902 | 25,889 | 42,548 | 1431 | 268,886 |
| 2015 | 20,843 | 26,362 | 38,318 | 1295 | 274,400 |
| 2016 | 21,414 | 29,110 | 37,813 | 1464 | 282,531 |
| 2017 | 22,366 | 32,509 | 37,114 | 1374 | 294,652 |

*Source* Vlaamse Havencommissie (2018d)

products, etc. It is an important industrial complex at European level (Vlaamse Havencommissie, 2018b).

Zeebruges finally is the North-West-European market leader for car traffic, and hence ro/ro activities. Its location close to the UK makes it extremely well-suited for ro/ro trade with the UK, and furthermore also Scandinavia and the Iberian Peninsula. Furthermore, Zeebruges also has an important role in importing LNG, with its capacity doubling in 2009 (Vlaamse Havencommissie, 2018c).

At European level, the Belgian seaports are typically not big passenger hubs. With regular ferry services calling at the ports of Zeebruges and Ostend, both ports featured substantial passenger turnover in the 1980s and 1990s, leading to a total of more than five million passengers in 1980 and over 3.6 million in 1990. With the disappearance of most regular ferry lines, passenger traffic dropped to below one million passengers. Only since 2016, the threshold of one million passengers was reached again, nearly entirely ascribed to the port of Zeebruges (Vlaamse Havencommissie, 2018e).

Total direct employment generated by the four Belgian ports (including Ostend) is 103,332 jobs in 2016, while indirect employment adds another 127,008 jobs (Table 11.2). Antwerp is the biggest employer with 60,849 direct jobs and 82,209 indirect jobs. Ghent is the second biggest employer with 27,983 direct jobs and 36,210 indirect

**Table 11.2** Employment by Belgian seaports

| | Direct | | | Indirect | Overall total |
|---|---|---|---|---|---|
| | Maritime cluster[a] | Non-maritime cluster[b] | Total | | |
| 2011 | 38,973 | 62,639 | 101,612 | 126,162 | 227,774 |
| 2012 | 39,223 | 64,375 | 103,597 | 128,421 | 232,018 |
| 2013 | 39,043 | 64,830 | 103,873 | 125,514 | 229,387 |
| 2014 | 38,571 | 65,282 | 103,852 | 126,941 | 230,793 |
| 2015 | 38,030 | 64,866 | 102,895 | 127,057 | 229,952 |
| 2016 | 38,320 | 65,012 | 103,332 | 127,008 | 230,340 |

*Source* Vlaamse Havencommissie (2018f)

[a]Shipping, terminals, warehousing, dredging, fishery and maritime services

[b]Industry, trade, land transport and logistics services

**Table 11.3** Value added by Belgian seaports (million euro, 2016 values)

| | Direct | | | Indirect | Overall total |
|---|---|---|---|---|---|
| | Maritime cluster | Non-maritime cluster | Total | | |
| 2011 | 4028.1 | 10,538.3 | 14,566.3 | 12,736.5 | 27,302.9 |
| 2012 | 4357.6 | 10,330.4 | 14,688.3 | 12,726.8 | 27,415.1 |
| 2013 | 4313.8 | 10,362.1 | 14,675.9 | 12,413.9 | 27,089.7 |
| 2014 | 4375.0 | 10,706.1 | 15,081.2 | 13,046.7 | 28,127.8 |
| 2015 | 4865.2 | 11,415.5 | 16,280.6 | 14,214.8 | 30,495.4 |
| 2016 | 4794.5 | 11,392.2 | 16,186.7 | 13,674.9 | 29,861.8 |

*Source* Vlaamse Havencommissie (2018g)

jobs. Overall, it can be observed that employment has not grown in line with traffic growth (Vlaamse Havencommissie, 2018f).

Total direct value added for the four Belgian seaports (including Ostend) is more than 16 euro in 2016, with another 14 billion euro of indirect value added (Table 11.3). With nearly 11 billion euro, Antwerp is the biggest generator of direct value added, and over nine billion euro indirect value added. Ghent has the second-largest value added, with nearly four billion euro directly, and over four billion euro indirectly. Value added grows more or less in line with traffic (Vlaamse Havencommissie, 2018g).

Finally, also the number of ship calls is considered. It can be seen that over the past decades, the number of calling ships has decreased in all Belgian ports. Combining this with the throughput increase observed in Table 11.4, it can be derived that the average vessel (and call) size has increased.

## Port Regulation and Planning Tools

The Belgian ports of Ghent and Antwerp have always had a very decentralized character, where management was organized locally, although public funding was required to finance the ever-larger public infrastructure that was needed. Zeebruges, initially also a locally run port, has

**Table 11.4** Ship calls at Belgian seaports

| | Antwerp | North Sea Port Flanders | Zeebruges | Ostend | Total |
|---|---|---|---|---|---|
| 1980 | 17,151 | 3260 | 9550 | 6797 | 36,758 |
| 1990 | 16,764 | 3694 | 11,321 | 4899 | 36,678 |
| 2000 | 16,105 | 2892 | 10,689 | 4103 | 33,789 |
| 2010 | 14,783 | 3436 | 8863 | 2554 | 29,636 |
| 2011 | 15,240 | 3351 | 8351 | 2201 | 29,146 |
| 2012 | 14,556 | 3125 | 7797 | 4425 | 29,903 |
| 2013 | 14,220 | 2949 | 7654 | 4358 | 29,178 |
| 2014 | 14,009 | 2893 | 7720 | 3779 | 28,401 |
| 2015 | 14,417 | 2847 | 7888 | 2687 | 27,839 |
| 2016 | 14,473 | 2891 | 8467 | 3406 | 29,237 |
| 2017 | 14,223 | 3093 | 8427 | 4050 | 29,793 |

*Source* Vlaamse Havencommissie (2018e)

developed over time a more strategic role of national military importance. Among others for that reason, the level of national involvement in Zeebruges, wider than just subsidies, has always been larger than for the two other Belgian ports.

Initially, the Belgian Minister of Traffic and Transport, who was in charge of transport policy, also covered port policy. The Belgian Minister of Public Works was in charge of the development of transport and port infrastructure. This situation necessitated a level of co-ordination and, in a later phase, organized deliberation on seaport-related policy. To that purpose, in 1963, the National Commission for the Enhancement of Port Interests was established. In 1978, it was reformed into the National Commission for Port Policy. The purpose was to create a consultative body for representatives of the ports and the most important ministries involved. Port undertakings were, however, clearly underrepresented.

In 1980, the second State Reform was voted in Belgium, with the establishment of regions and communities. As a consequence, since 1 January 1989, the Flemish Region is in charge of the seaports on its territory, more in particular for public works in the ports, on the access waterways, towage and pilotage services towards the ports and salvage services.

Also in 1989, the Flemish Port Commission (FPC) was launched. The FPC is an advisory body to the Flemish Government, which needs to be consulted for any strategic decision issue. It is composed of the representatives of employers and employees and has the following tasks:

- Elaborating general policy goals for infrastructure and exploitation of ports.
- Elaborating general proposals for competition conditions between the ports (financing, subsidies and co-operation agreements).
- Designing proposals for promoting co-ordination between port policy, concertation and re-inforced co-operation between the ports.
- Elaborating proposals for hinterland connections of the ports.
- Preparing interregional and international concertation.
- Elaborating general policy objectives in concrete infrastructure plans and projects for the entirety of ports.

Since 2 March 1999, the Flemish port policy got more structure by the Port Decree, which pays particular attention to port autonomy, unified operational conditions, more flexible labour management at the ports, mandatory corporatization of the port authorities, rules for co-operation between government and port management and financing policy. Port authorities are defined as authorities in charge of ports, with following competences (Belgian Official Gazette, 1999):

- Managing and exploiting the public and private port area.
- Fixing and collecting port dues.
- Providing port-related services to port users as well as the fixation and organization of use conditions.
- Providing special administrative police.

The Decree also defines the geographical port zones of the ports of Antwerp, Ghent, Zeebruges and Ostend. Equally, it defines the different types of infrastructure and superstructure, which will be the basis for the financing arrangements.

In 2001, the Port Decree gets modified with respect to the financial provisions.

In 2004, the European Commission approves the principles of government financing of the Flemish seaports, whereby a funding package by the Flemish government to its seaports is defined for construction and maintenance on the maritime side, in the port and on the landside access. In the same year, new modifications to the Port Decree are made, granting the port of Antwerp the competence to maintain the port inner docks.

In 2006, a new Decision by the Flemish Government decides on the maritime access ways and the components of the port infrastructure.

In 2007, Flanders Port Area is set up, an initiative that was part of the wider Vlaanderen in Actie and Flanders Logistics programme. The programme had three main objectives:

- Re-inforcing the societal support to Flemish ports
- Fixating the Flemish ports in logistics networks
- Re-inforcing the competitive position of Flemish ports

In 2008, the Port Decree gets modified in order to allow transforming the Belgian port authorities into autonomous municipal port companies.

Given the above, Belgian port entities themselves are governed in comparable ways, be it with slight differences, but with common responsibilities.

The Antwerp Port Authority got transformed in 1997 into the Municipal Port Company Antwerp. Till then, the port was governed directly from the City of Antwerp. In 2016, the Municipal Port Company Antwerp got transformed into the Anonymous Society of Public Law 'Port Company Antwerp'. The company's sole shareholder is the City of Antwerp. With that 2016 reform, the Port Company's Board, which till then was solely constituted of municipal politicians, got changed with the introduction of business people, which now make up six of the 11 Board positions.

The Port of Zeebrugge is since 1895 managed by the Maatschappij van de Brugse Zeehaven (MBZ). The City of Bruges now is the sole shareholder. The MBZ board is fully politically composed.

North Sea Port is the result of the merger between the Port of Ghent and Zeeland Seaports. The entity, establishes as a European Anonymous Society, functions as a holding on top of both existing port entities, and has eight shareholders. On the Dutch side, these are the Province of Zeeland (25%) and the municipalities of Borsele, Terneuzen and Flushing (each 8.33%). On the Flemish side, it concerns the City of Ghent (48.52%), the municipalities of Evergem (0.03%) and Zelzate (0.05%), and the Province of Eastern Flanders (1.444%). A supervisory body was erected for the holding entity. Both the Dutch and the Flemish shareholders each propose four members for that, of which maximum two each time are politically active.

## Financial Tools

The basic rule since the Port Decree of 1999 is that in Belgium all basic infrastructure, including maritime access ways, locks, harbour dams, dredging works, road networks, inland waterway connections and the like, is financed for 100% by the Flemish Region. It is to be noted that railways are a Federal matter in Belgium, and therefore funded by the national railway network manager Infrabel. Additional infrastructure in the port areas, like quay walls, is financed for 60% by the Flemish Region, the remaining 40% being covered by the Port Company itself. For renovation works and smaller seaports, the proportion is 80–20%. Superstructure is not subsidized, with the exception of superstructure which the port authority requires to fulfil its public duty. Typically, as all Belgian seaports work under a landlord system, with concessions granted to operators, terminal superstructure typically is financed by the concessionaires. Since 2001, with the modification of the Port Decree mentioned in section 2, the 60/40 rule for additional infrastructure got replaced by an 80/20 division.

A special case for maritime access infrastructure is the ports of Ghent and Antwerp, which are only accessible to sea-going vessels via the Scheldt, a tidal river. A large part of the river (known as the Western Scheldt) lies in Dutch territory. The status of the Scheldt was fixed under the Belgian-Dutch Separation Treaties of 1839–1843. Pilotage, concreting and maintenance of the fairway on the Western Scheldt are supervised by a council of permanent commissioners made up of two Dutch and two Belgian members. A radar system was constructed along the Scheldt and its maritime access channels, together with an information processing system. The Flemish Region takes 90% of the construction and operational costs on Dutch territory for its account and the full cost on Flemish territory.

The port of Ghent is connected with the Western Scheldt via the Ghent to Terneuzen canal. The Belgian section of the maritime canal to Ghent is regional property, so that it is maintained and improved at the expense of the Flemish Region. The Dutch section is owned by the Dutch state. Improvement works, including the construction of locks at Terneuzen, are subject to negotiation between Belgium and the Netherlands. On the basis of the treaty of 20 June 1960, Belgium contributes 80% of the costs of works in the Netherlands, while Belgium contributes an annual sum to maintenance.

In reality, other constructions are also applied. First of all, for specific projects (e.g. Deurganckdock in Antwerp, Kluizendock in Ghent, Ghent-Terneuzen Canal, etc.), the Flemish region can decide to fully finance the infrastructure works and have them carried out under its own direct management. After completion, ownership or exploitation of the port infrastructure can be transferred to the port authority. Second, the Port Companies may decide to execute projects themselves, calling for subsidies from the Flemish Region. Third and finally, more and more PPPs are being rolled out in Belgian seaports (Kieldrecht Lock Antwerp, Terneuzen Lock and Liefkenshoek Rail Tunnel).

Obviously, in any of the above constructions, Belgium needs to comply with EU legislation concerning State Aid, PPPs, VAT applicability, etc.

Table 11.5 gives an overview of the amounts of capital the Flemish Region has invested in Flemish ports over the period 1989–2017.

## Investments in Belgian Ports

The largely decentralized decision and promotion nature of Belgian seaport governance has proven useful in being agile in attracting foreign investment. Currently, all major container terminals are under concession with big international terminal groups (DP World and PSA in

Table 11.5 Flemish region seaport expenditure (million euro, 2017 prices)

| | Antwerp | North Sea Port Flanders | Zeebruges | Ostend | Total ports | Maritime access | Overall total |
|---|---|---|---|---|---|---|---|
| 2010 | 77.61 | 32.57 | 50.50 | 17.05 | 177.73 | 202.46 | 380.19 |
| 2011 | 83.76 | 23.58 | 57.52 | 8.66 | 173.52 | 189.40 | 362.93 |
| 2012 | 78.26 | 9.04 | 31.42 | 10.74 | 129.45 | 232.82 | 362.27 |
| 2013 | 110.32 | 4.35 | 27.37 | 12.88 | 154.91 | 250.97 | 405.89 |
| 2014 | 63.76 | 6.12 | 21.15 | 16.62 | 107.65 | 362.13 | 469.78 |
| 2015 | 60.49 | 17.06 | 17.47 | 16.75 | 111.77 | 156.93 | 299.85 |
| 2016 | 65.42 | 3.94 | 16.05 | 5.96 | 91.37 | 293.64 | 426.86 |
| 2017 | 68.87 | 7.90 | 38.47 | 5.17 | 120.40 | 254.96 | 414.91 |
| Total since 1989 | 2642.14 | 705.23 | 955.89 | 437.64 | 4740.90 | 6062.73 | 10,916.17 |

*Source* Vlaamse Havencommissie (2018g)

Antwerp, Cosco Pacific in Zeebruges, most often supported by international shipping company involvement). Given the above-described port governance, those international operators are only investing in terminal superstructure. The international involvement is a positive development to the extent that it enables investments that would not have been possible by local players. As opposed to this, the negative aspect is that involving foreign partners leads to loss of local control, which has a clear impact among others on the functioning of the local port community. Looking at general cargo and bulk (dry and liquid), it is observed that the operators in all Belgian ports tend to be more local players.

More recently, as one of the solutions introduced in section "Financial Tools" for financing of specific projects, PPPs were mentioned. That implies a more active involvement in ports of players from outside the port sector, mainly from the construction sector. Those are Belgian but also non-Belgian. A main reason for the application of PPPs is the huge amounts of investments needed, in times of financial shortages with European public governments, combined with debt restrictions imposed by EU legislation.

The decentralized character of Belgian seaport policy also enables co-operation at international level. A clear example is the freedom that the

Port of Ghent got in deciding on its mergers with Zeeland Seaports. Another example is the setup of an international branch as part of the Antwerp Port Company, called Port of Antwerp International, which develops financial participations in strategically interesting overseas ports. Finally, there is also the example of MBZ in Zeebruges that is going for stronger ties with Chinese companies like Cosco Shipping in local investment.

A final international impact comes through international security legislation. Programmes like ISPS, CT-PAT, etc. necessitate additional investments, imposed by international frameworks and agreements or by individual countries (e.g. the US).

## Critical Discussion

It is clear that port regulation, if not well-suited, can hamper port development. The advantage of giving the local decision levels a lot of responsibility in port development is that the needs and interests are clearly sensed and identified and also translated in suitable projects. These are the types of projects that are then submitted, for instance, to the European Commission (as part of TEN-T programmes, CEF funding calls, etc.) or the European Investment Bank. Sometimes, this is done in competition with other Belgian ports, but to that extent, competition has the positive effect of improving the quality of the submitted files and make them based on real needs in the port.

A drawback of this decentralized approach is that at a higher level, a strong co-ordination is needed, so as to prioritize projects at national level to some extent. In that respect, Belgium has a difficult governance structure overall. There is no 'unicity of command'. Ports became physically a responsibility of the Regions in Belgium, so Flanders in the case of the named ports, and more in particular the Minister of Mobility and Public Works. That Minister is also in charge of road and inland waterway hinterland connections, be it with separate administrations behind, which do to some extent compete with each other. However, also the Minister of Spatial Issues in Flanders is very relevant for ports, as (s)he determines the allocation of land for port expansion. Furthermore, rail in Belgium is a Federal matter, so that transport policy is spread over various government levels, which are not always unanimous, sometimes for well-grounded contents reasons, sometimes for political reasons. Moreover, these higher government levels often lack the budgets to respond to the full needs that ports have. This makes that port needs are not always served to their best interest, and that probably opportunities and inflow of international investments are missed.

It can therefore be concluded that Belgian port governance without a doubt is strongly beneficial to port development and its flexibility and agility, but at the same time, that is negatively impacted on by the dispersion of policy views at higher government levels. So far, Belgian ports manage to keep a strong position within Europe and globally, but the question is to what extent that will remain the case in the future, and to what extent decision power over the Belgian ports' position will still be local or rather be directed from elsewhere in the world.

## Literature

Belgian Official Gazette. (1999). Decreet houdende het beleid en het beheer van de zeehavens.

GeoBasis-DE/BKG. (2018). Vlaamse Havendag – Welkom in jouw haven op 17 september 2017! consulted at http://www.vlaamsehavendag.be/ on 10 December 2018.

Port of Antwerp. (2018). Geschiedenis, consulted at https://www.portofantwerp.com/nl/havengeschiedenis on 1 December 2018.

Port of Zeebruges. (2018). Geschiedenis, consulted at https://www.portofzeebrugge.be/nl/de-haven/geschiedenis on 1 December 2018.

Vanelslander, T. (2005). *The economics behind co-operation and competition in sea-port container handling*. Ph.D. University of Antwerp

Vlaamse Havencommissie. (2018a). Steekkaart Haven van Antwerpen, consulted at http://www.vlaamsehavencommissie.be/vhc/pagina/haven-antwerpen on 1 December 2018.

Vlaamse Havencommissie. (2018b). Steekkaart North Sea Port Flanders, consulted at http://www.vlaamsehavencommissie.be/vhc/pagina/north-sea-port-flanders-haven-gent on 1 December 2018.

Vlaamse Havencommissie. (2018c). Steekkaart Zeebrugge, consulted at http://www.vlaamsehavencommissie.be/vhc/pagina/haven-zeebrugge on 1 December 2018.

Vlaamse Havencommissie. (2018d). Statistieken Vlaamse zeehavens – Ladingen en lossingen, consulted at http://www.vlaamsehavencommissie.be/vhc/thema/statistiek-vlaamse-havens/ladingen-en-lossingen on 1 December 2018.

Vlaamse Havencommissie. (2018e). Statistieken Vlaamse zeehavens – Passagiers, consulted at http://www.vlaamsehavencommissie.be/vhc/thema/statistiek-vlaamse-havens/passagiers on 1 December 2018.

Vlaamse Havencommissie. (2018f). Statistieken Vlaamse zeehavens – Werkgelegenheid, consulted at http://www.vlaamsehavencommissie.be/vhc/thema/statistiek-vlaamse-havens/werkgelegenheid on 1 December 2018.

Vlaamse Havencommissie. (2018g). Statistieken Vlaamse zeehavens – Toegevoegde Waarde, consulted at http://www.vlaamsehavencommissie.be/vhc/thema/statistiek-vlaamse-havens/toegevoegde-waarde on 1 December 2018.

# 12

# The French Port System: Forty Years of Port Governance Reforms

**Laurent Fedi, Pierre Cariou, and Jason Monios**

Until the beginning of the twenty-first century, the French port system was characterised by the dominance of the 'tool port' model (Brooks & Pallis, 2012; World Bank, 2013). The concepts of 'public port service' and related 'general interest' have shaped the development of French ports for decades. Compared to other European seaports, the key changes in the French port system occurred later and were undertaken in a fragmented way. Successive law reforms have been adopted with the aim to modernise the status of French seaports facing stronger competition and

L. Fedi (✉) · P. Cariou · J. Monios
Kedge Business School, Marseille, France
e-mail: laurent.fedi@kedgebs.com

P. Cariou
e-mail: pierre.cariou@kedgebs.com

J. Monios
e-mail: jason.monios@kedgebs.com

© The Author(s), under exclusive license to Springer Nature Switzerland AG 2022
C. Ferrari et al. (eds.), *Regulation and Finance in the Port Industry*, Palgrave Studies in Maritime Economics,
https://doi.org/10.1007/978-3-030-83985-7_12

market share erosion, notably in the container segment (Cariou et al., 2014; Court of Auditors, 2006; Lacoste & Douet, 2013). In 2008, a significant port reform was announced and came into force in 2011 after tough negotiations characterised by numerous strikes and lock-outs (Fedi & Rézenthel, 2011). The 'landlord port' model has finally been introduced for major metropolitan commercial seaports (so-called 'Grands Ports Maritimes'—GPMs), which remain state-owned public bodies like the majority of European seaports (ESPO, 2016). Following a clear trend of devolution (Debrie et al., 2017), all other French commercial seaports and fishing ports have been under local administration, mostly Regions and Departments, since January 2007 (Debrie & Lavaud-Letilleul, 2010).

## The French Port System Description

France represents the second largest maritime domain after the United States of America, with 11 million square kilometres. Thanks to the Overseas Departments, France has a large number of ports from the Indian Ocean to South America, passing through the Caribbean. The entire maritime activity (fleet, ports, fisheries, naval industry, shipyard, research and tourism excluded) represents more than 336,000 direct jobs in the local basins (French Maritime Cluster, 2018) and industrial activities employ more than 90,000 people. The turnover of French seaports was € 830 million in 2016 and commercial seaports (Table 12.1) are divided into three main categories:

- the 'decentralised ports'
- the 'autonomous ports'
- the 'major maritime ports' ('grands ports maritimes' GPMs in French).

**Table 12.1** Typology of the French seaports

| Category | Decentralised ports | Autonomous ports | Major ports (GPM) |
|---|---|---|---|
| Main regulations | 1983, 2002, 2004, 2015 | 1965, 1994, 1999 | 2008, 2012, 2016 |
| Number | 500 | 2 | 11 |
| Status | Public body | Public body | Public body |
| Ownership and control | Local authorities: Regions, Departments, Agglomeration Communities, CCI | French state | French state |

*Source* Adapted from Cariou et al. (2014)

**Table 12.2** French port traffics in million tonnes

| | 2000 | 2005 | 2010 | 2015 | 2017 | AAGR 2000–2017 (%) |
|---|---|---|---|---|---|---|
| European Union (EU15)[a] | 3,012,086 | 3,433,446 | 3,358,165 | 3,500,521 | 3,607,446 | 1.1 |
| France | 325,789 | 341,470 | 316,137 | 297,880 | 302,840 | −0.4 |
| Marseille | 91,279 | 93,308 | 82,427 | 77,479 | 75,617 | −1.1 |
| Le Havre | 63,885 | 70,801 | 65,946 | 62,946 | 66,104 | 0.2 |
| Dunkirk | 44,318 | 48,503 | 36,309 | 36,906 | 39,085 | −0.7 |
| Nantes Saint-Nazaire | 31,263 | 34,043 | 30,582 | 24,878 | 29,307 | −0.4 |
| Others | 95,044 | 94,815 | 100,873 | 95,671 | 92,727 | −0.1 |

[a]Belgium; Denmark; Germany; Ireland; Greece; Spain, France; Croatia; Italy; Netherlands; Portugal; Finland; Sweden, United Kingdom; Iceland
*Source* Eurostat (2019)—https://ec.europa.eu/eurostat/data/database

The *decentralised ports* represent more than 500 small trading and fishing ports. As public entities, these ports are devolved to local government[1] such as Municipalities, Regions, Departments and Chambers of Commerce and Industry (CCI). Taking into account their modest traffic, usually less than five million tonnes per year except for the port of Calais,

[1] The French administrative organisation is divided between the central government and local governments or authorities that are the Regions, Departments and Muncipalities respectively. They have specific competencies and port management especially.

they are considered secondary ports. On the other hand, the *autonomous ports* and the *major maritime ports* (GPMs) represent the largest French ports handling more than five million tonnes a year. As public bodies, they belong to the French State and are directly monitored by the central administration. Only two inland river ports, Paris and Strasburg, belong to the *autonomous* port taxonomy implemented by the Law no. 65-491 (JORF, 1965). Prior to the latest reform in 2008, large French ports were operated under this framework that set up the tool port regime. It means that the port authority is involved in commercial operations at the same time as traditional port authority activities (e.g. safety and security). In addition, there are seven metropolitan GPMs: Marseille-Fos, La Rochelle, Le Havre, Nantes Saint-Nazaire, Bordeaux, Dunkirk and Rouen. In 2016, these ports represented more than 74% of the French ports' total volume. Four overseas major maritime ports are also operational: Guadeloupe, Guyanne, Martinique and Port Réunion. In 2017, 365 million tonnes were handled by French ports (Ministry of Ecological Transition, 2020).

One of the key advantages of French seaports is very good nautical accessibility, allowing them to welcome the largest containerships (20,000 TEUs) in particular in Le Havre, Dunkirk and Marseille, very large crude carriers (400,000 GRT) notably in Nantes Saint-Nazaire, and Marseille, which is the third busiest European oil terminal, handling large LNG tankers and the biggest cruise ships (Ports de France, 2016). In addition, numerous ports[2] benefit from efficient port community systems (PCS) connecting internal and external port stakeholders (Fedi et al., 2019; Mahé des Portes, 2013). Moreover, 26 French ports are identified as Trans-European Transport Network (TEN-T) ports, some of them positioned within TEN-T Corridors (EU Commission, 2014) and the Belt and Road Initiative (BRI) (Port of Marseille, 2018). Lastly, France provides a central system of large maritime ports in Europe with good connection to the major routes, motorways, railways and inland waterways (Seine and Rhône).

[2] Le Havre, Marseille-Fos, Dunkirk, Fecamp, Bordeaux, Nantes, Caen, La Rochelle, Lorient, Saint-Malo, Sète. Two French leading providers of cargo community system are established in France : MGI in Marseille https://www.mgi-ci5.com/en/ and SOGET in Le Havre: http://www.soget.fr/en/solutions.html.

**Table 12.3** Quality of port infrastructure—World Economic Forum ranking

| | EU | France | Netherlands | Belgium | Germany | Spain | Italy |
|---|---|---|---|---|---|---|---|
| 2007 | 4.82 | 5.87 | 6.7 | 6.4 | 6.5 | 5.3 | 3.1 |
| 2017 | 4.86 | 5.10 | 6.8 | 6.1 | 5.5 | 5.5 | 4.4 |

*Source* World Economic Forum (2019)—https://data.worldbank.org/indicator/IQ.WEF.PORT.XQ?year_high_desc=true

Despite these key advantages, the analysis of the long-term evolution of French port traffic (Table 12.1) depicts a declining trend, with an Average Annual Growth Rate of −0.4% against 1.1% for EU 15 countries from 2000 to 2017. France handles less than 10% of EU 15 port traffic, and within France, Le Havre and Marseille account for approximately 50% of total French traffic.

The World Economic Forum (WEF) survey on the Quality of Port Infrastructure (from one for underdeveloped to seven for well-developed and efficient) at the country level provides another basis of evaluation (Table 12.3). In 2007, the WEF index that measures business executives' perception of their country's port facilities was 5.87, France being number ten in the World Ranking and number seven in Europe. In 2017, France was number 28 in the world and 14 in Europe with an index of 5.1 out of seven.

## The French Port Regulation and Planning Tools

The current French model of port governance is based on successive reforms that have been initiated in the last century as summarised in Table 12.4. As regards secondary ports, two regulations in 1983 (JORF, 1983a, 1983b) started the transfer of competences from the State to Departments (for trading and fishing ports) and to Municipalities (for marinas). The Law of 13 August 2004 relating to the responsibilities of local authorities (JORF, 2004a) transferred the 18 ports of 'national interest' representing 20% of goods traffic and 80% of passenger traffic to local authorities and their groupings. The ownership and management of these ports (development strategy, investment, maintenance,

**Table 12.4** The main successive modifications of the French legal framework on seaport management

| Decentralisation secondary ports | Dock workers reform | Public domain and public investments | Terminal operating agreement | Reform of major ports (GPMs) |
|---|---|---|---|---|
| **Law 1983**<br>• Transfer from the State to Public entities: commercial ports (Departments) and fishing ports (Municipalities) | **Law 1992**<br>• Reform of the port workers' status<br>• Implementation of the 'monthly principle'<br>• Severe reduction of the number of dock workers | **Law 1994**<br>• Granting more rights to private operators/investors operating the port public domain<br>• Rights *in rem* recognised:<br>e.g. mortgage on buildings (warehouse) | **Decree 1999**<br>• Creation of a new contract: 'Terminal operating agreement'<br>supposed to progressively replace concession contracts | **Law 2008**<br>• New 'brand' and missions for previous 'autonomous ports'<br>• Landlord port model<br>• New governance bodies<br>• Environmental requirements<br>• Strategic plan |
| **Law 2002**<br>• Transfer from the State to 'Collectivité Territoriale de Corse': Ports of Ajaccio and Bastia | | **Law 2006**<br>• Creation of port companies | **Bylaw 2009**<br>• Standardisation of 'Terminal agreement' with specific clauses (i.e. standardised contract) became mandatory | **Law 2012**<br>• Four oversea ports : Fort-de-France (Martinique), Degrad-des-Cannes (Guyanne), Port –Réunion (La Réunion) and Pointe-à-Pitre (Gaudeloupe) became major ports |
| **Law 2004** | | | **Law 2019** | **Law 2016** |

| Decentralisation secondary ports | Dock workers reform | Public domain and public investments | Terminal operating agreement | Reform of major ports (GPMs) |
|---|---|---|---|---|
| • Transfer of secondary ports in full ownership to local authorities Regions, Departments, Agglomeration Communities, CCI | | | • New rules for port terminal management | • Additional measures on the composition of governance bodies<br>• Reinforcement of the Regions' representativeness<br>• Creation of Commission on investments |
| **Law 2015**<br>• Transfer of departmental ports to regions or local authorities or groupings | | | **Decree 2020**<br>• Adaptation of the 'Terminal agreement' conditions | |

*Source* The authors

etc.) are performed by local authorities either Regions, Departments or mixed associations including different local authorities while the CCI is still involved as concessionaire. According to Debrie et al. (2017), this devolution has provided a 'three-dimensional port model' incorporating the State, the new concessioning authorities (local authority) and the concession holder (CCI). Whereas the State remains in charge of activities in the public interest (safety, security, public order and environmental protection), the concessioning entity owns the port domain, takes over the port development planning and is considered as the port authority (PA). The concessionaire operates handling equipment, cranes, warehouses and facilities. The latest modification to the new administrative organisation of the French territory (JORF, 2015) allowed a possible transfer of departmental ports to Regions or local authorities from 1st January 2017.

Concerning the largest French ports, several reforms occurred in order to modify their legal environment. The first reform dealt with the port labour regime aiming at allowing dockers to become salaried employees of handling companies (JORF, 1992). In 1994, a reform of the public domain was enacted (JORF, 1994) with the purpose to promote the public port domain and to grant more securities—real rights—for private investors (Fedi & Rézenthel, 2007b). In 1999, the 'terminal operating agreement' was established (JORF, 1999) in order to modernise the legal framework of port land management (Fedi & Rézenthel, 2007a; Rézenthel, 2010) and to take into consideration the worldwide terminalisation of seaports (Slack, 2005).

Finally, a profound reform occurred between 2008 and 2011 transforming the existing 'autonomous ports' into 'large maritime ports' (GPMs). The law no. 2008-660 of 4 July 2008 replaced the 'tool port' organisation with the 'landlord port' model with the implicit aim to restore the French ports' competitiveness (Cariou et al., 2014). In 2011, notwithstanding severe social tensions (Fedi & Rézenthel, 2011), the reform took place with a dedicated framework applicable to the local context of each GPM (Lacoste & Douet, 2013; Debrie et al., 2017). The key features of this reform lie in different aspects in particular: transfer of full ownership of the State's infrastructure and facilities to the GPMs, new PA missions, sale and transfer of port equipment, transfer of port workers to private operators, new governance bodies designed to improve the decision-making process, generalisation of terminal operating agreements, integration of environmental protection and stronger compliance with competition rules.

The fundamental change of the 2008 reform was the adoption of the landlord port regime setting out the principle that GPMs cannot operate equipment designed for handling and storing goods. They instead focus on development, promotion and regulation. GPMs take charge of the construction, operation and maintenance of maritime access routes, port safety and security. Moreover, GPMs are also responsible for the administration and development of the whole port domain under their jurisdiction, the construction and maintenance of port infrastructure, the planning and management of industrial or logistic zones linked to port activities (Rézenthel, 2008a). In addition, GPMs take over development of infrastructure networks, rail and inland waterways to promote intermodality to support the development of the container industry (Cariou et al., 2014).

As regards the new governance bodies, the reform created a three-level structure made up of a *board of directors*, a *supervisory board* and a *development council* (Fig. 12.1). The board of directors is the executive body managing the day-to-day activities of the port and carries out the

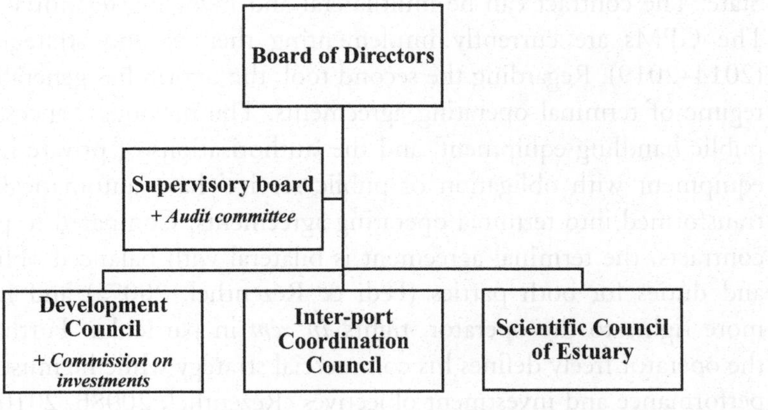


**Fig. 12.1** The structure of the GPM's governance (*Source* The authors, based on Law No. 2008-660 and Law No. 2016-816)

decisions taken by the supervisory board. The supervisory board sets up strategies and monitors the board of directors. Following the example of joint-stock companies, the new structure separated the responsibility for control and management (Fedi & Pignatel, 2011). An *audit committee* attached to the supervisory board performs the financial supervision of the GPM and provides information to the central government (JORF, 2016). An *inter-port coordination council* can be set up to encourage synergies between seaports and waterway ports such as Seine and Rhône and Atlantic (Gallais-Bouchet, 2013) as well as a *scientific council of estuary* that gives advice on ecological concerns and carries out environmental studies with the aim to orientate the choices of supervisory councils (Lacoste & Douet, 2013). A synthesis of this new organisation structure is presented in Table 12.5.

Concerning the planning tools, the reform has provided two key instruments: the *strategic plan* and the general application of *terminal operating agreements*. The strategic plan formalises a pluri-annual contractual relationship between the GPMs and the State that 'redefines the port authorities' missions and activities' (Cariou et al., 2014). Drafted for five years, the strategic plan requires each port to set up its strategy including its main orientations, the conditions of actions notably as regards planning and sustainable development policy, rail and inland waterway strategy, a business plan and a plan for estimating dividends to the State. The contract can be multilateral and involving territorial bodies. The GPMs are currently implementing their second strategic plans (2014–2019). Regarding the second tool, the reform has generalised the regime of terminal operating agreements. The previous 'concessions of public handling equipment' and the 'authorisations of private handling equipment with obligation of public service' have automatically been transformed into terminal operating agreements. Compared to previous contracts, the terminal agreement is bilateral with balanced obligations and duties for both parties (Fedi & Rézenthel, 2007a) and it grants more rights to the operator, rights *in rem* in particular. Furthermore, the operator freely defines his commercial strategy while he must respect performance and investment objectives (Rézenthel, 2008b, 2010). Even though the terminal operation agreement cannot avoid compliance

**Table 12.5** The organisation structure of GPMs

| Post-reform: 2008–2011 and 2016 | |
|---|---|
| Bodies and functions | Number of members |
| ***Supervisory board***<br>Defines strategic orientations, controls the board of directors | **18**<br>• Five state representatives<br>• Five local communities<br>• Three port employees<br>• Five qualified persons or experts (appointed by state) |
| **+ Audit Committee**<br>Performs the financial supervision | One Region's representative at least |
| ***Board of directors***<br>Management body: manages and carries out the supervisory council's decisions | **Three or four members**<br>• Chairman is appointed by French State<br>• Other members: appointed by Supervisory board |
| ***Development council***<br>Advisory body that gives advice to the supervisory board | **20–40 members**<br>Appointed by the Prefect (State) |
| **+ Commission on port investments** | Two colleges of investors (one public and one private) |
| ***Scientific council of estuary***<br>Optional, gives advice on ecology concerns | Undetermined number, not legally detailed |
| ***Inter-port coordination council***<br>Optional, proposes strategies for maritime and inland waterways or river port issues | Undetermined number, not legally detailed |

*Source* The authors based on Law No. 2008-660, Law No. 2016-816 and adapted fromCariou et al. (2014)

with competition rules, this new regime translates a liberalisation of conditions of occupation of the port public domain (Rézenthel, 2008b).

## The Financial Tools of the French Seaports

The funding options of the French seaports are diverse and can be categorised as self-funding, government funding and EU funding as shown in Table 12.6. As regards self-funding, decentralised ports and GPMs are legally entitled to collect:

**Table 12.6** Main funding sources of French seaports

| Self-funding | Governmental and regional funding | EU funding |
|---|---|---|
| • Port dues<br>• Services to ship<br>• Concession/Terminal agreements royalties<br>• Port land royalties<br>• Port companies | • Operating funding<br>• Maintenance funding<br>• CPER<br>• CPiER<br>• AFITF | • TEN-T Programme<br>• CEF<br>• ERDF<br>• EIB |

*Source* The authors

- port dues (on ships, goods, passengers and ship-generated waste) that represent their primary source of funding, i.e. more than 50% (Court of Auditors, 2017),
- concession and terminal revenues (royalties),
- revenues from the port domain,
- revenues from docks and storage areas.

For the period 2008–2015, the revenues from concession contracts and the leases of port domain represented an average of 25% of the annual turnover of Le Havre, Marseille, Rouen, Nantes Saint-Nazaire, La Rochelle and more than 35% for Bordeaux and Dunkirk (Court of Auditors, 2017).

Government funding comes from the central State through allocation budgets for facility maintenance and investments considered as fundamental 'to maintain the French port competitiveness and their capacity to regain market shares vis-à-vis other European ports and Northern seaports in particular' (Ministry of Ecological Transition, 2020). Operating and investment funding allows seaports to secure their maritime access (dredging), reinforce their multimodality and develop processing capacities of goods notably for container traffic which is a key component of the French ports' economic model (Le Havre, Marseille and Dunkirk in particular). The second financing source lies in co-funding between the State, the Regions and the local authorities. The State's contributions to ports' investments must be registered in 'State-region project contracts' (CPER) or in 'State-interregional project contracts' (CPiER). For the period 2015–2020, the latest contracts have represented around

€2 billion for the development of logistics activities and massification of flows. The State's contribution to these operations is roughly €360 million. Furthermore, the *French Infrastructure Transport Funding Agency* (AFITF) launched in 2004 (JORF, 2004c) also contributes to the funding of port infrastructure and in particular large projects of national and international interest such as Port 2000 in Le Havre and Fos 2XL in Marseille.

Additional financing can also be adopted. For example, a plan of economic revival (2009–2013) permitted to support port development up to €271 million in order to accompany the GPMs' reform. Nonetheless, these funding sources must comply with the European rules on State aid and not consequently distort competition (art. 107 TFEU). Furthermore, the French government sustains project leaders in attracting European funds in particular through the mechanism of 'Connecting Europe Facilities' (CEF), the Trans-European Transport Network (TEN-T) Programme where 26 French ports are concerned (EC, 2014) and that co-financed several projects on Sulphur (SOx) mitigation (Fedi & Cariou, 2015), the European Regional Development Fund (ERDF) or from the European Investment Bank (EIB).

Additionally, according to the latest provisions of the 2008 reform, GPMs can act inside or outside port limits and own shares in commercial, logistics firms, Economic Interest Groups (GIE) or Public Interest Groups (GIP) with the aim to pool activities and enhance the development or modernisation of the port. This principle was already set out by the Law no. 2006-10 that allowed autonomous ports to create 'port companies' (JORF, 2006; Vantorre & Rézenthel, 2006). Along the same lines and as derogation to the principle of prohibition to perform commercial activities, GPMs can temporarily operate terminals in case of failure of tenders and a subsidiary controlled by a port authority can be set up for strategic interest (e.g. oil products supply). The port of Marseille established 'Fluxel' a subsidiary owned at 66% dedicated to oil terminal operations (Cariou et al., 2014; JORF, 2004b). In 2015, the PA of Le Havre launched a tri-modal terminal and owned 49% of the capital. Furthermore, GPMs can hold minor shares in a private handling company such as the Port of Marseille with Intramar STS and the port of Dunkirk which holds an interest in the coal terminal (GIE Sea Bulk) and in the container terminal (Transmanche Terminal). Consequently, these investments allow ports additional financing.

## Links Between Local and National Port Regulation and the International Framework of Ports

Like other EU and global seaports (Notteboom, 2007; World Bank, 2007), the large French ports have experienced the development of public–private partnerships (PPPs) for a long time and before the 2008 port reform (Rézenthel, 2007). The reasons justifying the development of PPPs in French ports are similar to other countries (Notteboom & Winkelmans, 2001; Wang et al., 2010): the decline of public funds, greater competition, the need to improve service levels for infrastructure users, various types of highly specialised port terminals and consequently to enhance efficiency in operations (Merlin, 2009).

Private companies were already active prior to the port reform in operating several terminals; nonetheless, thanks to the implementation of the new framework, the partnerships with the private sector have been implicitly reinforced insofar as private entities are supposed to manage commercial activities. GPMs have indeed lost the right to handle cargoes except in some specific cases. In addition, the new legislation has generalised the terminal operating agreement in replacement of the former contracts such as the traditional *public service concession* or *private equipment with public service*. According to some experts the terminal operating agreement represents the main strategic tool for establishing a PPP (Merlin, 2009, 2013). The key principle of the terminal agreement is sharing risks between the PA and the private operator. Even though these risks are numerous for both parties, especially when the terminal is not yet built at the time the agreement is signed, they are mostly financial, commercial, operational and legal risks (Notteboom et al., 2012). To summarise, since the operator is ready to carry out investments in facilities (gantry cranes, rail cranes, straddle carriers, etc.), to satisfy performance objectives and to pay royalties, it can benefit from port infrastructure in the long-term (20–30 years) and from a large operational and commercial freedom. For its part, the PA must finance and build infrastructure (quays, yards, land connections—road and rail), dredge docks, maintain nautical access to the terminal and allow rights *in rem* on constructions realised by the operator. Finally, the new terminal operating agreement allows both parties to build a balanced and sustainable partnership while its economic equilibrium lies mainly in third parties who are shipping lines calling at the terminal (Merlin, 2013). Shipping lines are in reality directly involved in terminal operations as illustrated by the two main container terminals of the Port of Marseille-Fos: 'Terminal de la Mediterranée' operated by Seayard *(owned 50% by Terminal Investment Ltl (MSC group), 42% by AP Moller-Maersk Terminal and* 8% by COSCO) and 'Fos 2XL' operated by PortSynergy/Eurofos managed by a consortium made up of CMA CGM, DP World and China Merchants. More than €200 million of private funding were invested for Fos 2 XL (Merlin, 2009).

Furthermore, the existing concession contracts with private operators at the time of the entry into force of the 2008 reform were prorogated and turned into terminal operating agreements. It was the case for the container terminals of Le Havre operated jointly by the leading worldwide shipping lines Maersk, MSC, CMA CGM and the local stevedoring companies TN and GMP, the iron terminal of Dunkirk operated by Arcelor Mittal or the oil terminals of Le Havre-Antifer operated by CIM-CCMP. In addition, the development of logistics platforms established close to ports have attracted international companies and new investments. During the last decade, the Distriport platform next to the container terminals of the port of Marseille-Fos has welcomed large companies, notably Mattel, Danone, Ikea, Maisons du Monde, CEVA, Mediaco Vrac, Daher and XPO Logistics. To conclude, the 2008 law reinforced the relationships between the PAs and the private sector and implicitly encouraged the port managers to become more customer-oriented (Cariou et al., 2014).

## Critical Discussion

The different reforms have enabled a greater liberalisation of port activities and simplified the French port system with two main categories of port (state and decentralised ports). One can conclude that GPMs are henceforth positioned at the same 'standards' as other European ports. Their new sphere of intervention and cooperation allows greater commercial opportunities at national and international level (Gallais-Bouchet, 2013). HAROPA (Le Havre, Rouen, Paris that merged in June 2021), NORLINK (Haut de France ports: Dunkirk, Calais, Boulogne-sur-Mer, Eurotunnel dry port) and MEDLINK (Rhône Saône Mediterranean Ports) illustrate three successful actions of regional port strategies with the aim to pool and rationalise actions both commercially and logistically. At the international level, other cooperations are developing, enabling stronger lobbying and visibility, such as *Intermed Gateway* joining Marseille, Barcelona and Genoa. Nevertheless, some weaknesses remain in particular for the public domain management and the capacity of PAs to set up efficient commercial and financial strategies.

First, it should be stressed that the French traditional key legal principles governing the public domain are still in force and constrain port managers. The current regime of the public port domain jeopardises ports' competitiveness when confronted with fierce competition in a market economy (Naudin, 2013). For instance, private investors are subjected to the 'precariousness principle' of the occupation of publicly owned domain. Furthermore, the urban planning law and the port domain law set out numerous rules that often overlap and the provisions on environmental protection are stricter than those of European neighbours (Rézenthel, 2017). Although the Supreme administrative court recognised that the mission of valorisation of port land by major ports justified the freedom of choice of the land regime (Conseil d'Etat, 2015), the recent decision of the same court that requalified a 'terminal operating agreement' in a 'service concession' (Conseil d'Etat, 2017) indubitably showed a clear resistance to the liberalisation of the port public domain. This decision dealt with the container terminal of the Verdon (GPM of Bordeaux) that faced significant delay in its commissioning and finally led to a loss of traffic. Consequently, this policy of 'port land sanctuary' can have counter-productive effects and lead to a marginalisation of the public domain while it is necessary to promote it today more than ever. In addition, the Supreme administrative court still considers that the port management constitutes a public service (Conseil d'Etat, 2009) in contradiction with the European law (ECJ, 1997, 2003). While the EU Regulation n° 2017/352 establishing a framework for the provision of port services recognises that the Member States are entitled to impose public service obligations to port providers, it is merely an option and not a prerequisite for sinequanon (Fedi & Rézenthel, 2017).

Second, although GPMs are allowed to take equity investments in the capital of companies, they remain specific public shareholders. Pursuant to the Code of Transports, the supervisory board has to approve these participations (acquisition, extension or transfer) since they must comply with the purpose of 'the speciality' of the PA and are not merely speculative. Moreover, this financial strategy must be approved by the *State Agency of Participations* (JORF, 2004b) and when a PA is a major shareholder of companies located in the port area, the PA cannot discriminate in their favour pursuant with EU competition rules. The respect of transparency of State aid regulation and the use of competitive procedures (calls for proposal) must be followed.

To conclude, the current status of GPMs is indubitably hybrid and at an intermediate stage of corporatisation confirmed by the new governance bodies similar to private companies and possible equity investments inside or outside the port limits. Paradoxically, whereas GPMs have an apparent financial autonomy, set up commercial strategies and undertake promotion activities at international level, a close monitoring by the central State remains regarding the budget and the strategic orientations on economic, commercial and environmental aspects. This political intervention also characterises Italian ports and certainly with a higher acuity (Parola et al., 2012, 2017). Finally, the rules applied are still governed by the administrative law and the broad notion of public service subjected to numerous constraints that slow down decision-making.

The successive waves of laws adopted in the last 40 years illustrate clearly the 'atomised' approach of French port governance to the detriment of a more comprehensive policy. Nonetheless, law alone cannot solve everything and obviously these 40 years of reforms have not attracted greater traffic and have not prevented 'a worsening of deindustrialisation processes' (Debrie et al., 2017). According to a recent report of French Court of Auditors: '[...] implementation of provisions are unequal, with high potential costs, the effects on competitiveness have not been forthcoming and new evolutions are necessary. Competitiveness and performance objectives are not satisfied' (2017).

The greatest French port reform has now lasted ten years. Although the new governance model of the GPMs has improved their situation, the rules applied are still rooted in a 'bastion' of conservatism. Notwithstanding some measures of liberalisation, the key principles governing the port public domain and related public service raise difficulties for port managers in the valuation of the port land. The attractiveness of the French ports for foreign investors lies in the right balance between general and particular interests (Rézenthel, 2018). In addition, while the State's investments have progressively declined in the two last decades (Debrie et al., 2017; Lacoste & Douet, 2013), notwithstanding a lack of national port strategy (Court of Auditors, 2017), the public role remains significant in the port governance. The latest modification introduced by the Law on the Blue Economy (JORF, 2016) has indeed strengthened public representation within the GMPs' governance and has implicitly demonstrated that seaports remain strategic infrastructure for the French government that wants to maintain a close monitoring on their daily management.

## Bibliography

Brooks, M. R., & Pallis, A. A. (2012). Port governance. In W. K. Talley (Ed.), *The Blackwell companion to maritime economics* (pp. 491–516). Wiley-Blackwell.

Cariou, P., Dagnet, F., & Fedi, L. (2014). The new governance structure of French seaports: An initial post-evaluation. *Maritime Policy and Management, 41*(5), 430–443.

Conseil d'Etat. (2009). CE, Sect. des travaux publics, 14 avr. 2009, avis n° 382.669, EDCE n°61, *La Documentation Française*, 2010, p. 432.

Conseil d'Etat. (2015). CE, 27 mars 2015, société Nautech c/ Grand port maritime de Marseille, requête 388831.

Conseil d'Etat. (2017). CE 14 fevrier 2017 Grand port maritime de Bordeaux et société SMPA, requête 405157 et 40518. *Droit Maritime Français*:791 460-470, obs. Bordereaux.

Court of Auditors [Cour Des Comptes]. (2006). *Rapport public thématique sur les ports français face aux mutations du transport maritime: l'urgence de l'action.* Juillet 2006, p. 187.

Court of Auditors [Cour Des Comptes]. (2011). *Rapport public annuel de la Cour des Comptes, Tome 2: Le Grand port maritime de Marseille: blocage social et déclin.* February 2011, p. 21.

Court of Auditors [Cour Des Comptes]. (2017). Rapport public annuel 2017. *Le bilan de la réforme des grands ports maritimes : une mise en oeuvre inégale, des effets modestes, une attractivité insuffisante.* février 2017, p. 46.

Dagnet, F. (2010, July 7–9). *The cube: A comprehensive tool for port management*. Paper presented at the IAME Conference, Lisbon, Portugal.

Debrie, J., Gouvernal, E., & Slack, B. (2007, June 24–28). *Downloading public ports: Challenges of governance for lower tiers of public administration.* Paper presented at the WCTR conference 2007, University of California, Berkeley.

Debrie, J., Lacoste, R., & Magnan, M. (2017). From national reforms to local compromises: The evolution of France's model for port management, 2004–2015. *Research in Transportation Business & Management, 22*, 114–122.

Debrie, J., & Lavaud-Letilleul, V. (2010). *La décentralisation portuaire: réformes, acteurs, territoires*. L'Harmattan.

Debrie, J., Lavaud-Letilleul, V., & Parola, F. (2013). Shaping port governance: The territorial trajectories of reform. *Journal of Transport Geography, 27*(2013), 56–65.

ECJ. European Court of Justice. (1997). *Judgment of the Court (Sixth Chamber) of 17 July 1997. GT-Link A/S v De Danske Statsbaner (DSB)* (*European Court Reports 1997 I-04449).*

ECJ. (2003). *Judgment of the Court (Fifth Chamber) of 27 November 2003. Enirisorse SpA v Ministero delle Finanze* (*European Court Reports 2003 I-14243).*

European Commission. (2007). Communication from the Commission on European Ports Policy, Brussels 18 October 2007, COM(2007) 616 final.

European Commission. (2013, May 23). *Europe's Seaports 2030: Challenges Ahead*. Memo 13/448. Brussels.

European Commission. (2014, April 28). *Ports 2030: Gateways for the Trans-European Transport Network*. Directorate General for Mobility and Transport (p. 26).

European Parliament. (2017, March 3). Regulation (EU) 2017/352 of the European parliament and of the Council of 15 February 2017 establishing a framework for the provision of port services and common rules on the financial transparency of ports, OJEU L 57/1.

ESPO. (2016). *European Sea Port Organisation: Trends in EU ports governance* (p. 15).

Fedi, L. (2009). Le régime de la responsabilité de l'opérateur de terminal pétrolier avant la mise en œuvre de la réforme portuaire : perspectives d'évolution [The regime of terminal operator's liability prior to the implementation of the port reform: The outlook of development]. *Droit Maritime Français, 706*, 731–743.

Fedi, L., & Cariou, P. (2015, August 23–26). *Shipping sulphur reduction policy in Europe: An analysis of the 2015 implementation.* In IAME 2015 Conference, Kuala Lumpur, Malaysia.

Fedi, L., Lavissière, A., Russell, D., & Swanson, D. (2019). The facilitating role of IT systems for legal compliance: The case of port community systems and container Verified Gross Mass (VGM). *Supply Chain Forum: An International Journal, 20*(1), 29–42.

Fedi, L., & Pignatel, I. (2011). The governance of ports in mediterranean: Mutations and challenges. In M. Bellalah (Ed.), *6th International finance conference on financial crisis and governance* (pp. 76–90). ISBN (10): 1-4438-3308-8, ISBN (13): 978-1-4438-3308-0.

Fedi, L., & Rézenthel, R. (2007a). *L'exploitation des terminaux portuaires face aux enjeux maritimes du 21ème siècle* [The operation of port terminals confronted to the stakes of the 21st Century]. *Droit Maritime Français,* 685, 828–837.

Fedi, L., & Rézenthel, R. (2007b). Le régime actuel du domaine public maritime portuaire [The current regime of port public domain]. *Droit Maritime Français, 680*, 360–367.
Fedi, L., & Rézenthel, R. (2011). Le droit de grève dans les ports et les terminaux de commerce: Une liberté à utiliser avec modération [The right to strive in ports and terminals: A freedom to use with moderation]. *Droit Maritime Français, 727*, 655–666.
Fedi, L., & Rézenthel, R. (2017). La fourniture de services portuaires et la transparence financière des autorités portuaires [The provision of port services and the financial transparency of port authorities]. *Neptunus, e.revue*, Université de Nantes (vol. 23), 2017/4.
Ferrari, C., & Musso, E. (2011). Italian ports: Towards a new governance. *Maritime Policy and Management, 38*(3), 335–346.
French Maritime Cluster [Cluster Maritime Français]. (2018). L'économie maritime 2018 [*2018 Maritime economy*]. https://www.cluster-maritime.fr/economie_maritime/
Gallais-Bouchet, A. (2013). *La coopération inter-portuaire en Europe : de nouveaux modes de fonctionnement pour quelles strategies?* [Inter-port cooperation in Europe: new types of functioning for what kind of strategies?] Annales IMTM 2013 (pp. 147–152).
Herviaux, O. (2014). Enjeux et perspectives de la réforme de la décentralisation [Stakes and perspectives of decentralisation reform]. Rapport final, 14 mars 2014 (p. 64).
JORF. (1965). Loi n° 65–491 du 29 juin 1965 sur les ports maritimes autonomes, JORF du 30 juin 1965.
JORF. (1983a). Loi n° 83–8 du 7 janvier 1983 relative à la répartition de compétences entre les communes, les départements, les régions et l'Etat, JORF 9 janvier 1983.
JORF. (1983b). Loi n° 83–663 du 22 juillet 1983 complétant la loi n° 83–8 du 7 janvier 1983 relative à la répartition de compétences entre les communes, les départements, les régions et l'Etat, JORF 22 juillet 1983.
JORF. (1992). Loi n°92–496 du 9 juin 1992 modifiant le régime du travail dans les ports maritimes, JORF n°133 du 10 juin 1992 and décret n° 92–1130 du 12 octobre 1992, JORF n° 238 du 13 octobre 1992.
JORF. (1994). Loi n° 94–631 du 25 juillet 1994 complétant le code du domaine de l'Etat et relative à la constitution de droits réels sur le domaine public, JORF 26 juillet 1994.
JORF. (1999). Décret n°99–782 du 9 sept. 1999 modifiant le Code des ports maritimes, JORF du 11 sept. 1999.

JORF. (2004a). Loi n° 2004–809 du 13 août 2004 relative aux libertés et responsabilités locales, JORF n°190 du 17 août 2004.

JORF. (2004b). Décret n°2004–963 du 9 septembre 2004 portant création du service à compétence nationale Agence des participations de l'Etat, JORF du 10 septembre 2004.

JORF. (2004c). Décret n° 2004–1317 du 26 novembre 2004 relatif à l'Agence de financement des infrastructures de transport de France, JORF du 1er décembre 2004, modifié par plusieurs décrets, notamment les décrets n° 2006–894 du 18 juillet 2006, et n° 2012–1247 du 7 novembre 2012.

JORF. (2006). Loi n°2006–10 du 5 janvier 2006 relative à la sécurité et développement des transports, JOFR 6 janvier 2006.

JORF. (2008). Loi n°2008–660 du 4 juillet 2008 portant réforme portuaire, JORF n° 156 du 5 juillet 2008.

JORF. (2012). Loi n°2012–260 du 22 février 2012 portant réforme des ports d'outre-mer relevant de l'Etat et diverses dispositions d'adaptation de la législation au droit de l'Union européenne dans le domaine des transports, JORF n° du 25 février 2012.

JORF. (2015). Loi n° 2015–991 du 7 août 2015 portant nouvelle organisation territoriale de la République, JORF n°0182 du 8 août 2015.

JORF. (2016). Loi n° 2016–816 du 20 juin 2016 pour l'économie bleue, JORF 21 juin 2016.

Lacoste, R., & Douet, M. (2013). The adaptation of the landlord port model tolerance's major seaports: A critical analysis of local solutions. *Maritime Policy and Management, 40*(1), 21–47.

Mahé des Portes, F. (2013). *MGI AP+ Port Community System.* Annales IMTM 2013 (pp. 109–112).

Merk, O., & Comtois, C. (2012). *Competitiveness of port-cities: The case of Marseille Fos–France* (OECD Working paper) http://www.oecd-ilibrary.org/docserver/download/5k8x9b92cnnv.pdf?expires=1359103688&id=id&accname=guest&checksum=E711AF1FF6FC67DC1E3D408A028923F4

Merlin, C. (2009). *Public-private partnerships in the Port of Marseille.* Thesis, Euromed Management (p. 330).

Merlin, C. (2013). *L'outil contractuel majeur en France: La convention de terminal* [The main contractual tool in France: The terminal operating agreement]. Annales IMTM 2013 (pp. 113–130).

Ministry of Ecological Transition. (2020). Données et études statistiques. Chiffres clés du transport - Édition 2020. https://www.statistiques.developpement-durable.gouv.fr/chiffres-cles-du-transport-edition-2020

Naudin, C. (2013). *La domanialité publique portuaire* [The public port ownership]. Annales IMTM 2013 (pp. 141–146).

Notteboom, T. E. (2007). Concession agreements as port governance tools. In: Devolution, port governance and port performance. *Research in Transportation Economics, 17*, 347–455.

Notteboom, T. E., & Winkelmans, W. (2001). Structural changes in logistics: How will port authorities face the challenge? *Maritime Policy and Management, 28*(1), 71–89.

Notteboom, T. E., Verhoeven, P., & Fontanet, M. (2012). Current practices in European ports on the awarding of seaport terminals to private operators: Towards an industry good practice guide. *Maritime Policy and Management, 39*(1), 107–123.

Parola, F., Tei, A., & Ferrari, C. (2012). Managing port concessions: Evidence from Italy. *Maritime Policy and Management, 39*(1), 45–61.

Parola, F., Ferrari, C., Tei, A., Satta, G., & Musso, E. (2017). Dealing with multi-scalar embeddedness and institutional divergence: Evidence from the renovation of Italian port governance. *Research in Transportation Business & Management, 22*, 89–99.

Ports de France. (2016). *Les ports français en 2016: le point, le cap*. By Jacques Trorial (p. 19). http://www.port.fr/sites/default/files/fichiers/2016-11-30-j.trorial_academie_marine_upf.pdf

Port of Marseille. (2018, May). *Global port: Your strategic European gateway on the new Silk Road*. Brochure (p. 17).

Rézenthel, R. (2007). Le partenariat public-privé dans les ports maritimes [The public-private partenrship in seaports]. *La Revue du Trésor*, 252–254.

Rézenthel, R. (2008a, September–October). La création des grands ports maritimes [The creation of major maritime seaports]. *Revue Française de Droit Administratif*, 969–977

Rézenthel, R. (2008). Une nouvelle stratégie pour le développement des grands ports maritimes français [A new strategy for the development of French major maritime seaports]. *Droit Maritime Français, 643*, 1060–1066.

Rézenthel, R. (2010). La convention de terminal portuaire [The terminal operating agreement]. *Droit de la voirie et du domaine public, 146*, 140–143.

Rézenthel, R. (2013). *Le partenariat en matière portuaire* [The partnership in the port field]. Annales IMTM 2013 (pp. 131–140).

Rézenthel, R. (2014). Les projets portuaires à l'épreuve des procedures. Revue Navigation et Industries, Février 1–2.

Rézenthel, R. (2017). L'avenir de la gestion du domaine public portuaire. *Droit de la voirie et du domaine public*, 198, 134–139.

Rézenthel, R. (2018). La réforme portuaire a dix ans [The ten years of the port reform]. *Droit Maritime Français, 804*, 650–658.
Slack, B. (2005, December 12–14). *Terminalisation of ports: An academic question?* Paper presented at The international workshop on new generation of port-cities and their role in global supply chains (pp. 20–30).
Vantorre, F., & Rézenthel, R. (2006). Les sociétés portuaires et aéroportuaires et le droit communautaire [The port and airport firms and the European Law]. *Droit Maritime Français, 672*, 637–644.
Verhoeven, P. (2009). European ports policy: Meeting contemporary governance challenges. *Maritime Policy and Management, 36*(1), 79–101.
Verhoeven, P. (2010). A review of port authority functions: Towards a renaissance? *Maritime Policy and Management, 37*(3), 247–270.
Verhoeven, P. (2011). *European port governance: Report of an inquiry into the current governance of European seaports* (The ESPO Fact-Findings Report). Brussels, Belgium: European Sea Ports Organisation.
Wang, J., Olivier, D., Notteboom, T. E., & Slack, B. (2010). *Ports, cities and global supply chains*. Ashagat.
World Bank. (2007). Port Reform Toolkit PPIAF, World Bank (2nd ed.). https://ppp.worldbank.org/public-private-partnership/library/port
World Bank Port Reform Toolkit. (2013). http://www.ppiaf.org/sites/ppiaf.org/files/documents/toolkits/Portoolkit/Toolkit/index.html

# 13

# Regulation and Finance in the Port Sector: Current Practices in Germany

Michele Acciaro, Lars Stemmler, Katharina Renken, and Jan Christoph Ahting

## Introduction: The German Port System

Germany is the largest economy in Europe and the fourth largest economy globally. Notwithstanding some economic difficulties in the last part of 2018 and early 2019, German manufacturing is a major driver of the country's economic performance, represented in particular by its global position in the automotive industry, but also in exports of

M. Acciaro (✉) · K. Renken
Hapag-Lloyd Center for Shipping and Global Logistics, Kühne Logistics University gGmbH, Hamburg, Germany
e-mail: michele.acciaro@the-klu.org

L. Stemmler
bremenports GmbH & Co. KG, Bremen, Germany

J. C. Ahting
University of Naples "Parthenope", Naples, Italy

© The Author(s), under exclusive license to Springer Nature Switzerland AG 2022
C. Ferrari et al. (eds.), *Regulation and Finance in the Port Industry*, Palgrave Studies in Maritime Economics,
https://doi.org/10.1007/978-3-030-83985-7_13

chemicals, machinery and household equipment. As a major industrialized country, Germany's prosperity depends, among other things, on global trade and the German economy relies on a highly developed logistics industry. The World Bank Logistics performance index for Germany is the highest globally (at 4.20 in 2018), while the UNCTAD Liner Shipping Connectivity Index for Germany, and indicator of the degree of maritime connectivity of a country, is among the highest globally and it increased from 76.6 in 2004 to 97.1 in 2018. Logistics and transport are important enablers to the German economic powerhouse.

Germany benefits also from a highly developed infrastructure network, of which ports are a critical component. While German manufactures can also make use of ports located in other countries, primarily in the Netherlands, but also Belgium, Slovenia and Italy, the large portion of overseas export transit through the seaports on the North Sea and the Baltic Sea. Germany is a Federal Country and ports are located in the five northern coastal states (or *Bundesländer*, in German, plural of the German word *Bundesland* = federation member state). Two of the coastal states are the port city-states of Hamburg, the largest port in Germany and the third largest in Europe, and Bremen, that includes the coastal exclave of Bremerhaven. Similarly, to the main ports in Belgium and the Netherlands, the two largest ports in Germany, Hamburg and Bremen are located upstream the river Elbe and Weser, respectively, although in the case of Bremen, considerable activities have shifted downstream to the jointly managed port of Bremerhaven.

German ports are divided between the North Sea and the Baltic Sea coast, with the largest ports facing the North Sea. In addition to Hamburg, and Bremen/Bremerhaven already mentioned, the other larger North Sea ports are located in Lower Saxony (Wilhelmshaven and Cuxhaven), while the main ports in Schleswig–Holstein (Lübeck and Kiel) are on the Baltic Sea. The other main German ports on the Baltic are in Mecklenburg West-Pomerania (Rostock, Wismar and Sassnitz) and went through various waves of reform after the reunification of Germany in 1990 (Fig. 13.1).

In terms of throughput the largest German ports are Hamburg and Bremen/Bremerhaven followed by Wilhelmshaven, Rostock and Lübeck (Table 13.1). In 2017, according to the German national statistics,

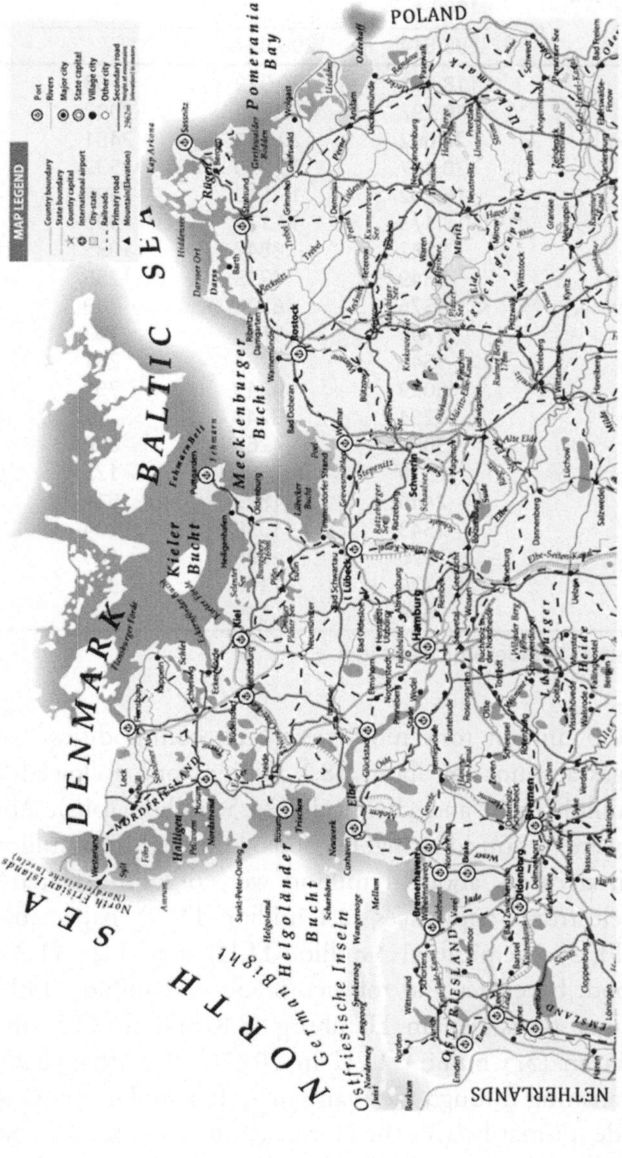


Fig. 13.1 German ports (*Source* Authors)

**Table 13.1** Throughput German ports (2017–2016, million tons and percentage)

| | 2017 | 2016 | Change | |
|---|---|---|---|---|
| | 1000 t | | | % |
| Total | 299,514 | 296,347 | 3167 | 1.1 |
| Hamburg | 118,761 | 120,319 | −1558 | −1.3 |
| Bremerhaven | 49,292 | 52,294 | −3002 | −5.7 |
| Wilhelmshaven | 22,662 | 20,181 | 2481 | 12.3 |
| Rostock | 20,427 | 20,959 | −532 | −2.5 |
| Lübeck | 16,202 | 15,510 | 692 | 4.5 |
| Bremen | 13,173 | 12,174 | 999 | 8.2 |
| Brunsbüttel | 9882 | 8847 | 1035 | 11.7 |
| JadeWeserPort | 5549 | 4293 | 1255 | 29.2 |
| Brake (Unterweser) | 5575 | 6324 | −749 | −11.8 |
| Stade | 5796 | 5633 | 163 | 2.9 |
| Fehmarn | 5545 | 5284 | 261 | 4.9 |
| Emden | 5039 | 4249 | 790 | 18.6 |
| Wismar | 3254 | 3243 | 11 | 0.3 |
| Kiel | 5063 | 4263 | 800 | 18.8 |
| Cuxhaven | 2510 | 2685 | −175 | −6.5 |
| Nordenham | 2446 | 1827 | 619 | 33.9 |
| Sassnitz | 1543 | 1339 | 204 | 15.2 |
| Stralsund | 970 | 865 | 105 | 12.2 |
| Duisburg | 770 | 1107 | −337 | −30.4 |
| Brünzow | 468 | 599 | −130 | −21.8 |

*Source* Statistisches Bundesamt (Destatis)

out of the 300 million tons most were bulk commodities. Coal, oil and natural gas account for about 38.1 million tons, followed by iron ores (33.2 million tons) and chemicals (24.5 million tons). About 74 million tons were of non-identifiable goods. Out of the 15 million TEU of containerized cargo, about 4 million were of non-declared goods, followed by electronic appliances (2.1 million TEU), paper and wood (1.6 million TEU), chemicals (1.3 million TEU), machinery (1.2 million TEU) and food, beverages and tobacco (about 1.1 million TEU). The largest container ports remain Hamburg (8.8 million TEU in 2017) and Bremerhaven (5.5 million TEU in 2017). More than half of the total cargo transiting through German ports (171 million tons) is intra-European trade, primarily with the Nordic countries (75.4 million tons), Russia (27 million tons) and the United Kingdom (17.8 million tons).

The rest is trade with Asia (56 million tons, of which 22 million with China), followed by the USA (16.5 million tons) and South America (16.1 million tons). German ports also registered about 30.8 million passengers (excluding cruise passenger visits) in 2017, primarily through the Fehmarn link to Denmark (5.9 million in 2017), but also Rostock (3.1 million in 2017), Kiel (2.1 Million) and the linkages with the East Frisian Islands (most notably Norden and Norderney with 2.6 million and 2.3 million passengers yearly, respectively).

Given the high level of devolution in Germany, the German port system is regulated differently in the five coastal *Bundesländer*, and as such the governance and financing structure of the ports differs substantially from port to port. In most ports a mixture of public and private actors are involved in the operations and management of the port, with a considerable involvement of the private sector in cargo handling operations and a critical role for the public sector in the management and development of port infrastructure. The governance of German ports can be subsumed under the "landlord" model, i.e., basic infrastructure is provided by the public sector, part of which is then leased to the private sector in exchange for a concession fee. The private sector in most cases is also responsible for providing superstructure and equipment and is the main employer of most of the workforce.

Within this simple setup German ports differ considerably to the degree of private sector involvement at least for two reasons. Firstly, port administrations have been gradually transformed or corporatized through the creation of port authorities' and port managing companies. Secondly, port activities have been gradually divested by transferring the ownership of port handling companies to private forms of organization. These processes resulted in a diverse set of governance structures among German ports that overlaid on the already different *Bundesland* port laws and are the result of different priorities set by local governments and citizens during the privatization processes. The process of privatization has been generally accompanied by political disagreement and labor disputes, and, similarly to other countries, was motivated by the limited financial means of most *Bundesländer* and increasing competitive pressure, both within Germany and from other European ports.

Similarly, to other European countries, there is no legal limitation to the degree of privatization for port cargo handling companies that can be achieved in Germany, if the public entity owning them has the willingness to sell them. So, fully private terminal operators coexist next to partially public ones, while in some ports, port authorities still carry out terminal handling operations directly. The largest terminals, however, even when controlled by the public sector are incorporated as private companies and part of their shares are owned by private investors.

## Port Finance in Germany

The overall framework for port financing is regulated in Germany by the Maritime Responsibility Act (*Seeaufgabengesetz*),[1] which defines responsibilities between the Federal Government and the Länder involved. Further provisions are made in the policy paper, *Joint Platform of the Federal Government and the Coastal States on German Seaport Policy*,[2] which defines that the responsibilities for port financing are shared among the Federal Government, the *Bundesländer* and the users, with the public entities acting within the framework of services of general public interest. This has been interpreted so that the Federal Government takes responsibility for the seaways and hinterland connections, most notably large part of the dredging of the river access to the ports of Hamburg and Bremen. The *Bundesland* has responsibility for the construction and maintenance of the basic port infrastructure, while the users are responsible for the construction and operation of the superstructure and equipment. Private companies can participate in port financing as there are no specific laws preventing access to private capital in port infrastructure financing.

[1] Seeaufgabengesetz (Maritime Responsibilities Act) in the version promulgated on 17 June 2016 (Federal Law Gazette I p. 1489), last amended by Article 3 of the Act of 30 June 2017 (Federal Law Gazette I p. 2190).

[2] Gemeinsame Plattform des Bundes und der Küstenländer zur deutschen Seehafenpolitik by Federal Ministry of Transport and Digital Infrastructure (1999).

German ports, even if entirely or partially controlled by the public sector, operate as private companies and show primarily four different ownership models:

- Ports owned by a *Bundesland* that largely or entirely coincides with a Municipality, such as Hamburg and Bremen;
- Ports owned by a Municipality, such as Kiel and Lübeck;
- Ports owned by a *Bundesland*, such as Wilhelmshaven or Emden;
- Ports owned by a limited liability company, such as Wismar or Rostock;
- Ports owned by a private company where the state has no share, such as Nordenham and Brunsbüttel and the Puttgarden ferry port owned by Scandlines.

In most of the German ports, the public sector is responsible for port administration, while port services are provided by private companies that have been the result of privatization of former public port handling companies. This implies that in any case port superstructure and equipment are financed exclusively by the operating companies. It should also be noted that until recently port administration did not have their own budgets for infrastructure investments and also no profit-loss account. These were provided ad hoc by the respective public authorities that had to be decided by the respective state parliaments.

A specific characteristic of the German system is the allocation of funds made possible by the "*Länderfinanzausgleich*" (LFA), a financial tool devised to reduce inequality among *Budesländer* and that allowed the coastal states to receive annual financial support by the other members of the federation for building and maintaining the port infrastructure from which also the other state benefit. The system has been extensively criticized and it is the subject of an acrimonious political debate in anticipation of its re-evaluation in 2020.

Given the importance of ports for the competitiveness of Germany, the federal government developed and published in 2016 its *National*

*Strategy for Sea and Inland Ports 2015*,[3] which expanded the first strategy published in 2009. The document outlines 155 measures aimed at strengthening the position of German ports by:

- Developing port infrastructure to meet the country's needs;
- Increasing the competitiveness of ports, promoting collaboration in a network perspective;
- Contributing and shaping proactively European and international port policy;
- Protecting the environment and reducing impacts on the climate;
- Promoting the use of alternative fuels and offshore wind energy;
- Continuing to secure qualified training and good jobs in the ports;
- Ensuring adequate safety and security;
- Improving port policy coordination.

The Strategy aims at strengthening coordination at a federal level in terms of port infrastructure development and planning, that is primarily the responsibility of individual *Länder*, although in recent years, demands have been advanced to provide federal funding for supporting offshore wind projects, LNG refueling points and onshore power supply installations. Furthermore, port investment needs to be coordinated with federal infrastructure development projects that make a contribution to strengthening the links to and from the hinterland of the ports. In particular, agreement was reached among the transport ministers of the *Bundesländer* on two lists of 60 strategic rail, road and inland waterway projects ("Ahrensburg List" and "Düsseldorf List") that would strengthen the connectivity among German ports and northern German States, and in general among ports and the rest of the Country.

[3] *Nationales Hafenkonzept für die See- und Binnenhäfen 2015* by Federal Ministry of Transport and Digital Infrastructur.

## Governance and Financing Examples of German Ports

In what follows, an overview of the structure of ports in the five coastal states will be discussed, with particular attention to the larger ports in each coastal *Bundesland*.

From the Table 13.2, it is evident that governance and ownership models in Germany vary from port to port, with the largest ports managed through companies controlled either by the municipalities or the *Bundesland* (when the two do not coincide) or a mixture of the two. Smaller ports are managed by a mix of public and private entities.

### Port of Hamburg

The largest port in Germany is the Port of Hamburg, a multipurpose port that is managed by the Hamburg Port Authority (HPA). The Port of Hamburg is among the top 20 container ports globally and the third in Europe after Rotterdam and Antwerp, with a throughput just about nine million TEU. The port overall throughput has remained stable in the last decade just below 140 million tons, with a slight imbalance on imports over exports. About 45 million tons are bulk commodities, primarily dry bulk, while containers are the largest share of the total port throughput at just below 90 million tons. The largest part of container traffic (61.8%) is gateway traffic and 38.2% transshipment. The port modal split favors truck over rail, but the port has one of the highest percentage globally of rail hinterland transportation (42%) and a minimal part of river traffic (2.2%).

Port operations are carried out by private companies, who rent out space provided by HPA. Given the importance of container transport, two major container operators are active in Hamburg: *Hamburger Hafen- und Logistik AG* (HHLA) and *EUROGATE Container Terminal Hamburg GmbH*, entirely controlled by the Eurogate Group. HHLA controls three container terminals (Tollerort, Altenwerder and Burchardkai) and a variety of other activities, primarily intermodal transport and logistics. HHLA has been listed on the stock

**Table 13.2** Representative examples of governance in German ports

| Port examples | Coastal state | Governance | Control of port managing company |
|---|---|---|---|
| Hamburg | Hamburg | Landlord | Free and Hanseatic City of Hamburg (100%) |
| Bremen and Bremerhaven | Bremen | Landlord | Free and Hanseatic City of Bremen (100%) |
| JadeWeserPort | Lower Saxony | Landlord | State of Lower Saxony (50.1%), Free and Hanseatic City of Bremen (49.9%) |
| Norden, Emden, Cuxhaven, Brake and others (joint management) | Lower Saxony | Landlord/Tool port | State of Lower Saxony (100%) |
| Nordenham | Lower Saxony | Private | Private (Rhenus Midgard GmbH & Co. KG, 100%) |
| Oldenburg, Papenburg, Leer and other ports | Lower Saxony | Public | Managed by respective municipalities through the Association of Public Inland Harbours (Bundesverband Öffentlicher Binnenhäfen e.V.) |
| Kiel | Schleswig–Holstein | Landlord | State Capital City of Kiel (100%) which also one of the operators in the port |
| Brunsbüttel, Glückstadt, Rendsburg | Schleswig–Holstein | Private | Private (SCHRAMM Ports & Logistics Sweden AB, 100%) |

(continued)

**Table 13.2** (continued)

| Port examples | Coastal state | Governance | Control of port managing company |
|---|---|---|---|
| Lübeck | Schleswig–Holstein | Landlord | Hanseatic City of Lübeck (62.5%); Private (RREEF Pan-European Infrastructure Two Lux S.a.r.l., 37.5%) |
| Puttgarden | Schleswig–Holstein | Private | Private (Scandlines Deutschland GmbH, 100%) |
| Rostock | Mecklenburg West-Pomerania | Landlord | State of Mecklenburg West-Pomerania (25.1%) and Hanseatic City of Rostock (74.9%) |
| Wismar, Sassnitz | Mecklenburg West-Pomerania | Landlord | State of Mecklenburg West-Pomerania (10%) and respective Cities (90%) |
| Stralsund | Mecklenburg West-Pomerania | Landlord | Hanseatic City of Stralsund, though SWS Stadwerke Stralsund GmbH (100%) |

*Source* Compiled by the authors on various sources

exchange since November 2007 and is 68% owned by the Hanseatic City of Hamburg through the HGV (*Hamburger Gesellschaft für Vermögens- und Beteiligungsmanagement GmbH*). The remaining 32% are in free float, of which 9% are private investors and 23% institutional investors. Part of the publicly held shares (Class S), relate to real estate and in particular historical building and urban redevelopment projects. In addition, one of HHLA's three container terminals in the Port of Hamburg, the Altenwerder Terminal, is operated as a joint project between HHLA and Hapag-Lloyd who has a share of 25.1%.

Until 2005 the Port of Hamburg was exclusive responsibility of the Senate (i.e., the Hamburg State Parliament) that, following the port law of 1971 and amended in 1982, had the duty to maintain port infrastructure, ensure nautical safety, act as port regulator and manage and rent port areas. These responsibilities were shared between the Ministry of Economic and Labor Affairs (BWA) and the Ministry of Finance. In November 2004, the Hamburg Senate, decided that in the following year, the public administrations with port responsibility would be merged to create a separate legal entity with own budget resources. The objective of the reform was the application of business principles, increasing organizational efficiency and higher flexibility, so that also other sources of funding could be obtained. The Hamburg Port Authority was created on 1st October 2005 as a public corporation (*Anstalt des öffentlichen Rechts* or *AöR*) and is managed according to commercial principles. Employees, land as well as public functions were transferred to the newly created Authority. It should be noted in particular provisions of the Port Development Act of 1982 prevent port land from being sold.

In 2008 following the HPA 2010 project, the company was restructured to improve management activities and eliminated outdated administrative structures. Today, HPA has around 1800 employees. It is envisaged that the HPA will finance the operation of the port infrastructure solely with income from the port industry. In recent years an increasing distinction has been made between commercial and public functions. In 2017 total capital expenditure by the HPA was € 174.7 million, almost 20% lower than in the previous year. Of this amount, € 111.9 million was attributable to the commercial business segment and € 56.3 million to the public business segment.

It is important to observe that HPA does not carry out container loading and unloading activities that are entrusted with the *Hamburger Hafen und Logistik AG* (HHLA), also owned by the city. HHLA is the largest terminal operator in the Port of Hamburg and offers integrated logistics services, hinterland rail freight transport and advisory services through Hamburg Port Consulting. As of 2018, the Free and

Hanseatic City of Hamburg still held 68% of the HHLA shares (the remaining 32% are in free float). The free float is divided between 9% private investors and 23% institutional investors. Terminal operations were assigned to HHLA already in 1971, but the company was thoroughly restructured in 2003 in four segments container handling, intermodal, logistics and real estate.

The reorganization in 2003 was the result of the desire to expand the activities of the company and originally the Hamburg Senate allowed for the partial sale of up to 74.9% of the company share. The port at the time had foreseen an expansion plan with the construction of a new terminal for a total of € 2.25 billion. The plan announced in 2006, would have allowed a private investor to acquire up to 49.9% of the shares of the company and was well received with over 100 international companies expressing interest (including Macquarie Bank, Dubai Ports and Deutsche Bahn). The project, however, was abandoned following criticism from the workers' union and a stark opposition by the public.[4]

The workers' union threatened to strike potentially paralyzing the port and the Hamburg Senate decided in 2007 to sell only up to 30% of the shares held by the city on the stock exchange. Some of the shares were reserved for small investors and generated about € 1.2 billion. The construction of the new terminal in Steinwerder was then abandoned and the area used for cruise vessels. HHLA pursued further diversification after acquiring a terminal in Odessa in 2001 that was expanded in 2005 and HHLA TK Estonia AS, that was acquired in 1996. The group also has a variety of other activities, from container repair, to bulk operations (Hansaport), fruit handling (HHLA Frucht) and rail connections (e.g., METRANS). The Steinwerder project was revamped in 2017 following an international competition for ideas, where China Communications Construction Company (CCCC) proposed the construction

[4] Federal Ministry of Transport and Digital Infrastructure (BMVI), *Hafenprivatisierung in Deutschland*, Research Information System (FIS) published by the Federal Ministry of Transport and Digital Infrastructure, https://www.forschungsinformationssystem.de/servlet/is/252887/ page created on: 22-02-2008 and last updated on the 06-09-2018.

of a new container terminal in the area. Again, stark public opposition seems to have stalled the potential investment.[5]

## The Ports of Bremen and Bremerhaven

The Ports of Bremen and Bremerhaven form the second largest port group in Germany and are among the most important European transshipment and gateway ports. Annually, around 6000 ships deliver and collect approximately 66 million tons of cargo (2020). The Free Hanseatic City of Bremen as landlord and competent authority, together with bremenports, the infrastructure manager, provides for capable marine infrastructure and, thus, ensures efficient maritime logistics via both ports.

Under Articles 30, 70 and 74 of the German constitution, the federal states are responsible for port development and port finance under predominantly landlord-port models.[6] Each federal state has established its own legislative framework for this. Bremen set up three legal entities to manage its port-related obligations. Those entities include the port infrastructure, bremenports GmbH & Co. KG (bremenports) as managing body of the infrastructure and the port authority. In addition, there are several private companies that provide essential ancillary services, such as pilotage and tugging to the port community.

The port-related long-term assets, such as locks, quay walls as well as rail and road access links, are held in public conduits which are at the same time separate from the budget and part of it. Those conduits are separate as they require individual accounting; they are part of the public budget as they are financed by the former out of the general budget of

[5] Louppova, J. 2017, Chinese consortium to build new container terminal in Hamburg? in port.today, https://port.today/cccc-builds-container-terminal-hamburg/posted posted 21-07-2017 and accessed 26-03-2019.

[6] There are just a few privately run ports, such as Puttgarden, Brunsbüttel and Nordenham. Although in the latter two the infrastructure is privately run by the terminal operator, there are public transfers towards the costs of maintaining the infrastructure. Furthermore, in Brake, the public infrastructure manager provides cranes and crane-drivers to the terminal operators, effectively turning the port into a tool port.

the federal state. Income generated by those assets, such as harbor dues or lease rentals for real estate, is accrued towards those conduits.

Bremen continuously invests in maintaining and expanding the port infrastructure to meet the needs of the maritime industry. However, the Ports of Bremen and Bremerhaven provide maritime logistics and infrastructural services which benefits go beyond the city limits. Other federal states enjoy avid exporters which send their goods via Bremen and Bremerhaven. Nevertheless, Bremen bears port development costs which those other especially land-locked, German states do not. As such, a functioning port infrastructure is in the interest of all German states. To compensate Bremen for this, all German federal states run a pooling arrangement, whereby Bremen is entitled to a financial allowance towards the ports out of this pool.

The landlord-port structure foresees that publicly owned land is rented out to private parties. This is also the case for Bremen and Bremerhaven. Plots are rented out to terminal operators, logistics services providers and the like under long-term land lease agreements. Those agreements normally stipulate that the lessee is responsible for providing the required logistics suprastructure. In Bremen, this amounts to all immovable assets up and including the pavement of the land, plus of course providing for all mobile equipment.

In the Ports of Bremen and Bremerhaven, several terminal operators provide services for containerized logistics as well as for the break-bulk, bulk and roll-on/roll-off segments. The most important ones are the BLG Logistics Group, Rhenus, Eurogate, North Sea Terminals and MSC Gate. Although some of them are, at least in part, state-owned, cargo handling and logistics are completely formally a private matter.

Back in 1877, when the first artificial harbor installations started to emerge in Bremen, local cotton merchants decided to jointly establish the "Bremer Lagerhaus Gesellschaft (BLG)" (Bremen warehousing company), which later became the BLG Logistics Group, to make the most of the newly built common-user port infrastructure by being able to issue storage warrants to its members. Consequently, the senate of the city assigned all port operations obligations to the BLG.

The marine infrastructures as well as the land leases are managed by bremenports GmbH & Co. KG. It is 100% owned by the Free

Hanseatic City of Bremen. Some 400 staff at bremenports are responsible for the development, operation, maintenance and repair of the complex public port infrastructure. In accordance with local laws the company is tasked with managing the public port conduits. bremenports maintains close contact with the shipping and logistics industries to ensure that port development in Bremen is systematically planned to meet demand. Experts of bremenports plan and implement construction projects such as Container Terminal 4 (completed in 2008) and Kaiserschleuse lock (2011) to ensure that the world port on the Weser is fit to cope with future requirements. Tasks also include international marketing activities for the Ports of Bremen and Bremerhaven.

Bremenports is also assigned with collecting the harbor dues from vessel agents. Those statutory fees apply for using the public areas of the port only. In addition, private handling charges apply as well as charges for obtaining pilots, tug boats and longshore men.

The company has managed the port infrastructure in Bremen and Bremerhaven on behalf of the Free Hanseatic City of Bremen since January 2002. At that time, bremenports was formally privatized into a private legal form in order to become more flexible and to offer infrastructure management and consulting services to clients outside of the port. Organizing bremenports in the legal form of a "GmbH & Co. KG"—a limited commercial partnership with a limited liability company as a general partner—was a milestone in the history of port management in Germany: the company is a powerful and flexible provider of public infrastructure with a clear focus on economic efficiency.

Statutory tasks of running a large international port, such as ensuring safety and security, immigration and health checks as well as vessel management in all harbor areas, are assigned to a dedicated port authority with the Harbormaster as its head, which is an independent public body from bremenports. In practice, experts of bremenports and the port authority work literally side-by-side, for example, when operating the five large sea locks of the ports.

The constitutional assignment of port responsibilities to the federal states dates back to the times of the Hanseatic Leagues, when cities like Bremen and Lübeck played a major role in this merchant´s union. At that time, Hanseatic cities established their own legislative power directly under the German emperor. Even the chaotic aftermath of WWII did not change this; moreover, the Americans insisted on its own port within the British-held territory in northern Germany, effectively carving out today's Bremen and Bremerhaven from neighboring Lower Saxony.

## Ports in Lower Saxony, and JadeWeserPort

The most important ports in Lower Saxony are owned by Niedersachsen Ports GmbH & Co. KG, a 100% state company that emerged in January 2005 from the former Port and Shipping Administration of the State of Lower Saxony. The state has transferred 15 state-owned ports to the company. It is responsible for the construction, maintenance and operation of the port system. Other public seaports in Lower Saxony are owned by the respective municipalities (Oldenburg, Papenburg and Leer) or by private companies (Nordenham).

*Niedersachsen Ports GmbH & Co. KG* (NPorts) with its main office in Oldenburg was founded in 2005 by the State of Niedersachsen (Lower Saxony). The state of Lower Saxony is since then the owner of this group combining 15 ports in Lower Saxony under one roof, both as a limited partner and as sole shareholder of the general partner GmbH. The company consists of a supervisory board and a shareholder meeting. The shareholder meeting is manned and provided by the Ministry of Finance of the State of Lower Saxony.

The 15 ports have been independent before the founding of the federally owned company, but have been themselves owned by the federal government. Now, the 15 ports have a common organization and share supporting departments such as the central controlling, a central human resources department and other administration (Niedersachsen Ports GmbH & Co. KG).

Each port, as they have been independent actors beforehand, has its own history. The bigger ports in this group are:

- the port of Norden (established around the year 1200),
- the port of Emden (established around the year 800),
- the port of Wilhelmshaven (established around the year 1860),

- the port of Brake (established in the midst of 1700), and
- the port of Cuxhaven (established around 1900) with
- the port of Stade (early forerunners of a port since the year 650).

Within this network, the ports have not only a diverse history but are also specialized in certain logistical tasks. From the location in Norden, the island traffics are managed, which on average transport more than nine million passengers each year. The port of Emden mainly serves RoRo ships providing facilities and storage space for the export of cars, while also playing a significant role in the wind energy market. The ports at Wilhelmshaven provide deep waters, handling crude oil, petroleum products, coal and chemical products at its outer port among other products on its premises. At the port of Brake, feedstock, grains and forestry products as well as steel and iron are handled. Handling of steel products is also a main competence in the port of Cuxhaven, in combination with RoRo traffic and the traditional role as fishing port. In Stade, situated between Hamburg and Cuxhaven, handling and storage of bulk and general cargo are the main activities (Niedersachsen Ports GmbH & Co. KG). Currently, a combined number of 700 employees work at the 15 ports, with a total length of quay wall of 26 km and 79 km in rail network. Forty thousand ships called the ports in the year 2016 with more than nine million passengers and almost 25 million tons handling volume. Niedersachsen Ports usually owns the land, the quay and other infrastructure, as well as cranes and other moving equipment in some ports. However, terminal operators often own parts or all of the cranes and storage facilities themselves.

A novelty in Lower Saxony was established with the JadeWeserPort located by the deep seawaters in Wilhelmshaven, as this green field project opening in 2012 was founded and financed jointly between the State of Lower Saxony (share 50.1%) and the City-State Bremen (share 49.9%) (Container Terminal Wilhelmshaven JadeWeserPort-Marketing GmbH & Co. KG). Mainly containers are imported and exported here, but there have also been some wind energy modules and other project cargo crossing this quay with a length of 1725 meters. The infrastructure, streets and land, are managed, maintained and owned by the landlord. As terminal operator, *EUROGATE Container Terminal Wilhelmshaven*

*GmbH & Co. KG* owns the superstructures, such as cranes and straddle carriers.

In all 15 ports in Lower Saxony plus the JadeWeserPort, the terminal operator has long-term leases for the quay and yard and pays a fee. Visiting ships pay a demurrage charge additionally where required. As most ports in Lower Saxony are owned by publicly owned companies, port planning is conducted by government entities. Budget plans involve maintenance and expansion projects where extensive pre-planning is often involved. Typically, port operators, which are generally privately owned companies, voice their expansion needs to the port managing companies. In some cases, where business development has been entrusted with specific companies, such as *Wilhelmshavener Hafenwirtschafts-Vereinigung* (WHV), it is these entities that lead the local infrastructure development process, as exemplified by the JadeWeserPort case.

Planning procedures take long and are unpredictable. Especially, as environmental aspects of each project are taken into account very seriously. The government mostly executes the port projects, as they are of infrastructural nature. Investments from the private sector usually address superstructure.

## Ports in Schleswig–Holstein: Lübeck and Kiel

The large ports in Schleswig–Holstein are managed by municipalities and the *Bundesland* has largely withdrawn from ownership and responsibility for the ports. There are several ports in the State, including Büsum, Husum, Flensburg, Kiel, Lübeck and Rendsburg on the Kiel Canal (*Nord-Ostsee-Kanal*). Some of the smaller ports are privatized, including Brunsbüttel, Glückstadt and Rendsburg, which are controlled by *SCHRAMM group GmbH & Co. KG*. Among those the largest ports are Lübeck that is Germany's largest port operator on the Baltic Sea, and Kiel, that is an important passenger hub. The private passenger port of Puttgarden is the largest ferry port in Germany with over seven million passengers and is located on the German side of the *Fehmarnbelt* and is owned by Scandlines, as a result of the privatization of the ferry activities of the *Deutsche Reichsbahn* und *Deutsche Bundesbahn*, that were then merged with the Danish ferry operator to create Scandlines.

The port of Lübeck handled over 16 million tons of cargo and its terminal facilities are operated primarily by the *Lübecker Hafen-Gesellschaft mbH* (LHG). LHG ownership is shared between the Hanseatic City of Lübeck and the private *RREEF Pan-European Infrastructure Two Lux S.a.r.l*, a subsidiary of Deutsche Bank. The process of privatization of LHG started in 2001, but negotiation procedures for more substantial privatization were initiated in 2006. The municipal government was willing to sell up to 90% of the company, but the LHG employees opposed the sale and threatened strike action. As a compromise initially only 25.1% were sold for €30 million. Today the Hanseatic City of Lübeck owns 62.5% of LHG and RREEF 37.5%. LHG, which was founded in 1934, also controls the *European Cargo Logistics GmbH*, a large forest product distributor and third-party logistics service provider and *Lübeck Distribution Gesellschaft mbH*, that handles bulk cargo.

The port of Kiel is an important passenger port with about 2.1 million passengers yearly. The port is owned and operated by the State Capital City of Kiel that is the sole shareholder of the *Seehafen Kiel GmbH & Co. KG.* that carries out the stevedoring activities, and 33.33% of the *Seehafen Kiel Cruise GmbH & Co. KG* that deals with the cruise ship handling. The city also controls the airport.

## Ports in Mecklenburg West-Pomerania: Port of Rostock

The ports of Mecklenburg—West-Pomerania are in municipal and private ownership with state interests in the ports of Rostock, Wismar and Sassnitz. The port of Rostock is Germany's fourth largest sea port by cargo volume. It is the largest universal port and the only deep-water port on the German Baltic Sea coast. It is located in a sheltered location at the mouth of the river Warnow into the Baltic Sea. The sea channel passage takes 3.6 km with a draught of 14.5 m. These conditions allow maximum ship dimensions of 300 m length, 45 m width and 13 m draught. A deepening of the sea channel at 16.5 m is planned for the future.

With an area of 750 ha, Rostock is the largest German Baltic Sea port. On more than 11 km of quay, 47 berths are available. The port railway consists of a marshaling yard with a track length of about 180 km. In addition, there are another 54 km of tracks on the port area by which the ship berths and plants are directly accessible. About 20% of all goods handled are transported in and out by rail.

With an estimated 205 ship calls in the year 2018, Rostock-Warnemünde is one of the major German cruise ports. Recording 766,000 passengers in 2016, it ranked 13th among the busiest European cruise ports.[7] Warnemünde Cruise Center is able to accommodate three cruise ships simultaneously. Additional cruise ships can be berthed at the ferry terminal in the sea port.

During the times of the former German Democratic Republic (GDR), the port of Rostock was organized as a nationally owned company, the *VEB Seehafen Rostock*. It was thus completely under state control in form of the Minister of Transportation. A so-called "Kombinat," which is comparable to a corporation, centralized the marine and port management for all marine and port companies. Within the centralized economic system of the GDR, the port of Rostock served as the central maritime import–export hub and found itself in a monopolistic situation.[8]

Shortly before German reunification the VEB underwent a harsh adaptation process from a shift of a centralized economy towards free-market economy. During this process the VEB was converted into a public limited company in May 1990. A year later it became the "Seehafen Rostock GmbH." In 1994, responsibilities were split between two new and independent companies:

[7] https://www.cruisetricks.de/die-groessten-kreuzfahrt-haefen-weltweit-in-der-karibik-und-in-europa/.

[8] Prause (2010, p. 372).

1. The *Seehafen Rostock Verwaltungsgesellschaft*, which operated later on under the name *Hafenentwicklungsgesellschaft Rostock mbH* (HERO) and which is since 2017 officially called *Rostock Port GmbH*, and
2. The *Seehafen Rostock Umschlagsgesellschaft* (SHRU), which is now called *Euroports Germany GmbH & Co. KG.*[9]

Nowadays, the Federal State of Mecklenburg West-Pomerania and the Hanseatic City of Rostock are the owners of the port of Rostock. Their interests are represented by the infrastructure/port development company Rostock Port GmbH with a 25.1% share on behalf of the Federal State of Mecklenburg West-Pomerania and a 74.9% share of the Hanseatic City of Rostock.

As the owner of the infrastructure and platform for all port companies, Rostock Port GmbH holds the status of a landlord port authority under private law. Its principal tasks are:

- Administration, development and maintenance of port infrastructure
- Lease of land and the rental of real estate for new settlements in the commercial area "Seaport Rostock"
- Provision of services and utilities
- Location marketing

The company is certified according to ISO 9001 and 14,001. It is committed to being competitively neutral to all companies operating in the "Seaport Rostock." Rostock Port GmbH owns the land, the quays and water surfaces in the sea port. Rostock Port GmbH acts as the sole operator of the ferry terminal at the sea port and the cruise terminal at the seaside district of Warnemünde. In addition, it is a shareholder of the operating company for combined freight transport. In order to strengthen its competitive position, Rostock Port GmbH may establish, acquire or have a share in companies, establish, acquire or lease auxiliary companies and open branch offices. As far as these are cargo handling services or storage activities/treatment of goods, the company

[9] Holst and Wolf (2018, p. 34).

may neither engage in this activity by itself nor may it own a majority share in a company engaging in such kind of activities.

Besides Rostock Port GmbH, there is another part of operators at the sea port. These are logistics companies and port service providers who care for handling, distribution and storage of goods. They are 100% privately owned and act independently from the infrastructure company Rostock Port GmbH.

In addition to the sea port, there are additional port sites. These are the chemical port, the cargo and fishery port, the city harbor, the industrial port of the metal company *Alba Metall Nord GmbH* as well as the two maritime industrial areas *MAGEB Süd* and *MAGEB Nord* close to the Warnemünde shipyards.

The port is the economic center of Rostock with more than 150 companies from the sectors "port economy," "shipping" and other industrial sectors. In the area the number of employees which are directly and indirectly employed by the port economy amounts to about 16,000 (status as of 2013). The biggest employers are: *EEW Special Pipe Constructions GmbH*, *Euroports Germany GmbH & Co. KG* and subsidiaries, *Gesamthafenbetriebsgesell-schaft Rostock mbH*, *Getreide AG/Power Oil Rostock GmbH*, *Großtanklager Ölhafen Rostock GmbH*, *Kloska SVR Schiffsversorgung Rostock GmbH* as well as *Liebherr-MCCtec Rostock GmbH*.

On the area of the sea port, a number of industrial companies have settled in recent years, e.g., a malt factory, a crane manufacturer, a building materials manufacturer, several disposal companies, an oil mill, a producer of biodiesel, a large pipe manufacturer and a specialist company for corrosion protection.

Around 8000 ferry, ro-ro, general cargo and cruise ships are handled per year. Rostock has a classic universal port which handles ro-ro cargo, liquid and dry bulk, general cargo and project cargo. The sea port consists of the following parts: ferry terminal, ro-ro terminal, intermodal terminal, general cargo terminal, industrial and bulk terminal, oil port and chemical port. Ferry services to Sweden and Denmark operate several times a day. Regular ro-ro connections to Finland and Denmark are offered several times a week. In addition, there is a conventional liner service to Norway.

## Discussion

From this overview it should be clear that ports in Germany have followed a very diverse pathway to privatization that has led to a variety of ownership structures and governance mechanisms. While most ports can be considered landlord ports, there are examples of fully privatized ports and of the involvement of the public sector in terminal handling activities. Most cases of privatization were opposed by workers' unions and by the public, which has often resulted in the public sector retaining majority shares in some of the port activities.

The involvement of the public sector, however, especially in the ports of Bremen and in Hamburg, can be a signal of the importance attributed by the public to the port. Having maintained substantial control of not only the port authority, but also terminal operations, logistics and intermodal activities, municipal governments have the possibility of maintaining long-term control of port developments and steering is so that in the long term it still generates benefits for the local economies.

It is also interesting that the German port sector has shown an advanced degree of integration. Prime examples are the port of Lübeck, managed and operated by a subsidiary of the municipality, HHLA, that is the operating arm of the Hamburg municipality (although part of the company's shares are in the hands of private investors), and the BLG case in Bremen. The history of development and growth of these companies is the result of compromise between public interests, the need to increase the efficiency of operations as well as increase private sector investment.

## References

bremenports GmbH & Co. KG. (2017). *Annual report 2017*.

Container Terminal Wilhelmshaven JadeWeserPort-Marketing GmbH & Co. KG. (undated). JadeWeserPort Wilhelmshaven: Historie. Abgerufen am 03. December 2018 von Hafen in Aufbruchstimmung: http://www.jadeweserport.de/hafen-betrieb/historie/

Federal Ministry of Transport and Digital Infrastructure (BMVI), *Seehäfen*, Research Information System (FIS) published by the Federal Ministry of Transport and Digital Infrastructure, https://www.forschungsinformationssystem.de page created on: 17-07-2003 and last updated on the 25-10-2018.

Holst, A., & Wolf., A. (2018). *Kreuzfahrthäfen im Wettbewerb*. de Gruyter.

Niedersachsen Ports GmbH & Co. KG. (kein Datum). Nidersachsen Ports: Organization. Abgerufen am 03. December 2018 von Company Bodies: https://www.nports.de/en/company/organization/

Niedersachsen Ports GmbH & Co. KG. (undated). Niedersachsen Ports. Abgerufen am 03. December 2018 von Ports: https://www.nports.de/en/ports/

Prause, G. (2010). Logistics-related entrepreneurship and regional development—An empiric study. In *Baltic Business and Socio-Economic Development 2007: 3rd International Conference Tallinn, Estonia, June 17–19, 2007* (p. 361). BWV Berliner Wissenschafts-Verlag, Berlin.

Senator für Wirtschaft, Arbeit und Häfen. (undated). Bremisches Hafenkonzept 2020/25, Bremen.

# 14

# Regulating and Financing Greek Ports

Athanasios A. Pallis and George K. Vaggelas

## Introduction

An insular country with a lengthy coastline, Greece has an extensive network of seaports varying in size, importance and governance schemes. With Greek islands accounting for 19% of the country's area and 7.6% of the population living on 112 inhabited islands (HAS, 2019), ports are essential facilitators of trade, economic growth and social cohesion; 18% of imports and 25% of the national trade are seaborne,

A. A. Pallis (✉)
Department of Port Management and Shipping, National and Kapodistrian University of Athens, Athens, Greece
e-mail: apallis@uoa.gr

G. K. Vaggelas
Department of Shipping, Trade and Transport, University of the Aegean, Mytilene, Greece

© The Author(s), under exclusive license to Springer Nature Switzerland AG 2022

C. Ferrari et al. (eds.), *Regulation and Finance in the Port Industry*, Palgrave Studies in Maritime Economics,
https://doi.org/10.1007/978-3-030-83985-7_14

facilitated by Greek ports (HRADF, 2012). In addition, following a long-lasting privatisation, Piraeus, the country's major port, has emerged as a transhipment hub, which since 2019 is the top container port in the Mediterranean Sea in terms of container throughput served per annum.

This chapter discusses the evolution of the contemporary regulatory regime governing Greek ports system, detailing the structure of the system, some key port data and the governance model in place. It then presents the financial tools available for Greek ports, discussing how these tools have been strongly affected by the economic recession that hit the Greek economy and forced a pursuit of private financing mechanisms.

## The Greek Port System

The regulatory foundations of the Greek port system are dated back to 1923, with the establishment of the first authorities responsible for the management and development of port infrastructures. Since then, Greek ports experienced several transformations aiming to address the emerging challenges.

Today, out of more than 1000 ports and port installations that exist in Greece, 585 ports are managed by a port entity (Vaggelas et al., 2018). Two of them are ports of international importance (Piraeus and Thessaloniki). Ten other ones are classified as of 'national importance' (Alexandroupolis, Kavala, Igoumenitsa, Corfu, Volos, Elefsina, Rafina, Lavrion, Patra, and Heraklion) and operate as corporate entities. In total, 13 port authorities operate as Societe Anonymes (S.A.), facilitating the majority share of the country's seaborne trade and passenger traffic. Figure 14.1 details the spatial distribution of the 13 corporatised Greek ports as well as the types of the traffic each port facilitates.

The bulk of them are multipurpose ports (Table 14.1), with the exceptions of Corfu, Rafina, and Igoumenitsa, which are passenger ports facilitating Ro-Pax and cruise vessels. Piraeus is the major container port in Greece holding 91.8% of the total container traffic for 2019, with 83.8% facilitated by the COSCO subsidiary PCT (Piraeus Container Terminal S.A.) and 8.0% by Piraeus Port Authority S.A. This is also the only port with a car terminal. Thessaloniki holds the second place as

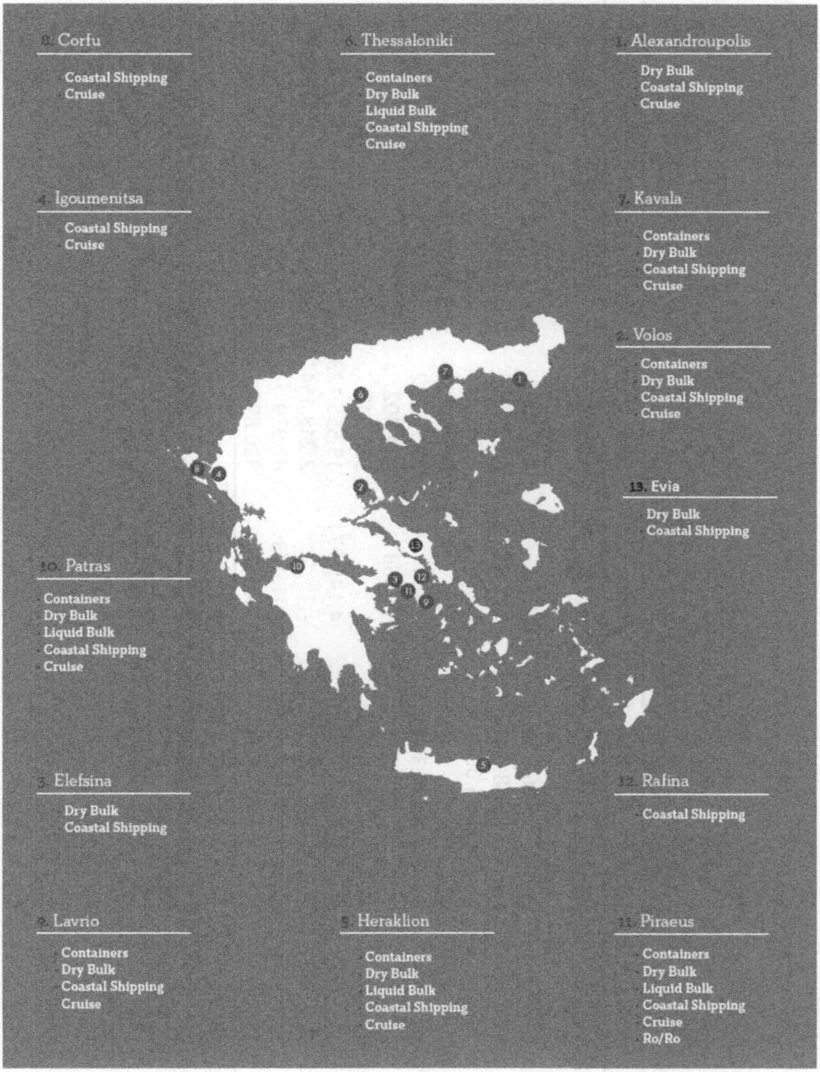


**Fig. 14.1** The major Greek ports

**Table 14.1** Greek port authorities—Characteristics and traffic data (2017)

| Port Authority S.A | Number of ports | Dry bulk (tn) | TEUs | Ferry (pax) | Cruise (pax) | Cars (units) |
|---|---|---|---|---|---|---|
| Alexandroupolis | 1 | 118.965 | - | 146.208 | | - |
| Corfu | 6 | - | - | 1.840.975 | 679.681 | - |
| Elefsina | 5 | 426.817 | 420 | 452.659 | - | - |
| Evia | 18 | 428.008 | - | 1.631.306 | - | - |
| Heraklion | 1 | 85.803 | 21.353 | 1.542.244 | 181.693 | - |
| Igoumenitsa | 1 | - | - | 2.677.303 | 9.088 | - |
| Kavala | 4 | 629.308 | - | 2.173.582 | 3.226 | - |
| Lavrio | 1 | 13.687 | 15.463 | 464.402 | 17.406 | - |
| Patras | 1 | 191.671 | - | 521.349 | 952 | - |
| Piraeus | 1 | - | 4.145.071 | 15.555.123 | 1.055.559 | 431.157 |
| Rafina | 2 | - | - | 2.248.454 | - | - |
| Thessaloniki | 1 | 3.186.888 | 401.473 | 47.939 | 2.424 | - |
| Volos | 1 | 867.102 | 19.017 | 330.896 | 7.618 | - |

*Source* Vaggelas and Pallis (2018)
*Note* Liquid bulk cargoes (oil and oil products) are facilitated through private port infrastructures owned by the companies operating the country's refineries

regards container traffic while serving as the major dry bulk port of the country. In aggregate, in 2017 all Greek ports handled 32.63 million tonnes (excluding liquid bulk terminals operated by refineries) and 62.13 m passengers (Vaggelas et al., 2018). Containerised trade reached 4.60 m TEUs (Vaggelas & Pallis, 2018), while cruise passenger movements reached 4.62 m passenger movements (Hellenic Ports Association, 2018).

This categorisation however is under reconsideration. According to the most recent National Port Policy plans detailed by the Ministry of Shipping and Insular Policy (MSIP, 2012) the Greek port system will eventually be restructured with 57 ports forming its backbone: 16 ports of international importance, 16 ports of national importance, and 25 of local importance. Yet in late 2019, the newly elected government set this plan under revision.

## The Regulatory Framework

Greece embarked on the (on-going) port governance reform in the late 1990s, with the conversion of 12 ports of national interest from 'public law undertakings' to government-owned port corporations. Surprisingly, this reform is still in progress. Table 14.2 presents the timeline of port reforms over these two decades, while Fig. 14.2 illustrates the structure of the port governance in Greece as it stands in 2019.

The first initiatives (1999) considered the two 'trans-European port organisations' of the country. The ports of Piraeus and Thessaloniki became corporations at that time, wholly owned by the Greek State (Law 2688/1999). Following a later decision these ports were listed in the Athens Stock Exchange (Thessaloniki since 2001; Piraeus since 2003). Being the owner of the land, the State signed long-term concession agreements with the respective port authorities which gained the exclusive right of use and exploitation of land, buildings, and infrastructure within the port zones, in order to operate as 'common user' ports, i.e. providing port services to all potential port users on an equal basis. In return port authorities pay to the State a concession fee standing at 2% of the annual operating income. The State retained at the time 75% of their shares for

**Table 14.2** Timeline of Greek port reform

| | Year | Reform |
|---|---|---|
| First Round | 1999 | Piraeus Port Authority (PPA) and Thessaloniki Port Authority (ThPA) converted to Sociétés Anonymes (S.A.) (Law 2688/1999) |
| | 2001 | Ten Port Authorities converted to S.A.s (one share owned by the state) (Law 2932/2001) |
| | | Establishment of the General Secretariat of Ports and Port Policy (Law 2932/2001) |
| | | ThPA S.A. listed in Athens Stock Exchange (state retains 74.27%, of shares) |
| | 2003 | PPA S.A. listed in Athens Stock Exchange (state retains 74.14% of shares) |
| Second Round | 2008 | Public tenders for the concession of (i) Thessaloniki Container Terminal; (ii) Piraeus Container Terminal Pier II (operation); and Container Terminal Pier III (greenfield) |
| | 2009 | Piraeus Container Terminal (PCT) S.A., a COSCO Pacific subsidiary, commences operations of Pier II |
| | 2010 | National economy experiences crisis—intervention of International Monetary Fund (IMF) and European Institutions (European Commission; European Central Bank) |
| | 2011 | PPA commences operation of Container Terminal Pier I |
| | 2012 | "Friendly agreement" between PPA S.A. and PCT S.A. to revise concession terms |
| | 2013 | All shares of Port SAs transferred to Hellenic Republic Asset Development Fund (HRADF) |
| | | One more port is transformed to S.A. (Evia Port Authority) |
| | | Non S.A. ports capacity to operate under a Port Authority S.A. form (Law 4150/13) |
| | 2014 | Establishment of the Ports Regulatory Authority (controlled by Ministry of Mercantile Marine) |
| | | Second "Friendly agreement" between PPA S.A. and PCT S.A. to revise concession terms |
| Third Round | 2016 | China COSCO Shipping Corporation Limited wins a tender call for buying 67% of the shares of the PPA SA. Greek Parliament endorses the decision |
| | | Conversion of the Ports Regulatory Authority to an independent authority |
| | | Establishment of a Public Port Authority (PPA) having one branch (Piraeus, PPA) |

(continued)

Table 14.2 (continued)

| Year | Reform |
|---|---|
| 2018 | South-Europe Gateway Thessaloniki wins a tender call for buying 67% of the shares of the Thessaloniki PA SA. Greek Parliament endorses the decision |

*Source* Adjusted from Pallis and Vaggelas (2017)

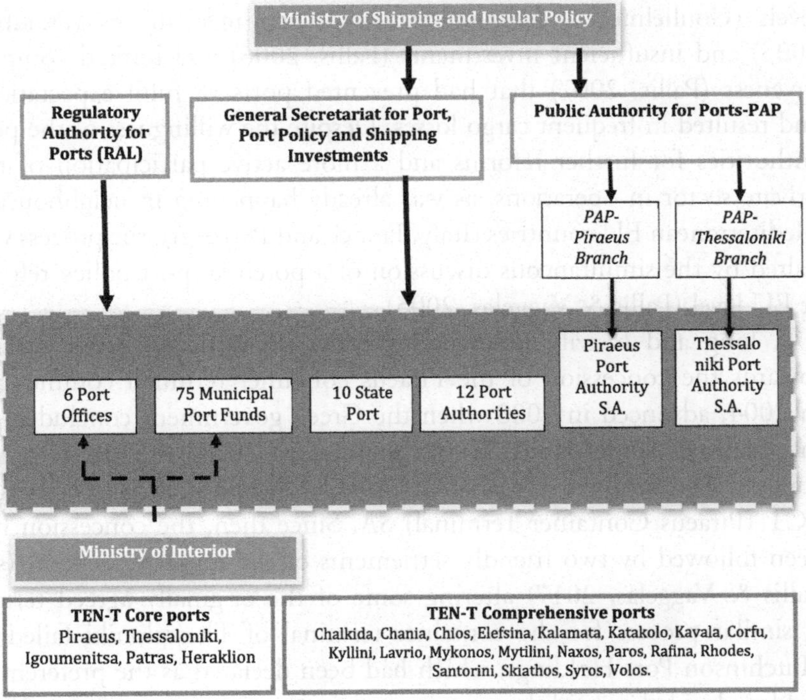


**Fig. 14.2** Structure of port governance in Greece (2019) (*Source* Authors)

almost 15 years—i.e. until the decision to sell 51% to the private sector (see below).

In 2001, ten more ports of national interest have been converted from limited companies (Law 2932/2001), supervised by a Secretariat for Port, Port Policy, and Shipping Investments. Each company has one share that is owned by the State. The scope is to generate a degree of autonomy regarding port management and operation. These ports are supposed to operate as 'private sector' businesses with the objective to develop infrastructure and offer qualitative and competitive services. Local and municipality authorities undertook the management of the remaining Greek ports, replacing managing boards directly appointed by the central administration.

The motive for this 'port devolution' (Baltazar & Brooks, 2001; also: Brooks & Cullinane, 2007) was the need to reverse low productivity levels (Goulielmos, 1999), ineffective pricing mechanisms (Psaraftis, 2005) and insufficient investments (Pallis, 2006) and limited competitiveness (Pallis, 2007) that had prevented ports to fulfil expectations and resulted in frequent cargo losses. Despite the willingness of the port authorities for further reforms and a more active participation of the private sector in operations, as was already happening in neighbouring Mediterranean EU countries (Italy, France and Portugal), the process was halted by the simultaneous discussion of a potential port policy reform at EU level (Pallis & Vaggelas, 2005).

A long and heavily politicised process (Psaraftis & Pallis, 2012), towards the concession of the Piraeus container terminal commenced in 2004, advanced in 2008 when the Greek government concluded an international tender, and was put in force in 2009 with the terminal concessioned for 35 + 5 years to a COSCO Pacific subsidiary company PCT (Piraeus Container Terminal) SA. Since then, the concession has been followed by two friendly settlements of the initial agreement (see Pallis & Vaggelas, 2017) altering some of the originally agreed terms. A similar process for the container terminal of Thessaloniki failed as Hutchinson Port Holdings, which had been declared as the preferential bidder, decided to withdraw its interest in the light of the 2008–2009 global financial crisis.

The recession of the national economy and the fiscal adjustment programmes had an impact on the regulatory framework of the Greek port system. Severely impacted by the global financial crisis of 2008–2009, and the breakdown of the country's fiscal policies in the early 2010s, successive Greek governments decided, or were obliged by the institutions monitoring the Greek economy (International Monetary Fund (IMF), European Commission, and the European Central Bank), to further exploit public assets, including ports, aiming at increasing state revenues but also generating conditions for economic development. Among others, this changed the financing mix of an industry that had been dominated by public control and financing.

The shares of all the corporatised Port Authorities, bar one which of regional nature (the recently established Evia Ports SA), were transferred to the Hellenic Republic Asset Development Fund (HRADF). HRDAF acts as the statutory body in charge of the exploitation of all assets owned by the State in all sectors of the economy and any corresponding privatisation programmes. An independent regulatory authority, the Greek Regulatory Authority (RAL), was established in 2013 to supervise legislation compliance, abuse of dominant position, port tariffs, and other regulatory implementation (Law 4150/2013).

In 2016 China Cosco Shipping Corporation Ltd, as the only bidder, bought 51% of the Piraeus Port Authority SA, with an option for acquiring an additional 16%. The Chinese government-owned company accompanied the offered price with a commitment for a series of compulsory investments. The same year, Law 4389/2016 established a Public Port Authority (PAP) responsible for safeguarding the 'public goods' produced in the country's privatised ports and for supervising the internal market in the respective ports. Today (2017), PPPAP has two branches, one operating in Piraeus and one operating in Thessaloniki. A similar selling process was completed in 2018, when a consortium of three companies including the port arm of CMA-CGM Terminal Link (33%), Deutsche Invest Equity Partners (47%), and a Greek investor (20%), bought 67% of the Thessaloniki Port Authority shares.

For the remaining ports that operate as corporate entities, the government has expressed plans to launch international tender processes for the concession of port areas and port activities. However, the new government that was elected in mid-2019 stated its intentions for revisiting these plans. The potential to endorse a privatisation strategy based on the selling of port authorities ownership, as has happened in the case of the two major ports of the country has re-emerged, even though this prototype of port governance stands as a practice that has been unprecedented at European Union level and has a limited application around the globe (for a multi-country comparison: Brooks et al., 2017). Irrespective of the outcome, it is evident that engaging further the private sector in the ownership and management of Greek ports remains part of a reform agenda that has yet to conclude.

Similarly, the restructuring of the governance of those secondary ports currently operating as state or municipal port funds, and the identification of additional financing tools for port investments with an eye on the modernisation of port infrastructures and port services, are also in the pipeline. The existing governance schemes of these ports generate conflicts and further inefficiencies between four different institutions, either ministries or regulatory authorities, involved in regulating and supervising their operations, with overlapping responsibilities and functions (Pallis & Vaggelas, 2017). This has led to thoughts for reforming the current governance model aiming at increasing their performance, their revenues, and their attractiveness for investments.

As regards port planning, this results via a process that applies to all ports, irrespective of the governance scheme in place. Each port authority must develop (a) a long-term master plan, which includes the upgrade of existing and/or the development of new port infrastructures, and superstructures, in order to serve best the forecasted port traffic and (b) a short-term (five years) business plan. These plans are subject to approval by a special Port Planning and Development Committee (PPDC) whose members are representatives of eight different ministries. This Committee is responsible for the general planning of the country's ports, the monitoring and the implementation of the endorsed port programmes by the port authorities, and the allocation of public financing to port infrastructure projects.

## Financial Tools

The financial tools available for investments in port infrastructure and, in some cases, for port operations, are grouped in four major categories. The first one refers to investments via the use of the port's own funds. The magnitude of these resources depends on the revenues that a port generates. A second group is the public funding via the capital allocated by the State budget. This financing path includes several alternatives, with the major one being the annual Public Investment Programme (PIP), the major governmental tool for financing public works. The third one is private funding in all its potential forms. For the moment, private financing of port development applies to the two major ports of the country only. The fourth category includes the financing tools developed by the EU.

The funding of port investments is strongly related with the governance model of each port management authority. Among the variety of (co)-financing tools for transport projects of the EU, three instruments are used by the 25 Greek ports belonging to the core and comprehensive Trans-European Transport Network (TEN-T) only (Fig. 14.2): These are the so-called Juncker Plan; (b) the Connecting Europe Facility programme; and (d) the European Structural and Investment Funds (ESIF). There are also additional EU financing tools available, including the mobilisation of capital via the Cohesion Fund, the European Regional Development Fund, as well as tools including the financing of feasibility studies and research dealing with the transport sector. It is worth noting that in the early days of the economic crisis that the country experiences, the then publicly owned Piraeus Port Authority secured, exceptionally, a 95% EU funding for the construction of a new cruise terminal having a total cost of €141 million. The construction of this terminal has still to commence.

Table 14.3 summarises the available financing tools, and the extent that each one applies to the Greek ports depending on different governance models in place.

## How Sustainable Is the Current Model?

In Greece the majority of port projects have been financed by the State through the Pubic Investment Programme (PIP) and through the ESIF, as the Greek port system followed for long the public service port management model (see The World Bank [2000] taxonomy). Since 2010 the mix of port financing in Greece has changed. The fiscal adjustment programme resulted in a 36% reduction of the PIP from €9.3 billion in 2009 to just €5.95 billion in 2017, with only a limited share heading

**Table 14.3** Financial tools available for Greek ports

| Financing tool/Port governance model | Port Authority S.A. (public) | Port Authority S.A. (private) | Municipal port fund | State port fund |
|---|---|---|---|---|
| Own funds | | | | |
| Cash and cash equivalents | √ | √ | √ | |
| State funding | | | | |
| Ministry of Shipping and Insular Policy | √ | | | √ |
| Ministry of Interior | | | √ | |
| Ministry of Transport and Infrastructures | √ | | √ | √ |
| Regions | √ | | √ | √ |
| Municipalities | | | √ | |
| Private funding | | | | |
| Stock Exchange | | √ | | |
| Bonds | √ | √ | | |
| Concessions | √ | √ | √ | √ |
| Bank loans | √ | √ | √ | √ |
| EU financing | | | | |
| Various tools | √ | √ | √ | √ |

*Source* Authors

to port-related investments. Consequently the Greek State sought for alternative sources of funding.

For the two major ports, the privatisation process produced the commitment of the new owners to proceed to necessary investments with their own funds. In Piraeus, according to the published financial accounts, between 2009 and 2017 the concessionaire of the container port invested €467 million, among others, in upgrading Pier II, the construction of Pier III and the procurement of new cargo handling equipment. Moreover, China Cosco Shipping is committed to invest €350 million until 2026, with the company's master plan foreseen the total investments to reach €800 million. In the case of Thessaloniki Port Authority, the new owner is committed to invest €180 million to upgrade port infrastructure and cargo handling equipment. The presence of international terminal operators in both ports creates conditions for further port development via Foreign Direct Investments (FDIs) and positive throughput trends.

However, at least for the moment, private investments remain focussed on the most profitable port infrastructures and operations. In the case of Piraeus, the vast majority of the investments refer to the container terminals. Only few of the other foreseen compulsory investments have been completed or at least are already on track. While it is too early to conclude on the actual reasons for this happening, delays in parts of port development plans are notable.

Private ownership has not been always enough to secure the advancement of private investments though. In the case of Piraeus the aforementioned applied planning procedures have led to controversies as regards certain types of port expansion, despite the willingness of the owner (Cosco) to finance them. The new owner developed within 15 months a master plan, yet more than a year later the designated public Committee (PPDC) has rejected the owner's proposals related to capacity expansion of both the container and the cruise terminals. The recent (October 2019) partial approval has been granted following a request to re-discuss several of the proposals, i.e. those for which local communities have expressed questions referring to commercial activities, such as malls and hotels. While the transformation of port-city relations to an area of conflict is not a rare phenomenon, the situation highlights that port governance and financing decisions remain embedded on the broader culture and institutional context within which the economy develops (Jacobs, 2007; Ng & Pallis, 2010; Notteboom et al., 2013). It remains to be seen whether this slow decision-making process observed is an ad hoc difficulty, or the present structures of private–public interests interactions limit the prospects of on-time port development.

The above is reconfirmed by the fact that private financing in Thessaloniki faces similar challenges. Two years since privatisation the major investments for the expansion of port infrastructures have yet to start. At the time of writing, early-2020 stands as the set day for this commencing. For the moment, the new owner has invested in some straddle carriers only, as they renegotiate with the government the initial agreement, and in particular the potential transfer of €20 million investments from real estate to investments in container terminal expansion. This request, which for the time being is rejected by the Greek State, would mean that €150 million out of the €180 million of compulsory investments will be allocated to the container terminal, reconfirming the priority that private investors assign to the particular market. Even in those cases that private financing seems to have been secured, the balanced development of all port units and markets, rather than the most profitable business alone, remains under question—bringing back in the discussion the need for mechanisms that would allow such balanced development to take place.

While sustaining financing of Greek ports' modernisation and development via FDIs is viable in the case of the two major ports, this potential stands questionable in the case of other major ports. Over the last decade, the expressed unsolicited private interest in investing in these ports has failed to turn to concrete actions. Conditioned by several factors, this interest might fail to materialise in the future as well. Still, financing for all Greek ports included in either the core or comprehensive European TEN-T seems probable via EU funds.

What remains as a major question is the development of the country's secondary ports. The majority of them do not have sufficient traffic; hence they lack the essential revenues. Yet they are vital from both economic and social perspectives. The increase of the PIP to €12.5 billion for 2019 provides some but not all funds needed. Private interest is absent thus financing their needs will continue to be covered by public funds. This increases the importance of applying a consolidation plan—i.e. through mergers—aiming at the formation of authorities having the potential to rationalise investment plans, improve the effectiveness and the efficiency of existing operations, improve day-to-day management practices, and, perhaps, systematically exploring the potential of further private investments in some of the Greek ports. A combination of economic and geographical proximity criteria would result in the formation of 13–15 new entities, rather than the 91 bodies that currently manage these ports in a costly and ineffective way.

## Concluding Remarks

The Greek port system has long relied heavily on the public sector; with the State being responsible for financing, managing, and operating all port projects. The port governance reforms of the last decade lifted the barriers for the involvement of the private sector in Greek ports.

This lifting had a significant impact on port development. The presence of an international terminal operator at Piraeus container port, whose parent company (China COSCO Shipping Corporation Ltd.) soon turned to owner, was accompanied by subsequent FDIs. Along with the integration of rail services to dry ports in central Europe and the contribution of the existing clustering (cf. Vaggelas et al., 2017), Piraeus emerged within a bit more than a decade to the fourth-biggest container port in Europe and the 28th biggest container port in the world in terms of TEU throughput. From a financing perspective, COSCO demonstrated the capacity to provide the essential port funds, taking into advantage its global reach. Given the commitment of the new owners, it is safe to conclude that similar will be the effects as regards the financing and development of the recently privatised Thessaloniki port. In addition, the presence of private operators has generated an euphoria as regards the prospect of both ports, accelerating both private and public plans for investments in logistics, supply chains, and the expansion of the overall port-related cluster (see Vaggelas & Pallis, 2019). All these in a period that the economic crisis limited the potential of public funding at an unprecedented lower level in the history of the country.

For Greece the change of port governance scheme has facilitated the financing of its two major ports, alas at the expense of losing public ownership control of the respective port authorities. Comparing to trends in other countries in Europe and beyond (see Brooks et al., 2017), the decision made was to follow a very 'Greek prototype' of port governance the real implications of which remain to be realised. The discussed disagreements between private interests and public perspectives need to be closely monitored and researched in order to accurately conclude on the actual magnitude of the expenses, if any, that the detailed governance model comes with.

It also remains to be seen whether this private interest will expand to the other ports of national interest, as currently projected, and in what terms. What is even more important, and perhaps questionable given the state of public accounts, is the identification of mechanisms that would allow the mobilisation of funds to maintain and improve the country's smaller ports, as well as the effective use of these funds at port level planning and implementation. While EU financial tools provide a potential mechanism for securing some of these funds, a reform of secondary ports governance that would include the merging of the too many small in size and low expertise authorities would work towards rationalisation of port planning and financing decisions.

## References


Baltazar, R., & Brooks, M. (2001). The governance of port devolution: A tale of two countries. In *Proceedings of the 9th World Conference on Transport Research (Cd-Rom)*. Seoul.

Brooks, M. R., & Cullinane, K. (2007). *Devolution, port governance and port performance*. Elsevier.

Brooks, M. R., Pallis, A. A., & Cullinane, K. (2017). Revisiting port governance and port reform: A multi-country examination. *Research in Transportation Business & Management, 100*(22), 1–10.

Goulielmos, A. M. (1999). Deregulation in major Greek ports: The way it has to be done. *International Journal of Transport Economics, XXV, I*(1), 121–148.

Hellenic Ports Association. (2018, June 4). *Cruise traffic at Greek ports for 2017*. Press Release. Piraeus, Greece.

Hellenic Republic Asset Development Fund (HRADF). (2012, September). *Background paper to the Hellenic Republic National Port Policy Paper* (Final Report). Athens.

Hellenic Statistical Authority (HAS). (2019). *2011 Population and housing census*. http://www.statistics.gr/en/statistics/-/publication/SAM03/2011. Accessed 30 Sept 2019.

Jacobs, W. (2007). Port competition between Los Angeles and Long Beach: An institutional analysis. *Tijdschrift Voor Economische En Sociale Geografie, 98*, 360–372.

Ministry of Shipping and Insular Policy. (2012, December). *National port strategy 2013–2018*. Piraeus.

Ng, K. Y. A., & Pallis, A. A. (2010). Port governance reforms in diversified institutional frameworks: Generic solutions, implementation asymmetries. *Environment and Planning A, 42*(9), 2147–2167.

Notteboom, T., De Langen, P., & Jacobs, W. (2013). Institutional plasticity and path dependence in seaports: Interactions between institutions, port governance reforms and port authority routines. *Journal of Transport Geography, 27*, 26–35.

Pallis, A. A. (2006). Port governance in Greece. *Research in Transportation Economics, 17*, 491–508.

Pallis, A. A. (2007). Whither port strategy? Theory and practice in conflict. *Research in Transportation Economics, 21*, 343–382.

Pallis, A. A., & Vaggelas, G. K. (2005). Port competitiveness and the EU 'port services' directive: The case of Greek ports. *Maritime Economics and Logistics, 7*(2), 116–140.

Pallis, A. A., & Vaggelas, G. K. (2017). A Greek prototype of port governance. *Research in Transportation Business & Management, 22*, 49–57.

Psaraftis, H. N. (2005). Tariff reform in the port of Piraeus: A practical approach. *Maritime Economics and Logistics, 7*(4), 356–381.

Psaraftis, H. N., & Pallis, A. A. (2012). Concession of the Piraeus container terminal: Turbulent times and the quest for competitiveness. *Maritime Policy and Management, 39*(1), 27–43.

Vaggelas, G. K., Kladaki, E., & Pallis, A. A. (2017, June 27–30). Unveiling configurations of shipping clusters: Challenges and opportunities in the case of Piraeus. In *International Association of Maritime Economists Conference*. Kyoto, Japan.

Vaggelas G. K., & Pallis A. A. (2018). *GREPORT—Report on Greek ports 2018* (in Greek). Ports and Shipping Advisory, Piraeus, Greece.

Vaggelas, G. K., & Pallis, A. A. (2019). Configuration and prospects of the Piraeus shipping cluster. *SPOUDAI-Journal of Economics and Business, 69*(1–2), 3–17.

Vaggelas, G. K., Papachristou, A. A., & Troumbetas, S. (2018). *Transformation of the port governance model—A study for the Ministry of Shipping and Insular Policy* (in Greek). Piraeus: Ports & Shipping Advisory.

World Bank. (2000). *World Bank port reform toolkit*. World Bank.

# 15

# Aims, Goals, and Results of Port Reforms in Italy

Sergio Prete and Alessio Tei

## Introduction

The Italian port system has often been criticised for its delay in adapting to new market challenges due to the limitations of a port law (i.e. law no 84/1994) designed when the port industry was substantially different

S. Prete (✉)
Port Network Authority of the Ionian Sea, Taranto, Italy
e-mail: presidente@port.taranto.it

A. Tei
Department of Economics, University of Genoa, Genoa, Italy
e-mail: alessio.tei@unige.it

S. Prete
University of Bari Aldo Moro, Bari, Italy

A. Tei
School of Engineering, Newcastle University, Newcastle upon Tyne, UK

© The Author(s), under exclusive license to Springer Nature Switzerland AG 2022
C. Ferrari et al. (eds.), *Regulation and Finance in the Port Industry*, Palgrave Studies in Maritime Economics,
https://doi.org/10.1007/978-3-030-83985-7_15

from what it has turned to be in the new millennium (e.g. Ferrari & Musso, 2011; Valleri et al., 2006; MIT, 2015). Despite this, and after decades of discussions, in 2016 a drastic modification of the port law generated a novel landscape, promoting the aggregation of Port Authorities (e.g. Parola et al., 2017). In its current form, the Italian port system is characterised by 16 "Port Network Authorities" that replaced the 24 port authorities present up to 2015. The aggregation has been pushed by the Central Government in order to solve some critical issues, such as the small size of many Port Authorities in respect to international competitors, the need for rationalising and prioritising investments, and the needed administrative and bureaucratic simplification.

Figure 15.1 shows the 2019 traffic per Network Authority, highlighting how, despite the reduction of port authorities, the Italian port system is still characterised by mainly two medium-sized ports (i.e. Authority of the Mar Ligure Occidentale and Authority of the Mar Adriatico Orientale) while almost all the other Network Authorities manage relatively small areas and infrastructure, with only a few highly specialised exceptions (e.g. Gioia Tauro for containers, Mar Tirreno Settentrionale for Ro-Ro activity, and Mar di Sardegna for Liquid Bulk). Similarly, while most Italian ports handle passenger traffic, only a few of them report statistics on, for instance, the cruise market, that is, mainly

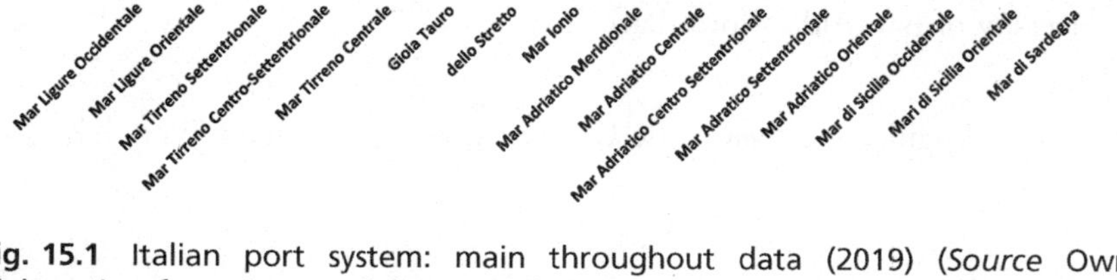


**Fig. 15.1** Italian port system: main throughout data (2019) (*Source* Own elaboration from Assoporti data, 2020)

concentrated in just a few ports (e.g. Mar Ligure Occidentale, Mar Tirreno Centro-Settentrionale, and Mar Adriatico Settentrionale).

In the last recorded year, 2019, the Italian port system handled about 480 million tonnes, i.e. all Italian ports together recorded just a bit more than Rotterdam—the biggest port in EU. In the same period, the biggest Port Network Authority (i.e. Mar Ligure Occidentale) was representing one-sixth of Rotterdam. The relatively small size of the Italian ports has affected the capability of attracting investments over the years, with only a few ports having been capable to attract major international operators.

Figure 15.2 shows the overall market trends, underlining the general stagnation of the Italian port industry, with all major traffic categories demonstrating a declining trend.

From the picture above, it is possible to underline that the Italian port system is currently struggling to keep up with major European competitors (e.g. other major Mediterranean ports have all registered growing trends in the past 3–5 years, with only a few exceptions). Looking at single ports, while the national trends are quite negative, all main ports (e.g. Mar Ligure Occidentale) actually recorded a growing trend in all major traffic categories. This latter fact is linked with a polarization of the traffic on a few main gateways capable of attracting main companies and investments from both the sea and landside.

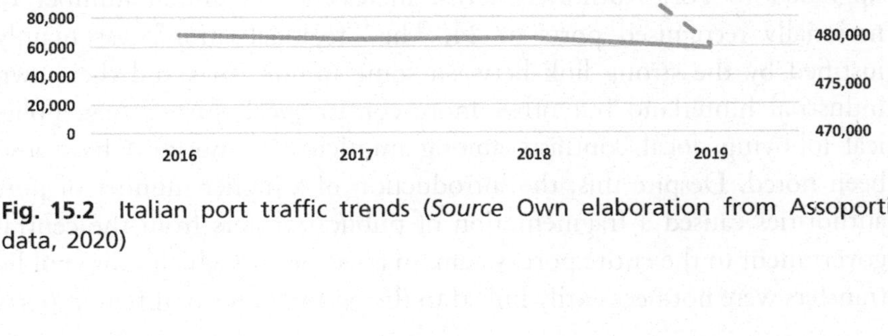


**Fig. 15.2** Italian port traffic trends (*Source* Own elaboration from Assoporti data, 2020)

## The Italian Port System

Since 1994, the Italian Port System has been characterised by the s.c. "port reform bill", i.e. Law No. 84/1994 (Carbone & Munari, 2006). This regulation was first introduced to align the Italian port governance system to the European legislation in terms of competition and market access. As such, starting from 1994, the port system abandoned the public port governance model in order to introduce the landlord model. In the new system private companies started investing in Italian Port Authorities thanks to the provision of the law that only private operators had the possibility to handle the cargo (Parola et al., 2012). In fact, Port Authorities were a special non-economic public body of national relevance having the duty of administrating, organising, and regulating the port area but without any budgetary autonomy. At the beginning of the 1994 regime, Italian ports were capable of attracting significant investments from national and international companies (e.g. PSA, Carnival, and Contship), especially in the container sector. In this period, the first privatised terminals were introduced in Genoa, while the biggest Mediterranean transhipment hub (Gioia Tauro) at that time was created by the conversion of a small industrial harbour.

Starting from the mid-2000s though, the concessioning system failed to promote efficiency among port operators, with difficulties in promoting intermodal transport and integration along the different supply chains. This aspect was mainly linked to the small size of many Port Authorities (i.e. serving local and regional markets) and to the legislative limitations that slowed down investments in the hinterland. Moreover, in the early-2000s, some further local ports were also upgraded to Port Authority status, increasing the initial number of nationally recognised ports to 24. This "regionalisation" was mainly justified by the strong link between some minor ports and their own industrial hinterland but other more controversial reasons (e.g. political lobbying, local contrasts among municipal authorities) have also been noted. Despite this, the introduction of a higher number of port authorities caused a fragmentation of public transfers from the central government to the entire port system, in a scenario in which those public transfers were not necessarily linked to the performance of different ports but just to redistribution purposes (Caballini et al., 2009). Moreover, the lack of financial autonomy and the strong reliance on central government funding caused long timeframes for project implementation that was often associated with a lack of an overall port vision at a national level due to the formal independence of different port authorities (Carbone & Munari, 2006; Ferrari & Musso, 2011).

In the same period, as shown in Fig. 15.3, most European port systems experienced steady growth (e.g. Spain, Greece, Germany, and The Netherlands), thus showing the need for further reform (Parola et al., 2017).

Thus, starting from 2016, the new legislation forced the consolidation of most port authorities in order to increase both the size of their infrastructure and their capability of promoting and rationalising investments in wider regions. As such, well known ports, such as Genoa or Trieste, have now been included in wider entities (e.g. Autorità del Mar Ligure Occidentale [*Authority of the Western Ligurian Sea*] in the case of Genoa). Figure 15.4 shows the transition between the old and the new system.

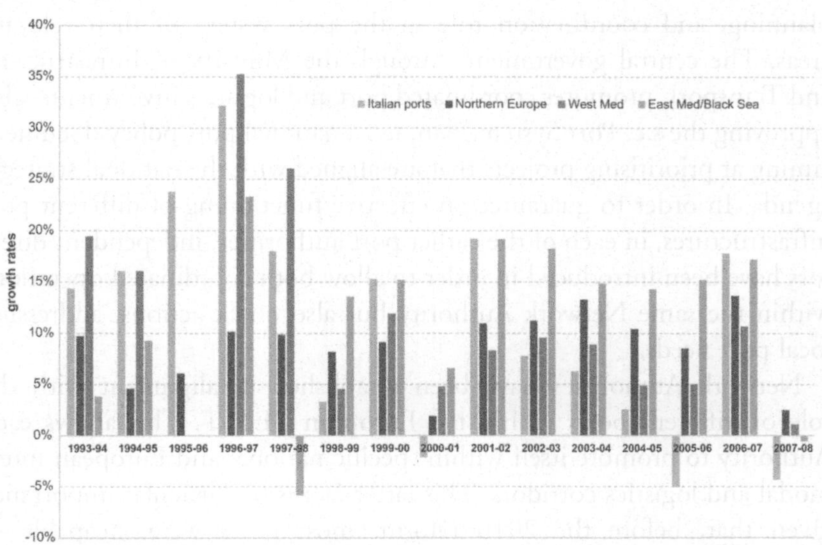


**Fig. 15.3** Italian port performance against other EU port systems (*Source* Parola et al., 2017)

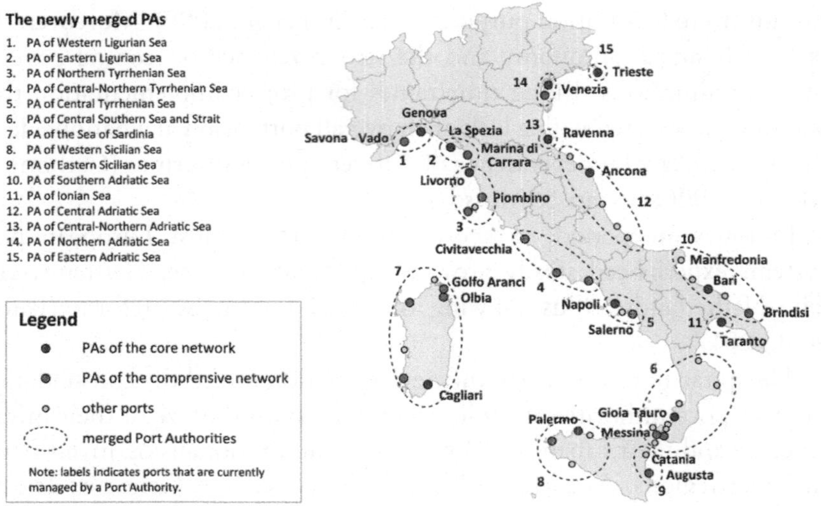


**Fig. 15.4** Italian Port system (*Source* Parola et al., 2017)

The current 16 Port Network Authorities have now a strategic policy, planning, and coordination role in the port system of their relevant areas. The central government, through the Ministry of Infrastructure and Transport, promotes coordinated port and logistics investments, also approving the s.c. Port System Plan, i.e. a national port policy document aiming at prioritising projects that are aligned with the national strategic agenda. In order to guarantee an effective functioning of different port infrastructures, in each of the earlier port authorities, independent directors have been introduced in order to allow both coordinated operations within the same Network Authority but also quick actions, addressing local port needs.

Network Authorities have been established in alignment with the role of different ports within the European TEN-T. This allows each Authority to promote itself within specific national and European intermodal and logistics corridors. This latter fact is of particular importance given that, before the 2016 reform, most ports were incapable of promoting intermodal transport corridors.

## Port Investment and Finance in the Italian Port System

As highlighted above, the port authorities introduced in 1994 were Special-State non-economic public bodies with no financial autonomy. As such, most of their financial capability is derived either from concession fees of different port areas (around 30–50% of many ports' balance sheet) or central government transfers (Parola et al., 2012).

Over the years, port authorities obtained a wider degree of financial independency, with current Network Authorities now enjoying the possibility to directly retain part of the port dues and other taxes.

In all Italian Network Authorities, the central government still needs to grant approval for any major infrastructure intervention, even when local authorities or the Network Authority itself is financially responsible for the execution of infrastructures works. Every year, the central government highlights funded interventions to be carried out in alignment with the Network Authorities' proposals, all presented through their own three-year operative plan.

The involvement of private funding is allowed and promoted through specific public–private partnerships. In such a scenario, private investors may partially or totally finance and construct port infrastructure within their own administrated area (e.g. warehouses, yards, and docks), in accordance with the Network Authorities' plans and the concessioning system. If the amortisation of the investment is not complete at the end of the concession period, the private company can either be reimbursed by the Network Authority or can apply for an extension of the concession period.

Starting from 1994, several private companies decided to invest in Italian ports through public–private partnerships, regulated by the terminal concession system. The first international groups investing in Italian ports were horizontally integrated operators, such as the Singaporean PSA (in both Genoa and Venice) or Hutchinson in Taranto, while national stevedoring companies were promoting "local" horizontal integration with the aim of establishing national champions (e.g. Contship handling cargoes in La Spezia, Gioia Tauro e Ravenna, GIP handling cargoes in Leghorn (Livorno) and Genoa). Starting in early 2000s, vertically integrated companies started investing in Italian ports, even if mainly through either long-term partnerships with specific terminals (e.g. MSC in Genoa) or direct ownerships (e.g. Evergreen in Taranto). Despite this, right before the economic crisis of 2008, most international carriers decided to slow down investment in Italian ports, with also some few main actors selling their shares in key terminals (e.g. both Gioia Tauro and Taranto registered several ownership issues). Only after the 2016 reform a novel wave of investments has been recorded. As such, MSC took control of the terminal in Gioia Tauro[1] and started a new investment in Genoa (with a new terminal due to start operations in 2022), while APMT (Maersk) started operating a novel 900,000 TEU terminal in Savona in late 2019.

Passenger terminals experienced similar developments: vertical integrations were particularly common in Italian ports, with most main cruise terminals directly owned by cruise operators (Carnival through its subsidiary Costa Crociere, MSC Cruises, and Royal Caribbean) and similar partnerships in the ferry market.

Since most of the Italian Port Network Authorities have been profiled in accordance with the role of key ports within the TEN-T, starting from 2016 some Italian ports were also capable of promoting improved connections with the hinterland. This fact also attracted the attention of other foreign investors and many Italian ports have been considered as potential candidates for developing cooperations within the Chinese Belt and Road Initiative. As a result, in autumn 2016, COSCO Shipping Ports bought 40% of the new APMT container terminal in Savona. Moreover, COSCO has also expressed interest in developing a hub in the North Adriatic Sea, exploiting some of the investment plans introduced by the Venice Port Authority (Costa et al., 2020). Such interest has been partially confirmed (switching from Venice to Trieste), during the visit of President Xi in Italy in Spring 2019, with Trieste preferred to Venice because of its interconnection with the Central and Eastern European markets.

[1] In June 2020, P. Maccarini, the head of MSC terminal investment, publicly stated that the company's plan is to promote further investments on Gioia Tauro in order to turn it into the main Mediterranean containter hub in the next future (Capuzzo, 2020).

## Port Operations in the Italian Port System

Port operations in the Italian port system are highly regulated, particularly as regards critical services that are either directly provided by pubic authorities (e.g. services of general interest) or concessioned to third parties operating as "regulated monopolies" (e.g. technical-nautical services). This element is mainly connected to the fact that, within the Italian system, Port (Network) Authorities cannot directly provide any business-oriented service, maintaining only a planning, regulatory, and administrative duty to pursue.

As such, terminals are operated by private companies that have an exclusive right to cargohandling. Terminal operators have their own staff and resort to the port pool during peaks. Port pools exist in most Italian ports through a homogeneous system that recognises these private legal entities as the major labour source for handling cargo besides direct terminal employees (Ferrari & Musso, 2011; Valleri et al., 2006). Within such system, main port services have regulated tariffs agreed between the providers (e.g. pools, pilotage, and tugs) and the Port (Network) Authority, while stevedoring companies can negotiate their own prices with shipping companies.

In accordance with Italian legislation, terminal concessions should have a duration of maximum 30 years apart from exceptions caused by special investments that need longer amortisation periods. Despite the general stipulation, all major terminals have concessions longer than 30 years (e.g. the major container terminal in Genoa was granted a concession lasting more than 60 years), thus creating a concentrated situation that impacts the actual possibility for new comers to compete for terminal areas (Parola et al., 2012). Similarly, while the general law does not allow terminal operators to own more than one terminal—per traffic category—within the same port, exceptions can be seen (e.g. both PSA and MSC own shares in two terminals in Genoa), causing further concentration within the market.

Within this situation, the capability for evaluating terminal performance and influencing terminal management seems to be a critical governing element for the Italian Port (Network) Authorities. As argued by Ferrari et al. (2013), while the concession system encouraged private investments, the Italian system did not allow Port Authorities to collect enough information, so as to provide an effective concession management system. This led to the incapability of most Authorities to either evaluate terminal performances or to provide an incentive system capable of pushing operators to improve their competitive position. This latter element is of particular importance since (i) in the current legal system, port concession details cannot be easily changed (i.e. they are assimilated to *public acts*) and (ii) the concession fee is normally based only on the historical construction costs of the terminal, with many ports that consider alternative factors (e.g. land use value or operational characteristics) but without any link with the related terminal performance. Given these two elements, the current concession regime does not allow the Port (Network) Authority to modify concession elements in order to either incentivise the private operator to improve its performance or adapt the concession to potential market changes. This is causing several potential problems. For instance, Ferrari et al. (2013) showed how—in the Italian port system—certain stevedoring operators could benefit from an increased dwell time and, therefore, from a sub-optimal situation. This lack of incentives has been seen as one of the major weaknesses of the current system, as also highlighted by the Italian Transport Regulation Authority in 2018 (ART, 2018).

While the regulatory system did not always allow Port (Network) Authorities to introduce incentives to terminal operators so as to improve their operational efficiency, their status as regulatory and planning authorities allowed many Italian ports to promote technology platforms to serve the port community to improve several alternative business areas. As such, both Bari and Venice have introduced innovative environmental and flow management systems to allow for a better port management, while the biggest Italian ports all introduced public Port Community Systems that allowed for an optimised in- and outflow cargo management.

## Challenges for the Future of the Italian Port System

Italian ports have always been characterised by their relatively small size, with only a few ports capable of competing at international level. The "regionalisation" of most port authorities assisted many Italian ports to establish stronger links with their hinterlands despite the difficulty in integrating several players along their supply chains. Such difficulties have also been present in the latest port reform, with all relevant Port Network Authorities having been embedded in specific TEN-T corridors. In spite of this, the fragmentation of the market still presents a major challenge for many Italian ports: the existence of Port Network Authorities ensures an evenly distributed system with the possibility for better serving local industries. Nevertheless, in the past years, major port companies invested only in a few key Port Authorities, highlighting the need for a more effective hierarchisation among the Italian ports. This latter fact is not only linked to the necessary private investments but it is also determined by the development of the National System Plan and the related need for a clear prioritisation of funding.

Moreover, while the current system tries to encourage private involvement in the port operations, the current regulation still lacks clear targets with respect to the port goals to be achieved. This latter element generates concession agreements that are quite difficult to adapt to the changing market conditions or to promote specific port strategies. Despite this, it is interesting to underline how the current system was indeed capable of attracting all major shipping and port players, allowing the market to generate a hierarchy among different ports and investments.

## References


ART—Transport Regulatory Authority. (2018). *Metodologie e criteri per garantire l'accesso equo e non discriminatorio alle infrastrutture portuali. Prime misure di regolazione* [Methodologies and criteria for granting a fair market access to port infrastructure]. http://www.autorita-trasporti.it/notizie/porti-art-approva-misure-di-regolazione-per-garantire-laccesso-equo-e-non-discriminatorio-alle-infrastrutture-portuali/

Assoporti. (2020). *Annual statistics*. https://www.assoporti.it/en/autoritasistemaportuale/statistiche/statistiche-annuali-complessive/autorita-di-sistema-portuale-movimenti-portuali/

Caballini C., Carpaneto L., & Parola F. (2009). Italian port authorities approaching the post-reform: The Ligurian case. In T. Notteboom, P. de Langen, & C. Ducruet (Eds.), *Ports in proximity: Competition and coordination among adjacent seaports* (pp. 191–208). Ashgate.

Capuzzo N. (2020). Gioia Tauro boss vows to give Piraeus a giht for box business. *Splash247*. https://splash247.com/gioia-tauro-port-boss-vows-to-give-piraeus-a-fight-for-box-business/

Carbone S. M., & Munari F. (2006). *La disciplina dei porti tra diritto comunitario e diritto interno*.

Costa P., Haralambides H., & Roson R. (2020). From Trans European (Ten-T) to Trans Global (Twn-T) transport infrastructure networks: A conceptual framework. In F. Cerniglia & F. Saraceno (Eds.), *European public investment outlook*. Open Book Publishers. (forthcoming).

Ferrari, C., & Musso, E. (2011). Italian ports: Towards a new governance? *Maritime Policy & Management, 38*, 335–346.

Ferrari C., Puliafito P. P., & Tei A. (2013). Performance and quality indexes in the evaluation of the terminal activity: A dynamic approach. *Research in Transportation Business & Management, 8*, 77–86.

MIT—Italian Ministry of Transport. (2015). *Iniziativa di studio sulla portualita italiana, department for planning and coordination of the economic policy*. Italy.

Parola, F., Ferrari, C., Tei, A., Satta, G., & Musso, E. (2017). Dealing with multi-scalar embeddedness and institutional divergence: Evidence from the renovation of Italian port governance. *Research in Transportation Business & Management, 22*, 89–99.

Parola, F., Tei, A., & Ferrari, C. (2012). Managing port concessions: Evidence from Italy. *Maritime Policy & Management, 39*, 45–61.
Valleri, M. A., Lamonarca, M., & Papa, P. (2006). Port governance in Italy. *Research in Transportation Economics, 17*, 139–153.

# 16

# The Dutch Port System: Regulation and Planning Issues

Claudio Ferrari, Bart Kuipers, and Alessio Tei

## Introduction

The current chapter is going to discuss the current port management system in The Netherlands highlighting the general regulatory and funding frameworks as well as some peculiarities related to the main national port, i.e. Rotterdam.

C. Ferrari · A. Tei
Department of Economics, University of Genoa, Genoa, Italy
e-mail: ferrari@economia.unige.it

B. Kuipers
Erasmus Centre for Urban, Port and Transport Economics, Erasmus University, Rotterdam, Netherlands
e-mail: bkuipers@ese.eur.nl

A. Tei (✉)
School of Engineering, Newcastle University, Newcastle upon Tyne, UK
e-mail: alessio.tei@unige.it

© The Author(s), under exclusive license to Springer Nature Switzerland AG 2022
C. Ferrari et al. (eds.), *Regulation and Finance in the Port Industry*, Palgrave Studies in Maritime Economics,
https://doi.org/10.1007/978-3-030-83985-7_16

In fact, the Dutch port system is quite heterogenic since different ports are applying different governance and managerial solutions (e.g. ISL, 2006; de Langen & van der Lugt, 2006, 2017) with the development of Rotterdam that has often been required special planning solutions (e.g. Kuipers & Jonkhoff, 2011). The influence of the national government is quite limited—with the exception of the port of Rotterdam, where the national government is a 30% shareholder, next to the municipality of Rotterdam—while local authorities have a substantial role in shaping the regulation of different ports. Currently, the Dutch port system is composed of 15 main corporatised ports that perform several industrial as well commercial activities. According to the National Port Council (ISL, 2006), these ports can be divided by specific geographical areas (also shown in Fig. 16.1), depending on the region they are located to but also on the main hinterland served:

- Northern ports (Delfzijl & Eemshaven, Harlingen, Den Helder);

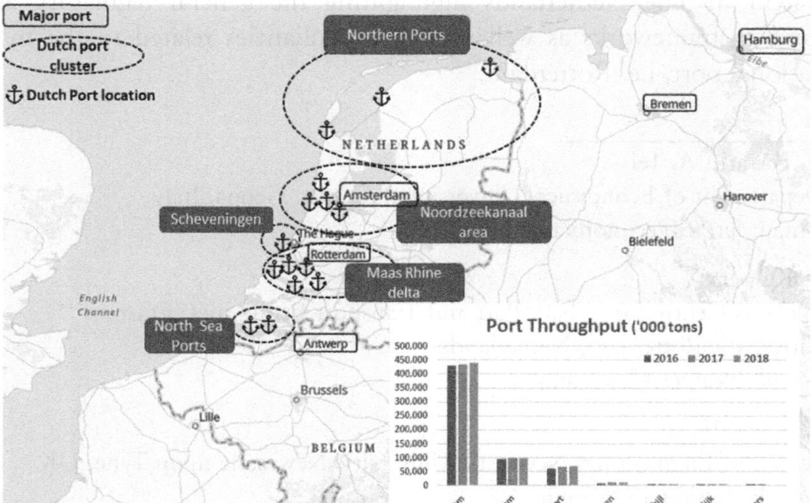


Fig. 16.1 Dutch seaports, location and throughput (*Source* Own elaboration based on Eurostat data, 2019)

- Noordzeekanaal area (Velsen/IJmuiden, Beverwijk, Zaanstad and Amsterdam), also referred to as Amsterdam Ports;
- Maas/Rhine delta (Vlaardingen; Schiedam; Rotterdam; Dordrecht; Moerdijk);
- Mouth of the Scheldt river (Vlissingen, Terneuzen and the Belgian port of Ghent, operating under the unified North Sea Port Authority);
- Other (Scheveningen).

As part of the unique managerial characteristics of the Dutch port system, some of the national ports are administrated by joint port authorities, such as in the case of Delfzijl and Eemshaven that belong to the Groningen Seaports Port Authority as well as Vlissingen, Terneuzen and Ghent, that are operating under the unified North Sea Port Authority—a rare example of an international joint venture between adjacent ports, next to Copenhagen Malmö Port. The rationale for the joint port authority is to rationalise the use of resources as well as to promote investment that could achieve a greater impact within a certain economic region/cluster.

As it is shown in Fig. 16.1, most of the traffic is concentrated in two ports: Rotterdam and Amsterdam. The former one is the biggest port in Europe (Eurostat, 2019) and it is formed by a plurality of different terminals located on the river Maas. The latter one is mainly connected to bulk traffic, even if there are also several other liner services.

Overall the Dutch ports have registered a general increase in cargo throughput in the past five years (Eurostat, 2019) with Rotterdam accounting for more than 70% of the overall handled traffic. Figure 16.2 shows the split between main traffic categories among the two main ports and the rest of the maritime gateways. Given its dominant role within the national port system, Rotterdam enjoys a special status within the National policies, often being characterised by specific rules and funding schemes that differentiate it from the other harbours.

Apart from the main two ports, other Dutch port facilities are small-medium-sized ports with marginal contribution to the overall port system, being normally highly specialised and often representing examples of single-user ports (e.g. de Langen & van der Lugt, 2006, 2017: ISL, 2006). Moreover, it is important to highlight how while

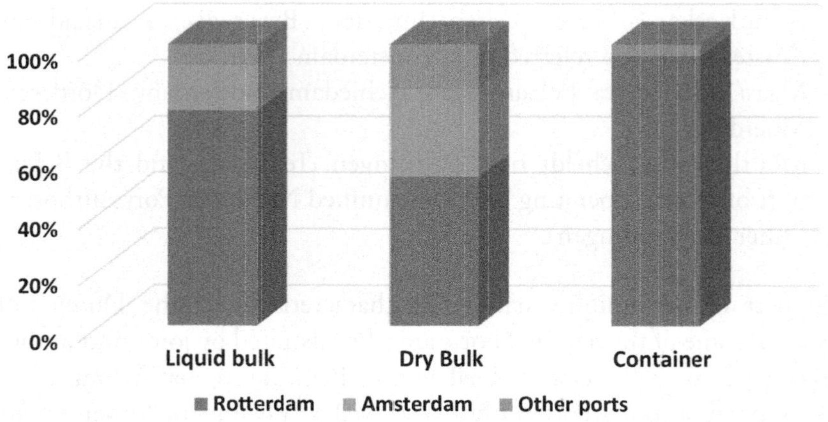


**Fig. 16.2** Split among traffic categories (2018) (*Source* Own elaboration from Eurostat data, 2019)

the smallest Dutch ports mainly serve local industries, the biggest ports serve wider areas with dedicated infrastructure that allow, for instance, Rotterdam to serve Central and Eastern Europe as well as to act as a main European transhipment point (e.g. Merk & Notteboom, 2015). The definition of the reference market allows the Dutch port to have dedicated investments in specific infrastructure as well as to promote special collaborations with key partners, such as the strategic partnership between Groningen Seaports and the ports of Northern Germany, Niedersachsen Ports and in particular the port of Emden, that aims at achieving full integration among the listed partners. Moreover, the advanced logistics services present in the region make The Netherlands a unique port and logistics platform within the European Union (e.g. Geerlings & Kuipers, 2013; Roso et al., 2009; van der Lugt et al., 2014; Wiegmans et al., 2014). In order to deal with this complexity, port authorities often act as promoters of local businesses (e.g. Port Development Companies as defined by de Langen & van der Lugt, 2017) more than simple port administrative bodies.

## The Dutch Governance System

Concerning the governance model, the landlord port model is the dominant one in large and medium-sized Dutch ports but small ports can also act as either public or more or less private ports (de Langen & van der Lugt, 2006, 2017). In this sense, the current national policy does not have a clear and strict set of rules in relation to the governance models that Dutch seaports should follow: it is generally recognised much flexibility to the regional and local governments to establish whether or not port authorities should be characterised by a certain degree of private involvement as well as on the degree of public control. The only strict constrain is that port management bodies should always guarantee that public interest is secured, as for the Dutch Ministry of Transport guidelines (2004). Thus, under the Dutch landlord model, a port authority is usually a separate legal entity with the capacity to conclude contracts (including concession agreements) and to enforce standards. Given this possibility, most of the biggest ports have been corporatised in the past decade, with both Rotterdam (from 2004) and Amsterdam (from 2013) ports that are from the group of ports that have changed their organisational structure into public limited companies (often defined as Port Development Companies) in which the shareholders remain key public institutions (mainly the local authority and in Rotterdam next to the municipality the national government) but assuring a more effective strategic behaviour thanks to the status of private company in respect to the more traditional "public authority" role.

Nevertheless, even if port authorities are highly commercialised entities, public influence is indirectly assured by the ownership interests that the Dutch state (or the regional governments) maintain in these public limited companies. Although legal title to the land in the port areas remains with the municipal government, in most cases the port authorities of Rotterdam and Amsterdam have leased this land in perpetuity. These lease agreements with the relevant municipal governments therefore allocate the economic ownership of the port area to the Port Authorities. The Port Authorities then can award specific portions of the port area to stevedore operators for the management (or the construction) of a terminal facility. Those concessions are normally awarded by either a competitive process (e.g. international tenders) or private agreements, depending on the size of the terminal. These issues are normally treated under the Dutch Public Procurement Act that represents an inclusion in the national law of several directives derived from the EU legislation (i.e. the EU Directives on public procurement [e.g. European Parliament, 2004a, 2004b] should be respected). No specific national laws affect port governance, with the exemption of the general organisation. Since the Port Authorities are considered privatised entities, they do not have to fully respect the majority of the public laws and there is an absence of specific legislation on the internal port organisation, despite this all main EU competition laws as well as environmental rules are directly applicable to the port sector. General EU guidelines and competition rules are also applicable for many marine services, such as dredging, mooring, pilotage, etc. Small ports are normally managed by special agencies within municipalities remits and for this reason are normally directly subject to the local political power.

As said, even if the Port Authorities are private commercial companies with a relatively reduced share owned by the central state, public shareholders are normally owning the strict majority of the shares (e.g. thanks to the role of the local authorities) determining a strong influence of the public governments on every port development process. Despite this, the private form allows port authorities to invest on the market also outside the port domain (e.g. inland ports and logistics parks) as well as the possibility to invest in international markets (as normally done by the Port of Rotterdam signing special agreements or even buying shares of other port companies). For instance, on 1 January 2018, the ports of Vlissingen, Terneuzen and Ghent merged into North Sea Port while the port of Rotterdam started a collaboration with several ports (e.g. in Brazil and in the Middle East) in order to better exploit network economies (de Langen & Heiji, 2006, 2017; Dooms et al., 2013). This form of investment and collaboration also came from the need of achieving a certain financial performance, derived for the corporate governance that most of the ports are subject to. De Langen and Heiji (2014) argued that the corporatisation determined a financial success for the port of Rotterdam while de Langen and van der Lugt (2017) registered that financial performance for other Dutch ports could be under dispute due to some underperforming year of some other port development companies (e.g. Zeeland Seaports recorded a loss after the first year of privatisation). Moreover, the special status the Dutch ports enjoy has generated the possibility for them to avoid corporate taxes and this situation is currently disputed at EU level given the potential distortion in terms of EU competition (e.g. TradeWinds, 2019).

## Dutch Investment Strategies and Port Tariffs

Concerning general tariffs and port costs, main ports—being independent private entities—have differentiated tariffs and they are free to impose different level of fares depending on their own strategic view. Nevertheless, the government maintains a supervisory role in order to assure a transparent decision-making process even if no specific regulation is present. Similarly, public–private partnerships in the port sector are neither regulated nor incentivised; despite this, main Port Authorities promote PPPs within their specific port strategy: Maasvlakte 2 in Rotterdam is an example of public–private participation, often using a design-built-finance-maintain(-own) scheme. Concerning this issue, foreign investments are not limited, even when they are connected to state-owned companies. Nevertheless, they are subject to a specific review process in order to assure that those investment are not against the national interest.

Currently, 2300 private companies operate in the port of Rotterdam and 1400 in the port of Amsterdam (among which 135 and 61 involved in terminal operations, respectively). Most of the terminals are operated by international specialised companies, such as APM-Maersk for the Maasvlakte 2, often benefitting from integrated industrial strategies, as in the case of the bulk terminals that among their shareholders see main multi-national cargo owners (e.g. Cargill in Amsterdam grain terminal and Arcelor Mittal in the Rotterdam metal terminal as well as Aramco, BP, Total and Shell for different oil terminals). In relation to linear shipping terminals, most of them are managed by vertical integrated companies, such as Maersk and CMA-CGM in the case of containers and Stena Liner for the Ro-Ro traffic. Nevertheless, many international stevedore companies have also recently invested in the Dutch ports, as in the Rotterdam World Gateway (RWG) terminal. RWG is an international consortium consisting of four globally operating container shipping companies—APL, MOL, HMM and CMA-CGM—and terminal operator DP World. The RWG-terminal is also located at Maasvlakte 2.

Every local municipal government issues several regulations regarding the ports within their jurisdiction, such as the Port Management By-Laws. Some municipalities have chosen to harmonise their regulations with those of other municipalities in the region, especially in case of joint port authorities, as in the case of Groningen and North Sea Port. The local regulations are only in addition to the various international and national safety and environmental rules applicable within all port areas and on waterways.

The Dutch port system is funded by different finance routes depending on the goals of the work. Investments related to issues that affect the overall functioning of the port area (e.g. dredging, natural defences, breakwaters and access to the infrastructures) are normally funded by the central government either directly (e.g. tenders for civil works) or indirectly (e.g. through the Port Authority). This funding route is quite similar for all the Dutch ports, independently to the size or the role of the port. Moreover, general national rules for procurement of civil works and use of public finance are applied in these cases. According to de Langen and van der Lugt (2006, 2017) the ministry inserted a special clause in its funding guidelines: after the evaluation of several investment options, in every situation in which the cost/benefit ratio is equal for an alternative that includes Rotterdam, this latter project will have the priority being developed within the "Dutch main port".

Similarly, land access to ports is normally a responsibility of the public entities (e.g. State, Provinces and Municipality) in charge of manage or built the specific transport infrastructure (e.g. rail or road) and the decision-making process normally involves Port-related representatives but only as a consultation exercise. Other investments and maintenance costs are normally related to the sole responsibility of the specific Port Authority (e.g. port internal road system, warehouses and quays) but many of these projects are normally part of concession agreements with the private companies actually managing the port activities and operations.

Often, new terminal projects supported by public–private agreements involve an investment also in port general facilities (e.g. roads) and then to the port authorities remains just the planning and organisational functions. For this reason, big port investments—managed through a design–build–finance–manage agreement—often include ancillary works (such as land reclamation) for which the private company can reclaim the expenses or ask for an extension of the concession period. Terminal superstructures and equipment are normally the sole responsibility of the private company awarded of a certain terminal area.

All contractors in either public or private companies have to comply with national rules on construction standards and the related labour and environmental legislation. Independent certification is often seen as a compulsory requirement to avoid specific liabilities. It is important to underline that in most cases Port Authorities can rely only on their own finance without any specific transfer from local or national governments. For this reason, the role of private operators is increasingly important.

Table 16.1 resumes main financial responsibilities, even if—as said—actual arrangements might vary, depending on specific agreements among the parties.

**Table 16.1** Investment duties in the Dutch port sector

| Type of infrastructure | Responsibility |
|---|---|
| General works (e.g. breakwaters) | Central Government |
| Access infrastructure (both by sea or by land) | Central Government (or other public bodies) |
| Terminal related infrastructure | Port Authority |
| Port internal works | Port Authority |
| Terminal superstructure and equipment | Private companies |
| | Tailor-made arrangements by Port Authority |

*Source* (ISL, 2006)

## Port Operation Management Legal Systems

Port operations are directly performed by private companies with only a few exemptions in the smallest Dutch ports. The concession contract gives them the right to a private operator to develop its own terminal activity with the restriction of the port area (and often of the cargo category) in which the company can operate.

Port Authorities and other public entities do not normally interfere with daily terminal operations even if the harbourmaster can normally arrange specific visits and controls for the agreed standards (e.g. labour and environmental goals) as well as the Port Authority has the right to check the achievement of the promised commercial outcomes (e.g. traffic goals). Specific penalties are foreseen by the Port Authorities in case of failure in respecting standards or in achieving goals and in extreme circumstances the Port Authority can take over the port operations. Concession agreements act as leasing contract under Dutch regulation and for this reason all the agreed elements might change over the time if either agreed by the parties or judged by a court for which a specific clause shouldn't be in place anymore. Concessions normally last for more than a decade and there is not specific reference duration foreseen by the law. Since the duration is normally agreed by the parties based on the amount of the investment, specific termination clauses can also be included in the concession contract. In order to allow the development of the agreed port operations, the Port Authority has a general commitment in assuring a correct functioning of all the port facilities directly connected to the terminal while National Government has a general commitment of assuring a good performance of the hinterland transport infrastructure. While terminal operations are performed by stevedoring companies, marine services are normally performed by separate private companies in a legal monopoly situation. These services are regulated under the EU legislation and the Port Authority has a regulatory power on the providers of those services with the aim of assuring high quality and high standard services. The nature (and the market organisation) of marine services varied a lot during the last 15 years, passing from a public provided service to a competitive market to the current market structure.

Concerning the superstructures and other terminal facilities, the terminal operator is free to invest in the necessary equipment or facilities, but it has the duty to return the land to the Port Authority at the same conditions of the beginning of the concession. Despite this, Port Authorities are free to make special agreements on case-by-case situations, assisting terminal operators in making their investments or in arranging special conditions at the end of the concession agreement. Similarly, there are no financial constraints in terms of terminal agreements or creation of special joint venture with other operators (or even Port Authorities) allowing terminal companies to increase their commercial value.

## Port Planning and Shoreline Resource Protection Legal Systems

Port planning is developed by the Port Authority in accordance with national and international regulation and based on port development plans. Main ports have multi-years strategic plans that reflect medium-long-term planning for the port infrastructure and general facilities. Similarly, Ministries publish guidelines and policy papers aiming at leading future developments in the port sectors, often in relation to a multitude of issues that concerns the maritime industry (e.g. "The Dutch Maritime Strategy 2015–2025" published by Directorate for Maritime Affairs of the Ministry of Infrastructure and Water Management [2015]).

Currently both Amsterdam and Rotterdam are undergoing major infrastructure developments that are heavily transforming the administrated shorelines. Generally, every major work is allowed only after the verification of compliance to the Nature Conservation Act. This permission has the role of assuring the respect of the port-related environment or the inclusion of compensation measures that assure an adequate protection of the natural resources involved in the port development. Compensation measures can be related to specific preservation works (e.g. in case of special areas populated by animals or plants), monetary refunds for damaged communities (e.g. in case of economic damage or need for relocation of certain activities) or creation of special protective zones in which—despite the port development—specific higher environmental standards must be met by the concessionaires. In order to respect the abovementioned environmental constraints, special clauses and goals are normally included in the tendering offer made to select the awarded operators for the specific development project. Thus these environmental issues represent part of the awarding procedure together with other operational or financial parameters. For instance, in the tender's offers for the Maasvlakte 2 the sustainability issues weighed around 20% of the overall score of the different offers.

Moreover, the harbourmaster is normally in charge to verify the respect of the agreed standards and in case of not respect, specific penalties—or even the withdraw of the concession—can be applied.

## Conclusions

The Dutch port system is characterised by a unique governance model in Europe that stands in between private (e.g. The United Kingdom) and more traditional landlord models (e.g. France, Italy and Spain). This approach makes port planning and operations capable to adapt to market changes as well as to promote the proactive involvement of port managers in many cooperation strategies (e.g. horizontal integrations, involvement of industrial companies in the port planning operations, port authorities long-term strategies outside the administered ports). This unique way to promote port business, allowed major ports to attract several investments, mainly in terms of public–private partnerships, as demonstrated by the Maasvlakte 2, in Rotterdam. Moreover, the integration of ports along different logistic corridors as well as the clear business orientation of corporatised Port Authorities did not affect the public ownership of major ports with related direct link to local (public) shareholders. The benefits of such approach are mainly connected with the preservation of a local interest without affecting the possibility to attract multi-national private operators interested in the highly specialised logistics services located in the Dutch region. The cooperation of major ports with relevant regional players (e.g. with both Flemish and German ports) also facilitated the establishment of efficient integrated solutions, improving the overall national logistics performance.

## References

De Langen, P. W., & Heij, C. (2014). Corporatisation and performance: A literature review and an analysis of the performance effects of the corporatisation of port of Rotterdam authority. *Transport Reviews, 34*, 396–414.

de Langen, P. W., & van der Lugt, L. (2006). Governance structures of port authorities in the Netherlands. *Research in Transportation Economics, 17*, 109–137.

de Langen, P. W., & van der Lugt, L. (2017). Institutional reforms of port authorities in the Netherlands: The establishment of port development companies. *Research in Transportation Business & Management, 22*, 108–113.

Directorate for Maritime Affairs. (2015). *The dutch maritime strategy 2015–2025*. Directorate for Maritime Affairs.

Dooms, M., van der Lugt, L., & de Langen, P. W. (2013). International strategies of port authorities: The case of the Port of Rotterdam Authority. *Research in Transportation Business & Management, 8*, 148–157.

Dutch Ministry of Transport. (2004). *Zeehavens: Ankers van de economie*. The Hague.

European Parliament. (2004a). *Directive n. 2004/17/EC, coordinating the procurement procedures of entities operating in the water, energy, transport and postal services sectors*. European Directive.

European Parliament. (2004b). *Directive n. 2004/18/EC, coordination of procedures for the award of public works contracts, public supply contracts and public service contracts*. European Directive.

Eurostat. (2019). http://ec.europa.eu/eurostat. Accessed September 1 2019.

Geerlings, H., & Kuipers, B. (2013). Smart governance and the management of sustainable mobility: An illustration of the application of policy integration and transition management in the Port of Rotterdam. In T. Vanoutrive & A. Verhetsel (Eds.), *Smart transport networks* (pp. 224–247). Edward Elgar.

Kuipers, B., & Jonkhoff, W. (2011). Ex post evaluation of Rotterdam port investment. In W. Manshanden & W. Jonkhoff (Eds.), *Infrastructure Productivity Evaluation* (pp. 47–64). Springer.

ISL—Institute of Shipping Economics and Logistics. (2006). *Public financing and charging practices of seaports in the EU*.

Merk, O., & Notteboom T. (2015). *Port Hinterland connectivity*. ITF Discussion Paper No.13, International Transport Forum, Paris.

Roso, V., Woxenius, J., & Lumsden, K. (2009). The dry port concept: Connecting container seaports with the hinterland. *Journal of Transport Geography, 17*, 338–345.

TradeWinds. (2019). www.tradewindsnews.com. Accessed September 1 2019.

Van der Lugt, L., Rodrigues, S., & van den Berg, R. (2014). Co-evolution of the strategic reorientation of port actors: Insights from the Port of Rotterdam and the Port of Barcelona. *Journal of Transport Geography, 41*, 197–209.

Wiegmans, B., Witte, P., & Spit, T. (2014). Inland port performance: A statistical analysis of Dutch inland ports. *Transportation Research Procedia*. European Transport Conference 2014.

# 17

# Regulation and Finance in the Norwegian Port Sector

**Axel Merkel and Ziaul Haque Munim**

## National Port System Description

Norway has a long tradition as a maritime nation, housing a large shipping sector with a highly international profile. Around the end of the nineteenth century, shipping services accounted for as much as 40% of the country's total exports (Hodne & Grytten, 1992, p. 47). It currently ranks in ninth place in terms of fleet ownership, controlling roughly 3% of world dead-weight tonnage (UNCTAD, 2018), though this figure is considerably down since 50 years ago when Norwegian ownership accounted for as much as 12% (Fearnley and Egers Chartering Co.

A. Merkel (✉)
Swedish National Road and Transport Research Institute, Linköping, Sweden
e-mail: axel.merkel@vti.se

Z. H. Munim
University of South-Eastern Norway, Notodden, Norway

© The Author(s), under exclusive license to Springer Nature Switzerland AG 2022
C. Ferrari et al. (eds.), *Regulation and Finance in the Port Industry*, Palgrave Studies in Maritime Economics,
https://doi.org/10.1007/978-3-030-83985-7_17

Ltd., 1968, as cited in Tenold, 2001). The administrative bodies of historically important ports such as Oslo and Bergen trace their history back to 1735, when port authorities were established by royal decree. A national administrative body for ports, primarily tasked with controlling and exercising national authority over municipally governed ports, was established in 1841 (Norwegian Coastal Administration, 2014).

Today, there are some 130 ports of varying size and commercial importance that handle cargo. Of these, 27 ports have terminals that are classified as being *key* parts of the transport network (Ministry of Transport and Communications, 2015a). While the central government does not exercise direct influence over cargo ports (e.g. through port infrastructure investments), these key ports are prioritized in terms of providing adequate connecting infrastructure such as fairways, roads and railways. Such investments are carried out by the government and indicated in advance through the ten-year National Transport Plan (NTP), which is ratified by parliament every four years. Figure 17.1 illustrates the evolution of port throughput in Norway since 2002. In tonnage terms, the two largest ports are those of Bergen (48 million tonnes in

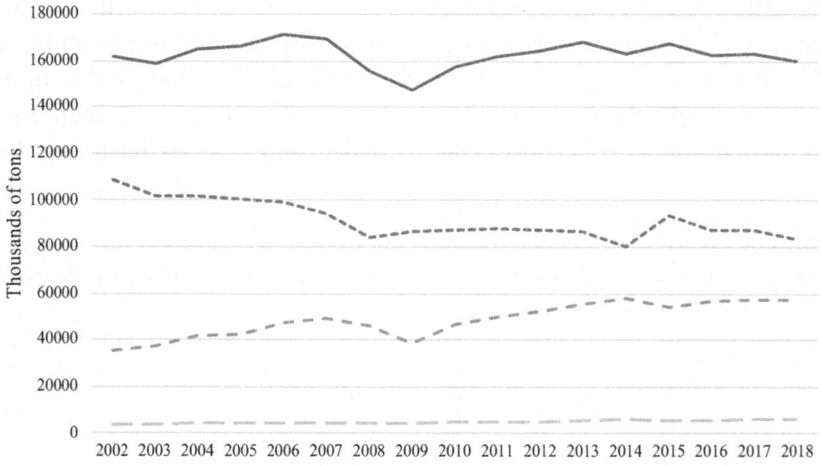


**Fig. 17.1** Evolution of port throughput in Norwegian ports 2002–2018 (*Source* Own elaboration of Eurostat [2019])

2017) and Narvik (21 million tonnes) (Statistics Norway, 2018). This is partly because they deal with very large export-generating regional customers (Ministry of Transport and Communications, 2015a). A large share of Bergen's volumes is related to the nearby private oil terminals. In the case of Narvik, the vast majority of its tonnage comes from the iron ore industry in northern Sweden. In tonnage terms, liquid and dry bulk cargo together constitute most of the goods handled in Norwegian ports. In 2017, more than 50% of total tonnage handled was liquid bulk cargo (liquid gas, crude oil, petroleum and other) (Statistics Norway, 2018). Dry bulk (ore, coal, agricultural products and other) accounted for 35%, while containerized goods only accounted for roughly 4% of total tonnage (in value terms, containerized goods naturally account for a significantly larger share).

Geographically, liquid bulk transports are concentrated mostly to the lower continental shelf, as can be seen from Fig. 17.2. As can also be seen from that figure, the most geographically concentrated region in terms of the number of ports is in and around the Oslo fjord, where seven ports (Grenland, Larvik, Tønsberg, Borg, Moss, Drammen and Oslo) are located in close proximity. This is also where handling of containerized cargo is mostly concentrated. In addition to the aforementioned key ports, there is also a large amount of small local ports, fishing ports and pleasure craft ports. A substantial number of fishing ports are owned by the government and managed by the Norwegian Coastal Administration. While there are some privately owned ports and terminals, public ownership at the municipality level is by far the most common in Norwegian ports (Ministry of Transport and Communications, 2015a). In this regard, Norway is similar to its neighbours in continental northern Europe and Scandinavia, where 80% of port authorities are municipality-owned (Verhoeven, 2011).

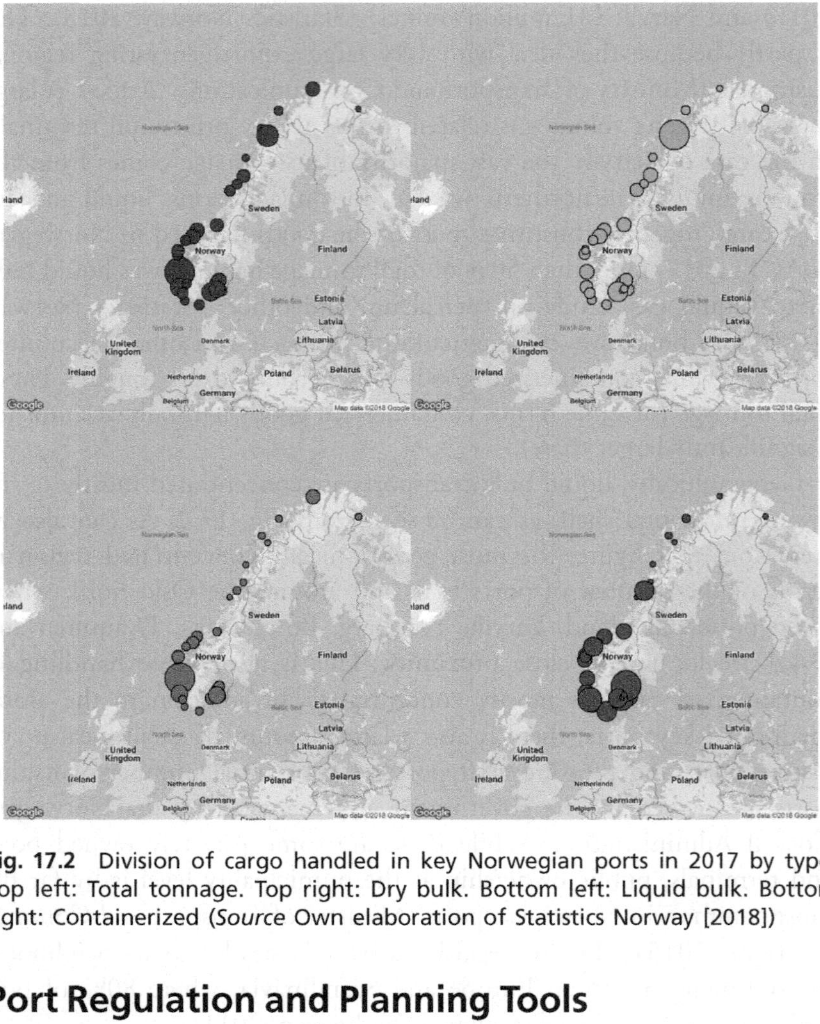


Fig. 17.2 Division of cargo handled in key Norwegian ports in 2017 by type. Top left: Total tonnage. Top right: Dry bulk. Bottom left: Liquid bulk. Bottom right: Containerized (*Source* Own elaboration of Statistics Norway [2018])

## Port Regulation and Planning Tools

Port-owning municipalities have some degrees of freedom in determining how to organize their activities. Municipalities can choose among a variety of governance structures, which are prescribed by the Local Government Act (1992). A port may be organized as an integrated part of the municipality administration, a municipal enterprise (ME), an inter-municipal (I-M) cooperation, an inter-municipal (I-M) company

**Table 17.1** Division ports by organizational structure (Ministry of Transport and Communications, 2015a). Note that minor changes have occurred since the list was compiled

| Organizational structure | Number of ports (share of total) | Degree of independence from municipality |
|---|---|---|
| Integrated in municipality administration | 79 (61%) | None |
| Municipal enterprise (ME) | 36 (27%) | Low |
| Inter-municipal (I-M) cooperation | 3 (2%) | Medium |
| Inter-municipal (I-M) company | 11 (7%) | High |
| Limited enterprise | 0 (0%) | Very high |

or as a limited liability (stock-based) enterprise. The observed frequency of each of these alternatives as of 2015 is reported in Table 17.1. The third column provides a characterization of the degree of autonomy provided by each organizational structure. We classify ports that are run as a part of the municipality administration as completely non-autonomous, since there is no independent entity appointed to handle port affairs. MEs are not legally distinct from the municipality itself, and hence the degree of autonomy is low, but it does have an appointed board of directors, which can act independently to some extent. For I-M cooperation ports, a board including representatives from the participating municipalities is appointed and given authority to make decisions regarding organizational and operational issues. By contrast, I-M companies are legally independent of its owners and are designed to have a high degree of functional autonomy. Finally, ports that are run as limited enterprises operate under the same conditions as any private company. Even in cases where the municipality is the majority (or the sole) shareholder, the board of directors typically has a higher degree of independence and freedom from political control than in an I-M company. While the first option listed in Table 17.1 is the most common, it is predominantly seen in small ports. Out of the previously mentioned 27 key ports, organization as a municipal enterprise is the most common, followed by organization as an inter-municipal company (Ministry of

Transport and Communications, 2015a). While the option of organizing as a limited enterprise appears rare, this might be on the verge of changing. The port of Bergen recently converted its organizational structure from that of an inter-municipal cooperation to a limited company jointly owned by Bergen and 11 neighbouring municipalities (Port of Bergen, 2019).

The division of responsibilities between municipalities and the state are to some extent geographically defined. The Ports and Fairways Act (2009) stipulates that municipalities are responsible for the safety and accessibility in ports and their immediately surrounding sea areas, as well as for operation and maintenance of ports and terminals so that the needs of port users are met in a secure and efficient manner. The responsibilities of the state, as delegated to the Norwegian Coastal Administration, include the safety and accessibility of waters outside port areas. Until recently, seven ports: Oslo, Kristiansand, Stavanger, Bergen, Tromsø, Trondheim and Bodø, were identified by the Ministry of Fisheries and Coastal affairs as being of special importance as hubs for domestic and international freight and passenger transport (Ministry of Transport and Communications, 2015a). This policy allowed the government to more directly regulate the governance mechanisms in such ports, in accordance with Ports and Fairways Act (2009). While this remains a potentially useful tool in Norwegian port policy, as of today no ports are classified in this way.

An important regulation stipulated by the aforementioned law is that all port capital, including accumulated revenues from port-related services, land rents, fees or other assets, can only be used for the purposes of port-related operations and development (a small number of exceptions non-withstanding). This means that any revenues or asset returns accruing to the port are effectively screened off from other areas of business or development in a municipality. On one hand, this may be motivated by concerns that ports would otherwise be incentivized to charge premium prices for port services in order to finance other municipal ventures. On the other hand, a likely consequence of the regulation of port capital is that the existing port structure becomes very difficult to change, e.g. through disinvestment in smaller ports combined with consolidation of capacity to benefit from economies of scale in port operations. It has also been suggested in a review of the current legal framework (NOU, 2018:4, 2018) that prohibiting the use of economic surpluses from port activities for other investments than those related to the port may result in over investment in port capacity. The reason is that when capital is not allocated to the highest yielding investments, but instead confined to a particular purpose, the marginal rates of return are likely to be lower than elsewhere in the economy. It has however also been argued (Marskar et al., 2015) that the regulations in place have led to increased opportunities to sustain a geographically dispersed and diversified supply of port services at low costs to users.[1]

## Financial Tools

The financial options and obligations of ports differ with regard to organizational structure. First, municipalities that own and/or operate ports need to follow the general regulations for financial management set out by the Local Government Act (1992), the Limited Liability Companies Act (1997), as well as the Accounting Act (1998). These general regulations have slightly different consequences depending on the chosen organizational structure. For organizational options 1–3 as listed in Table 17.1, the port is viewed as part of a municipality's business and there is an obligation every year to decide upon an economic four-year plan, as well as an annual budget, which should be balanced and based on 'realistic expectations' of future revenues and costs. Such a municipality-owned port may finance investments through loans but is required to manage its finances 'without considerable risk'. The law of inter-municipal companies (1999) regulates ports organized as option 4 in Table 17.1. The financial regulation of such an organization is largely similar to those of options 1–3, with the expectation that it is allowed under certain circumstances to pay dividends to its owners. Organizing as a limited company (option 5) comes with the benefit that the municipality can

[1] Since the writing of this chapter, an amended version of the Ports and Fairways Act was passed in 2019. The changes have some implications for the regulation of capital in municipal ports.

share port ownership with private actors. Ports organized as limited companies are subject to regulations in the public limited companies act (Limited Liability Companies Act, 1997), which stipulates among other things that the company is required to have a 'defensible' level of equity and liquidity with respect to its risk exposure. On top of these general regulations pertaining to the organizational structure of ports, every port is subject to the specific conditions of the Ports and Fairways Act (2009). Regardless of the chosen organizational structure of the port, its capital is restricted from other uses than those related to the operation, maintenance or development of the port. If the port is set up as a limited company where the municipality is not the sole shareholder, only the share of capital proportional to the municipality's stake of ownership is regulated as port capital.

Besides user charges, loans or private sector collaboration, governmental financial subsidization schemes are a channel through which ports may raise funds. There are a number of such schemes in place, directed for example to incentivize port cooperation and environmental schemes set to encourage the use of shore power. A scheme to provide financial support to port cooperation initiatives was established in 2015 and comprised a broad definition of cooperation, encompassing a total merger of ports' businesses and organization, a partial merger or the coordination of supporting and administrative activities (Norwegian Coastal Administration, 2018). The expressed purpose of the scheme has been to strengthen the competitiveness of maritime transport vis-à-vis other modes through quality-enhancing and cost-reducing cooperative solutions. Overall, the annual budget for this scheme has been roughly 10 million NOK.[2] The public subsidization of shore power initiatives, transmitted through the government enterprise Enova, has since its beginning in 2016 amounted to roughly 439 million NOK (Enova, 2016a, 2016b, 2017a, 2017b, 2018). Though this is a substantial amount, it does not constitute government subsidization in the general sense since it steers towards development initiatives that would otherwise not have been pursued, with the aim of improving the environmental performance of the transport system.

---

[2] 10 million NOK amounts to roughly 1.05 million EUR.

## Links Between Local and National Port Regulation and the International Framework of Ports

Due to the strategic role of ports in their home region or country, traditionally, ports worldwide have been regulated by central or local government, although their autonomy varies from country to country (Tovar et al., 2004). This is largely evident in the Norwegian governance models as depicted in Table 17.1, where the degree of autonomy varies from port to port. However, globally, the participation of private firms in port development and investment increased dramatically over the last two decades. Among the causes of increased private participation is to increase port efficiency, reduce the cost of port services, access new financial resources, transfer of expertise and technologies and reducing pressure on public sector budget (Dekker & Verhaeghe, 2012; UNCTAD, 2017).

Particularly, the *landlord port* model, in which a port authority enters into a concession contract or a public–private partnership or a combination of both with a private firm, is the most common with an estimated 85–90% global ports being landlord today (UNCTAD, 2017). In the landlord port model, the central government or municipality owns and manages the port land and infrastructures (including access to road, rail and air transport networks), while private firms are responsible for maintaining and operating port superstructures (e.g. equipment, cranes). Despite the majority of Norwegian ports being municipality-owned, the landlord port model is evident in major cargo handling ports. For example, the Sjursøya Container Terminal of the country's largest container port, the Port of Oslo, is maintained and operated by Yilport-Oslo, a subsidiary of a Turkey-based global terminal operator (GTO) Yilport Holding. Another port governance model, *tool port* in which port authority owns and maintains port infrastructure *and* superstructure while private firms provide port labour, is considered as an intermediary between service port and landlord port model. The container terminal at the Port of Kristiansand functions under the tool port model and is also operated by two private firms, Seafront and Green carrier. However, to the best of our knowledge, none of the leading global port investors such as AP Moller–Maersk, Port of Singapore, Hutchison, DP World, etc. (UNCTAD, 2017) are involved in the operation of Norwegian ports.

For port asset management, there exists two almost contradictory viewpoints: Anglo-Saxonian and continental. The first posits that ports should be financially self-sufficient while the latter emphasizes the social welfare of ports (Lee & Lam, 2015; Musso et al., 2006). While Norwegian ports do have a high degree of financial self-sufficiency, port governance is mostly characterized by the 'Hanseatic' style of governance that prevails in northern continental Europe and the rest of Scandinavia (Verhoeven, 2011). Government subsidies made available under different circumstances to minimize environmental impacts of port operation (such as the aforementioned shore power subsidization scheme) are an interesting example of how Norwegian policy is focused on social welfare. As mentioned earlier, there exists limited scale public–private partnerships (PPPs) and foreign direct investments (FDIs) in port development in Norway. As of PPPs, examples include the operations of Yilport at the Port of Oslo, privatization of the Port of Bergen and involvement of private firms at the Port of Kristiansand. However, such private involvements by means of concession contracts are not equivalent to *privatization* but should rather be called *partnerships* (Rodal & Mulder, 1993). Some privatization in the form of FDIs do exist in smaller ports such as the Port of Slagen. This small liquid bulk port is located on the west of Oslo Fjord, owned and operated by the Esso Norge AS that is owned by the USA headquartered oil and gas corporation ExxonMobil. Such a low degree of private sector participation in infrastructure development is consistent with the rest of Europe, which has the lowest rate of private participation in port infrastructure development projects globally. Europe and Central Asia combined had only 19 port development projects with private participation during 2000–2016 (UNCTAD, 2017). Meanwhile, Chinese companies have expressed their interest to invest in port infrastructure development in the Norwegian city of Kirkenes as a part of their plan to commercialize the Northern Sea Route (NSR) (Kynge, 2017). Although some regulatory issues exist, private participation has potential to boost further the competitiveness of the Norwegian port industry.

## Critical Discussion: How Can Port Regulation and Financial Practices Affect Local Port Development?

The current Ports and Fairways Act is currently being considered for revision. Among the proposed revisions is a liberalization of port capital usage, suggesting that municipalities should be given the freedom to extract accumulated port values and redeploy freely, as long as the financial needs of the port have been secured (NOU, 2018:4, 2018). There is an increased propensity in Norway as in the rest of Europe to devolve operational responsibilities to private terminal operators (Marskar et al., 2015). While the value captured by the port in terms of rental revenues is regulated as 'port capital', this means that the development of terminal operations and services, which are highly capital-intensive elements of port businesses, are being increasingly integrated with the private sector. An interesting question going forward is to what extent liberalizations and possibly increased private sector involvement can affect port development in Norway. In particular, the effect of liberalizing the usage of port capital on the intensity of port competition in Norway needs to be carefully evaluated. Since many regions of Norway lack the concentration of population necessary to support multiple competing ports of sufficient scale, there is a clear risk that policy changes that would induce a concentration of port capacity could lead to some ports having excessive market power.

Norwegian transport authorities have shown interest in PPPs only recently. PPPs would have not been possible 10 years back, but now it is deemed to be feasible, as initiatives are already taken to assess regulations concerning municipalities' port ownership (Ministry of Transport and Communications, 2015b). As mentioned in previous studies, among the major objectives of private participation in port infrastructure development (Baird, 2000; Dekker & Verhaeghe, 2012; UNCTAD, 2017), not many are relevant for Norway due to the socio-economic status of the country. There already exists about 130 ports in Norway for a population of 5.5 million: there is no substantial need to develop new ports from scratch. For future capacity expansion and development, ports utilize their accumulated capital, as well as government subsidies available for dedicated (social and environmental) purposes. Meanwhile, ports may still require funds from alternative sources. For example, the Port of Kristiansand initiated a real-estate project named 'Kanalbyen',[3] from which profit will be invested in the port's expansion. Involvement of the world's leading port investors and GTOs could benefit such projects greatly. One of the regulations that limit the involvement of global investors is the aforementioned limitations that apply to the usage of port capital. However, with the initiative of transforming the ownership of the Port of Bergen to a municipality-owned joint stock company, the number of ports organized as limited enterprises with private participation may increase in the future. Still, it is expected that the public sector will keep most control over investment, planning, development and regulation of ports as seen in the majority of countries worldwide (Baird, 2000).

Overall, major Norwegian ports are performing well in terms of connectivity (Jia et al., 2017) and efficiency (Schøyen & Odeck, 2013). In this context, the participation of GTOs in port operation can improve the competitiveness of Norwegian maritime transport through the transfer of know-how, the introduction of competition and increasing port throughput by establishing dedicated terminals. Due to the large geographical spread of GTOs, they are well accustomed to the latest technology and management tools. Also, competition among terminal operators or ports, if introduced through privatization, can improve service quality of ports. However, ports' size and their service types should be taken into account when analyzing the feasibility of competition (Tovar et al., 2004). Furthermore, GTOs, particularly those owned by leading shipping lines, can attract a large volume of container throughput via the establishment of their dedicated terminals at ports (Haralambides et al., 2002). For example, 50% of total container throughput in Northern Europe is handled by the four major GTOs (PSA, Eurogate, Hutchinson and HHLA) (Franc & Van der Horst, 2010). This also holds for ferry operators, as mentioned in Baird (2000) that P&O ferry subsidiaries managed 'terminal operations at more than ten ports throughout continental Europe, United Kingdom and Ireland' (p. 178).

[3] http://www.portofkristiansand.no/en/eiendom/kanalbyen/.

Finally, another argument in favour of PPP would be efficient project execution (Ministry of Transport and Communications, 2015b). Port infrastructure development projects are typically complex. Usually, such projects follow the iron rule of complex project management, that is, *Over Budget, Over Time, Over and Over Again* (Flyvbjerg, 2014, p. 6). In this regard, cooperation with GTOs through PPPs or concession agreements can benefit local port development projects due to their rich know-how.

Despite some potential benefits of private participation in port infrastructure development, potential drawbacks should also be considered. The result of large-scale privatization of UK ports did not yield a good outcome for the society (Baird, 2000). Ports with a higher degree of private involvement induce less local participation (Slack & Frémont, 2005). In a similar vein, Poulsen et al. (2018) found that there is significant potential for public port authorities to facilitate improved environmental performance in shipping. Furthermore, due to the nature of port investments, that is, high capital cost, long cost recovery period and the wider economic, social and environmental aspects (Baird, 2000), the continued role of public authorities should not be overlooked.

## References

Aksjeloven [Limited Liability Companies Act]. (1997). *Lov om aksjeselskaper (LOV-1997–06–13–44)*. https://lovdata.no/dokument/NL/lov/1997-06-13-44

Baird, A. J. (2000). Port privatisation: Objectives, extent, process, and the UK experience. *International Journal of Maritime Economics, 2*(3), 177–194.

Dekker, S., & Verhaeghe, R. J. (2012). Port investment and finance. *The Blackwell Companion to Maritime Economics*, 623–637.

Enova. (2016a, March 11). *Enova kobler til 13 landstrøm-prosjekter*. http://presse.enova.no/pressreleases/enova-kobler-til-13-landstroem-prosjekter-1392206

Enova. (2016b, December 14). *140 millioner till landstrøm*. http://presse.enova.no/pressreleases/140-millioner-til-landstroem-1689508

Enova. (2017a, June 27). *20 landstrømprosjekter får Enova-støtte*. http://presse.enova.no/pressreleases/20-landstroemprosjekter-faar-enova-stoette-2019649
Enova. (2017b, December 20). *Enova støtter ni nye landstrøm-prosjekt*. http://presse.enova.no/pressreleases/enova-stoetter-ni-nye-landstroem-prosjekter-2325688
Enova. (2018, June 28). *Over 50 nye millioner til landstrøm*. http://presse.enova.no/pressreleases/over-50-nye-millioner-til-landstroem-2551693
Eurostat. (2019). *Gross weight of goods handled in all ports by direction and type of cargo—quarterly data*.
Flyvbjerg, B. (2014). What you should know about megaprojects and why: An overview. *Project Management Journal, 45*(2), 6–19.
Franc, P., & Van der Horst, M. (2010). Understanding hinterland service integration by shipping lines and terminal operators: A theoretical and empirical analysis. *Journal of Transport Geography, 18*(4), 557–566.
Haralambides, H. E., Cariou, P., & Benacchio, M. (2002). Costs, benefits and pricing of dedicated container terminals. *International Journal of Maritime Economics, 4*(1), 21–34.
Havne- og farvannsloven [Ports and Fairways Act]. (2009). *Lov om havner og farvann (LOV-2009–04–17–19)*. https://lovdata.no/dokument/NL/lov/2009-04-17-19
Hodne, F., & Grytten, O. H. (1992). *Norsk økonomi 1900–1990*. Tano.
Jia, H., Daae Lampe, O., Solteszova, V., & Strandenes, S. P. (2017). Norwegian port connectivity and its policy implications. *Maritime Policy & Management, 44*(8), 956–966.
Kommuneloven [Local Government Act]. (1992). *Lov om kommuner og fylkeskommuner (LOV-1992–09–25–107)*. https://lovdata.no/dokument/NL/lov/1992-09-25-107
Kynge, J. (2017, July 16). Chinese purchases of overseas ports top $20bn in past year. *Financial Times*. http://www.ft.com
Kystverket [Norwegian Coastal Administration]. (2014, May 9). *Historikk*. https://www.kystverket.no/Maritim-infrastruktur/Havner/Havnehistorie/
Kystverket [Norwegian Coastal Administration]. (2018, April 17). *Tilskot til hamnesamerbeid*. https://www.kystverket.no/Maritim-infrastruktur/Havner/Tilskuddsordning-for-havnesamarbeid/
Lee, P. T.-W., & Lam, J. S. L. (2015). Container port competition and competitiveness analysis: Asian major ports In C. Y. Lee & Q. Meng (Eds,), *Handbook of ocean container transport logistics*. International Series in Operations Research & Management Science. Springer.

Lov om interkommunale selskaper [Inter-municipal Companies Act]. (1999). *Lov om interkommunale selskaper (LOV-1999–01–29–6)*. https://lovdata.no/dokument/NL/lov/1999-01-29-6

Marskar, E., Askildsen, T., Markussen, G., Farstad von Hall, P., & Presttun, T. (2015). *NTP Godsanalyse. Delrapport 2: Offentlige godsterminaler. Struktur, eierskap, finansiering og drift*. Sekretariatet for nasjonal transportplan.

Musso, E., Ferrari, C., & Benacchio, M. (2006). Port investment: Profitability, economic impact and financing. *Research in Transportation Economics, 16*, 171–218.

NOU 2018:4. (2018). *Sjøveien videre—Forslag til ny havne- og farvannslov*. Ministry of Transport and Communications.

Port of Bergen. (2019). *Fakta om Bergen havn*. https://bergenhavn.no/om-bergen-havn/fakta-om-bergen-havn/. Last accessed on 2019.09.26.

Poulsen, R. T., Ponte, S., & Sornn-Friese, H. (2018). Environmental upgrading in global value chains: The potential and limitations of ports in the greening of maritime transport. *Geoforum, 89*, 83–95.

Regnskapsloven [Accounting Act]. (1998). *Lov om årsregnskap m.v. (LOV-1998–07–17–56)*. https://lovdata.no/dokument/NL/lov/1998-07-17-56

Rodal, A., & Mulder, N. (1993). Partnerships, devolution and power-sharing: Issues and implications for management. *Optimum, 24*, 27–27.

Samferdselsdepartementet [Ministry of transport and communications]. (2015a). *Nasjonal havnestrategi. Regjeringens strategi for effektive havner for å få mer gods på sjø*. Departementenes sikkerhets- og serviceorganisasjon.

Samferdselsdepartementet [Ministry of transport and communications]. (2015b). *Reforming and modernising the Norwegian transport sector*. Retrieved on December 5, 2018 from https://www.regjeringen.no/contentassets/7b538ed3b155426ab4c7447420f32d1f/83682_sd_brosjyre_uu.pdf

Schøyen, H., & Odeck, J. (2013). The technical efficiency of Norwegian container ports: A comparison to some Nordic and UK container ports using Data Envelopment Analysis (DEA). *Maritime Economics & Logistics, 15*(2), 197–221.

Slack, B., & Frémont, A. (2005). Transformation of port terminal operations: From the local to the global. *Transport Reviews, 25*(1), 117–130.

Statistics Norway (2018). 08923: *Maritime transport statistics. Goods, by ports, type of cargo, type of commodity, flag and domestic/foreign 2011K1 - 2018K2*. https://www.ssb.no/en/statbank/table/08923/

Tenold, S. (2001). *The shipping crisis of the 1970s: Causes, effects and implications for Norwegian shipping*. Doctoral dissertation, Norwegian School of Economics and Business Administration.

Tovar de la Fé, B., Trujillo, L., & Jara-Díaz, S. (2004). Organization and regulation of the port industry: Europe and Spain. In *Essays on microeconomics and industrial organisation* (2nd ed.). Physica-Verlag. A Springer-Verlag Company.

United Nations Conference on Trade and Development (UNCTAD). (2017). *Review of maritime transport*. UNCTAD.

United Nations Conference on Trade and Development (UNCTAD). (2018). *Review of maritime transport*. UNCTAD.

Verhoeven, P. (2011). *European port governance*. Report of an enquiry into the current governance of European seaports.

# 18

# Regulation and Finance in the Spanish Port Sector

Beatriz Tovar and Alan Wall

## Main Characteristics of Spanish State Port System

The Spanish State-owned Port System comprises 46 General Interest ports[1] that are managed by 28 Port Authorities (see Fig. 18.1). Since 1992, the coordination and control of the system is the responsibility of

[1] Ports with a relevance beyond local traffic that are property of the State and that must comply with a series of characteristics—see section "Governance Model" for more details.

B. Tovar (✉)
Tourism and Transport Research Unit, Institute of Tourism and Sustainable Economic Development, University of Las Palmas de Gran Canaria (ULPGC), Las Palmas de Gran Canaria, Spain
e-mail: beatriz.tovar@ulpgc.es

© The Author(s), under exclusive license to Springer Nature Switzerland AG 2022

C. Ferrari et al. (eds.), *Regulation and Finance in the Port Industry*, Palgrave Studies in Maritime Economics,
https://doi.org/10.1007/978-3-030-83985-7_18

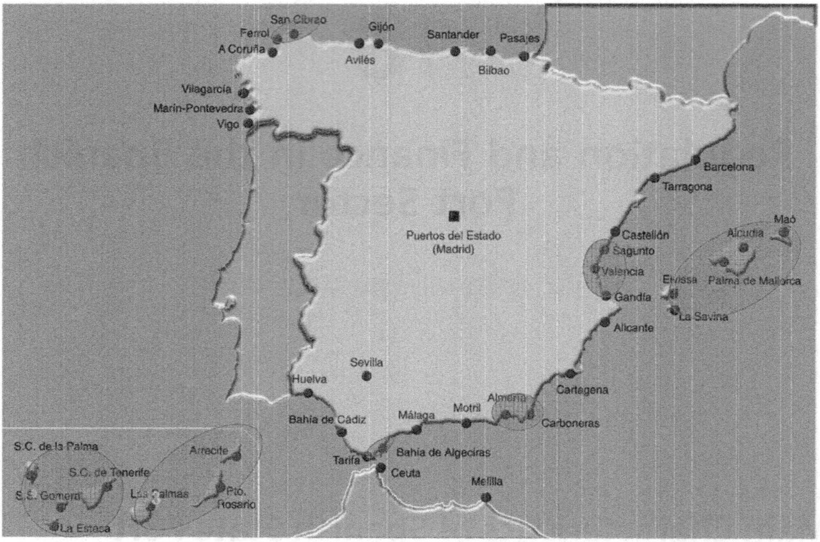


**Fig. 18.1** The Spanish state-owned port system[a] (*Source* State Ports Authority [*Organismo Público Puertos del Estado*]. [a]Port Authorities that manage more than one port [e.g., Balearic Islands] are circled)

State Ports Authority (*Organismo Público Puertos del Estado*), an organisation overseen by the Ministry of Public Works that executes government port policy.

Data from the State Ports Authority (Organismo Público de Puertos del Estado) (2016) highlight the importance of the Spanish port system for the economy. Thus, in 2015, 53% of Spanish foreign trade with the EU and 96% of non-EU trade was maritime, accounting for 60% of exports from and 85% of imports to Spain. The economic activity of the port system accounted for 20% of transport sector GDP,

Campus Universitario de Tafira, Módulo D, Las Palmas de Gran Canaria, Spain

A. Wall
Oviedo Efficiency Group, Department of Economics, University of Oviedo, Oviedo, Spain

**Table 18.1** Total port traffic in Spain by category in 2017

| Type of traffic | Quantity (tons) | % Total traffic |
|---|---|---|
| Liquid bulk | 178,592,743 | 32.8 |
| Solid bulk | 101,040,382 | 18.5 |
| General cargo: Break bulk | 71,085,676 | 13.0 |
| General cargo: Containers | 181,449,042 | 33.3 |
| Other goods | 12,789,539 | 2.3 |
| **Total Cargo Traffic** | **544,957,382** | **100.0** |
| Non cruise Passengers | 24,791,516 | 72.8 |
| Cruise passengers | 9,281,923 | 27.2 |
| **Total Passenger traffic** | **34,073,516** | **100.0** |

*Source* State Ports Authority (Organismo Público Puertos del Estado)

or 1.1% of Spanish GDP, and generated direct and indirect employment of 35,000 and 110,000 workers.

Table 18.1 shows the breakdown of port traffic—cargo and passengers—in Spain for 2017. As can be seen, total goods traffic in 2017 was 544.96 million tons. The largest type of traffic was containerised general cargo (33.3% of total), followed closely by liquid bulk (32.8%), solid bulk (18.5%) and break bulk (13%).

Over the last decade, there have been significant changes in the composition of Spanish port traffic. General cargo (break bulk and containerised) rose from 41.5% of the total in 2007 to 46.3% in 2017, whereas bulk cargo (liquids and solids) fell from 55.3% of the total in 2007 to 51.3% in 2017. Containerised traffic has grown considerably over the last decade, increasing from 139.3 million tonnes in 2007 (28.8% of total traffic) to 181.4 million tonnes in 2017 (33.3% of total traffic). Goods in transit also rose significantly from 18.4% of total traffic in 2007 (89 million tons) to 25.1% of total traffic in 2017.

Passenger traffic has grown significantly in recent decades. Ferry traffic, amounting to almost 25 million passengers in 2017, covers relatively short trajectories and is especially important in the Strait of Gibraltar and the Balearic and Canary Islands. The number of cruise passengers has risen dramatically over the last decade, with the Mediterranean seaboard accounting for the lion's share of this. Indeed, Barcelona and the Balearic Islands, with over 2.5 million and 2 million passengers respectively in 2015, were the busiest and fourth-busiest passenger port in Europe. The

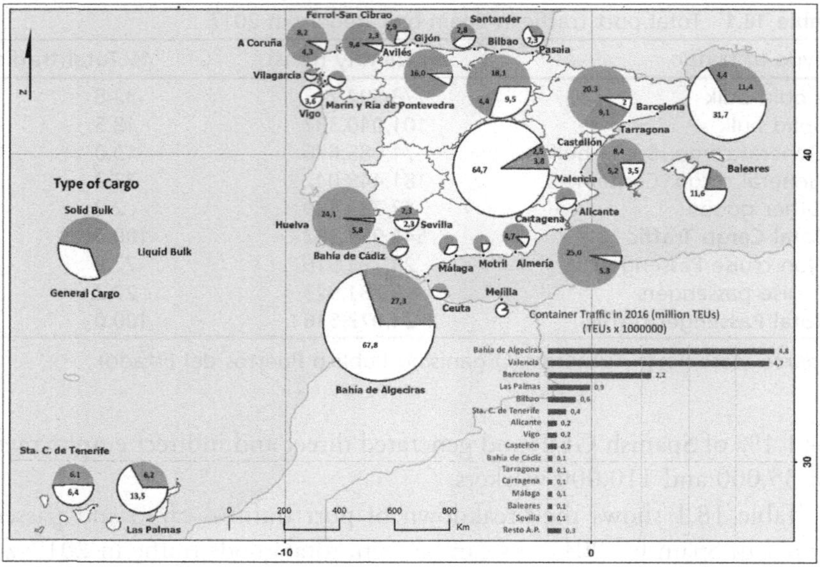


**Fig. 18.2** Spanish state port authorities: goods traffic in 2016 (million tons) (*Source* Elaborated from State Ports Authority [Organismo Público Puertos del Estado] data for the authors by Agustín Naranjo Cigala, Human Geography Department, ULPGC. This map complies with ETRS89 [European Terrestrial Reference System 1989])

Canary Islands, with 2.5 million passengers, is the third-largest market in Europe after the Mediterranean and the North Sea (Baños & Tovar, 2019).

Finally, the Spanish port system comprises port authorities of widely varying sizes and specialisations.[2] The differences in terms of size and composition of the goods traffic of individual Port Authorities is illustrated in Fig. 18.2. As can be seen, general cargo is dominated by the three largest ports of Algeciras, Valencia and Barcelona, which together account for almost 80% of container traffic.

[2] See Tovar and Wall (2017b, 2019) for analyses of specialisation in Spanish ports.

## Governance Model

Ports in Spain can be classified into two legal categories. *General interest ports* are the property of the State (depending on the Ministry of Public Works) and must comply with certain characteristics. These may include, among others, international maritime activity, provision of services of strategic national economic importance or port activity that affects several Autonomous Communities (regions). The remaining ports comprise *marinas, fishing ports and ports of refuge*, and are managed by regional governments. As these ports have relatively little commercial activity, our focus will be on the general interest ports. The power to change the status of a port to or from the category of general interest lies with the central government. Ports that lose general interest status are transferred to the Autonomous Communities.[3]

The central government, through the Ministry of Public Works, has exclusive control over the general interest ports.[4] These are directly managed by Port Authorities, which have a certain degree of autonomy, and the State Ports authority (Organismo Público Puertos del Estado), which is responsible for the coordination and efficiency of the port system. The State Ports Authority, which coordinates the 28 Port Authorities that manage the 46 general interest ports, possesses a series of legal powers including the execution of government port policy, the coordination and control of the efficiency of the state-owned port system and the coordination of the different State organs with port-related competences.[5] Regarding control functions, it acts as regulator and supervisor, proposing sectoral rules and norms and approving Port Authority financial plans and port investment projects. Its President is named by the government based on a proposal by the Ministry of Public Works, and its Governing Council comprises a minimum of 12 and a maximum of 15 members, appointed by the Ministry. Among other functions, the State

[3] Article 4 of the Consolidated Text of the Spanish State Ports and Merchant Marine Act (2011).

[4] Articles 12 and 13 of the Consolidated Text of the Spanish State Ports and Merchant Marine Act (2011).

[5] It is established as a separate legal entity dependent on the Ministry of Public Works with its own patrimony.

Ports Authority defines and endorses the objectives of the State-owned port system, as laid out in the Business Plans of the Port Authorities, and approves the financial and investment plans of the Port Authorities.

The governing council of the Port Authorities that manage the general interest ports comprises a President and 10–13 members, all appointed by the Autonomous Communities, as well as an ex officio member (Harbour Master). The Port Authorities, which are separate legal entities with a patrimony independent from that of the State, may manage one or several ports in a given region and are responsible for financing access routes to the ports as well as basic port infrastructure. The Port Authorities can be considered as *landlords*, as they have been ceded control (though not ownership) of port property by the State government. Law 33/2010 assigns them the role of facilitators of economic activity, as well as regulators and providers of infrastructure. The Port Authorities provide concessions to private operators, which have a minimum duration of 3 years.

Overall, the Spanish port system has followed the European-wide trend in recent decades towards greater decentralisation of port management, greater autonomy for ports and greater liberalisation of the services provided by agents involved in port-related activity.

## Financial Tools and Their Link to Governance Models and National Legislation

While coordination of the port authorities is the responsibility of the State Ports Authority, the port system does not receive direct subsidies from the Spanish government. Instead, it finances itself from the income it generates, external debt and special European Union subsidies. A consequence of this policy objective of self-financing is that there has been increasing emphasis placed in recent years on measures to improve the competitiveness of ports (Tovar & Wall, 2017a). This has been enshrined in a series of important legal reforms since the start of the 1990s.

The first of these major reforms was the Law 27/1992, which established the State Ports Authority and unified the existing management regimes into autonomous Port Authorities. Signalling the transition to a landlord system, this law specified that port authorities' management should be carried under the general principle of operational and financial autonomy for port authorities based on criteria of efficiency and productivity, without prejudice to the powers of the Ministry of Public Works exercised through the State Ports Authority (regulation of, coordination of and support for the system as mentioned in section "Governance Model"), or the Autonomous Communities.

While there was an emphasis on efficiency and self-financing, coupled with the consequent requirement that port authorities must generate a sufficient level of income to cover current as well as capital expenditure, port authorities had virtually no control over pricing policy. Law 62/1997, which modified Law 27/1992, reinforced the autonomy of Port Authorities and proposed freedom of rates. However, control over pricing remained almost completely beyond the control of ports. Law 48/2003 introduced a degree of control over prices but only for a limited range of services related to the use of cranes, storage or energy supplies. This law was modified by Law 33/2010, which gave increased autonomy and control over pricing policy to Port Authorities. Port Authorities were granted greater flexibility to set rates and greater managerial discretion to tailor their policies in order to differentiate themselves according to their needs. The law established a minimum target of 2.5% profitability for the system as a whole and the scope of individual ports to change rates is made conditioned on their profitability.[6] That said, in 2017 only 13 of the 28 Port Authorities complied with this target. A further 12 had positive profits below 2.5%, while 3 ports had losses. The Royal Legislative Decree 2/2011 approved the Consolidated Text of the Spanish State Ports and Merchant Marine Act in an attempt to bring together the previous legal reforms into a single text.

Law 33/2010 placed explicit emphasis on the role of private investment. Thus, general interest ports were assigned a leadership role in the involvement of the private sector in the provision of port services, and

[6] The profitability target can be revised by the State Budgetary Law. Annual profitability targets for each Port Authority are established in their Business Plans.

exhorted to do as much as possible to attract and maintain private investment in port infrastructure. To this end, the Law eliminated certain port rates (the so-called general service rate) and amended others (occupancy and activity rates) in order to show loyalty to firms that had already invested and to promote new private investment. This goal of encouraging private investment was reinforced more recently by Law 8/2014, enacted during a period of economic crisis in Spain. This Law provides additional incentives to private investment by permitting the possibility of extending concession periods for up to 50 years conditional on the private operator committing to substantial investment in the port area, partially financing ports' landside communication links or making reductions in the prices they charge for their services. Law 33/2010 also obliges the Port Authorities to publish an annual Environmental Sustainability Report, which includes a series of environmental indicators that are monitored, and provides for the possibility of reducing rates for agents engaging in environmentally friendly practices.

Finally, Decree Law 8/2017 proposes a modification of the process of contracting stevedores. While not directly related to financing, this law, which has the objective of bringing Spanish legislation in line with Article 49 of the Treaty on the Functioning of the European Union, continues the process of liberalisation of services forming part of port activity.

The objective of self-financing for individual ports is aided by the existence in Spain, since 2003, of an Inter-Port Compensation Fund. This Fund is defined in Article 159 of Royal Legislative Decree 2/2011 as an instrument for the distribution of resources of the State Port System to be administered by the Organismo Público Puertos del Estado. The Fund is financed in large part by contributions by each Port Authority of a minimum of 4% (up to a maximum of 12%) of their yearly income, with the exception of the insular ports and Ceuta and Melilla which contribute a minimum of 2%. Basically, the fund uses contributions from ports with surplus income to finance investments and other expenditure at ports with a shortfall. Moreover, these compensatory transfers with the fund guarantee the economic viability of some of the smaller Port Authorities in the Spanish port system that are limited in their ability to generate resources.

Complementary sources of funding include subsidies through the European Regional Development Fund (ERDF), as well as private financial institutions. Specific fiscal policy measures have also been used to encourage certain types of traffic or environmentally friendly practices. For example, the importance of the cruise sector for the Spanish economy has led to special tax treatment for cruise ships, with reductions of 70% in basic vessel charges at stopover ports and a further 56% reduction of the remaining charge for base ports.[7] Regarding sustainability, the European Council recently gave authorisation for a plan promoted by the State Ports Authority to reduce taxes on electricity supply from €0.05/kWh to a 'symbolic' €0.0005/kWh for vessels that shut down their auxiliary engines and connect to the general network while at berth.[8]

## Public–Private Collaboration

The landlord model, where the public port authority acts as property owner and regulatory body while port operations are carried by private companies, has become the dominant global model of port governance (World Bank, 2007). Spain is no exception to this, with Law 48/2003 enshrining the landlord model as the one preferred for port governance. Subsequent legislation has further emphasised the role of the private sector. The regulation of contracts between the public and private sectors is provided by the Consolidated Text of the Spanish State Ports and Merchant Marine Act (2011), which actively encourages public–private partnerships (PPPs), under a regime of regulated free access. The Port Authorities provide concessions to any and all companies that comply with the conditions set out in sectoral, national and European legislation and that comply with the specific contractual clauses (*Pliego de Prescripciones Particulares*) set out by the Port Authority and approved in turn by the State Ports Authority. A public call for tenders is published in the

[7] https://www.diariodelpuerto.com/ver/208748/ventajas-a-los-cruceros-en-los-puertos.html.

[8] Organismo Público Puertos del Estado 11/10/2018. www.puertos.es/es-es/Paginas/Noticias/ProyectoOPS2018.aspx.

Official State Bulletin and, when the value of work to be carried out is greater than €5 million, in the Official Journal of the European Union. Subject to a favourable prior report by the State Ports Authority (and, in cases where an environmental impact assessment is needed, a report from the Ministry of Agriculture, Food and the Environment), concessions are awarded by the Port Authority. Concession fees are established as coefficients applied to the value of the goods or resources being used or occupied by the company, which can be separated into land, port waters and installations and infrastructure. The valuation of waters and land is determined by the Ministry of Public Works, while that of infrastructure and installations is established by the Port Authority.

A recent speech by the President of the State Ports Authority deemed public–private partnerships (PPPs) as crucial for achieving the objectives of the newly planned Strategic Framework.[9] The explicit functions of the private sector were specified as: planning and provision of own infrastructure and installations; providing port services to meet demand with a high quality/cost ratio and a focus on generating value added; and ensuring efficiency of port operations through appropriate management of resources. Explicit mention was also made of the importance of working with the private sector in the design of port terminals' trading and marketing strategies.

The PPP experience in Spain since the port reform legislation of the 1990s came into effect has been analysed in detail by Cabrera et al. (2015). They find that the contracts were overwhelmingly Design, Build, Finance, Operation and Maintenance (DBFOM), and that two-thirds of the contracts were related to ports and one third to terminals. Large DBFOM contracts were provided by large construction operators and worldwide conglomerates such as Abertis, FCC or OHL, and the tender processes were generally carried out by regional governments. One of the characteristics of this process is that PPP contracts in Spain do not face a negotiation process because, as Cabrera et al. (2015) point out, the administration submits the contract and bidders accept along with the terms of tender. This has led to some notorious and well-documented

[9] http://www.puertos.es/es-es/Documents/INTERVENCION_ORNELLA_PRESIDENTA.pdf.

cases of over-spending as contracts are 'renegotiated' over the duration of the contract.[10]

As for the future of PPPs, Cabrera et al. (2015) raised concerns about competition, failure to meet expectations and the role of risk allocation. The role of risk in port PPPs is considered crucial to the success of the landlord model (Oliveira Cruz & Cunha Marques, 2012). However, episodes such as the bailout of the debt-laden Gijón port authority, as well as the cost overruns and renegotiations documented on Cabrera et al. (2015), would seem to indicate that risk is being reassigned to the taxpayer rather the private sector.[11]

## Challenges and Proposals for Reform

### Overcapacity

As a consequence of the fact that Spanish ports were subject to legislation which left them no control over pricing policies until the year 2003, ports' competitive strategy centred on investment policy, the main variable under their control. The result was a huge increase in infrastructural investment over the period 1993–2008, with major expansions in port capacity (Tovar & Wall, 2015). This overcapacity is reflected in the capacity utilisation rates. According to the Platform of Investors in Spanish Ports (PIPE), the level of capacity utilisation for containers for the system as a whole was estimated at 36%, with several container terminals with rates below 20%.[12] Similarly, Esparza et al. (2017) found an average unweighted idle ratio of port facilities designed for container traffic of over 60% in the eight main ports. This in turn led to a substantial increase in costs.[13]

[10] In the case of the enlargement of the port of Gijón, the EU has reclaimed €250 in overspending which it attributed to fraud.

[11] The effect of Directive 2014/23/EU on the award of concession contracts, which was approved into Spanish Law by Congress in late 2017, will be of interest in future research.

[12] http://www.plataformaipe.com/retos-y-dificultades/.

[13] Díaz-Hernández et al. (2014) calculated the efficiency of the provision and utilisation of infrastructure of Spanish ports for the period 2000–2007, and found that the improper use of

As the port devolution process in Spain is similar to other Mediterranean countries in so far as it is characterised by financial centralisation and increasingly political decentralisation, political as well as economic factors will likely play a role when it comes to investment. In this context, Castillo-Manzano and Fageda (2014) find that economic considerations play an important role in investment in ports, but that the reform processes aimed at greater political, as opposed to financial, decentralisation give greater weight to tactical political criteria such as the same political party being in power in both the regional and local governments.

However, recent developments show that there is a desire to tackle the problem of overcapacity. In February 2018, the State Ports Authority sent out a request for tender for a study on port capacity and investment planning.[14] The purpose of the study was to identify the physical installations of the Spanish port system catering for commercial traffic, define their theoretical capacity and compare this to the real (or estimated) traffic data available and generate software tools to organise and manage the data generated. The idea of this is to assist the State Ports Authority in forming a position with regard to decisions on planned investments and the possible inclusion of these in the Business Plans of each port authority.

## Proposals for Change in Governance and New Strategic Framework

Highlighting overcapacity in the Spanish, a recent detailed review of the Spanish port system called for specialisation of ports and advocated a series of reforms regarding governance, organisation and planning, arguing that governance model should evolve to a corporation model based on public–private management with Port Authorities unified under corporations or seaboard logistics authorities (Cerbán-Jiménez & Ortí-Llatas, 2015). A reform of the system is currently being negotiated.

quasi-fixed inputs contributed to inefficiency in the form of an increase in costs by an average of almost 8%. See also Tovar and Wall (2015).

[14] Published in the Official State Bulletin (*BOE*) on 05/02/2018.

Thus, In October 2018, the State Ports Authority initiated a process of consultation with the 28 Port Authorities of the general interest port system with a view of developing a new Strategic Framework to substitute the existing one that has been in place since 1998. The objective of this process was to permit the Port Authorities to express their opinion and provide proposals for improvement with regard to the functioning and development of the port system, which would provide the basis for the new Strategic Framework to be elaborated by the State Ports Authority in conjunction with the port authorities. The process was carried out using a questionnaire sent to the port authorities and the results became available in January 2019.

The consultation process revealed differences among the Port Authorities with regard to comprehensive reform of the port system. Two main streams of thought were uncovered. On one side were large and/or economically powerful port authorities that proposed some type of segregation, classification or aggregation of general interest ports or port authorities with the aim of increasing managerial autonomy in order to gain competitiveness through being better able to adjust to market forces. On the other side were medium-sized or small port authorities who are more inclined towards reinforcing the existing system to guarantee equilibrium in the port supply under criteria of general interest including territorial cohesion. However, despite these differences in opinion, there was consensus among the Port Authorities on a series of issues, including the need for mechanisms to promote greater collaboration among the Authorities to place them on a more equal footing with increasingly concentrated large global operators, the need to plan port enlargements in line with technical and economic considerations and the need for formulas that enhance public–private collaboration. The Port Authorities recognised the advantages of the landlord model but also the lack of inter-port competition, which will need to be addressed in order to comply with EU legislation. Finally, the Port Authorities manifested their openness to financing from foreign sources.

# References


Baños, J. F., & Tovar, B. (2019). Explaining cruisers' shore expenditure through a latent class tobit model: Evidence from the Canary Islands. *Tourism Economics* (pp. 1–29). https://doi.org/10.1177/1354816618823599

Cabrera, M., Suárez-Alemán, A., & Trujillo, L. (2015). Public-private partnerships in Spanish ports: Current status and future prospects. *Utilities Policy, 32*, 1–11.

Castillo-Manzano, J.-I., & Fageda, X. (2014). How are investments allocated in a publicly-owned Port System? Political factors versus economic criteria. *Regional Studies, 48*(7), 1279–1294.

Cerbán-Jiménez, M.-M., & Ortí-Llatas, J. (2015). *Infraestructuras portuarias. Análisis del sistema portuario español: Contexto internacional y propuestas de reforma*. FEDEA.

Díaz-Hernández, J.-J., Martínez-Budría, E., & Salazar-González, J. (2014). Measuring cost efficiency in the presence of quasi-fixed inputs using dynamic Data Envelopment Analysis: The case of port infrastructure. *Maritime Economics and Logistics, 16*(2), 111–126.

Esparza, A., Cerbán, M. M., & Piniella, F. (2017). State-owned Spanish port system oversizing: An analysis of maximum operational capacity. *Maritime Policy and Management, 44*(8), 995–1011.

Oliveira-Cruz, C., & Cunha-Marques, R. (2012). Risk-sharing in seaport terminal concessions. *Transport Reviews, 32*(4), 455–471.

State Ports Authority (Organismo Público de Puertos del Estado). (2016). *Annual report*.

State Ports Authority (Organismo Público de Puertos del Estado). (2017). *Annual report*.

Tovar, B., & Wall, A. (2015). Can ports increase traffic while reducing inputs? Technical efficiency of Spanish port authorities using a directional distance function approach. *Transportation Research Part A, 71*, 128–144.

Tovar, B., & Wall, A. (2017a). Competition strategies in the Spanish port system and their relationship with port authority efficiency. In S. Pettit & A. Beresford (Eds.), *Port management: Cases in port geography, operations and policy*. Kogan Page. ISBN: 978–0749474324.

Tovar, B., & Wall, A. (2017b). Specialisation, diversification, size and technical efficiency in ports: An empirical analysis using frontier techniques. *European Journal of Transport and Infrastructure Research, 17*(2), 279–303.

Tovar, B., & Wall, A. (2019). Are larger and more complex port more productive? An analysis of Spanish port authorities. *Transportation Research Part A: Policy and Practice, 121*, 265–276.

World Bank. (2007). *Port reform toolkit*. World Bank.

# 19

# Port Regulation and Finance in Turkey

**Soner Esmer and Seçil Sigali**

## Introduction

Turkey's port industry has been built by government intervention since the 1920s as in many countries, due to high investment costs and relatively low returns. However, the structure of the port industry has changed rapidly since the 1990s and the process of reform of the port sector started.

A port cluster involves all economic activities and public/private organizations including cargo handling, transport, logistics, manufacturing and trade activities related to the arrival of ships and cargo in ports (de Langen, 2004; de Langen & Visser, 2005). For this reason, the increase in the handling volumes has caused the formation of a cluster of ports,

S. Esmer (✉) · S. Sigali
Maritime Faculty, Dokuz Eylul University,
Izmir, Turkey

© The Author(s), under exclusive license to Springer Nature
Switzerland AG 2022
C. Ferrari et al. (eds.), *Regulation and Finance in the Port Industry*,
Palgrave Studies in Maritime Economics,
https://doi.org/10.1007/978-3-030-83985-7_19

which has been triggered by logistics services in the hinterland (Notteboom & Rodrigue, 2005; Pettit & Beresford, 2009). Especially in such regions as Istanbul and Kocaeli (Izmit), where industrial development is high, this change has clearly been observed and appreciable.

Since the involvement of the public sector in the port business in 1924, and the first industrial port in 1987, port business development in Turkey has continued and advanced with the contribution and involvement of private ports, to provide port services as a core field of economic activity. Gemport that started providing services in 1992 is the first private port investment in Turkey. After this period, all major port investments have been made by the private sector in the coastal area of Turkey.

The efficiency and service quality of private ports perceived by port users has led the privatization process to continue in the following periods. Privatization process of Turkish public sector ports officially began in 1997. In the Turkish port privatization model, the control of operations and management is transferred to the private enterprises for a specific period of time (30, 36 or 39 years); additionally, requirements of new capital assets are set, and these assets are expected to be transferred to the government by the end of the contract period. The contracts require not only the protection but also the modernization of the port infrastructure, superstructure and equipment. At the end of the contract, port facilities must be returned at the quality level of the delivery time (Esmer & Duru, 2017).

Considering these developments in both economic and social scale, this paper briefly describes the current status of the regulations and finance structures in Turkish port sector and explains the national port system. In the study, the role of privatized ports and the global terminal operators operating in Turkey are highlighted. Finally, the complexity of the financial structures and public governance model in the national port industry is discussed in terms of PPPs, FDI and the role of both local and international players within the national port sector.

## The National Port System

Turkey is located on the Far East-Europe (East–West) main sea trade route with a low deviation distance and also on the Black Sea–Mediterranean Sea (North–South) maritime routes. In this sense, Turkey is a country with easy access to major maritime (also land) routes and has an increased potential for local and transit cargoes (Fig. 19.1).

Even though ports have been operated in the coast of Turkey since ancient times, the first port (Port of Haydarpasa) has been operated by related bodies of the Republic of Turkey since 1924. The port investments of the public sector increased especially in the 1950s, and today's major public sector ports were built in this period. After the 1970s, some piers have been built in the coastal areas to meet the needs of the manufacturing companies, and they have started to serve third parties since 1987 with special permission from the government. Finally, in the early 1990s, the first private port (Gemport) was founded and after five years, the privatization process of public-owned ports was initiated in 1997 (Fig. 19.2).

As seen in Fig. 19.3, there are six main port clusters in Turkey and more than half of the cargo are handled in these regions. As showed

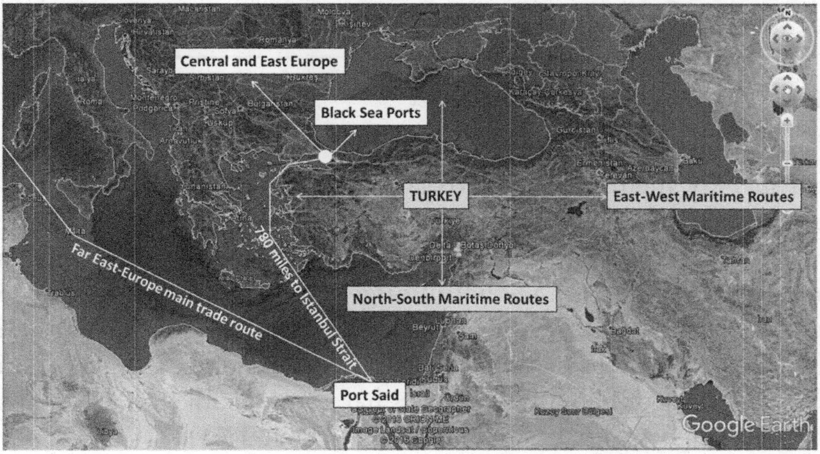


**Fig. 19.1** Turkey's location on the trade routes

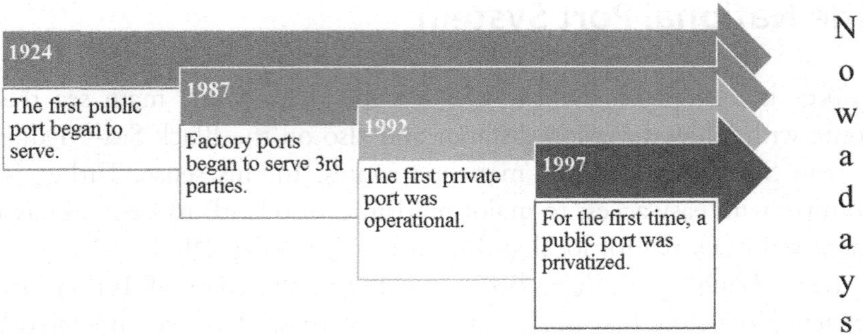


Fig. 19.2 Milestones of port operations in Turkey

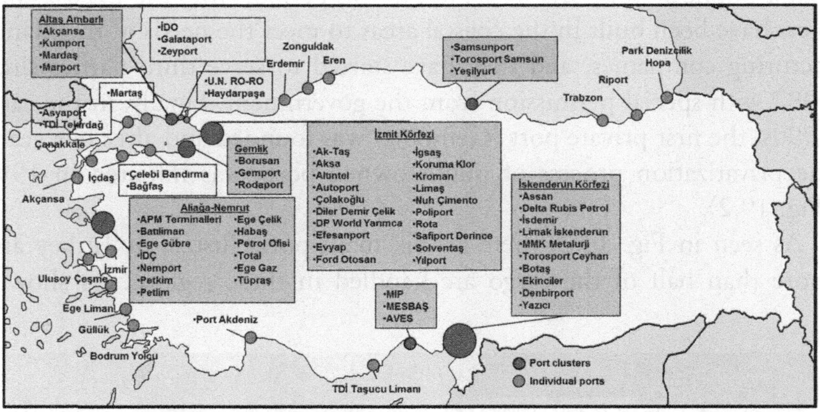


Fig. 19.3 Ports and terminals in Turkey

in Fig. 19.3, the rest of the ports are stretched through Turkey's coastal areas.

In 2017, according to the statistics of the Ministry of Transport and Infrastructure, the total amount of cargo handled has been 471 million tonnes in 187 ports. Liquid cargoes are the most handled cargoes in Turkish ports, while dry bulk cargoes are second. For instance, 153 million tonnes of liquid bulk cargoes have been handled as followed by dry bulk cargoes with 129 million tonnes (Table 19.1).

While the total cargo development can be seen in Fig. 19.4, the main characteristics of container handling are demonstrated in Fig. 19.5.

**Table 19.1** Handling figures by cargo types (2017-Tonne)

| Cargo types | Export | Import | Cabotage | Transit | Total |
|---|---|---|---|---|---|
| Liquid bulk | 21,255,057 | 64,856,860 | 19,645,258 | 47,140,172 | 152,897,347 |
| Dry bulk | 21,150,627 | 91,671,208 | 15,964,245 | 56,635 | 128,842,715 |
| Container | 44,433,316 | 37,275,863 | 10,059,528 | 16,149,201 | 107,917,908 |
| General cargo | 21,931,364 | 35,521,956 | 14,610,309 | 83,557 | 72,147,186 |
| Ro-Ro | 4,921,704 | 4,330,137 | 116,739 | 160 | 9,368,740 |
| Total | 113,692,068 | 233,656,024 | 60,396,079 | 63,429,725 | 471,173,896 |

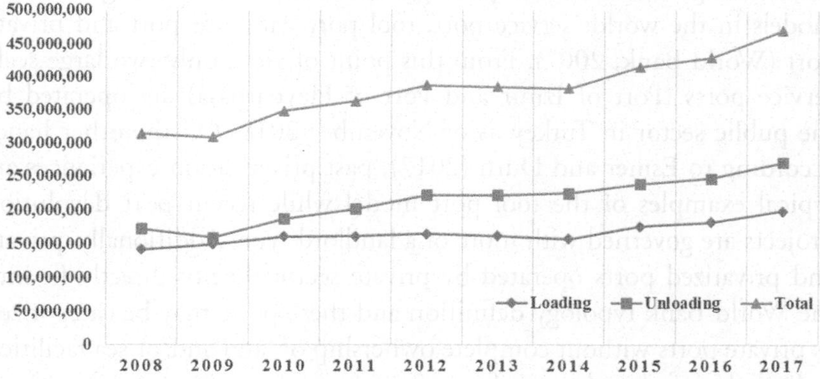


**Fig. 19.4** Cargo handling figure in Turkish ports (2017)

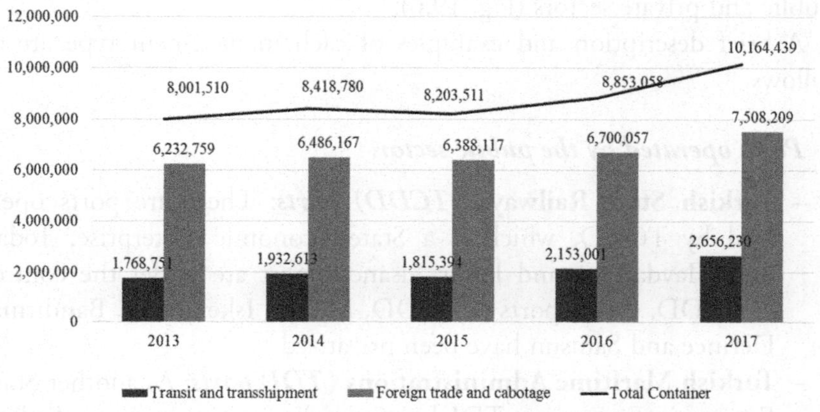


**Fig. 19.5** Container handling figures of container terminals in Turkey (Turklim, 2018; TEU)

As previously mentioned, due to its location on the major trade routes, Turkey has become a transhipment hub for transit cargoes originated to/from the Black Sea countries. In 2017, total containers handled over 10 million TEU while almost 25% of containers (2.6 million TEU) are transhipment cargo (Fig. 19.5).

## Three-Port Regulation and Planning Tools

Considering World Bank typology, there are four basic governance models in the world: service port, tool port, landlord port and private port (World Bank, 2007). From this point of view, only two large-scale service ports (Port of Izmir and Port of Haydarpasa) are operated by the public sector in Turkey as of November 2018. On the other hand, according to Esmer and Duru (2017), past privatization experiences are typical examples of the tool port model while recent port devolution projects are governed with more of a landlord type. Additionally, private and privatized ports operated by private sector do not directly fit into the World Bank typology definition and these ports may be categorized as private ports without complete ownership of land and/or sea facilities.

In light of the above information, management types of ports in Turkey can be grouped into two main categories: ports operated by public and private sectors (Fig. 19.6).

A brief description and examples of each management type are as follows:

- ***Ports operated by the public sector***:
  - **Turkish State Railways** (***TCDD) ports***: These are ports operated by TCDD, which is a State Economic Enterprise. Today only Haydarpaşa and İzmir Alsancak port are under the control of TCDD. Other ports of TCDD, Mersin, İskenderun, Bandırma, Derince and Samsun have been privatized.
  - **Turkish Maritime Administrations** (***TDI) ports***: As another State Economic Enterprise, TDI has controlled many ports in Turkey. Most of the high-capacity TDI ports have been privatized (Trabzon,

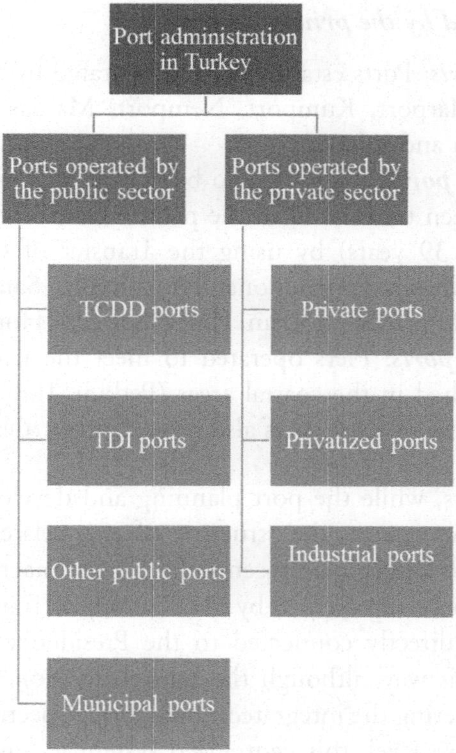


**Fig. 19.6** Classification according to the operators of ports in Turkey (Karataş Cetin, 2012; Yeni, 2017)

Rize, Sinop, Alanya, Marmaris, Kuşadası, Dikili, Hopa, Antalya, Çeşme and Tekirdağ ports) and privatization process of the non-privatized TDI ports is still ongoing (SEKA Tasucu, Kabatepe, Gokceada Kuzu, Sarayburnu, Gokceada Ugurlu, etc.).

– ***Other public sector ports***: These are ports operated by other state-owned enterprises except TCDD and TDI such as Petroleum Pipeline Cooperation (BOTAŞ) and Turkey Hard Coal Enterprises (TTK). These ports handle the loads of the factory/mine/industry to which they are partly or fully connected.
– ***Municipal ports***: Small-scale ports operated by municipalities such as Ayvalık, Gemlik Belediye and Ordu.

- ***Ports operated by the private sector***:
  - ***Private ports***: Ports established and operated by the private sector (Such as Marport, Kumport, Nemport, Mardaş, Solventaş, TCE EGE, Assan and Yılport).
  - ***Privatized ports***: They used to belong to TCDD and TDI ports but have been transferred to the private sector for a certain period (30, 36 or 39 years) by using the Transfer of Operating Rights method. (Mersin International Port (MIP), Samsunport, Celebi Bandırma, Limak Iskenderun, Park Denizcilik Hopa and Egeports).
  - ***Industrial ports***: Piers operated to meet the needs of the factories established in the coastal areas (Petkim, İDÇ, Ege Gübre and Habaş). Some of these piers also serve third parties.

In recent years, while the port planning and development issues are of increasing importance, the structure of port-related public institutions has changed and is mainly centralized at the macro level. Maritime governance has been represented by the Ministry of Transport and Infrastructure and is directly connected to the Presidency of the Republic of Turkey. In this way, although the central decision making has been enhanced considering the integrated transport perspective and port planning at the macro level, this centralized system is sometimes criticized by the transport-related private sector, non-governmental organizations and non-governmental communities with the loss of port and maritime focus.

## Ownership and Financial Structures of Ports and Related National Regulations in Turkey

The continuing privatization process of ports in Turkey that are owned by Turkish Maritime Administrations (TDI) and Turkish State Railways (TCDD), aims to improve the level of port efficiency and performance. Within the 187 ports that are located at Turkey's coastal line, 75% of the ports in Turkey are currently operated by private companies, while 25%

are managed by related public bodies and municipalities (Cetin et. al., 2017).

Although the privatization process started in 1997, the major ports in Turkey were privatized after 2005, starting with the 2005/54 numbered regulations of Privatization High Council. When the privatization process is analysed, it can be observed that the major privatization cases have been TCDD ports of Mersin International Port (MIP) with privatization price of USD 755 million in 2007, Derince Port with USD 543 million in 2012 and İskenderun Port with USD 372 million in 2015. These ports have been privatized through the transfer of the "*operation right method*" for the duration of 36–39 years.

The ownership changes in the port environment and the privatizations have been supported by the regulatory developments and institutional changes in Turkey with the purpose of attracting foreign direct investments (FDI). FDI Law (Law No. 4875) in Turkey was put into force in 2003 and aimed to protect the rights of foreign investors. According to Article 3 of the FDI law, "*Foreign investors are free to make foreign direct investments in Turkey and Foreign investors shall be subject to equal treatment with domestic investors*" and "*Foreign investors can freely transfer abroad: net profits, dividends, proceeds from the sale or liquidation of all or any part of an investment, compensation payments, amounts arising from license, management and similar agreements, and reimbursements and interest payments arising from foreign loans through banks or special financial institutions*". Additionally, in line with the privatization process and to ensure the protection of foreign capital, the banking and the accounting system in Turkey has changed dramatically. International Financial Reporting Standards (IFRS) were adopted in 2005 and communique′ on Independent Audit was effective in 2006 first for the public companies, while Capital Markets Board of Turkey (CMB) issued the Corporate Governance (CG) Principles based on the CG Principles of OECD. The consensus in Turkey on the significance of CG principles led to a change in Turkish Commercial Law, and the new Commercial Code No. 6102, which came into effect on 1 July 2012 (Balsari & Varan, 2014). These regulatory developments led foreign investors to increase their investments in the country. According to the Ministry of Trade, the number of companies with foreign capital in Turkey increased to 58,422 as of December 2017 from 5600 in 2002.

The post-performance of the port privatization process in Turkey has been empirically examined by Varan and Cerit (2014), and it is found that the port privatization process has stimulated private sector investments and competition, led to a declining concentration trend amongst Turkish container ports towards a modest concentration and that the newcomers as private port owners have the largest competitive advantage in Turkey.

When port privatizations are analysed in terms of FDI, it can be seen that the global terminal operators are mainly interested in container ports. Table 19.2 presents the main global terminal operators in Turkey.

Although the ownership and the financial structure of the ports in Turkey are opaque, Table 19.2 intends to show the relevant information on port-related FDI that is available to the public. In regards to the capacity, MIP is the greatest amongst these ports. Regarding the ports in Table 19.2, solely MIP's audited IFRS reports are publicly available. When the financial highlights of MIP are analysed for 2017 and 2016, return on equity capital (ROE) is 19 and 20%, and return on assets (ROA) is 9 and 8%, respectively. MIP is financed by equity 45% for 2017. The debt to assets ratio is 55% for 2017 and 55% for 2016. On 12 August 2013, MIP issued corporate bonds with maturity date on 12 August 2020 and a nominal amount of USD 450,000 (issue price: 99.576%) at an interest rate of 5.875% to be paid in every six months and is listed on the Irish Stock Exchange (Mersin International Port (MIP), 2017). DP World Yarımca discloses that all of the investment was made with DP World equity capital. According to Kumport Sustainability Report, 2017, USD 50 million of investments were made during the 2013–2017 period, and USD 100 million of investment in the budget for the 2018–2021 period.

Although the information regarding operational performance is publicly available for ports that are operated in Turkey, the financial performance and ownership structure figures are generally opaque and the public ownership is rare. According to the Public Disclosure Platform of Turkey, solely Trabzon Port has public ownership and discloses audited IFRS financial reports.

**Table 19.2** Main global terminal operators in Turkey

| Port | Ownership structure | Country (Headquarters) | Max. capacity (TEU)* |
|---|---|---|---|
| MIP | PSA (50%) + IFM Investors (40%) + Akfen (10%) | Singapore and Australia | 2,600,000 |
| Asyaport | Global Terminal Investment (GTL) (70%) + Soyuer Family (30%) | Switzerland | 2,500,000 |
| Marport | Terminal Investment Limited (TIL) (%50) + Arkas (%50) | Switzerland | 2,400,000 |
| Kumport | China Merchants (26%) + Cosco Pacific (26%) + China Investment Corporation (13%) + Oman State GR Fund (35%) | China | 2,100,000 |
| APM Terminals İzmir | SOCAR-APM Terminals | Azerbaijan and Netherlands | 1,300,000 |
| Limak Iskenderun | Limak (80%) + Inframed (20%) | Luxembourg | 1,300,000 |
| DP World Yarımca | DP World (100%) | Dubai | 1,300,000 |
| TCEEGE | TCEGE Ltd | Spain | 1,000,000 |
| Assan Port | Kibar Holding (51%) + TIL (49%) | Switzerland | 400,000 |
| Total Capacity (TEU) | | | 14,900,000 |

*Including current and planned capacity
*Sources* Ministry of Trade (2018) and Turklim (2016)

Trabzon Port was privatized in 2003 for 30 years of duration to the Albayrak Group, the investment was totalled to USD 20 million and 30% of its equity is publicly offered and traded in Borsa İstanbul by the 24 January 2018. When the recent financial figures are analysed for 2017 and 2016, ROA is 23 and 19.7% and ROE is 48 and 38%, respectively. Trabzon Port is financed by 49% equity and 51% debt by 31 December 2017 (Trabzon Port Annual Financial Reports, 2017).

According to Haralambides (2002), to succeed in fair competition amongst ports, stronger policy intervention in order to ensure greater transparency of port accounting systems and better and more harmonized port statistics are necessary. Literature suggests that sound corporate governance and transparency of financial results leads to a decrease in agency costs and in the cost of capital, and an increase in shareholder value. Turkey's global competitiveness amongst port investments calls for more transparency in ownership structures and financial reports.

## Conclusion

Turkey, as a newly industrialized and developing country, has a steady increase in the volume of trade and cargo handling. This increase leads to significant growth in the logistics sector. Therefore, the need to invest in port infrastructure has been increasing every day. As a result of the significant increase in cargo volume, global terminal operators have also been interested in Turkish ports and makes direct investments. Today, especially container terminals are mainly operated by the global terminal operators and these investments can be made through an acquisition of an existing port as well as new port investments.

Unlike the past, the port investments are now being carried out by the private sector in Turkey. The public institutions related to the port sector serve as a controller and competition regulator. At this point, some expectations of the private sector appear and the most important one is that the public establishes the rules that will ensure the continuity of port investments. In order to do this, it is necessary to re-evaluate and redesign the national port policy, all legal regulations and the bureaucracy regarding ports.

Although the ownership structure of ports in Turkey has changed dramatically since 1997 as presented in this paper, measuring the effects of this change on financial performance and comparing this performance with the global competitors is a challenging task for the academic literature and the practitioners due to the lack of financial data.

Considering the global financial environment after the 2001 and 2008 financial crises, banks substantially have turned off the loan limits and businesses have been forced to seek alternative financing sources in capital markets as bond issues and public/private equity offerings. Nevertheless, corporate governance principles and FDI flows have gained more significance for the emerging economies. In Turkey, especially after 2005, the reforms in the banking, accounting and capital markets regulations, and the new Commercial Code shows the determination for the sound corporate governance practices and also for "attracting foreign capital" for all sectors.

Although the regulatory actions have resulted in attracting a high amount of FDI, the global capital providers seek more stable financial markets and a financial system that ensures "*the protection of capital*". The concept of "*the protection of capital*" necessitates more transparency in port corporate governance structures and the independently audited financial figures. Additionally, re-evaluation of the national port policy and the bureaucracy regarding ports are necessary actions to lower the cost of capital and improve Turkey's global competitiveness in port investments.

## References

Balsari, C. K., & Varan, S. (2014). IFRS implementation and studies in Turkey. *Accounting and Management Information Systems, 13*(2), 373.

Cetin, İ. B., Balcı, G., & Esmer, S. (2017). Uzayan Liman Özelleştirme Sürecinin Etkileri: İzmir Alsancak Limanı Vaka Çalışması. *Dokuz Eylül Üniversitesi Denizcilik Fakültesi Dergisi, 9*(2), 112–134.

de Langen, P. W. (2004). *The performance of seaport clusters, a framework to analyze cluster performance and an application to the seaport clusters of Durban, Rotterdam, and the Lower Mississippi*. Rotterdam, ERIM PhD series.

de Langen, P. W., & Visser, E. J. (2005). Collective action regimes in seaport clusters: The case of the Lower Mississippi port cluster. *Journal of Transport Geography, 13*(2), 173–186.

Esmer, S., & Duru, O. (2017). Port governance in Turkey: The age of the global terminal operators. *Research in Transportation Business & Management, 22*, 214–223.

Haralambides, H. E. (2002). Competition, excess capacity and the pricing of port infrastructure. *International Journal of Maritime Economics, 4*, 323–347.

Karataş Cetin, C. (2012). *Limanlarda Örgütsel Değişim ve Değer Zinciri Sistemlerinde Etkililik Analizi*. Dokuz Eylül Üniversitesi Yayınları.

Kumport Sustainability Report. (2017). http://www.kumport.com.tr/resources/files/documents/surdurulebilirlik_raporu_v2.pdf

Mersin International Port (MIP). *Annual financial reports 2017*. https://en.mersinport.com.tr/images/PartDocuments/MIP%20_31_12_2017_IFRS_Report.pdf

Ministry of Trade, Turkey. (2018). *Foreign trade statistics*. https://www.trade.gov.tr/fdi/statistics

Notteboom, T. E., & Rodrigue, J. P. (2005). Port regionalization: Towards a new phase in port development. *Maritime Policy & Management, 32*(3), 297–313.

Pettit, S. J., & Beresford, A. K. C. (2009). Port development: From gateways to logistics hubs. *Maritime Policy & Management, 36*(3), 253–267.

Trabzon Port Annual Financial Reports. (2017). http://trabzonport.com.tr/yatirimci/TrabzonLimanDenetimRaporu_31122017.pdf

Turklim. (2016). *Turkish port sector report*. Istanbul.

Turklim. (2018). *Turkish port sector report*. Istanbul.

Varan, S., & Cerit, A. G. (2014). Concentration and competition of container ports in Turkey: A statistical analysis. *Dokuz Eylül Üniversitesi Denizcilik Fakültesi Dergisi, 6*(1).

World Bank. (2007). Port Reform Toolkit PPIAF, 2nd Edition.

Yeni, K. (2017). Liman Hizmetlerinde Fiyatlandırma: Türkiye İçin Ampirik Bir Uygulama. Dokuz Eylül Üniversitesi Sosyal Bilimler Enstitüsü Doktora Tezi, İzmir.

# 20

# The British Port System: Current Organisation and Regulatory Challenges

Alessio Tei

## The UK Port Governance Model

The United Kingdom is the main private port system in Europe and one of the main full corporatized port sectors worldwide (e.g. Baird & Valentine, 2007; Monios, 2017). The governance model is substantially different from the main European port governance models and it is based on three main managerial solutions (e.g. ISL, 2006):

A. Tei (✉)
Department of Economics, University of Genoa, Genoa, Italy
e-mail: alessio.tei@unige.it

School of Engineering,
Newcastle University, Newcastle upon Tyne, UK

© The Author(s), under exclusive license to Springer Nature Switzerland AG 2022
C. Ferrari et al. (eds.), *Regulation and Finance in the Port Industry*, Palgrave Studies in Maritime Economics,
https://doi.org/10.1007/978-3-030-83985-7_20

- Private ports (this category represents the majority of the big UK ports, some of them are managed by holdings quoted at the stock exchange market);
- Trust ports (ports administrated by trusts, sometimes with a public participation too);
- Municipality ports (smaller ports directly managed by small city councils).

Starting from the 1970s, the British port system underwent a series of legislative modifications that—with the aim of boosting investments, increasing efficiency, and reducing the public debt—pushed ports to embrace a more commercially focussed management (Baird, 2000; Monios, 2017). The corporatisation process has been sequentially developed, with most of the ports that either became privately owned or they have been managed by trusts that allow ports to act as a private entity. This privatisation process has been often criticized for its disputable outcomes (e.g. Baird [2000] suggested that the financial countervalue raised by the public authorities in selling main port infrastructure was 80–90% lower than the actual asset value and Pettit [2008] highlighted as the incoherence of certain decentralised policies cause an ineffective use of resources in the planning of port activities): despite this, in 2018, seven of the UK top ten ports were privately owned ports while the remaining three ports were trust ports (Department for Transport, 2019a).

Moreover, given the private nature of the port system (even if in some cases administrated by public bodies), since the final phase of the privatisation process, there is no major national legislation or common national port policy (Baird & Valentine, 2007) influencing British ports while the devolution occurred in the 1990s created also a series of different authorities in the decentralised UK regions (i.e. England, Wales, and Scotland) that supervise specific port-related aspects. Formally, each port is administrated by a Competent Harbour Authority (CHA) that is the managing body of the port. This authority is the representation of the port-owning company (or trust or public authority) and each CHA is in charge of the port planning and development as well as of the introduction of the relevant set of rules to manage the port. Currently, the central government practice is to release only few port-related rules, devolving to most CHAs the regulatory power on the related administrated area and generating a heterogeneous port environment.

The Department for Transport (DfT) is the governmental ministry in charge of developing the transport policy and related strategies (Department for Transport, 2019b). Nevertheless, the DfT provides only general guidelines directly applicable to the UK port sector while most of the binding regulations are present to general laws, such as safety and security or environmental issues (e.g. Monios, 2017). Similarly, channels and rivers are often managed by public authorities with the only aim to preserve fair access to the market as well as the protection of common areas of interest, such as the environment. An example is the role of Port of London Authority for the management of the navigation along the Thames (PLA, 2019).

Private port associations (e.g. UK Major Ports, for instance, include the biggest nine port companies managing the majority of British-based port facilities) have a role of representation of the ports to the government, developing lobby activities as well as proposing integrated policies and strategic investments.

## The UK Port System

The private nature of the British ports allows investors to create transport conglomerates that are normally uncommon in other parts of Europe and that manage integrated transport services. ABP, for instance, is one of the leading companies in the sector, managing 21 port facilities over the UK, a rail operator, and several logistics and port service providers (e.g. ship's agency and dredging). Among the port facilities managed by ABP are both Immingham and Southampton (i.e. the first and fourth national ports) and a series of other medium-sized ports, like Hull and Plymouth (ABP, 2019).

Apart from privately owned ports, other governance models include the municipality-managed ports—that are often customized solutions for regional and small ports (but with a few exceptions of medium-sized ports, like Portsmouth)—and trust ports that are a group of heterogenic ports that also includes various major specialized ports, such as Dover, Milford Haven, and Belfast (Maritime UK, 2019).

While the government statistics counts for 120 commercial port facilities around the country (also counting some fish-based harbours or offshore facilities), according to Eurostat, UK port system is characterized by 55 ports, in 2017 the top ten ports handled more than 70% of the overall freight cargo, determining a quite concentrated market in which only nine ports exceeded 20 million tonnes. Nevertheless, the privatized structure of the port governance generates a quite different situation in comparison with other EU port systems: UK main ports are normally highly specialized in a few traffic categories—often linked to specific regional industrial characteristics—and there is not an overall main port that represents the national gateway for main traffic categories (e.g. as in the cases of Rotterdam and Hamburg for The Netherlands and Germany, respectively). This situation strongly affects other port operation aspects, such as the planning and the possibility of attracting national funding for the land infrastructure.

Figure 20.1 shows the location of the main UK ports as well as the traffic trend for different cargo categories.

While big multi-purpose ports (such as Liverpool or London) represent an exception to the main scenario, the presence of specialized and privately owned ports generated a coherent stream of investments also in the related hinterland infrastructure and economic environment (e.g. specialized logistics services). This can be easily observed in Felixstowe (for the container) or Immingham (for the liquid bulk traffic).

The peculiar governance structure affects the management system and the possibility to pursue specific investments: while there is no need for specific regulation for modifying the port areas and activities performed within the port, any activity outside the port has to be agreed with the relevant public authority, often generating a delay in relevant land transport investment (e.g. road and rail connection) given the lack of a major national vision for the port system (e.g. Pettit, 2008). In order to cope with this issue, the DfT launched a series of coordination programmes that are currently under development. The most famous action was taken in 2012 (Department for Transport, 2012) with the discussion in the Parliament of the "National Policy Statement for Ports" [NPS].

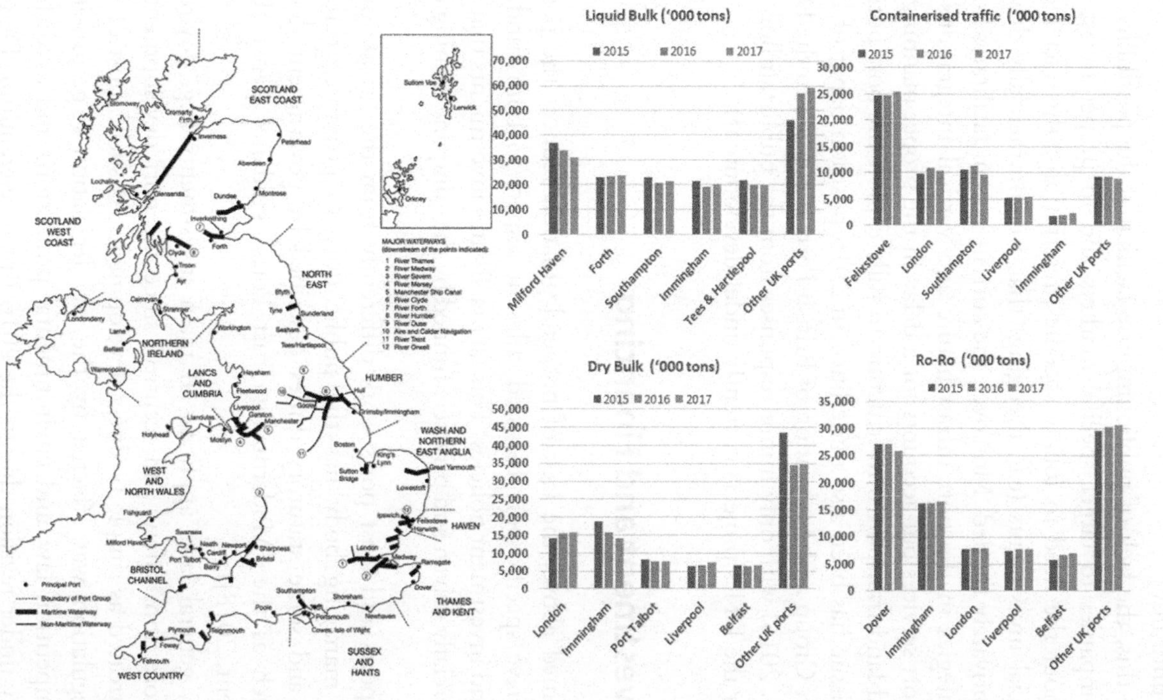


**Fig. 20.1** Port location and cargo throughput of UK seaports in 2015–2017 (*Source* Own elaboration from DfT and Eurostat data, 2019)

Nevertheless, the intention of achieving a national policy has been not successful until now.

Despite this, the lack of public impulse facilitated the possibility for private companies to target specific markets and to proper invest on them without the need to follow specific prescriptions: this fact facilitated special investments (e.g. dredging) that are commercially driven and fully privately funded. Moreover, the current system facilitates horizontal strategies in the port infrastructure and vertical integrations in the transport services but accounts for a delay in the proper planning of the needed land transport infrastructure to fully exploit the port potential. This issue has been also underlined in 2016 position paper of UK Major Port Group and Association of British Ports presented to the DfT (UKMPG, 2016) with only minor responses from the public authorities (except for the DfT's projects currently under development).

## Port Investment and Financing

As underlined above, the lack of proper legislation reduces the possibility to have specific port focussed rules in respect to both funding schemes and investment policies. This fact facilitates investments that are all commercially driven and privately funded by the company owning the port.

Public ports and trust ports work differently from the private ones since the managing body has the public duty to guarantee certain standards and some statutory duties described by government documents (such as the "Modernizing Trust Ports" guidance paper [UK Government, 2018]).

Overall, general laws apply to all main investments (e.g. environmental protection, safety, and security) since the port development is generally treated as simple business development. As such, most of the current regulation was affected by the EU legislation (e.g. procurement, competition law, and environmental protection) and as such it is currently under revision due to the 2016 Brexit referendum. Despite the relative freedom in upgrading existing port infrastructure, big investments (or new port facilities) have to comply with the Planning Act

(UK Government, 2008) that regulates the procedure for investments that can have a national effect or interest. This process normally involves a governmental procedure to allow private companies to go on with the investment. Together with this authorisation, environmental regulation states that any major work that might affect the environment should also obtain a special license from the Marine Management Organization (MMO) that verifies the environmental sustainability and the compliance with the Marine and Coastal Access Act (UK Government, 2009).

Given the privatised system, there are no restrictions on investment in port companies by either private or public partners. This also applies to foreign investments but restrictions could be here introduced in relation to negative effects on national interests. Despite this, the lack of national regulation and the possibility for the port company to be on the stock exchange market facilitates the attraction of funds and the possibility to foster both collaborations and specific investment projects. Often these funds are either speculative or specialised funds attracted by stable rate of returns. An example of such situation is the history of Association of British Ports (*The Telegraph*, 2015) that was on the stock exchange until 2006 when it was bought by several capital funds (among which specialised investors, such as InfraCapital, and sovereignty funds, such as the Singaporean CIG) and then changed its ownership again in 2015; thanks to a nearly two billion dollars investment of two major pensions schemes. Together with financial investors, international shipping and terminal companies have also invested in the UK port sectors, often through either brownfield investments (e.g. the Hutchinson purchase of the port of Felixstowe) or through the development of greenfield projects (as in the case of the London Gateway owned by DP World).

The abovementioned framework also results in differentiated approval processes in terms of port projects planning, since within the NPS different guidelines are provided to make a case-by-case process to the relevant government body. The case-by-case status for the approval process generates the absence of specific construction requirements or standards but they are normally evaluated, following NPS guidelines, during the overall investment assessment by the Planning Inspectorate, in accordance with the investment goals. Within the initial investment evaluation project (for any investment that has a national interest), NPS provides also the possibility for the private operator to require specific land links to connect the new port (or terminal) to the national transport network. These further investments are normally assessed separately and not within the same evaluation process.

Moreover, the abovementioned framework generates differences with other EU port systems in terms of impossibility to have a national concession term or the difficulties to account on Public–Private Partnership given the low interest of public bodies to invest in ports. Nevertheless, some ports CHAs release lease contracts to third parties in order to operate within the managed port. These agreements are all private contracts and general commercial law is then applied.

The lack of any public service duty leads UK ports to seek private funding and no government schemes are currently entirely dedicated to port maintenance or related projects. Similarly, tariffs are not subject to specific regulations apart from general competition rules and through the revenue stream (or loans) the port companies are normally funding all the relevant works.

## Port Operations

All port actors must comply with EU and general national legislation in terms of both safety and security. Each CHA has the duty to implement an internal regulation that has to at least guarantee national and international standards. Nevertheless, many port activities are fully devolved to the CHA supervision (e.g. piloting) and for this reason every port has a variety of different standards with no specific national benchmark or regulation. Harbourmasters are appointed by relevant national authorities (e.g. UK government) only in ports in which the presence of the navy generates the need for it (e.g. Plymouth). In all other situations the CHA is in charge of publishing port regulations and to supervise the regular respect of those rules. Among these self-published regulations, some of them have to be in line with relevant policy documents and codes (such as the Merchant Shipping Act or the Port Marine Safety Code), determining a minimum level of consistency among the different

UK ports. Nevertheless, some general differences can be also observed in the different UK devolved areas (e.g. Scotland, Wales, England, and Northern Ireland) in which specific aspects (e.g. environment and security) of port regulation can also be under further regional legislations, requiring further authorisations or controls to be performed. These differences are promoted also by the fact that all main national rules have a guidance role with only few of them having the full power of law.

The existence of private companies that manage a plurality of ports (e.g. ABP) generates homogenise rules for the port administrated by the same private company but overall the UK system is characterised by a plurality of standards as well as technical solutions. Nevertheless, some sector associations provide guidelines that tend to promote consistency among different ports. Despite this, the commercial status of most ports and related marine service providers affects the possibility of modifications, in terms—for instance—of handling tariffs that are normally under the simple supervision of national competition authorities (and often included in an agreement between the CHA and the relevant parliamentary commission).

A specific Harbour Act (UK Government, 1964) dictates general principles in relation to the harbour dues. Her Majesty's Revenue and Customs (HRMC) is in charge of custom controls and other checks on the freight cargo, in collaboration with the Border Force. Many administrative processes are directly offered as commercial services by relevant private companies, in collaboration with HRMC and other local authorities that are specialised in specific controls. For instance, the Food Standards Agency (FSA) and the Department for Environment, Food and Rural Affairs (Defra) are normally in charge to release guidelines and general rules for import of food, plants, and animals (with relevant checking for health hazard). Thus, each port has normally a local Port Health Authority that performs the controls (often in collaboration with HRMC) while the Association of Port Health Authorities assures the coordination of different checks in different national ports. At the national level, the Customs Handling of Import and Export Freight (CHIEF) system provides a unique informatics tool to input data of freight passing through UK ports and starting the custom procedures.

UK has been part of the EU custom union but the 2016 referendum ended this status with effect from beginning of 2021, generating modifications on the structure of port controls on goods and creating delays and operational barriers to all cross-channel operations.

## Conclusive Remarks

The UK port system is characterised by a general integration of the logistics activities within main port operations thanks to the privately owned nature of its main gateways. The absence of physical barriers (such as mountains) also favoured intermodal transport that is encouraged by several political strategies (e.g. Department for Transport, 2019b). Moreover, the land transportation and related infrastructure enjoy better national planning—in respect to the maritime sector—and are able to improve coordinated investments (something generally missing in the maritime industry, as demonstrated by relevant analyses [e.g. Monios, 2017]). Despite this, the lack of coordinated policies between port actors and transport investments has created several issues in terms of outdated infrastructure that increase congestion and delays in shipping cargos (UKMPG, 2016). Mangan et al. (2008) highlighted how port logistics in UK has great potential but added value services are still in a latent phase due to critical market issues. Nevertheless, the privatised nature of key ports facilitated the development of specialised supply chains with related logistics services. Similarly, ports as the London Gateway and Hull have been developed as "distripark-ports" in which highly specialised services are designed to serve specific markets with ad hoc logistics activities as well as dedicated infrastructure (Pettit & Beresford, 2009). On the one hand, the development of such ports demonstrates the potential benefits for private investments in the UK port sectors. On the other hand, the current situation highlights the potential unbalanced issues that a missing planning could cause: extra costs generated to the broader sector due to a missing coordinated strategy, together with the presence of worldwide companies that can benefit from their own market position. As discussed above, current government attempts (e.g. Department for Transport, 2019b) are trying to fill the gap left by the missing planning, coordinating public and private sectors in order to enhance the current situation. The recent political issues (e.g. Brexit) also generated a local debate in terms of the key role that ports will enjoy in the future of the UK economy, helping in introducing longer term plans—as in the case of the Maritime 2050 document (Department for Transport, 2019b)—that might change the current approach to both port regulation and finance.

## References

ABP. (2019). *Association of British ports*. www.abports.co.uk

Baird, A. (2000). Port privatisation: Objectives, extent, process, and the UK experience. *International Journal of Maritime Economics, 3*, 177–194.

Baird, A., & Valentine, V. (2007). Port privatisation in the United Kingdom. *Research in Transportation Economics, 17*, 55–84.

Department for Transport. (2012). *National policy statement for ports*. Dft.

Department for Transport. (2019a). *Port freight statistics*. DfT.

Department for Transport. (2019b). *Maritime 2050—Navigating the future*. DfT.

Eurostat. (2019). https://ec.europa.eu/eurostat/home

ISL—Institute of Shipping Economics and Logistics. (2006). *Public financing and charging practices of seaports in the EU*. Bremen.

Mangan, J., Lalwani, C., & Fynes, B. (2008). Port-centric logistics. *The International Journal of Logistics Management, 19*, 29–41.

Maritime UK. (2019). https://www.maritimeuk.org/about/our-sector/ports/

Monios, J. (2017). Port governance in the UK: Planning without policy. *Research in Transportation and Business, 22*, 78–88.

Pettit, S. (2008). United Kingdom ports policy: Changing government attitudes. *Marine Policy, 32*, 719–727.

Pettit, S., & Beresford, A. (2009). Port development: From gateways to logistics hubs. *Maritime Policy & Management, 36*, 253–267.

PLA. (2019). *Port of London authority*. www.pla.co.uk

*The Telegraph*. (2015). *Associated British Ports stake sold for £1.6bn*. Accessed online on October 2019. https://www.telegraph.co.uk/finance/newsbysector/industry/11505859/Associated-British-Ports-stake-sold-for-1.6bn.html

UK Government. (1964). *Harbour act*. Accessed in September 2019 at: http://www.legislation.gov.uk/ukpga/1964/40/contents

UK Government. (2008). *Planning act*. Accessed online in September 2019 at: http://www.legislation.gov.uk/ukpga/2008/29/contents

UK Government. (2009). *Marine and coastal access act*. Accessed in September 2019 at: http://www.legislation.gov.uk/ukpga/2009/23/contents

UK Government. (2018). *Modern trust ports*. Accessed online in September 2019 at: https://assets.publishing.service.gov.uk/government/uploads/system/uploads/attachment_data/file/677494/mtp-good-guide-to-governance.pdf

UKMPG. (2016). *Delivering value, creating prosperity*. UK Major Ports Group. https://www.britishports.org.uk/system/files/documents/blueprint_for_ports_policy_0_0.pdf

# Part III

## The Port of the Future and Financial Solutions

# 21

# Port Development, Regulation and Financial Approach

Giovanni Satta and Alessio Tei

## Introduction

Governance models represent regulatory frameworks for better organising rights, benefits, tasks and duties of different economic actors involved in specific markets. As introduced in Chapter 1, first port reforms have been promoted in order to both increase port efficiency and reduce public debt, funding new investments leveraging on alternative financial sources. For instance, Parola et al. (2012) underline how during

G. Satta · A. Tei (✉)
Department of Economics, University of Genoa, Genoa, Italy
e-mail: alessio.tei@unige.it

G. Satta
e-mail: giovanni.satta@unige.it

A. Tei
School of Engineering, Newcastle University, Newcastle upon Tyne, UK

© The Author(s), under exclusive license to Springer Nature Switzerland AG 2022

C. Ferrari et al. (eds.), *Regulation and Finance in the Port Industry*, Palgrave Studies in Maritime Economics,
https://doi.org/10.1007/978-3-030-83985-7_21

the transition phase between the public governance model adopted in Italy until 1994 and the subsequent landlord model, the sources of funding drastically changed reducing over 50% of the central government transfers to port authorities. Similarly, De Langen and Heij (2014) argue that some governance models, as in the case of The Netherlands, allow different ports within the same regulatory framework for using special public funding schemes in order to promote strategic improvements as well as for granting the possibility of speeding-up needed investments. Moreover, as mentioned by early studies on port reforms (e.g. Goss, 1990), one of the reasons for introducing the landlord model was the modification of the decision-making process with port (public) authorities capable of promoting investments within the port area and the private operators in charge for developing projects looking at the whole logistics corridors rather than just at the port node. Similarly, the possibility of promoting private company participation for certain investments has been linked not only to the need for new financial resources but also to the possibility of attracting needed know-how. Every national regulator then allows for different solutions, as mentioned in the different chapters of part II of the present book. Despite the peculiarity of different approaches, certain patterns and specific solutions emerge and this is the purpose of this chapter. For instance, on the one hand, recent terminal investments and transport infrastructure links have often been promoted by either private companies (e.g. private funding, bonds and joint-ventures) or through public–private cooperation schemes (e.g. Public–Private Partnerships [PPP]); on the other hand, a series of key port common-user investments (e.g. breakwater, dredging, gates and digitalisation) are still left to public intervention, at least in the majority of the port systems worldwide (e.g. a partial exception, for instance, can be observed in the UK port system). Thus, market-driven actions seem to link to a more market-oriented financial solutions while common port infrastructure, superstructure and facilities are still funded through government resources.

Within this framework, an important finding in the comparison of the major port systems is the link between recent port expansions, governance models, port planning and alternative funding schemes. Even though this link is also mentioned by the World Reform Tool Kit (World

Bank, 2001) where different funding schemes are described and linked to different governance models as well as to specific investment typologies, the application of different port governance models is generating a variety of applied solutions (e.g. Brooks & Pallis, 2012) in which both public and private actors differently define their boundaries in respect with key investment and port development strategies. This discrepancy between ideal port governance classification and actual empirical applications impacts also on different capabilities of using alternative funding schemes for long-term port strategies. Nevertheless, as underlined by Chen and Everett (2014), several port reforms have pushed port authorities to corporatise themselves adding business goals (e.g. revenues and rate of investment) to the more traditional ones (e.g. maximisation of welfare, accessibility and throughput). As such, in several country-specific settings, port authorities are more and more similar to "port development companies" rather than simple public authorities (e.g. de Langen & van der Lugt, 2017) for which a variety of development strategies (together with the usual planning tools) and financial solutions (jointly with the traditional port duties and public government transfers) are needed in order to fulfill port goals. As such, a variety of local approaches have been promoted to either increase financial performance or productivity of port infrastructure (e.g. the case of the merge between Dutch port authorities mentioned in Chapter 17; the full privatisation of many ports in the UK mentioned in Chapter 21; the coordinated system of the South African ports described in Chapter 5; the foreign direct investments promoted by several port authorities).

This chapter discusses such financial tools discussing their impact on port planning and long-term development.

## Governance, Planning and Finance in Ports

Depending on the governance model, public finance has substantially influenced the capability of ports to plan area redevelopments, new terminal expansions and maintenance operations. As mentioned in Everett and Robinson (2006), the first wave of port reforms in the 1970s and 1980s was strictly motivated by: (i) the need for reducing public expenditure in running port businesses and (ii) the increasing demand for novel investments in specialised shipping and port sectors (e.g. automation and containerisation). Before those early reforms, traditional public support was delivered through public transfers (i.e. direct funding coming from central governments) to be managed by (public) port management bodies without the need for specific rate of returns or performance goals. The introduction of corporatised ports allowed for novel solutions in terms of funding schemes: most of the port authorities saw their public transfers reduced drastically (e.g. Everett & Robinson, 2006; Parola et al., 2012) with funding being predominantly dedicated to pre-listed kinds of investments (e.g. periodic maintenance). Despite this, the "privatisation" of certain port operations, raised the possibility for either directly (e.g. port duties) or indirectly (e.g. concession fee) collect money from the activities delivered by private parties now involved in the port operations. Thus, the shift in terms of duties (i.e. from performing port operations to planning and regulating them) changed the financial sources as well. In such general scenario, different port reforms established both different forms of public funding sources and decision-making processes for having access to them (e.g. priority funding for national champions [e.g. Chapter 17] and introduction of Central government agencies for the rationalisation of port investments [e.g. Chapter 5]). A key element in such scenario is the level of decisional and financial independency of different port authorities in respect to central government and the impact that such independence could generate in terms of overcapacity (i.e. no coordination among investments), financial capability (i.e. no rationalisation, hierarchisation and long-term strategies for the use of collected financial resources) and wider economic elements (e.g. link between port investments and other regional logistics characteristics). In order to prevent some of those critical issues (e.g. doubling similar investments within the same port region, therefore generating inefficiencies in port investments at regional and national level), national governments have often introduced national coordination agencies in order to filter funding distribution among the controlled port authorities. Despite this, while those agencies are normally capable of influencing public expenditures (e.g. the Spanish "Puertos del Estado"), they only seldom have the power to stop local (private) investments planned by the single port authorities. Similarly, special national and regional funding is often still an option for port development, irrespectively from the governance model applied, for the achievement of special national goals, such as the environmental challenges as well as inter-regional accessibility policies (e.g. for promoting certain transport links rather than others). In parallel with these government funding schemes, special emphasis should be placed on certain international initiatives, such as the Trans-European Transport Network (that funds project within Europe with the aim of increasing connectivity and accessibility) and the Belt and Road Initiative (mainly supported by Chinese-related institutions) having the capability, under certain bilateral agreement, to provide public funds to port managers and port companies for the development of either novel or upgraded infrastructure irrespectively from the governance model applied.

Within this general framework, some regulators allowed for either the full or the partial privatisation of the port infrastructure. In such scenario, ports have been "sold" to private companies and all involved financial resources linked to port planning and development are seen as part of the port business activity and, as such, they depend on the port owner only without any recurring public funding to support them. Exceptions from such fully private cases are the land common infrastructures (e.g. roadways and railways) as well as the possibility for applying to special national funding. Examples of such situation could be found in both UK (e.g. Baird, 2013) and Australia (e.g. Everett & Robinson, 2006) port systems. As part of this governance setting, the possibility to apply for bonds or stock market is often allowed, as part of the financial strategy of the companies involved in the business. In addition, a number of port-related companies are grounding on Initial Public Offering (IPOs) and subsequent follow-on in order to gather fresh equity sources from financial markets, as demonstrated by the Chinese, the Vietnamese and the Greek cases (Satta et al., 2017).

Other governance models (e.g. The Netherlands, Germany) allowed for the privatisation of certain business-oriented ports (i.e. industrial terminals) but such infrastructure can still be eligible for public funding, determining a mixed approach in which private infrastructure are still capable of receiving government funding for performing certain long-term investments.

Despite the possibility of having privatised solutions, most port reforms still push towards a public port manager. As such, planning activities are still largely supported by public funding schemes while operations and terminal expansions need to be supported by private capital as well. Among the most commonly used financial solutions that impact on port planning and development, the public–private partnerships (PPP) are having today a great impact on the industry. Within the PPP framework, a series of alternatives can be found in which port authorities can attract investments—or disinvest from a certain asset in order to collect needed financial resources or know-how—for the development of certain port areas. For their role within the industry, PPPs have been deeply analysed over the last decade by both academics as well as practitioners and policymakers (World Bank, 2007). According to the United States Department of Transportation, PPPs are agreements that allow private companies to take on traditionally public roles in infrastructure projects, while keeping the public sector ultimately accountable for a project and the overall service to the public. More in detail, in PPPs, a government agency typically contracts with a private company to renovate, build, operate, maintain, manage or finance a (transport) facility. Within the port domain, public authorities see PPP as a mean to overcome budgetary constraints (Flinders, 2005; Hammami et al., 2006), specifically when it comes to large and technically complex port development project, as this instrument allows to compensate their lack of expertise in operations, to boost economic growth and foreign direct investments (Parola et al., 2013). New governance settings that are fuelling the development of a huge amount of new terminal infrastructure projects or the renewing of existing facilities are stimulating the private involvement through PPP arrangements, due to the high degree of complexity which characterise these projects in terms of amount and variety of required resources (e.g. financial investment, management skills, personnel, technology, etc.) (Fung et al., 2011).

Within the PPP setting, port infrastructure can be either totally or partially funded through private funds, with the infrastructure that can remain under the jurisdiction of the public authority, being an effective tool for the promotion of the port planning activity. Most concession agreements then fall within this category and related contracts specifically detail financial and operational characteristics of both public and private actors involved. As such, PPPs are the common financial tools connected to landlord models and most of the recent port investments (e.g. Maasvlakte 2 in Rotterdam) are linked to such kind of solution. Despite this, some authors (e.g. Theys et al., 2010) highlight that some of the critical issues of PPPs are due to the misalignment in long-term goals between port authorities and private partners, for instance, in the specification of investment duties (e.g. port shared services and infrastructure, targeted KPIs) or the needed contract renewal conditions. Moreover, whenever PPPs have been applied for public disinvesting procedures, privatisations (at least part) of the port assets have also been introduced, as in the case of the port of Piraeus in which a private liner (i.e. COSCO) now "directly owns" all port assets (Chapter 15), therefore using PPPs as a more extensive way for pushing towards different governance models without the lengthy processes generated by port reforms.

## Financing Port Development: The Role of Private Parties

After the first phase of port reform worldwide, private companies largely shaped the port sector through a series of investments that allowed the industry to renew key infrastructure, increase the size of the facilities and update most of the involved port services. In order to achieve such goals, a series of financial tools have been introduced to the market, each of them with specific characteristics and impact on the port development capability and the related terminal sector, as discussed below.

### Public–Private Partnerships

As previously mentioned, PPPs have been a viable and effective tool for the promotion of port investments. While PPPs represented a way for replacing public funding and acquiring know-how, for private operators they acted as a solution for effectively entering the port industry. In this perspective, the growing need for private investments in building and operating major transport infrastructure projects, especially in developing economies, has given momentum to PPP arrangements (Guasch, 2004), thus determining an increase in participation of the private sector. Recent port projects, in addition, expose the parties involved to a range of commercial, technical, regulatory, political, financial and environmental risks (Rodrigue et al., 2011; Van Ham & Koppenjan, 2001), thus suggesting the need for new risk identification, assessment and hedging tools that PPPs are capable of guaranteeing (World Bank, 2007).

Methods and money used in each PPP arrangement strongly depend upon the mission of the PPP itself and specifically on the field the project belongs to (e.g. specific businesses) and on "life-cycle" of the port infrastructure: greenfield, upgrading/upsizing and brownfield projects. In this perspective, for example, Fig. 21.1 shows the most diffuse PPP methods

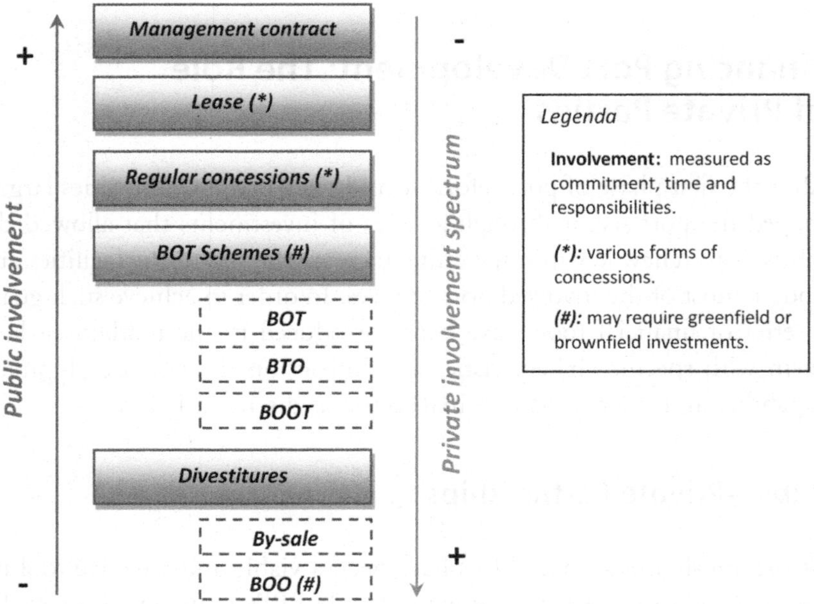


**Fig. 21.1** PPPs' alternatives in the port domain (*Source* Satta & Parola, 2012)

adopted in the port container industry.

Relatedly, the specific funding mechanisms and schemes adopted in the port industry for supporting PPP arrangements could significantly vary according to country-related specificities and port business' features. In this vein, the PPP arrangement clauses have to set which investments have to be financed by public sources and which through private sources. Indeed, the public involvement is based on several alternative mechanisms such as: public direct investment (equity stake), tools, buying back of the port infrastructure at the end of the contract, tax incentive (e.g. tax exceptions, tax credits, etc.), grants, security instruments and ad hoc pricing policies. Conversely, the private involvement in the funding of port infrastructures grounds on both traditional private finance (equity and debt) as well as dedicated financial instruments from special financial intermediates such as the World Bank, the European Investment Bank (EIB) or other multilateral financial institutions and development banks.

New port governance settings and development strategies worldwide have generated valuable investment opportunities for private companies, especially multinational enterprises (MNEs) eager to invest in the port domain. The container port industry (Bichou & Bell, 2007; Parola et al., 2013; Peters, 2001) and the cruise industry (Pallis et al., 2018), in particular, emerged as the most attractive port business for private investors. In this vein, for example, PPP solutions have been extensively adopted by private operators for enlarging the portfolio of container facilities managed during the first decade of the century as reported in the following Fig. 21.2,

Since the early 2000s, the high market growth rate and the valuable profitability reached by companies operating in several port-related businesses triggered an increasing number of financial operators to enter the port industry, seeking for investment opportunities. Among them, institutional investors, i.e. specialised financial institutions that manage savings collectively on the behalf of small investors, heading a well-defined objective in terms of reasonable risk, return maximisation and maturity of claims, have been committed in several port infrastructure markets. Notably, institutional investors active in port infrastructure include a broad range of financial operators typologies such as pension funds and insurance companies (e.g. Ontario Teaching Pension

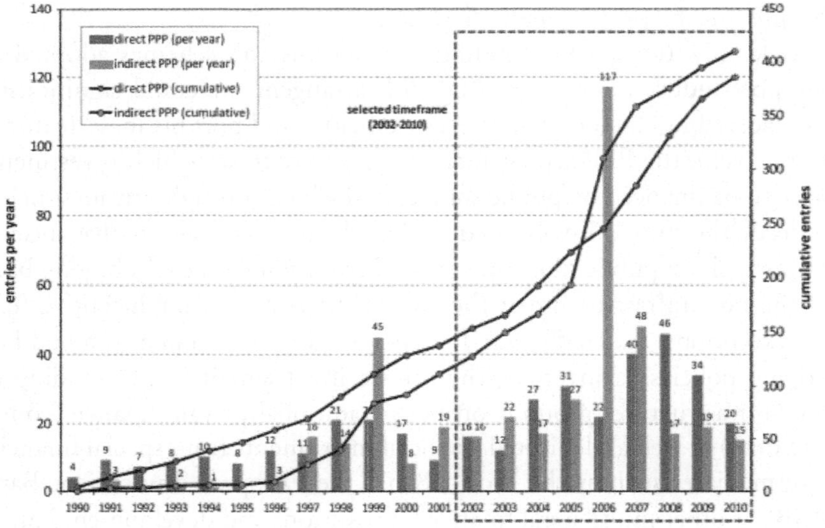


**Fig. 21.2** The evolution of PPP foreign entry strategies in the container port industry (1990–2010) (*Source* Parola et al., 2013, p. 74)

Plan, Borealis Infrastructure—OMERS, Highstar Capital—AIG group, etc.), sovereign wealth funds (e.g. Government of Singapore Investment Corporation, Abu Dhabi Investment Authority, Oman Investment Fund, etc.), investment banks and private equity funds (e.g. Citi Infrastructure Investors, Goldman Sachs, Macquarie, Morgan Stanley, Deutsche Bank—RREEF, Bank of China, JP Morgan Chase—Noatum, etc.) as well as investment holding companies (e.g. China Merchants Holding International, Wharf Holdings—Modern Terminal Limited, NWS Holdings, etc.). These private financial investors are dramatically shaping the port industry by pursuing aggressive growth strategies in several port infrastructure markets such as the container port industry and the cruise terminal sector (Satta et al., 2020).

## Project Financing

In the last two decades, within the overall framework provided by PPP schemes, the port industry has benefited worldwide from the increasing role played by project financing, in line with what has happened in other transport sectors.

Several alternative definitions of project financing exist in the extant academic literature. According to Bouzguenda (2014), for instance, project financing is "*the long-term financing of infrastructure and industrial projects based upon the projected cash flows of the project rather than the balance sheets of its sponsors. Usually, a project financing structure involves a number of equity investors, known as 'sponsors', a 'syndicate' of banks or other lending institutions that provide loans to the operation. They are most commonly non-recourse loans, which are secured by the project assets and paid entirely from project cash flow, rather than from the general assets or creditworthiness of the project sponsors, a decision in part supported by financial modeling*".

Grounding on previous academic contributions, four key features characterising project finance can be identified: (i) the role of special purpose vehicle (SPV) and the concept of "ring fencing"; (ii) the cash flow-based nature of the project; (iii) the relationships existing among lenders (debt financiers), risks and the security package and (iv) contractual agreements related to sponsors and their impact on risks and returns dimensions.

When it comes to the first issue (i), for the infrastructure design, construction and/or management, an "ad hoc", separate, legally and economically independent entity/company is established. It is owned by the sponsor/s (who usually takes an active role in the management of the project) and often it has a hybrid public–private nature. Typically, it is a limited company (LTD) in the form of Public Limited Company (PLC) or Limited Liability Company (LLC) and is named SPV (Special Purpose Vehicle), Special Purpose Company (SPC) or NEWCO (New Company). By this way the ring fencing principle is satisfied, meaning that the economic and financial equilibrium of the SPV and the sponsors are independent as well as SPV's assets couldn't be legally attached by third parties holding a credit towards the sponsors and vice versa.

With regard to the second dimension (ii), in this type of port projects, the providers of the funds (financial intermediates, institutional investors, bond markets and equity markets) look primarily to the cash flow from the project as a source of funds to service their loans and provide the return of and a return on their equity invested in the project. In this vein, the project "bankability" mainly grounds upon the projected cash flows of the project rather than the balance sheets of its sponsors. Therefore, capital invested and loans are secured by the project assets, rather than from the general assets or creditworthiness of the project sponsors, This determines two valuable consequences: (a) business plan development and the financial modelling (assumptions; forecasts and sensitivity analysis) are fundamental for attracting private financial resources; (b) in the port domain, often the duration of the "concession" needs to be consistent with the port infrastructure payback period (PBP).

The third dimension (iii) highlights that the lenders are given a lien on all of the SPV's assets and are able to assume control of a project if the project company has difficulties complying with the loan terms. In this perspective, debt funds gathered for the project are predominantly designed as "non-recourse" finance (but also "limited-recourse" funds could be included). This type of project can also exploit bank fiancé and bond issuing. In all the cases, a key role is played by the security package defined within the contractual agreement, which can include several "collateral assets" and security pillars, such as: mortgage on the SPV's assets, revenue-producing contracts and insurance assigned to the lenders, covenants on obligations, pledge of share, bank or insurance guarantees and contractual arrangements for risk mitigation or risk transfer to specialised third parties.

Finally, when it comes to the last issue (iv), as the sponsors' responsibility is limited to the equity they invested in the project, the investment in this port project should become more attractive for private investors. In particular, the financial leverage is used for increasing private investors' returns. In particular, according to relevant industry reports (e.g. the one published in 2017 by Deloitte and Louis), the debt/equity ratio in port project financing has been around 3.29 in the 2002–2016 timeframe.

## Project Bonds

After the 2008 global financial crisis, financial institutions and banks have started to face stricter regulations and lending requirements. The new Basel III regulation has determined stricter monitoring and disclosure clauses, higher capital costs and higher capital requirements. As a result, large infrastructure projects are facing additional difficulties in being funded by traditional debt alone. In such circumstances, by accessing the institutional bond market, companies operating in the infrastructure domain are potentially able to reduce the project funding cost (and increase the internal rate of return). In particular, project bonds offer an opportunity for institutional investors to participate in infrastructure projects through listed, tradable securities that can offer superior risk-adjusted returns.

Nonetheless, the adoption of project bonds as a funding mechanism for large port infrastructures may be unattractive to investors with low appetite for risk given the inherently high-risk level characterising the construction and development phase of these projects. Therefore, not all debt portions of international port mega-project will be able to take advantage of this financial source but this mechanism is expected to provide benefits to the project developers in the form of potentially enhanced returns due to the lower cost of capital, as reported by several advisory companies such as Deloitte (Baldi, 2017).

Project bonds, indeed, have been successfully used in Europe and America to fund port infrastructure projects, favoured by the positive momentum of the corporate bond markets. Relatedly, also some developing countries have started experiencing this form of funding in the port domain such as Kenya and Nigeria in Africa. When it comes to Europe, on 7 September 2010, the "Europe 2020 Project Bond Initiative" has been announced, aiming at providing EU support to project companies committed in issuing bonds to finance large-scale infrastructure projects (Bassanini et al., 2011). The "Europe 2020 Project Bond Initiative", in particular, has been directed to attract additional private sector financing of individual infrastructure projects by improving the rating of the senior debt of project companies, thus guaranteeing that it can be placed as "bond" financial instrument with institutional investors.

## Alternative Funding Schemes: The Role of Multilateral Financial Institutions and Development Banks

Notably, in addition to PPP schemes, traditional private investment solutions, project financing solutions and project bonds, several alternative funding schemes exists for supporting the development of ports for overcoming public budget constraints. In particular, a number of dedicated financial instruments provided by financial entities such as the World Bank, multilateral financial institutions and development banks are available for the industry. In this perspective, for example, the World Bank offers both downstream technical assistance for corporate finance as well as financial intervention instruments, which include among others:

- Capital markets solutions: capital markets framework for long-term finance, financial innovations and regulations to mobilise institutional investors (including credit enhancement and other risk-sharing instruments) both through debt and equity markets.
- Banking solutions: banking sector policies and prudential regulations, role of development banks in crowding in the private sector, risk management and hedging instruments and use of Islamic finance.
- Guarantee programs/facilities: capacity development of national development banks for catalytic role and/or supporting design and implementation of standalone facilities.
- Tailored financing solutions for LICs (Low Income Countries): these tools predominantly refer to the optimisation of blended financing and credit enhancements to crowd in private investments;
- World Bank loans and guarantees: which support interventions that leverage commercial investors (credit enhancements for obligators, offtakers and issuers, risk-sharing, refinancing, pooled financing vehicles, investment funds, green finance schemes, etc.).

Multilateral financial institutions and development banks are institutions established by more than one country that operate subject to international law. Predominantly, major shareholders are national governments and state-owned enterprises (SOEs). They are increasingly supporting the growth and development of port infrastructure by providing special funding schemes as well as professional advising. These institutions, typically, have a broad membership including both developed donor countries and developing borrower nations. They finance infrastructural projects by offering long-term loans at market rates, very long-term loans with below-market rates or grants. Multilateral development banks (MDBs) act as key co-investors in the port domain, funding both greenfield and brownfield projects in low- and middle-income countries (Satta et al., 2020).

Among the most active financial operators within the port domain, we can list the European Investment Bank (EIB), the European Bank for Reconstruction and Development (EBRD), the Asian Development Bank (ADB), CDC Group (formerly the Commonwealth Development Corporation) and the Investment Fund for Developing Countries. The EIB, for instance, works to overcome concerns that traffic-dependent revenue (tolls, fares etc.) may not reach medium-term targets. An example of dedicated financial instrument for transport infrastructure provided by EIB is the Loan Guarantee Instrument for Trans-European Transport Network Projects (LGTT) that can be used for partially cover risks for projects (or part-projects) that are deemed of common interest (as defined in Decision No. 1692/96/EC) and receive income from user-charges. This instrument allows to guarantee a maximum of 10% of senior debt (20% in exceptional instances) up to a maximum of €200 million per project with a duration which last from 5 to 7 years after project completion.

## Lessons to Be Learnt

The various port reforms and the corporatisation of many port sectors have deeply affected the funding strategies for key port investments. As mentioned, in the past most of the port authorities were directly funding key strategic expansions through public transfers from central government. Despite this, just a few port systems worldwide are still using central government money for (entirely) funding new project developments. Most of the current terminal expansions are promoted by port authorities and managers but funded through a differentiated array of financial solutions.

Looking at different port systems assessed within the current book, and matching these analyses with relevant financial solutions, a matrix of funding possibilities may be drawn (Fig. 21.2). Independently from the peculiarities of certain port sectors (e.g. industrial ports are normally keener than general port infrastructure to use bonds and other private sectors related tools), different tools are used with a different frequency depending on port governance models and related needed investments. As such, Fig. 21.3 shows the frequency [L(ow), M(edium) and H(igh)] of their adoption in the port industry.

Advantages and disadvantages of different solutions strongly depend upon local context and governance settings as well as industry-based specificities and trends. Despite this, the landlord model allows for greater flexibility in collecting differentiated financial resources, being capable of both assuring specialisation of assets and the possibility to

| Port Sector | | Public transfer | PPP: Disivestiture | PPP: Concession | PPP: Other | Project Financing | Project Bond | Other |
|---|---|---|---|---|---|---|---|---|
| Public Port | | H | X | X | X | X | X | X |
| Land Lord | Hanseatic | L | L | H | M | M | L | M |
| | Latin | M | X | H | L | L | X | M |
| | Asian | L | X | L | M | M | X | M |
| | Other | M | L | H | H | L | L | M |
| Tool Port | | H | X | L | L | X | X | L |
| Private Port | | X | H | X | | M | H | H |

Fig. 21.3 Port funding: matrix of viable financial solutions (*Source* Authors' elaboration from various sources. Legend: Xno funding example is currently in place; L—low use of the financial solution; M—medium use of the financial solutions; H—highly used financial solution)

interconnect a variety of stakeholders. This intrinsic characteristic is one of the reasons why most port reforms push towards landlord models, declined differently depending on the local context (e.g. Hanseatic vs Latin in Europe). On the other hand, the possibility to customise PPPs in relation to specific market and regulators' needs is the reason for the widespread use of such tool: PPPs have been used for attracting private financial partners often providing mixed approaches between joint-venture schemes, project financing and PPPs themselves. As such, most developing countries are attracting foreign direct investments through the use of PPPs (e.g. European, Australian and Asian banks funded port investments through minority shares in specific PPPs), while private operators try to promote horizontal and vertical integration strategies given the possibility to direct "own" or "operate" specific port facilities, e.g. most new passenger terminals (e.g. Cruise Terminals in the Med area) as well as cargo infrastructures (e.g. Japanese joint-ventures, Maasvlakte 2 in Rotterdam) have all been linked to industrial PPPs.

On the other hand, the rapid growth in terms of financial resources has also pushed towards the use of alternative instruments. These tools are still underused (e.g. bonds), but they are strongly linked to the growing need for either mitigating the risk of investing or increasing potential return for investment. Within this solution, the support of multilateral institutions or third country's support (e.g. Belt and Road Initiative) is of particular relevance for the development of the future port planning.

## References

Baird, A. J. (2013). Acquisition of UK ports by private equity funds. *Research in Transportation Business and Management, 8*, 158–165.

Baldi, F. (2017). *Gli Investimenti in Infrastrutture di Trasporto: Le Scelte di Finanziamento*. Deloitte & Luiss University.

Bassanini, F., Del Bufalo, G., & Reviglio, E. (2011). *Financing infrastructure in Europe project bonds, solvency II and the "connecting Europe" facility*. Paper prepared in occasion of the "Eurofi Financial Forum".

Bichou, K., & Bell, M. G. (2007). Internationalisation and consolidation of the container port industry: Assessment of channel structure and relationships. *Maritime Economics & Logistics, 9*(1), 35–51.

Bouzguenda, N. (2014). Project finance: Determinants of the bank loan spread. *International Journal of Business and Social Science, 5*(5).

Brooks M. R., & Pallis A. A. (2012). Port governance. In *The Blackwell companion to maritime economics* (pp. 491–516). Wiley-Blackwell.

Chen, S. L., & Everett, S. (2014). The dynamics of port reform: Different contexts, similar strategies. *Maritime Policy and Management, 41*, 288–301.

De Langen, P. W., & Heij, C. (2014). Corporatisation and performance: A literature review and an analysis of the performance effects of the corporatisation of port of Rotterdam authority. *Transport Reviews, 34*, 396–414.

de Langen, P. W., & van der Lugt, L. M. (2017). Institutional reforms of port authorities in the Netherlands; the establishment of port development companies. *Research in Transportation Business and Management, 22*, 108–113.

Everett, S., & Robinson, R. (2006). Chapter 12 port reform: The Australian experience. *Research in Transportation Economics, 17*, 259–284.

Flinders, M. (2005). The politics of public–private partnerships. *The British Journal of Politics and International Relations, 7*(2), 215–239.

Fung, K.-C., Garcia-Herrero, A., & Ng, F. (2011). *Foreign direct investment in cross border infrastructure projects* (ADBI Working Paper 274). Tokyo: Asian Development Bank Institute.

Goss, R. O. (1990). Economic policies and seaports: 4. *Strategies for Port Authorities, Maritime Policy and Management, 17*, 273–287.

Guasch, J. L. (2004). *Granting and renegotiating infrastructure concessions: Doing it right*. The World Bank.

Hammami, M., Ruhashyankiko, J. F., & Yehoue, E. B. (2006). *Determinants of public–private partnerships in infrastructure.*

Pallis, A. A., Parola, F., Satta, G., & Notteboom, T. E. (2018). Private entry in cruise terminal operations in the Mediterranean Sea. *Maritime Economics & Logistics, 20*(1), 1–28.

Parola, F., Ferrari, F., & Tei, A. (2012). Managing port concessions: Evidence from Italy. *Maritime Policy & Management, 39*, 45–61.

Parola, F., Notteboom, T., Satta, G., & Rodrigue, J. P. (2013). Analysis of factors underlying foreign entry strategies of terminal operators in container ports. *Journal of Transport Geography, 33*, 72–84.

Peters, H. J. (2001). Developments in global seatrade and container shipping markets: Their effects on the port industry and private sector involvement. *International Journal of Maritime Economics, 3*(1), 3–26.

Rodrigue, J. P., Notteboom, T., & Pallis, A. A. (2011). The financialization of the port and terminal industry: Revisiting risk and embeddedness. *Maritime Policy & Management, 38*(2), 191–213.

Satta, G., Notteboom, T., Parola, F., & Persico, L. (2017). Determinants of the long-term performance of initial public offerings (IPOs) in the port industry. *Transportation Research Part A: Policy and Practice, 103*, 135–153.

Satta, G., & Parola, F. (2012). *I processi di espansione internazionale nella container port industry: analisi delle determinanti delle scelte di ingresso* (Vol. 969). FrancoAngeli.

Satta, G., Parola, F., Musso, E., & Vitellaro, F. (2020). *Financial operators in port infrastructures: Typologies, objectives and global strategies*. Edward Elgar Publishing.

Theys, C., Notteboom, T. E. , Pallis, A. A., & de Langen, P. W. (2010). The economics behind the awarding of terminals in seaports: Towards a research agenda. *Research in Transportation Economics, 27*, 37–50.

Van Ham, H., & Koppenjan, J. (2001). Building public-private partnerships: Assessing and managing risks in port development. *Public Management Review, 3*(4), 593–616.

World Bank. (2001). *Port reform toolkit*. World Bank.

World Bank. (2007). *Public private partnerships: Reference guide*. The World Bank.

# 22

# Insights for Policymakers

Claudio Ferrari

## Seaport Governance: What For?

The present book focusses on the various port governance models adopted in several countries around the world. In a sense, it has deliberately skipped an issue extremely relevant, with an important impact on the governance model and even more on the possible role of policymakers: the nature and role of seaports. More specifically: if ports have a public role or if the port service may be treated as the provision of a usual private service.

This is not an academic discussion at all, and it had been already the main research question of the fourfold intervention of Richard Goss in *Maritime Policy and Management* in 1990. In those papers, Goss argued that the economic function of ports is to increase the surpluses

C. Ferrari (✉)
Department of Economics, University of Genoa, Genoa, Italy
e-mail: ferrari@economia.unige.it

© The Author(s), under exclusive license to Springer Nature Switzerland AG 2022

C. Ferrari et al. (eds.), *Regulation and Finance in the Port Industry*, Palgrave Studies in Maritime Economics,
https://doi.org/10.1007/978-3-030-83985-7_22

of consumers and producers using the ports. At that time, seaports were facing the spread of the containerization and the main pressure was on fostering the efficiency of port operations. Today that question still arises, probably with some additional characteristics. In fact, while the fundamental function of seaports remains the same as argued by Goss almost 30 years ago, the evolutionary framework of seaports is currently driven by new trends: the increased vertical and horizontal integration of the supply chains; the awareness of the importance of actions to reduce the carbon footprint of the industry; the importance of investment in port infrastructure and superstructures in order to keep the pace of the evolution of the shipping industry, the relevance of logistics services for a better satisfaction of the final consumer, etc.

The transition from the concept of the port as an emporium to the port as a node of a complex logistics chain has dramatically changed the nature of ports, also changing the type and intensity of the relationships that each port establishes with its hosting economic region as well as its hinterland. The scope of this transition was highlighted by the process of cargo containerization (Vieira & Kliemann Neto, 2016; Svindland et al., 2019).

The changes induced by containerization can be traced back to two. The first is the lesser relevance of the local economic impacts due to the existence of a port; certainly not because such impacts are insignificant, but rather because impacts, although fuelled and grown in accordance with the economic globalization, are currently more widely spread and in some way "diluted" in a wider hinterland, often contested by several seaports simultaneously (Acciaro et al., 2017; Hintjens, 2018). The second change regards the great emphasis put on the technical and economic efficiency of the movements of cargo from ship to berth and vice versa and the forwarding of cargo from/to the hinterland (Cullinane et al., 2006; Roll & Hayuth, 1993).

The growing interest in the efficiency of the port node fostered in several countries the adoption of the landlord port model, even with some (important) differences, in order to take into account national circumstances, while in some cases seaports have been involved in the corporatization of the port authorities (De Langen & Heij, 2014;

Everett, 2003; Tongzon et al., 2015). All in all, the private interests of port operators have gained importance over the public nature of seaports.

## Port Reform: A Never-Ending Story

Undoubtedly one of the main aspects characterizing the port sector is the necessity to adapt to a client—the shipping industry—that changes very rapidly, for example, in terms of number and scheduling of services, ship sizes, industry structure, etc. For instance, taking into consideration the containerized trade, as pointed out by Roe (2013) the quick evolution of the shipping industry makes port policies inadequate with regard to the requirements of the shipping industry. Some clear examples: the increasing average size of ships makes some terminals inadequate to serve the loops where the biggest full-containerships are deployed; carriers will inevitably replace those terminals with others, in the same port or in a neighbouring port. The same happens with the cascading effect, i.e. the process of deploying the new larger vessels on the more profitable routes moving the "old" (and smaller) ships to minor routes (OECD, 2015). Focussing on port governance rules, the attention paid in the 1990s on opening seaports to competition was aiming, in most cases, at the number of terminals in the same port competing for the same cargo demand. Today, due to the overlapping of port hinterlands, the same result is obtained with competition between terminals belonging to neighbouring seaports.

Ports and shipping industries play on different time and geographical scales (Pilcher & Tseng, 2017). In fact, the shipping industry is a globalized industry whose profit centre is represented by the ship that can be easily moved from one route to another and from one service loop to another, without excessive relocation costs. The shipping industry is international also for the role that multilateral institutions—as IMO, UNCTAD, etc.—play in shaping the sector with reference to several relevant topics. On the contrary, the port industry is characterized by a remarkable rigidity of structures and investments that are reflected in (and shape) its governance rules. For port activities, relocation is feasible, but extremely costly, mainly due to superstructures and labour. Moreover, changes need much more time to occur, they are characterized by a lumpy supply, and they usually happen in successive waves. In addition, in several countries port policies are general, they are issued pursuing a national perspective due to the relevance of the sector for the national economies and such policies apply to all domestic seaports possibly grouping them by size (or volume of throughput) or by the international, national or regional role of seaports. There are some important exceptions, even with different approaches, as for instance in Germany (see Chapter 14) and South Africa (see Chapter 5). Again, these characteristics support the idea of a never-ending run of port policies to adapt to changes in the shipping industry and to imitate the rules applied in other successful contexts and perceived as the best ones. It is then almost clear why in the literature we can easily find waves of papers that cyclically analyse how the port governance rules evolve in the most important maritime economies around the world (Brooks & Cullinane, 2006; Brooks & Pallis, 2012) as shown in Fig. 22.1.

Going somewhat further on the analysis of the set of papers indexed with "port governance" as a keyword on the database Scopus (733 documents published from 1990 on), the plotting of the main co-occurrences,

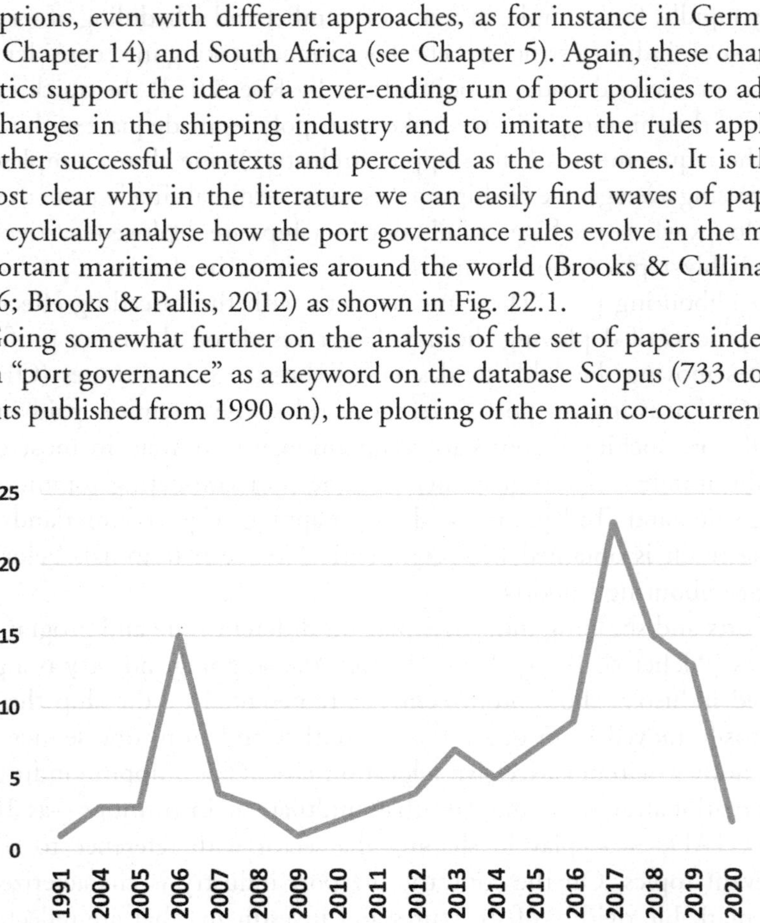


**Fig. 22.1** Number of papers recorded in the Scopus database from 1990 on, with the keyword "port governance" in the title (*Source* Own elaboration)

shown in Fig. 22.2, makes evident the existence of three different layers involved in the analysis of seaport governance:

- a strategic layer, aligning the performance goals of the port actors with the request for more sustainable economic environment;
- an industrial layer, in which the competitive forces coexist with the necessity of some forms of cooperation;
- an operational layer, represented by the port as the interface between ships and terminals; it is on this level that public and private interests must be balanced.

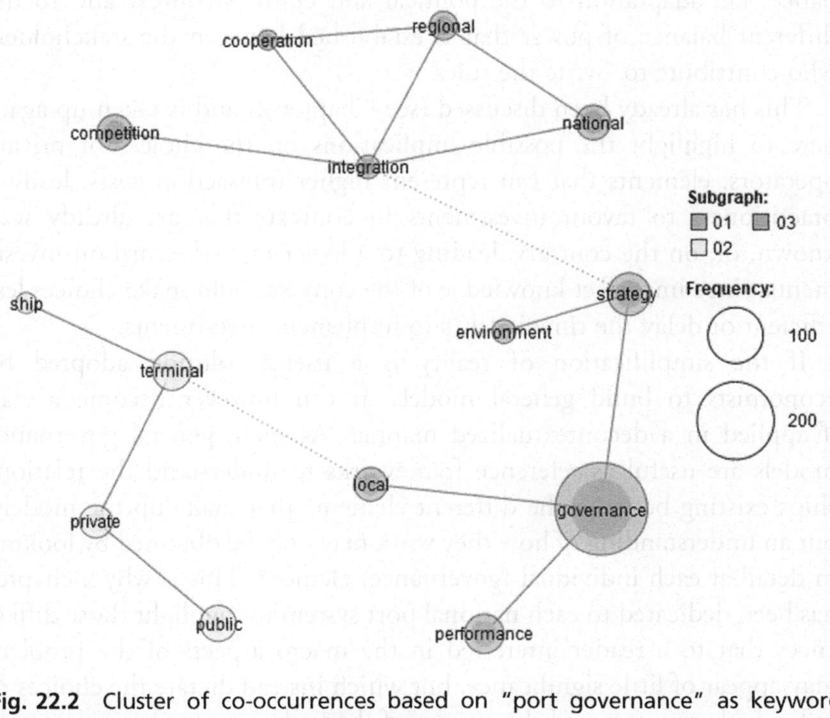


**Fig. 22.2** Cluster of co-occurrences based on "port governance" as keyword (*Source* Own elaboration on Scopus database)

## Implications for Practitioners

The role of private operators is crucial in the functioning of a modern port. The aim of port governance is to regulate their activity but at the same time to create the conditions to enhance their potential, while respecting a recognized—more general—interest.

Therefore, all three levels of analysis mentioned in the previous section have relevant implications for the management of individual port activities and full knowledge of them can be a competitive advantage for professionals called upon to make both strategic and tactical decisions.

Among the things that stand out from this book, there are different applications of the same theoretical and organizational archetypes that lead to quite substantial differences between one port and another, despite claiming to adopt the same governance model. In part, these differences can be explained by the concept of plasticity of governance, i.e. adaptation to the political and cultural context and to the different balance of power that is established between the stakeholders who contribute to "write the rules".

This has already been discussed (see Chapter 2) and is taken up again here to highlight the possible implications on the choices of private operators: elements that can represent higher transaction costs, leading practitioners to favour investments in contexts that are already well known, or, on the contrary, leading to a lower rate of return on investments, since imperfect knowledge of the context could make choices less efficient or delay the time it takes to implement investments.

If the simplification of reality is a useful solution adopted by economists to build general models, it can however become a trap if applied in a decontextualized manner. As such, general governance models are useful as reference frameworks to understand the relationships existing between the different elements that make up the models, but an understanding of how they work may only be obtained by looking in detail at each individual (governance) element. This is why a chapter has been dedicated to each national port system to highlight those differences that to a reader interested in the macro aspects of the problem may appear of little significance, but which instead dictate the choices of individual operators and the success of those choices.

## Further Considerations for Policymakers

Globalization has significantly improved the interdependence of the various economic and social systems, as unfortunately shown, in 2008, by the contagion of the economic crisis, triggered by the subprime mortgage bubble, and recently by the worldwide spreading process of the Covid-19 virus. This interdependence between economic systems has ensured rapid economic growth as evidenced by the fact that according to estimates made by the World Bank in 1990, world GDP, expressed in 2011 PPP US$, amounted to 43.3 trillion dollars, while at the end of 2018 it had risen to 120.8 with an average annual growth of 3.7% in the period. To signify the extent of globalization, it is noteworthy that in this 30-year period, the trend in GDP marked a decline only on the occasion of the 2009 economic crisis and only for the year 2009. So the capitalist system has developed in recent decades, thanks to the strong globalization, fed by an important logistics and transport network which, however, ultimately turns out to be rather fragile in the case of shocks, as it is unable, for example, to partition itself.

This fragility is simply the other side of the coin of the great strategic nature of the transport and logistics sector in general, without which it would be extremely difficult to feed the production process and guarantee the levels of well-being reached by now by a consistent part of the world population. So it becomes fundamental to understand who controls the network, who are the actors in it and in its various parts, who play dominant roles and thus understand the logic actors respond to.

Narrowing the field of observation to the maritime-port sector, as is the aim of this book, one cannot fail to detect the presence of varied situations. In fact, in highly overlapping markets—to the point that it is often claimed that the relevant market is actually only one: the global market—large private corporations compete with others, with public participation, some are vertically integrated and others are integrated horizontally. There is a significant number of companies, but very different in size from each other, with the simultaneous presence of a few giants sharing the market with many small operators. The regulatory and control authorities of the sector are sometimes global—as is the case of the IMO—but in other cases they have regional jurisdiction, as in the case of some antitrust authorities, or even national, as in the case of port governance rules which present a variety of models (as seen in the previous chapters). Such diversity applies also in countries with a strong level of economic integration such as those belonging to the EU.

Nowadays, the role of seaports cannot be limited to that of *interface* with the shipping industry. Ports represent the nodes linking the global shipping network to the logistics (inland) networks. The latter, even if interconnected, are made of several distinguished markets partially overlapping. In particular, the level of port efficiency contributes to define, together with its network of logistic services, the size of the seaport market area while the efficiency of logistics networks impacts on the level of competition among seaports serving the same market area.

Thus the intersection of different levels of government emerges, which should hopefully pursue the same goals while acting with different tools (as for instance port taxes, concession awarding criteria, etc.). The port strategy must therefore be expressed in specific actions and rules for the different levels of government, where the main criticality lies precisely in avoiding any kind of contradiction. For example, it is difficult to combine the search for scale economies due to the concentration of import and export container flows with constraints, at the level of the single port, to the integration of physically contiguous terminals.

Seaports changed dramatically over the last half-century. Important changes are occurring and many others are planned in order to better serve the demand. Most of these changes imply the involvement of private actors—due to the lack of sufficient public capital and due to the devolution process of many port operations to the private sector. This may represent a great opportunity for a quick improvement of port infrastructure but at the same time it requires some coordination actions for the achievement of the seaport's strategic goals.

In this perspective, it is noteworthy asking what economic logic does these industries and sectors respond to. Apparently they respond to a logic of maximizing long-term profit, but not to a logic of *Pareto optimality*. The maximization of long-term profit appears justified by the search to exploit economies of scale both by shipping lines and by port terminal operators, as well as the trend towards vertical integration which, by avoiding double marginalization, allows the integrated operator to gain a greater profit. Horizontal integration also responds to a profit maximizing logic as it allows the achievement of some kind of scale economy based on the volumes of production. These advantages for the operators are basically obtained by acting on the size of their production unit; this starts from the ships themselves and their sizes, and then gradually moving to investments in canals, waterways, and finally to ports and the terrestrial infrastructures and hinterland logistics nodes necessary for the forwarding by land of increasingly large cargo volumes.

Private investments in the mega-ships induce a series of investments in infrastructures, plants and technologies which in various cases use—entirely or largely—public capital. Moreover, the shipping industry is characterized by some forms of cooperation, in order to share among competitors the risk of such large investments (consortia were born precisely for this purpose; cf. Parola et al., 2014; Stopford, 2003). On the port side, often, there are no similar tools to rationalize or coordinate investments. This entails the real risk of generating an oversupply of productive capacity, incapable of matching demand because, for example, it consists of a number of terminals that are too small or inaccessible with regard to connecting land infrastructures (or too far from the main trunk routes), or because they are controlled or simply used by competing shipping companies. Some exceptions begin to appear, in the cases of South Africa and Belgium.

Similarly, infrastructural shortages lead to sub-optimal equilibria. As stated by Vanelslander and Sys (2020), if fundamental port infrastructure is not present, which can typically only come into place with public support, one risks having market players investing a lot of money and effort into sub-optimizing other parts of the chain, thereby seeing funds go lost that could be spent in the development of maritime supply ecosystems.

Thus, it seems important to rethink the governance of the port system, starting from a reflection on the etymology and the real meaning of the term. This derives from the Latin term *gubernare* that means the ability to mediate between opposing interests. In the case of seaports, such interests cannot be exclusively those of the supply chain operators but it is necessary to include also the interests of the communities involved, i.e.

the port ecosystem. In fact, the port ecosystem not only includes the users of port services and the consumers of the goods that are produced and transported along the supply chain but it also includes the regions (households and firms) enjoying the benefits and paying the costs (e.g. congestion and pollution) of the production of port services.

Different levels or "scale" that the port governance has to consider can therefore be identified. It is necessary to overcome a partial optimization approach, such as most of those adopted in past decades, which identified a problem—and restructured the governance accordingly. Such problems were sometimes represented by the need to introduce a private approach to the management of port operations, sometimes by the need to improve the berths' efficiency or even by the need to encourage the private participation to port investments. A similar approach was able to solve a problem but in most cases quite immediately highlighted other problems or inefficiencies. It is rather to be favoured an integrated approach that starting from the identification of a systemic balance—a clear vision of the port of the future is able to decline it at different scales and according to the different actors subject to the whole set of rules that are defined in order to achieve that vision.

Thus, the revision of the governance structure of seaports cannot be resolved at the level of the single port or the level of the seaports of a nation, but must involve the international institutions, those already usually involved in maritime and port issues—such as the IMO—as well as those dealing with international trade and competition rules—therefore, in particular, OECD, UNCTAD and antitrust authorities.

It is quite evident that this task is neither easy to achieve nor achievable in a short time. However, it appears necessary to optimize port investments, to reconcile seaports with their hosting local communities and with the environment, to make ports elements increasingly crucial in the process of creation of well-being and development for communities.

## References


Acciaro, M., Bardi, A., Cusano, M. I., Ferrari, C., & Tei, A. (2017). Contested port hinterlands: An empirical survey on Adriatic seaports. *Case Studies on Transport Policy, 5*, 342–350.

Brooks, M. R., & Cullinane, K. P. B. (2006). Devolution, port performance and port governance. *Research in Transportation Economics, 17*, 1–686.

Brooks, M. R., & Pallis, A. (2012) Port governance. In: W. T. Talley (Ed.), *Maritime economics—A Blackwell companion*. Blackwell Publishing.

Cullinane, K., Wang, T.-F., Song, D.-W., & Ji, P. (2006). The technical efficiency of container ports: Comparing data envelopment analysis and stochastic frontier analysis. *Transportation Research Part A: Policy and Practice, 40*(4), 354–374.

De Langen, P. W., & Heij, C. (2014). Corporatisation and performance: A literature review and an analysis of the performance effects of the corporatisation of port of Rotterdam authority. *Transport Reviews, 34*(3), 396–414.

Everett, S. (2003). Corporatization: A legislative framework for port inefficiencies. *Maritime Policy and Management, 30*(3), 211–219.

Goss, R. (1990a). Economic policies and seaports: 2 The economic function of seaports. *Maritime Policy & Management, 17*(3), 207–220.

Goss, R. (1990b). Economic policies and seaports: 2 The diversity of port policies. *Maritime Policy & Management, 17*(3), 221–234.

Hintjens, J. (2018). A conceptual framework for cooperation in hinterland development between neighbouring seaport authorities. *Maritime Policy & Management, 45*(6), 819–836.

OECD—International Transport Forum. (2015). *The impact of mega-ships*. Paris.

Parola, F., Caschili, S., Medda, F. R., & Ferrari, C. (2014). Measuring the scope of inter-firm agreements in the container shipping industry: An empirical assessment. *International Journal of Shipping and Transport Logistics, 6*(5), 466–487.

Pilcher, N., & Tseng, P.-H. (2017). Can we really measure the impact of port governance reform? *Maritime Policy & Management, 44*(8), 981–994.

Roe, M. (2013). Maritime governance and policy-making: The need for process rather than form. *The Asian Journal of Shipping and Logistics, 29*(2), 167–186.

Roll, Y., & Hayuth, Y. (1993). Port performance comparison applying data envelopment analysis (DEA). *Maritime Policy & Management, 20*(2), 153–161.

Stopford, M. (2003). *Maritime economics* (2nd ed.). Routledge.

Svindland, M., Monios, J., & Hjelle H. M. (2019). Port rationalization and the evolution of regional port systems: The case of Norway. *Maritime Policy & Management, 46*(5), 613–629.

Tongzon, J. L., Ng, A. K. Y., & Shou, E. C. (2015). Institutions, transport infrastructure governance, and planning: Lessons from the corporatization of port authorities in East Asia. *Environment and Planning C: Government and Policy, 33*(6), 1467–1483.

Vanelslander, T., & Sys, C. (2020). *Maritime supply chains*. Elsevier.

Vieira, G. B. B., & Kliemann Neto, F. J. (2016). Taxonomy for the classification of container ports: A contribution to port governance. *Espacios, 37*(3), 23.

# Conclusions—What's Next?

The book development experienced several disruptions in its writing up phase: lastly by the Covid-19 pandemic that impacted the lives of many. During 2020, the work organisation of several authors that contributed to the present volume was drastically changed, impacting the book development as well. The pandemic caused the delay of nearly a year of the present book, heavily affecting the port industry as much as the present volume. Despite this, the port sector never stopped during the pandemic, allowing many countries to go on with their main trades: similarly, we tried to keep the book production process as effective and meaningful as possible, despite the potential drastic changes that the pandemic could cause to the future of the maritime sector.

The contributions presented in the volume highlight how general recipes are often present only in theory, with national and regional regulators that adapt general planning tools and funding schemes to local needs, actually generating a diverse array of market practices. This element is evident when port systems using similar approaches are compared, as developed by the contributions in this book. As such, investment goals, investment plans, regulatory tools, concession schemes,

© The Editor(s) (if applicable) and The Author(s), under exclusive license to Springer Nature Switzerland AG 2022

C. Ferrari et al. (eds.), *Regulation and Finance in the Port Industry*, Palgrave Studies in Maritime Economics,
https://doi.org/10.1007/978-3-030-83985-7

and private company participation are all elements that differ quite substantially in each national port system. Thus, the present book highlights how the globalisation of the port and maritime industry has not necessarily brought a standardisation of local practices which indeed remain quite diversified. Moreover, the diversification is not only related to the different possibilities—in terms, for instance, of port planning tools—but also in respect of involved actors, powers, and goals (e.g. revenues vs social welfare). Most of the critical issues seem then related to local limits and cultural boundaries, affecting the complexity in finding the right balance among market needs and such critical issues.

As highlighted in the last chapter, it seems important to rethink the discussion on port governance, maybe adding to the discussion on general governance schemes the one on specific local regulatory solutions with the aim of identifying how local elements impact on the capability of different models to achieve the regulators' goals. Furthermore, in the case of seaports, conflicts of interest are often present: while regulators are normally public entities, port laws often take into consideration only the interests of the supply chain operators (e.g. stevedores and shipping companies) often not explicitly considering the communities involved, i.e. the whole port ecosystem. Only in few port regions, the legally recognised port ecosystem includes both the users of port services and also other local stakeholders that benefit and pay the related external costs of the production of port services. It is interesting to notice that often this recognition—where present—is not necessarily linked to a public own port, with different privatised bodies that recognise the presence of the port community; thanks to either an effective market regulation or to cultural elements.

Furthermore, in different port systems, the regulation offers only a partial optimization that impacts on available resources. Within these cases, regulators fail to understand the possible long-term goals and subsequent industry patterns, such in the case of environment, technological changes, and market macro-trends. While certain port systems have tried to cope with short-sighted strategies towards more market-oriented regulations, often national port systems lack an "integrated" and "systematic" approach: in our opinion, a key finding of the book is that a clear vision of the port of the future should be able to assess the port development strategies at different levels, for instance, by assessing the impact that regulation could have on different stakeholders' activities. Similary, a continuous check on the alignment among long-term port goals, as defined by the port management body's vision, and the port operators' objectives is needed in order to assure a sustainable port development.

Within this latter issue, some overarching industry opportunities/challenges—such as the environment—will stand as an implicit element to be taken into consideration in future port investment plans in all major port systems. Despite this, the way in which such issues are actually included in port investment plans is different from port to port and, as discussed in the present book, strongly dependent on local elements and regulations. This can be observed in the multitude of examples provided in the book chapters and—while the effects of the Covid-19 pandemic have not been directly treated—it impacts also on the capability of different port systems to promote innovative solutions to adapt to the external market shocks.

We hope that the insights provided by the current book will shed light on different "governance" alternatives, allowing policymakers for more evidence-based decisions, knowing pros and cons of different regulatory solutions. The book, though, does not represent just the final step of the project but an opportunity to promote further debate on the topic, hopefully allowing students and future scholars to go on in investigating the link between local practices and port planning tools in order to provide policymakers with precise guidelines that will help them in connecting long-term goals with optimal port management and organisation models.

# Index



© The Editor(s) (if applicable) and The Author(s), under exclusive license to Springer Nature Switzerland AG 2022
C. Ferrari et al. (eds.), *Regulation and Finance in the Port Industry*, Palgrave Studies in Maritime Economics,
https://doi.org/10.1007/978-3-030-83985-7

U



V



Y

The manufacturer's authorised representative in the EU is Springer Nature Customer Service Centre GmbH, Europaplatz 3, 69115 Heidelberg, Germany. If you have any concerns regarding our products, please contact ProductSafety@springernature.com

Printed and bound by CPI Group (UK) Ltd, Croydon, CR0 4YY
30/09/2026
02225459-0019